Financial Aid 101

Carlyn Foshee Chatfield

Former Assistant Director for
Student Financial Services
Rice University

PROPERTY OF
Baker College of Cadillac

THOMSON ★ PETERSON'S

Australia • Canada • Mexico • Singapore • Spain • United Kingdom • United States

About The Thomson Corporation and Peterson's

The Thomson Corporation, with 2002 revenues of US$7.8 billion, is a global leader in providing integrated information solutions to business and professional customers. The Corporation's common shares are listed on the Toronto and New York stock exchanges (TSX: TOC; NYSE: TOC). Its learning businesses and brands serve the needs of individuals, learning institutions, corporations, and government agencies with products and services for both traditional and distributed learning. Peterson's (www.petersons.com) is a leading provider of education information and advice, with books and online resources focusing on education search, test preparation, and financial aid. Its Web site offers searchable databases and interactive tools for contacting educational institutions, online practice tests and instruction, and planning tools for securing financial aid. Peterson's serves 110 million education consumers annually.

For more information, contact Peterson's, 2000 Lenox Drive, Lawrenceville, NJ 08648; 800-338-3282; or find us on the World Wide Web at www.petersons.com/about.

COPYRIGHT © 2004 Peterson's, a division of Thomson Learning, Inc.
Thomson Learning™ is a trademark used herein under license.

ALL RIGHTS RESERVED. No part of this work covered by the copyright herein may be reproduced or used in any form or by any means—graphic, electronic, or mechanical, including photocopying, recording, taping, Web distribution, or information storage and retrieval systems—without the prior written permission of the publisher.

For permission to use material from this text or product, contact us by
Phone: 800-730-2214
Fax: 800-730-2215
Web: www.thomsonrights.com

ISBN 0-7689-1240-7

Printed in the United States of America

10 9 8 7 6 5 4 3 2 1   06 05 04

First Edition

Contents

Introduction 1

1 Let's Get Started 5
Beware of the Myths 6

2 Financial Aid Basics 9
Need 10
Federal Methodology 11
Can I Negotiate a Better Deal? 12
Cost of Attendance 12
Public or Private Aid 17
Need vs. Non-Need Awards 17
Dependency Status 18
Academic Year vs. Award Year 18

3 Filling Out All Those Forms 21
Paper Pushing 22
FAFSA on the Web 23
Applying for a PIN 24
After Your PIN Information Is Submitted . . . 25
The Pre-Application Worksheet 26
The Paper FAFSA 26

Contents

Mailing the FAFSA 35
The Student Aid Report (SAR) 36
Blank EFC 37
College Scholarship Service CSS/PROFILE® 37

4 Federal Student Aid 39
Sources of Federal Aid 40

5 Institutional Aid and Private Scholarships 47
Finding Scholarships 48
Applying for Institutional Scholarships 51
Athletic Scholarships 52
Academic Scholarships 54
Other Scholarships 59

6 State Aid Programs 61
State Residency 62
Federally Assisted State Aid Programs 63

7 What a Deal! 99
The Checkbook Comparison 102
The Accountant Comparison 105
The Wall Street Comparison 109
And the Winner Is... 115

Contents

8 Can You Lend Me a Dollar? 117
Federal Perkins Loan   118
Stafford Loans   122
Parent Loans for Undergraduate Students (PLUS)   125
Alternative Loan Programs   127
State Loan Programs   129
What Is the Best Program for Me?   130
Guilt, Dreams, and Bankruptcy   131

9 Alternative Payment Plans 133
Other Ways to Finance Higher Education   134

10 What Do the New Higher Education Amendments Say? 141
Pell Grant   143
Federal Supplemental Opportunity Education Grant (FSEOG)   143
Federal Perkins Loan   143
Federal Work-Study (FWS)   144
Leveraging Educational Assistance Partnership (LEAP)   144

Epilogue 145
Appendix A: Key Terms 149
Appendix B: Financial Aid Calendar 167
Appendix C: Forms Bank 173
Appendix D: Additional State Aid Programs 199

If you're reading this book, you probably want a college education for yourself or for a member of your family and, like me, you are wondering how you can afford it. Okay, it's safe to say that we're in this together. Let's figure out a way to get what we want—the best opportunity for the college-bound students in our families.

This book will teach you not only how to stretch your resources to cover all the expenses you can but also how to ask for money. Don't worry. It's not like standing out on the street corner with a coffee can and a sign. There is actually a formal process for asking the government, your state, and your college for money.

Think about asking for a car loan or a mortgage. Sure, there is some paperwork you'd rather not have to deal with. But aren't the results worth it? Think about the kind of car you would be driving if you had to purchase the vehicle with the money you had in your checking account because you didn't want to ask for a loan.

While we're on the subject of loans, what do think about them? Most students and their parents end up taking out a loan to help finance all or part of a college education.

What are your thoughts on grants? A grant is like a gift because you don't have to pay it back. How about work-study? Are you comfortable accepting work-study? Surprise! We have just covered the "Big Three" in the world of financial aid: loans, grants, and work-study. Financial aid comes in one of these three forms. Loans may have many different names, depending on the sponsoring program or lender. Scholarships are another name for grant dollars because you don't have to pay them back. Some scholarships are awarded based on need, and others are based on merit. Merit scholarships are gifts that are earned by academic, athletic, extracurricular, or other accomplishments. Scholarships based on need are harder to discover, but they are available. Work-study dollars are sometimes called "student work portion" or "student work contribution" and how the funds are applied

Introduction

to a student's cost can be a bit tricky to understand. Don't worry. We'll walk you through each component of the "Big Three" later.

The complexity of the financial aid application process intimidates many families. If you are confused or overwhelmed by the paperwork and that is why you haven't applied for financial aid, then *Financial Aid 101* is a guide you can use to simplify the process. I promise you that this book will show you how to get the financial aid dollars you deserve. So turn the page and let's get started.

CHAPTER 1

Let's Get Started

Just as everyone dreams of owning their own car—usually before being licensed to drive—you or someone in your family is dreaming of and planning for a college education. Planning is the first step in your college preparation. If you are a senior in high school, or your child is, you obviously have less time to prepare and execute a financial plan than a parent (or a grandparent) of a 13-year-old does. Still, it is never too late to start planning for college.

But what can you expect in the way of financial aid? Every situation is different, but if you know you cannot write a check for your student's entire college tuition—even on an installment plan—then you probably need financial assistance. And even if you could pay the entire cost of your child's college education, why should you?

Beware of the Myths

Negotiate Your Financial Aid Package

When you begin to prepare, it is important that you are aware of the myths associated with the awarding of financial aid. One of the most common myths in the world of financial aid is the notion that you can *negotiate your financial aid package*. Just because you choose to not fully utilize your assets, your home equity, or even your annual income does not mean that you can persuade a financial aid officer to give you more grant money based on your skillful negotiations. In fact, very few financial aid officers can change a financial aid package. Just like CPAs, IRS auditors, and company controllers, financial aid officers are liable for the files and funds they manage, and they must have documentation proving the applicant's need for the dollars awarded. If a financial aid officer falsely awards federal financial aid dollars to applicants who are determined to be ineligible for aid, the institution is liable for all improperly administered funds received or returned under the federal student aid programs. Worse, the institution will probably lose its eligibility for federal aid funds. The U.S. Department of Education is the largest provider of

Let's Get Started

financial aid dollars for college students, and to be cut off from this source is catastrophic for any institution.

Wait Until You're Admitted

The faster you submit all the required documents to the financial aid office, the faster you will receive information about your financial aid awards. A financial aid myth that is especially damaging to prospective first-year students is the idea that applicants should *wait until they receive their admission decision before they apply for financial aid*. This sounds like a consultant's idea for reducing the workload in a financial aid office, but it certainly doesn't help anyone who is in need of financial aid. Any financial aid officer will advise students to apply for financial aid as soon as possible. FAFSAs can be filed on or after January 1 for the academic year, which begins July 1 of that same calendar year. Supplemental forms may be available as early as September or October of the year before the aid is available. To cover all your bases, research each of the institutions you hope to attend to determine their deadlines, suggested filing dates, and priority filing dates for financial aid applications. In most cases, you will submit your financial aid applications before you complete the admission application process, or at least before your admission decision is finalized. Institutions that make use of deadlines typically process students who meet the application deadlines first. Obviously, if the financial aid office has limited dollars to offer, these "first processed" students have the greatest chance of receiving aid to cover all of their demonstrated need. Don't think your admission application will be more appealing to the admission committee or handled with greater attention if you don't apply for financial assistance up front. As one financial aid officer at a prestigious university laments, "Every spring, I have sad conversations with families who were counseled to hold off on applying for aid until after they get into the university. The fact of the matter is that most, if not all, need-based aid is exhausted at that point."

There's Plenty of Money

One of the most popular myths is that *there are millions of dollars of financial aid lying around untapped each year*. Oh, yes. And I have a bridge over the Grand Canyon that I'd like to sell you. It is true that there are some highly selective funds that are not widely publicized. Many of these funds are available in the form of forgivable loans based on military service, teaching, law enforcement employment, or other careers

Financial Aid 101   www.petersons.com

Chapter 1

in national or community safeguarding or improvement. The best way to uncover untapped financial aid funds is to ask:

 Is there a family trust fund for education somewhere?

 Does my high school club, parent-teacher organization, or athletic team offer any scholarship opportunities?

 Is anyone in my family active in the Lions Club, the Rotary Club, a veteran's organization, or cultural awareness/enhancement organizations such as the League of United Latin American Citizens (LULAC) or the National Association for the Advancement of Colored People (NAACP)?

Ask your high school guidance counselor about scholarships for graduating seniors. If possible, you should ask your counselor about these scholarships as early as the fall semester of your freshman year. Usually if you ask about scholarships in April before you graduate in May, it's too late.

I'm Not a U.S. Citizen

The biggest myth that hurts financial aid applicants is a fear that *only U.S.-born residents are eligible for financial assistance*. The two questions on the FAFSA that touch on this area are question 14, which asks if the applicant is a U.S. citizen, an eligible noncitizen, or neither of the two. If a student is a U.S. citizen or an eligible noncitizen, his application is processed the same way. There are no special privileges awarded to U.S. citizens and there is no discrimination or withholding of aid for eligible noncitizens.

Okay, enough of the fairy tales. So far all you've gotten for your investment in this book is a few entertaining myths and the idea that it's never too late (or too soon) to start creating a financial aid plan. Now it's time to start creating that plan and increasing your knowledge of how the financial aid process can work for your family. Follow me to chapter 2.

CHAPTER 2

Financial Aid Basics

How do you increase your knowledge about a subject when you don't even know where to start? If you decided to help your son with a Boy Scout pinewood derby entry, where would you begin to find information on this type of race? If you decided to try to support your daughter in her science fair entry on thermonuclear energy, where would you go first to see what in the world she's talking about? Let your mind wander just a bit here and think about what you really want to know about financial aid. Are you asking yourself:

 How much money do I need?

 When do I need to apply?

 What is the first thing I need to do?

The theme here is *need*, so that is where we will begin.

Need

Need is the difference between the cost of a college education and the amount you are able to pay or your *Expected Family Contribution (EFC)*, which is based on a determination made by the federal government. Parents have been calculating their expected family contribution for years for everything from their kids' allowances to back-to-school clothes to birthday presents. In the same way, the government asks more than 100 questions to estimate how much of your annual income and assets can be directed toward your EFC.

Let's take the following example: If you expect you can pay $150 for back-to-school clothes for your children, and they pick clothes that cost $130, do you still have to spend $150? Of course not. Unfortunately, your kids will probably pick brand-name clothing that costs $180 and you'll have to negotiate with them to choose only the items that they "absolutely can't live without." That's because there is no financial aid for back-to-school clothes shoppers. In reality, if your child is accepted at a school

Financial Aid Basics

that costs $18,000 and your federal EFC is $15,000, then the $3,000 that falls beyond your family's ability to pay may be covered by financial aid. That $3,000 is the amount you need in order to pay for all of your child's college costs. Again, "need" is the difference between your EFC and the total cost to attend college. Congratulations! You've just completed your first course in financial aid.

Federal Methodology

The next topic we want to cover is something called federal methodology. Don't worry. It sounds more intimidating than it really is. Federal methodology is the U.S. Department of Education's formula for calculating a family's ability to pay for college. The college or university you are considering may start with the federal methodology formula and then factor in additional elements to determine your ability to pay for college. Home equity, noncustodial parent income and assets, business and farm income details, and private tuition for elementary, middle, or high school students are just a few of the elements institutions use. Your college or university may use its own financial aid formula to supplement the federal methodology calculation. Its private formula results in a calculation known as the local or college methodology. Regardless of which methodology your institution uses, the result is a number that shows the dollar amount your family can expect to contribute toward college expenses for that academic year.

Remember that the amount your family is expected to pay for college is called your expected family contribution, or EFC. Usually the federal methodology EFC is the lowest EFC of all the methodologies used to calculate a family's ability to pay. When you apply for financial aid, you must complete a Free Application for Federal Student Aid (FAFSA). The information you provide on the FAFSA is used in the federal methodology EFC calculation. Most financial aid officers think of the federal methodology EFC as simply the "federal EFC." This important number is not a secret to you. As soon as you complete the FAFSA online, you will be shown an estimated EFC. When your FAFSA is processed, you will receive a copy of the information you submitted in order to verify your answers. The copy you receive is called your Student Aid Record (SAR). The SAR includes a cover statement with a number in the top right-hand corner of the page. That number, prefaced with the abbreviation EFC, is your federal Expected Family Contribution. If the number is 923, for example, your expected family contribution for the student listed on the

Financial Aid 101   www.petersons.com

Chapter 2

application is $923 for a typical nine-month academic year. If the number is 45312, your expected family contribution is $45,312.

Can I Negotiate a Better Deal?

Although you cannot negotiate your financial aid package, you can appeal your situation to the financial aid officer for additional consideration. If your assets are tied up in such a way that you cannot access them or even borrow against them, make this information known to the financial aid officer.

Cost of Attendance

Another important term you should be familiar with is ***Cost of Attendance (COA)***, or total college costs. What makes up the COA at the college or university of your choice varies somewhat, but the six basic components of most institutions' annual cost of attendance are:

- *Tuition*
- *Fees*
- *Room and board*
- *Books*
- *Transportation*
- *Personal expenses*

Will you receive a bill from the school for each of these six components? Probably not. When calculating financial need, financial aid officers consider every expense, from soap and shampoo to textbooks and notebooks. The soap, shampoo, and even spending money are lumped into a category known as ***personal expenses***. Books and supplies are usually referred to as ***books***. ***Transportation*** is usually a sum that is based on the distance of a student's permanent home from the campus, but it can also be the calculation of the travel expenses for a commuter student on an annual basis. More than likely, none of these three COA components (personal expenses, books, transportation) will appear on your bill from the institution. For these three components, you will have to work out your own payment plan. The good part about these components is that the financial aid officer takes each of

Financial Aid Basics

them into consideration when determining how much the academic year is going to cost. The three COA items you can usually expect to see on your bill are *tuition*, *fees*, and *room and board*.

Tuition

Tuition is a school's charge for time spent in class for instruction (lecture), or instructional laboratory work (lab). Many colleges and universities charge on a semester-hour or credit-hour basis, so your tuition charge can increase or decrease each semester, depending on the number of credit hours you take. Other institutions charge a set amount for full-time (12 credit hours or more) registration regardless of the actual number of hours a student selects. In this case, students are expected to register for at least 12 hours, and stringent restrictions are usually in place to prevent students from registering for less. If a student appeals and drops below full-time status for some reason, tuition charges are usually revised to reflect less than full-time status. The good thing about this type of tuition charge is that a student can take additional courses without incurring any additional tuition expense. For more information on how various colleges and universities assess their tuition charges, refer to Peterson's *Four-Year Colleges* or www.petersons.com.

Fees

Fees are often associated with labs, Internet access, student activities, campus transportation, campus sporting events, and other opportunities and services provided to students on a daily, weekly, or seasonal basis.

Room and Board

The final component of your COA that will typically appear on your bill is *room and board*. However, depending on where a student lives, room and board can either be the charges you see on your bill for living and/or eating on campus or they can be an allowance that your financial aid officer includes in your total COA for the cost to live and eat off campus. Your bill will note charges for campus-run room and board plans. Typically, there will be no charges for non-campus-affiliated room and board charges. For instance, you may have missed the deadline for campus-based housing but have a confirmed place in a private dormitory. The private dormitory charges will probably be handled like an apartment lease with a contract, and they would not show up on your bill from the college or university. Perhaps you want the social connection that is often found in a college dining hall and you purchase a five-day campus meal plan for

Financial Aid 101　　　　　　　　　　　　　　　　　　　　　　　　　www.petersons.com

Chapter 2

the semester. Although the private dormitory charges are handled separately, the campus meal plan will show up on your semester bill.

> *Note:* If you commute to campus on a daily basis from home, the room and board amount budgeted into your cost of attendance will be much lower than that of a student residing in a campus residence hall or an individual or shared apartment close to the campus.

The lower allowance for a commuter's room and board expenses is tied directly to his decision to commute in order to reduce college expenses. Don't try to pull one over on the financial aid officer and say you will live on campus and require housing to get the higher allowance if you know you are going to commute. You will be falsifying information and can be heavily fined. On the other hand, if you don't know where you will live, indicate campus housing on your applications. If you don't end up living on campus, you can contact the financial aid officer when your housing arrangements are finalized.

You now know at least three key phrases to help guide you through conversations and correspondence with your financial aid officer: *Need, EFC*, and *COA. COA minus EFC equals Need* is the formula you should keep in mind when you begin to create your college financial plan. If you are rapidly approaching your first year of college, you have a pretty good idea of the cost of attendance at your top schools. If you are beginning this process as a freshman or sophomore in high school, you have more time to plan but a less concrete idea of what the cost of attendance will be. In either case, there are several tools you can use to help you forecast future costs, including:

 FinAid.org offers an EFC calculator at www.finaid.org/calculators/finaidestimate.phtml

 Collegiate Funding sponsors an EFC calculator at www.collegiatefunding.com/calculator.html

 College Savings Bank at www.collegesavings.com/create1.shtml

 Sallie Mae's Wiredscholar.com at www.wiredscholar.com/paying/lt_financial_planning/ltfp_collcost.jsp

 Education Services Foundation at www.esfweb.com/collegesavcalc.html

Financial Aid Basics

Many colleges and universities list the components of their COA in their literature and on their Web sites. For ease of comparison, make multiple copies of the table below or create it in Excel or any other electronic calculation tool.

Problem with COA

There are two problems with this simple *COA minus EFC equals Need* formula, and you may as well know about them now. The first one has to do with capacity. Although every institution wants you to have all the financial aid dollars you need to complete the payments for your education, most simply do not have the funds to meet 100 percent of each student's need. Only schools with extremely large endowments, alumni and donor contributions, or other financial foundation building blocks can promise to meet 100 percent of your demonstrated need. (These "100 percent" schools can be found at Peterson's *Best College Deals*®, available at www.bestcollegedeals.com.)

If your EFC is zero and your school's cost of attendance is $27,000, that means you have 100 percent need. Federal grant dollars might be used for one seventh

Cost of Attendance (COA) Estimator

Name of School:	
Tuition	_____
Mandatory Fees	_____
Room and Board	_____
Books	_____
Transportation	_____
Personal Expenses	_____
Other*	_____
Total COA for this school:	_____

* Expenses specific to this school that can be applied to the total cost of attendance calculated by your financial aid officer

Financial Aid 101   www.petersons.com

Chapter 2

or one eighth of those costs, but you still need more than $23,000 in additional financial aid. You may be offered a work-study award where you could earn financial aid dollars while you work a part-time job on or close to campus. That might bring the remaining financial aid dollars you'll need down to $20,000. Guess what form of financial aid you may be offered to fill the rest of your need? That's right—*loans*. On the other hand, if your school has any institutional funds available for needy students, part—or even all—of the remaining need might be met through local scholarships and grants. You can start investigating your top-choice schools right now to see if they meet 100 percent of demonstrated need. You can also start asking questions by e-mail, phone, or at college night presentations. Ask how much you would be expected to pay to the university if your EFC is zero. Then ask how much of the aid would be in the form of loans.

The second problem with *COA minus EFC equals Need* is that you may have a difficult time determining which methodology your institution uses to calculate your family's EFC. The federal EFC is only one of three major methodologies used by schools to calculate a family's ability to pay. The federal EFC must be used by every institution to award federal Pell Grants, and many institutions use it to determine who receives federal SEOG Grants and Federal Perkins Loans. However, your institution does not have to use a federal EFC to determine whether or not you are eligible for the institution's private funds or state-funded financial aid. Typically, the wording in institutional and state-based financial aid fund requirements indicates that the student must show need, but the requirements might not specify which methodology must be used to calculate the student's EFC and resulting need. One of the benefits that the College Board touts to member institutions is that using the CSS/PROFILE® financial aid application saves institutional dollars. This is accomplished by asking additional questions to ferret out previously overlooked sources of family contributions so that the student's EFC is increased. Remember that *COA minus EFC equals Need*. So if your family's contribution increases because your noncustodial parent has significant assets and income—a supplemental form associated with the CSS/PROFILE specifically targets noncustodial parents—the institution does not have to award you as much financial aid as the federal EFC would appear to indicate. So once again, start asking questions of your top three or five institutions now. Ask which methodology the school uses to calculate EFC. If the answer is not the federal EFC, you should inquire about the supplemental forms used by the school.

Financial Aid Basics

Chances are, even if supplemental forms are used, none of the additional questions may apply to your case, and your resulting EFC may be similar to your federal EFC. Unfortunately, the use of supplemental forms in public and private universities often signals increased EFC values, such as a minimum EFC for every student, regardless of the EFC assessed by the federal methodology.

Public or Private Aid

The reason why the methodology for your EFC is so important lies in the availability of public and private financial aid. If the only financial aid dollars available were the funds provided by the federal government (public financial aid), the only application form families would need to complete would be the FAFSA. Fortunately, private aid is also available, where individual donors, organizations, or foundations have given funds to a specific institution for financial aid purposes. Unfortunately, there is a limit to private financial aid dollars, just as there is a limit to federal and state grants, so institutions must use their own judgment to sift through numerous applications for the most qualified recipients.

For example, what if an institution has one $2,500 scholarship to award to a needy student and there are 358 students at that institution with EFCs below 1,000? Worse yet, 96 of those students have federal EFCs of zero. How is the institution going to select the most needy student? No one will be happy if the institution just selects a name at random, so the institution is probably going to ask for additional information about the applicants to assist with decisions like this. That is why many institutions require each applicant to submit a supplemental form, either an institutional form or a private form like the CSS/PROFILE®.

Need vs. Non-Need Awards

Outside funding is the term financial aid officers use to refer to awards you *bring with you* to your institution in the form of one-time or continuing scholarships. At this point, outside funding is usually not based on a FAFSA or other financial aid application. Outside funding does not usually require a financial aid application because the awards are usually not based on financial need. Typically, outside awards can come from local school support groups such as band booster clubs and parent-teacher organizations, local community organizations like the Lions Club or Rotary Club, or regional associations such as the Houston Livestock Show and Rodeo or the

Financial Aid 101   www.petersons.com

Chapter 2

Jones Foundation. Even national scholarships such as the Coca-Cola Scholarships or the Bill and Melinda Gates Foundation Scholarships are considered outside funding by your financial aid officer. Because scholarships such as these are often based on academic merit, community involvement, or other student accomplishments, the financial aid community refers to these awards as *non-need-based*.

However, this book is really intended to help you apply for need-based awards. Your institution may have private need scholarships, which means that donors have provided funding for scholarships that are primarily based on the student's financial need. But there may be a few strings attached. Public need awards include federal and state grants, loans, and work programs and are always based on a student's EFC.

Dependency Status

One of the primary areas that affect a student's EFC is dependency status. Obviously, a 35-year-old first-time college student is not going to submit her parent's tax information when she applies for financial aid. Where and when parental information is required depends on a student's dependency status.

Dependency is a concept based on parental responsibility to pay for an undergraduate degree for a child. Essentially, students are dependent on their parents and their own earnings to pay for their college expenses. Financial aid helps to fill the gap between the amount the family has a realistic capacity to pay and the expenses of the child's institution. For this reason, the FAFSA asks seven questions to determine where the college expense payment responsibility lies. If an applicant answers no to all seven questions, the primary responsibility to pay for an undergraduate degree lies with the applicant's parents as well as with the applicant, and the applicant is considered a dependent student. If the applicant answers yes to one or more of the seven questions, then responsibility to pay for the college education resides with the applicant, who is considered an independent student. After the dependency status is resolved, the ability to pay is calculated based on the responsible party's (or parties') income and assets. We will discuss dependency status in greater detail in chapter 3.

Academic Year vs. Award Year

Financial aid officers follow different calendars than the rest of us. Thanks to a fiscal year that runs from July 1 through June 30 for several federal financial aid

Financial Aid Basics

programs, financial aid officers had to learn how to distinguish the award year applications and funding used in January from the applications and funding that are available in December of the same calendar year. Ask a financial aid officer what year it is and you'll most likely hear something like, "Do you mean oh-three-oh-four or oh-four-oh-five?" Although it sounds nonsensical, the financial aid officer is simply trying to clarify your question. Are you inquiring about an award or application that is used in the 2003–04 award year, which runs July 1, 2003 through June 30, 2004, or about an award or application that is used in the 2004–05 award year, which runs July 1, 2004 through June 30, 2005?

You may also be confused by nine-month and twelve-month years. Academic years are often measured in nine-month periods. Award years, on the other hand, can be measured in up to twelve-month spans. Your nine-month academic year probably runs September through May and falls squarely within the fiscal award year of July through June. If you decide to take summer semester courses, any financial aid eligibility will be the result of both your EFC and the dollars of aid you use in the other nine months of the academic year. Perhaps a student is eligible for a Pell Grant of $800 for both the fall and spring semesters, but attends only half-time in the spring. His Pell Grants are $400 for the fall semester and $200 for the spring semester. The $200 in Pell Grant dollars that this student does not use in the spring might be available for use toward summer semester expenses.

However, another student might enroll in a quarter-based school that runs year-round. If this student enters school in July, his first nine-month academic year is over at the end of March, before the award year ends in June. Here, the same Pell Grant-eligible student from the previous example may have used all of his grant eligibility for the twelve-month award year in the first nine months of his courses. At that point, the student might receive only a loan offer for use between April and June. If this happens to you, don't lose heart. If your situation remains the same from one award year to the next, your grant eligibility will probably resume as soon as the new award year begins in July. Just remember to reapply for financial aid each year.

You have been reading and taking notes (hopefully) for a long time now. You need a break. Sleep on the information you've digested so far. The next chapter will lead you step-by-step through each of the primary applications you will probably use. So give yourself a rest. We'll see you in chapter 3.

Financial Aid 101   www.petersons.com

The *two primary* financial aid applications are the Free Application for Federal Student Aid (FAFSA) and the PROFILE® application from the College Scholarship Service. The FAFSA is the universal application for all federal financial aid programs. It is the primary application for most state and college financial aid. The PROFILE is a more comprehensive financial aid application that is used mostly at private, higher-cost colleges and universities to award nonfederal student aid funds. Many private scholarship programs also use the PROFILE. The FAFSA is free, but the PROFILE is not. It requires a registration fee and an additional fee for each school or program you select to receive your information.

Paper Pushing

Today, everyone seems to be going paperless. You can review your checking account information electronically or listen to your banking transactions over the phone. You can set up your mortgage or rent payments electronically and have your checking account debited on a specific day each month. Of course, you can file your tax returns electronically.

However, for many, paper is comforting. Paper is proof. When we've crashed our computer four times in one week or have forgotten where we saved the most recent version of our electronic phone book, we start to write things down and carry around little slips of paper in our pockets and purses. If you are a member of the "paper is proof" crowd, regardless of your age, you will be relieved to know that you do not have to apply for financial aid over the Internet. The last thing the U.S. Department of Education is going to do is provide financial aid only to people with computers. If you do not have access to the Internet, there are four easy ways to get a paper FAFSA, including:

 your high school guidance counselor

 your college or university's financial aid office

 your local library

 the Federal Student Aid Information Center (FSAIC) at 800-4-FED-AID

Filling Out All Those Forms

Although you have access to paper applications, you must realize that the paper FAFSA is processed in approximately three to four weeks, while the electronic application is usually processed in less than two weeks. However, as long as you plan ahead, you can still meet the state and institutional deadlines for applications. The longer processing time is simply a matter of manpower. If you submit an electronic application, you are keying in and checking all the information yourself. Even if you take two weeks to complete the application by working on a few questions at a time and saving your information at the end of each session, you are still the person who is touching the keys and submitting the information. Conversely, if you submit a paper application, an electronic scanning device reads your information and changes your handwritten answers into numbers and letters in an electronic format. If you leave a field blank, no one makes up an answer for you. If you write down that your adjusted gross income and tax paid are the same amount, no one is going to stop processing your application to phone you and ask you to check your answers. Furthermore, no one is going to read an appeal, notes written in the margins, or a cover letter. The data processor's only job is to feed your paper application through the scanner. Once the data is entered, the application is processed in the same amount of time as if you had entered the data yourself. So even if you submit a paper application, your information will still be processed electronically. Although the trend is toward filing online, we will focus most of our attention in this chapter on the paper FAFSA, because the online application is very user-friendly and explains each question in depth. Thus, we think it is important to offer the same kind of instruction for those of you filing a paper FAFSA.

FAFSA on the Web

Before we get to filing the paper FAFSA, we need to cover two important topics for those filing online. (Paper filers—skip ahead a few pages to the section titled *"The Paper FAFSA."*)

If you are filing online, the first thing you need to do is obtain a PIN (personal identification number). The PIN enables you to sign your application electronically and have your FAFSA processed immediately. It is used to:

 sign the FAFSA, make corrections, or process renewals electronically

 view the status and/or results of your FAFSA

Financial Aid 101   www.petersons.com

Chapter 3

 access the National Student Loan Data System (NSLDS) Web site (www.nslds.ed.gov) and view information about loans and other federal student aid

 access the Direct Loan Servicing Web site (www.dl.ed.gov) and view information about Direct Loans

 access the Direct Loan Consolidation Web site (www.loanconsolidation.ed.gov) to track the processing status of your online Consolidation Loan application

 e-sign a Federal Direct Loan (www.ed.gov/offices/OFSAP/DirectLoan) or Federal Family Education Loan (FFEL) Master Promissory Note

Note: If you are a dependent, your parent will also need to have a PIN, but the same one can apply to all college students in the family.

Using a PIN is the fastest way for your application to reach the institution of your choice. Yes, you can submit a FAFSA online if you do not have a PIN, but then you have to print the signature page that appears at the end of the data entry section, sign the page, and mail it in. Another option for non-PIN holders who submit the FAFSA online is to wait until they have received their initial Student Aid Report (SAR), which is the report that summarizes the data entered, reports your EFC, and gives you the opportunity to make any corrections. When satisfied with the accuracy of the document, you can then send in corrections or approval of the data with your signature.

Note: Remember that when you use an ink signature, your FAFSA information is not considered complete and an EFC cannot be calculated until the signatures are received.

Applying for a PIN

To apply for a PIN, simply log on to www.pin.ed.gov, click on **Apply for PIN** in the explanation paragraph, or click on the **Apply for PIN** icon at the bottom of the page. You will be directed to www.pin.ed.gov/appinstr.htm.

Navigation Tip: You can move from box to box using your mouse. Also, the tab key will move you from one box to the next throughout the page. Neither the Return/Enter key nor the Up/Down arrow keys work to navigate around this page.

Filling Out All Those Forms

Do Not Guess Your Social Security Number

If you have not had to write or type your social security number recently, take the time to look at your social security card and type the exact number. Also look at the name on your card. This is your official name for financial aid purposes. If your social security card was issued to Elizabeth Smith, do not complete applications as Betty Smith, even if that is what everyone calls you. If your name is Ann, but your social security card incorrectly has an extra "n" and an "e" on the end, your name for all government applications is Annne. This type of accuracy is necessary for financial aid purposes. The information you provide on the various applications must match your social security card exactly, because the U.S. Department of Education always compares financial aid applicants to the information in the Social Security Administration's database. If there is a discrepancy between the two systems, the processing of your financial aid application will be delayed, and you will probably be asked to submit more documentation—such as your social security card—to your financial aid officer. If you have lost your social security card, you should request another one at this time, because you may be asked to present your social security card as proof of identification a number of times during your college experience.

> *Note:* When asked for a password, choose one that is easy to remember, because there is no process for recovering this password in any of the U.S. Department of Education systems. If you forget it, you will have to start the PIN application process from the beginning—not a time-consuming process, but annoying.

After Your PIN Information Is Submitted...

If you are a dependent student, you will need to return to the PIN home page and complete the process again with a parent's personal data. It is a good idea for both parents to apply for a PIN. When the student and the parents have their own PINs, it is possible to complete future FAFSA applications or corrections from different computers. You can even submit information simultaneously. A student cannot submit or make corrections to parental data, such as adjusted gross income or other tax return information, so parents don't have to worry that their child will rush through the application and possibly guess their information in order to beat an application deadline. You will receive the student and parent PINs by e-mail within 24 hours.

Financial Aid 101   www.petersons.com

Chapter 3

The Pre-Application Worksheet

The second thing online applicants need to do is complete the *Pre-Application Worksheet*. On the Pre-Application Worksheet, the numbers in parentheses correspond to the question numbers on the paper FAFSA. (The questions on the worksheet itself were intentionally left unnumbered to prevent additional confusion.) The creators of the Pre-Application Worksheet did not begin with the personal demographic data requested in the first section of the FAFSA, so you might want to jot down all applicable social security numbers and driver's license numbers. The Pre-Application Worksheet is the best way to collect and organize the data required on the FAFSA. It is only a worksheet used to assist you in efficiently completing the FAFSA and is not forwarded or mailed. This is especially useful for first-time financial aid applicants, because it is a good way of organizing your information before filling out the actual FAFSA, and you will be able to zip through the data entry process. Also, if you are unsure about how to answer a specific question on the FAFSA, you can use the Pre-Application Worksheet to pinpoint the area of concern. However, if you have already submitted several FAFSAs, you may not need to take the time to complete this form.

When the worksheet is done, continue by clicking *Filling Out a FAFSA* and keying in the data from your Pre-Application Worksheet. If you have questions while completing the online form, there are help screens for each page, a link to a *Frequently Asked Questions* page, and a link to a page where you can send an e-mail for help. In addition, the following information about filling out the paper FAFSA form has lots of good tips and insider information about different fields on the FAFSA. After submitting all the required data, you will be able to access your Student Aid Report (SAR) in less than two weeks, which reports your Estimated Family Contribution (EFC).

The Paper FAFSA

The paper FAFSA consists of a page of general instructions; two pages of notes for the questions that require codes or explanations; the seven-step, four-page, 100-question FAFSA; Worksheets A, B, and C; and a mailing envelope and return confirmation postcard. The whole form is color coded, even the Notes pages, so that you can clearly see which information is required of the student and which information is required of the parent. As already noted, there are two pages of

Filling Out All Those Forms

explanatory notes about most of the questions, so there is no need to repeat them here. Instead, we are going to provide valuable tips and expert explanations on how to answer the questions most effectively.

> *Note:* For your convenience, a copy of the paper 2004–05 FAFSA can be found in Appendix C.

Step One
The first part of the FAFSA asks for some general information about the student, such as name, address, and social security number. There's nothing new here.

Citizenship
The answer you provide here is matched against the Social Security Administration's database and/or the Bureau of Citizenship and Immigration Services (previously the INS) database. If you do not select *U.S. citizen,* you will need to fill in your *Alien Registration Number* in the next question.

Marital Status
The next group of questions asks about the student's marital status.

Legal Residence
The questions about state of legal residence are also used for private, state, and local scholarship consideration.

Gender
Don't be offended by the gender question. Most males must be registered with the Selective Service in order to be considered for federal aid. If you haven't registered with the Selective Service, you may register now by answering yes to the next question. However, if you'd prefer to complete the registration yourself, you can either get a registration card at your local post office or you can register online at www.sss.gov.

Educational Plans
The first few questions refer to your educational plans for the academic year and your consideration of both loans and work-study as forms of financial aid. Regardless of your own personal definition of financial aid, both loans and work-

Financial Aid 101   www.petersons.com

Chapter 3

study are programs designed to assist you in paying for college. If you are simply not interested in loans or work-study, answer "no." Depending on the sophistication of your institution's financial aid management system, you may be offered these programs even if you answer "no." In addition, some schools include work and loans as the first two elements of any financial aid package, regardless of your answers to these questions.

Parents' Level of Education

Answering questions about your parents' highest level of education may help you win private scholarships or local or state scholarships designed for first-generation college students. Be as accurate as you can and pay attention to the word completed in the question.

Prior Convictions

At least three years of planning and revision have gone into the question about prior drug convictions. This is one of the only questions that you absolutely *MUST NOT LEAVE BLANK*. Most people can answer with a straightforward "no." However, even if you've had a prior conviction, you may still be eligible for aid. This question led to so many additional questions about the accuracy of the applicant's answers in the first two years it was used, that an entire worksheet has been developed to assist convicted persons to determine whether or not they are eligible for aid. If you answer "yes" to this question, you will be mailed a worksheet to fill out to determine if your conviction affects your eligibility for aid.

Step Two

To proceed, pull out your most up-to-date student tax returns, W-2s, and any documentation for untaxed income. Here, your answers will include a definite "yes," a definite "no," or a "promise of not yet, but I'll get to it eventually." To evaluate your family's ability to pay, the current federal EFC calculations use numbers from specific lines on your tax returns and boxes on your W-2s. Of course, other factors are also considered. But your answers to the following questions are critical to the success of evaluating your eligibility for federal financial aid:

 Has the student completed a 2003 IRS or other income tax return?
If the student has completed a tax return, regardless of whether or not it has been filed, select *Have Already Completed.* If the student's income

Filling Out All Those Forms

situation is such that he is not required to file a tax return, select *Not Going to File.* If the student doesn't fit either of these situations, select *Will File* and set a deadline to complete the tax return soon. Remember that some institutions will not process financial aid applications until they have received copies of the student's, spouse's, and/or parents' tax returns. Even though you select *Will File,* you may have other institutionally imposed deadlines that require the completed tax return. If you are one of the lucky tax-return nonfilers, you get to skip ahead six questions. Go ahead, we'll catch up later. For the rest of us, let's continue.

 What kind of tax return did you file or will you file?
Select your answer and move on.

 Were you eligible to file a 1040A or 1040 EZ?
The type of tax return you filed may not be the easiest or most simple tax return you are eligible to file. Perhaps your accountant just prefers 1040 tax returns to all others. The instructions in the notes pages provide some clarification on this question. The reason why the type of tax return you filed is important is that the current federal EFC calculations use shortcuts to calculate aid eligibility if a particular type of tax return is used. For example, families who earn below the adjusted gross income (AGI) ceiling of $50,000 and file only a 1040A or 1040EZ probably cannot afford to use any of their assets to pay for college. So a family that indicates it is eligible to file a 1040A or 1040EZ falls under the *Simplified Need* federal EFC calculation, and none of the family's assets will be used in the EFC calculation.

Student and Spouse Income

Now is when you really need the student's (and spouse's, if applicable) tax return and W-2s, plus any documentation about untaxed income. Simply follow the directions for each question. (Example: The dependent student's AGI comes from IRS Form 1040, line 4; from 1040A, line 21; from 1040EZ, line 4; or from TeleFile, line 1.) For the earnings from work questions, you *MUST ANSWER* these regardless of whether or not you are going to file a tax return. Add up the W-2s for the student if she worked several different jobs and do the same for the student's spouse, if applicable. If the student and/or student's spouse is going to file a tax return, add up the numbers

Financial Aid 101   www.petersons.com

Chapter 3

from IRS Form 1040 on lines 7, 12, and 18. If the tax return is an IRS 1040A, use the numbers from line 7; if the tax return is an IRS 1040EZ, use in the number from line 1. TeleFilers should just use the information from their W-2s.

Now you understand why a completed tax return is vital to answering FAFSA questions. Regardless of whether or not you have filed your tax return, requested your tax refund, or made your first payment on the remaining tax you owe, your completed tax return is going to provide you with answers you need for the FAFSA. But if you don't have it yet, go ahead and file for the FAFSA anyway—the sooner the better. Once you file your tax return, you can correct any income or tax information that may have changed.

Why Use a Previous Year's Income to Determine Financial Aid?

This time, accuracy and proof are twin answers. In a perfect world where there were no tax headaches, everyone would complete a tax return by midnight on December 31, so accurate data could be provided on financial aid applications on January 1 for an award year that runs January 2 through December 31. Just like IRS auditors, financial aid officers are required to audit some or all of their financial aid applications. The measuring tool for comparing the FAFSA answers to actual data is the most recently completed tax return. On the one hand, it is nice to have a deadline as late as April 15 for filing federal tax returns. On the other hand, the annual financial information on that tax return is already six months old by the time the financial aid year begins on July 1. Financial aid officers all understand this dilemma, but it is the best solution that the U.S. Department of Education has offered thus far. More importantly, it treats all applicants the same. Regardless of whether the family income is less than $30,000 or more than $300,000, everyone uses a completed tax return for the same tax year.

Worksheet A

Worksheets A, B, and C are next. For the purposes of the FAFSA, they are worksheets only and are not mailed. However, you should save them, because your school may ask to see them. Leave the answers blank or enter a zero if the question does not apply to your situation. If the independent student is married, her answers are combined with her spouse's answers. As you complete each worksheet, write the worksheet sum in the appropriate line on the FAFSA. Worksheet A collects information on government-provided (excluding veteran's benefits) income or income credits that were untaxed. Although the government is not benefiting from this income by generating tax dollars

Filling Out All Those Forms

from it, the government is already providing income support to the family, so this type of assistance is treated differently when it comes to assessing a family's ability to pay for college. Earned income credit and additional child tax credit are both types of income credit that are not available to families who do not file a tax return. Social security benefits are also accounted for here as well as *Temporary Assistance for Needy Families (TANF)* or other types of monetary welfare benefits. Food stamps or welfare housing subsidies are not included in Worksheet A.

Worksheet B

Worksheet B collects information about private or veteran's noneducational income and benefits that were untaxed. Strangely enough, even though six of the questions are drawn from specific lines on the tax return, these items are deducted from the income on which your federal tax is calculated. Although they appear on the tax return, they are, in fact, untaxed income. When it comes to assessing your family's ability to pay for college, all of the private sources of untaxed income are added to the family's total earnings, income, and/or dollar value of living allowances and benefits. This is where you show child support that you receive from someone else to support children in your own household. About the only untaxed benefits or income that don't get counted here are *flexible spending plans* and previously received student aid. Since child care and medical prescriptions, devices, and co-payments are already proving to be a steady drain on family income, any dollars you set aside in a flexible spending plan to help cover these consistent expenses will be protected from the calculation of your EFC. Also, if you received student aid last year, it was intended to help you pay for your college costs in that year and you don't have to count it in your calculation for the amount of money you can contribute toward your college expenses this year. Finally, if the student has a benefactor, such as a grandparent, aunt, uncle, or family friend who assists the student with living or educational expenses, that untaxed income value is entered into the last student answer in Worksheet B.

Worksheet C

Worksheet C allows you to include any child support or other taxes you pay that should not be included in the federal EFC calculation. There are four specific areas that are targeted here:

- education credits
- child support that comes out of your family's income

Financial Aid 101

Chapter 3

- ☑ taxable income from need-based employment programs (such as Federal Work-Study) and

- ☑ student grant and scholarship aid that was included in the student's or dependent student's parent's AGI.

Here is the simplest explanation of why you report them in Worksheet C. Last year you paid for college expenses for yourself or your dependent student. When it came to filing your tax return, the IRS gave you a break and said, "Take a certain amount of the money you spent on college expenses last year and deduct it from the amount of federal income tax you have to pay us for the same year." Since the government is trying to give families a small break on the amount of tax they have to pay if they are also paying for college expenses, it would penalize this family if the government were to include that tax credit in the calculation on how much the family can pay for college expenses this year. Similarly, even if a student paid tax on work-study earnings, grants, scholarships, fellowships, or assistantships, these dollars were tied to last year's college expenses, and the same dollars should not be included in this year's ability-to-pay calculation. Child support is another example of dollars that came out of the family's total income last year that are simply not available to draw upon for college expenses this year, so they are also deducted from the family's federal EFC calculation.

Student Assets

Now that you've danced through the three worksheets, you need to have some idea of what the student is worth on the open market. You'll have to estimate the worth by counting up financial assets. Of course, shoes, clothes, and electronic gadgets could be worth more than savings accounts and investments, but you can't count toys, sports equipment, or clothing.

> *Note:* These answers should not be revised by the student or parent in future FAFSA corrections. The FAFSA provides a snapshot of the student's financial worth, not real-time value. A student with $10,000 in savings on the day he completes the FAFSA cannot revise his answer if he spends the amount on a car or even tuition during his academic year because he had the money during the course of the year.

Estimate the market value of the student's current investments and then estimate the market value of the dependent student's business or farm.

Filling Out All Those Forms

Students who are receiving veteran's education benefits should note the number of months they will receive these benefits from July 1 through June 30. The monthly amount that you will receive for these benefits is the answer for the last veterans' question. If you are unsure of your veteran's education benefits, you should contact your nearest **Veterans Administration Office** or research your benefits by phone at 877-823-2378 or on the Web at www.gibill.va.gov. Congratulations! Step 2 is behind us and we're ready to move on to Step 3.

Step Three

Dependency Status

The answers in this section determine whether or not you are considered dependent or independent; answer all seven questions. Notice that there are no selections for *maybe* or *that depends.* In extreme circumstances, your financial aid officer may consider performing an override of your dependency status. Before you can ask a financial aid officer to review your circumstances, however, you must complete and submit the FAFSA. When your application has been processed and a copy of the data sent to your institution, you may then approach the financial aid officer about your situation. Depending on the answers you provide, you will be led through the rest of the application for the relevant sections for dependent students, independent students, and parents of dependent students. If you enter "yes" to any question, skip Step Four (a whole page of parental information!) and go to Step Five. If you answer "no" to all questions, complete Step Four and skip Step Five.

Step Four

Step Four is a whole page of data pertaining to parents. They may want to fill this out themselves. It is very similar to the information the student supplied up to now about himself and his income.

Tips for Parental Assets

- **What is your parents' total current balance of cash, savings, and checking accounts?**
  If, by chance, you have money that is a result of student financial aid in cash, in your savings, or in your checking account today, don't include these amounts here.

Financial Aid 101   www.petersons.com

Chapter 3

☑ **What is the current net worth of your parents' investments and real estate (not your home)?**

Subtract anything you owe on your properties or any outstanding loans you may have made against your investments. You'll want to include trust funds, money market funds, mutual funds, CDs, stocks, stock options, bonds, other securities, education IRAs, private college savings plans, installment and land sale contracts, commodities, and other similar investments. What you don't want to include is the home you live in, cash, savings and checking accounts, life insurance, retirement plans, pension funds, annuities, noneducation IRAs, Keogh plans, and, prepaid tuition plans (usually managed through your state).

☑ **What is the net worth of your parents' businesses and/or investment farms?**

Do not include a farm that you live on and operate. However, include the market value of business or investment farm equipment, land, buildings, machinery, inventory, and so forth. Many of us think of farmers and ranchers as the families who are doing their best to hold onto the home, land, and livelihood that they inherited from their parents and grandparents; these family farms and ranches are not included in this question. On the other hand, investment farms are included. Usually, investment farms and ranches are providing supplemental income and/or tax benefits for an individual or family who already has a homestead somewhere else. You have finished another section! The end is near; stick with us just a little longer.

Step Five

Complete this section only if you answered "yes" to any question in Step Three.

Step Six

Schools to Receive Results

How you complete this section determines which institutions will receive your financial aid application information and which housing plan you want to use to estimate your cost of attendance. You are asked to enter the six-digit federal school code and your housing plans. Look for the federal school codes at

Filling Out All Those Forms

www.fafsa.ed.gov, at your college financial aid office, at your public library, or at your high school guidance office. If you cannot get the federal school code, write in the complete name, address, city, and state of the institution. If you are unsure about your housing plans, or if they change before your begin classes, notify your financial aid officer. Finally, estimate your intention to enroll as a full-time, three-quarter, half-time, or less-than-half-time student for the start of the school year.

Read, Sign, and Date

Before your FAFSA is complete, you and your parent, if applicable, must sign and date the form. By signing the application, you certify that:

- You will use federal and/or state student financial aid only to pay the cost of attending an institution of higher education.

- You are not in default on a federal student loan or have made satisfactory agreements to repay it.

- You do not owe money on a federal student grant or have made satisfactory arrangements to repay it.

- You will notify your school if you default on a federal student loan.

- You will provide information that will verify the accuracy of your completed form, if asked.

- You understand that the U.S. Secretary of Education has the authority to verify information reported on the application with the IRS and other federal agencies.

Mailing the FAFSA

After you have completed your application, make copies of pages 3 through 6 for your records. Then mail the original pages 3 through 6 to:

Federal Student Aid Programs
P.O. Box 4691
Mt. Vernon, IL 62864-0071

Chapter 3

Your application should be processed in about four weeks. You can check on the status of your application online at www.fafsa.ed.gov or by calling 800-433-3243. If you provided an e-mail address in Step One, you will receive information about the application in a few days.

The Student Aid Report (SAR)

You will receive a *Student Aid Report (SAR)* by mail if there is not an e-mail address on file for you (remember that you could enter your e-mail address at the beginning of the paper FAFSA form) or if the signature, either electronic or ink, is missing. All others can check on the status and print out a SAR by going to the FAFSA *Follow-Up* section on the FAFSA Web site and following the instructions. If the SAR is complete and correct, you don't need to do anything. If you do need to make changes, you can do so either by writing them on the paper SAR, signing it, and mailing it back, or by going to the FAFSA Follow-Up section and following the instructions to make corrections electronically. Even if you used the paper form to submit the application, you can still make corrections online, but you'll need to create a PIN.

Each time you submit a corrected SAR, your transaction number will increase by one. For example, your first submission is always Transaction 1, and subsequent transactions are numbered 2, 3, 4, etc. When you submit corrections, you must include either the electronic signature (PIN) for each responsible party or the ink signature for each responsible party when you submit paper corrections. If your school verifies your file and finds an error, the school has the right to submit corrections based on their documentation (usually a copy of your tax return or W-2). For this reason, you may receive a new SAR. You may have sent your FAFSA information to six different schools. Each school has the opportunity to "correct" your data. Imagine if you entered your adjusted gross income as $49,500 and also indicated that the federal income tax you paid was $49,500. This is unlikely, and each of the institutions will question the information you submitted. Two of the six schools might have a policy of adjusting the taxes paid down to a calculated level even before they receive copies of your tax return. One or two of the institutions may correct the taxes paid field as soon as they receive copies of your tax return.

The remaining schools may not have caught the discrepancy in your taxes paid field but have caught other errors and submitted corrections in these fields.

Although the student's family in this example may have not submitted any corrections, if each of the institutions that received the student's FAFSA information submits a correction through their system, you could easily see six more transaction numbers in your SAR summary page. Probably each of the six schools is swamped with prospective freshman financial aid applications and do not submit corrections on the data they receive until after May 1 (the typical deadline for prospective students to commit to their institution). However, if you receive two or more corrected SARs that you did not submit, you should contact the financial aid officer at the institution that you plan to attend to find out if there is a problem with your application.

Blank EFC

If you receive a SAR with a *blank EFC*, there is definitely a problem with your application. It may be as simple as collecting mom or dad's signature (which of course means that mom or dad should review the SAR because the student may have rushed through the application process to meet a particular deadline without collecting a parent's signature). A blank EFC could also point to conflicting information. Sometimes students enter their birthday as October 4, 2003, or January 29, 2004, instead of using their correct birth year. Conflicting information is usually easy to find because questionable answers are in bold-faced type on the SAR.

College Scholarship Service CSS/PROFILE®

One of the institutions to which you are applying may require you to submit a *College Scholarship Service (CSS) PROFILE* application. You can register, complete, and submit the application online at www.collegeboard.com. You can also request a paper form through your high school guidance counselor or through the College Board by phone at 800-778-6888. Submit the application at least a week before your school's deadline. The College Board Web site maintains a list of all schools using the CSS/PROFILE and lists some of the deadline dates. Just as with FAFSA,

Financial Aid 101

the PROFILE application contains a Pre-Application Worksheet to make filling out the actual PROFILE application easier. For your convenience, we have included a copy of the 2003–04 Pre-Application Worksheet in Appendix C.

Registration Costs

Unlike the FAFSA, registering for the CSS/PROFILE is not free. Currently, the processing fees are $5 for initial registration ($7 if registering by phone) plus a processing fee of $18 for the first institution. At the end of the application process, additional institutions can be added for $18 each. However, you may be eligible for a fee waiver. Check with your high school guidance counselor for details.

> *Note:* If you are not ready to pay for additional institutions, you may add them at a later date. However, if you add institutions later, you will be charged a $7 processing fee each time you add institutions, in addition to the $18 for each institution. So if you can afford it, go ahead and list your top three or four institutions now.

Congratulations! You've just survived the most detailed chapter of the book. You should be commended for making it to the end. Next, you'll find much more interesting information on the various types of federal, state, institutional, and private student aid available. See you in chapter 4.

CHAPTER 4

Federal Student Aid

After you've completed all your forms and received your EFC, you can begin to study up on the types of aid you might receive through your institution. Notice the word through. Federal student aid is provided to you from the United States Department of Education. It is channeled to you through your institution. In addition to federal student aid dollars, remember that your institution may also be the channel for state financial aid dollars, private loans and scholarships, and institutional loans, scholarships, and work-study awards. There are many different combinations of aid and sources of aid, but this chapter will concentrate only on federal student aid. In the next chapters, we'll take a look at other sources and types of financial aid.

Sources of Federal Aid

The most popular federal student aid program is the Pell Grant program. A lesser-known federal grant program is the Supplemental Educational Opportunity Grant, or SEOG. Another widely recognized federal aid program is the Perkins Loan program. Finally, the programs that supply the most financial aid dollars each year are federal education loans. Basically, there are two types of education loans: student loans and parent loans. Student loans are usually referred to as Stafford Loans. Parent loans are usually called Parent Loans for Undergraduate Students, or PLUS. The loan applications you submit for Stafford and PLUS loans are processed either through the William D. Ford Direct Loan Program or by an independent financial institution through the Federal Family Education Loan (FFEL) program. You can read more about federal loans in chapter 8.

The U.S. Department of Education gathers annual research about each school that participates in federal aid programs and then uses this information to determine how much each school will receive (the school's allocation) in three different programs: *Pell Grant*, *Supplemental Educational Opportunity Grant (SEOG)* and *Work-Study*. Then the school determines which of its financial aid applicants receives an award from this allocation. As long as the school follows some broad-based guidelines, it has complete autonomy on how these three allocations are awarded and disbursed. The first of these federal aid programs we'll discuss is the Pell Grant.

Pell Grant

In 1965, a nonrepayment federal aid program called the Educational Opportunity Grant was initiated. In 1972, the program was replaced with a similar nonrepayment award, the Basic Educational Opportunity Grant (BEOG), and the BEOG was renamed the Federal Pell Grant in 1980. The Pell Grant is a federal entitlement award. That means that everyone who is entitled to the award receives it, regardless of the number of recipients each year. But what if many more families qualify for the award than the statistics forecast? Congress deliberates long and hard over how much the program can spend each year. While families and financial aid officers alike would like to see maximum Pell Grant awards go much higher than the current $4,050 a year, Congress continues to vote to keep the growth conservative. What does all this mean for you? The two things you need to remember are:

1. Undergraduate students with the greatest need (lowest EFC) are the most likely candidates for a Pell Grant.

2. A Pell Grant does not require repayment.

If the maximum Pell Grant award is $4,050, how can you estimate the amount you will receive? There are several charts used by financial aid officers to determine the amount of a Pell Grant for a student. These Pell Grant charts are published annually by the U.S. Department of Education and are available to the public. If you have access to the Internet, go to www.ifap.ed.gov and click on the links to *Pell Grant*. To make your research a little easier, we've included a sample Pell Grant chart on the next page for full-time students.

The Pell Grant charts for each year are released in the spring before the academic year begins. The 2004–2005 Pell Grant Payment Chart for Full-Time Students should be released in March or April of 2004. However, since Pell Grant amounts are expected to remain the same (according to the initial Reauthorization bills from the House and Senate), the 2003–2004 Pell Grant Chart provides information similar to the 2004–2005 chart.

Financial Aid 101

www.petersons.com

Chapter 4

Federal Pell Grant Program
Regular Payment Schedule for Determining
Full-Time Scheduled Awards in the 2003-2004 Award Period
February 2003

Important: schools must use the alternate schedule for students in the cells outlined above when tuition plus dependent care or disability related expenses are lower than $675.

Federal Student Aid

Two factors determine the amount of the Pell Grant award you may receive. These factors are your federal EFC and the COA at your school. Find your federal EFC (remember it was estimated for you when you completed your FAFSA online and it was printed on your SAR) in the columns at the top of the chart and then find your school's COA in the rows on the left-hand side of the chart. If you don't know the school's total cost of attendance, contact the financial aid office and ask. Confused? Don't be. Look on the Pell Grant chart for full-time students. Where your federal EFC column and your school's COA row meet is your estimated Pell Grant for 2003–04. For simplicity, only the full-time student Pell Grant chart is referenced in this book. In the real world, your financial aid officer must revise your Pell Grant award if you drop below full-time or if your federal EFC is revised due to changes on your FAFSA. For these reasons, there are charts for three-quarter-time Pell Grant awards, half-time Pell Grant awards, less-than-half-time Pell Grant awards, and alternative Pell Grant charts for very low tuition charge assessments. Also, if you use any of your Pell Grant eligibility at another institution during the school year, your Pell Grant for your current institution may be reduced. Relax. You don't have to know all the charts and rules; that's the job of your financial aid officer. The charts are only mentioned here to take away some of the mystery of the award process.

Supplemental Educational Opportunity Grant

The SEOG was designed to supplement Pell Grant awards. For families with very low EFCs, the Pell Grant is probably not enough to cover the cost of attendance for an undergraduate student. Ideally, these same families will receive additional financial aid dollars in the form of a supplemental grant, or SEOG. The maximum SEOG award is $4,000 annually, and the SEOG is a grant, which means repayment is not required. Unfortunately, many families with very low EFCs may not receive an SEOG if they miss their school's application deadline. The SEOG is often the smallest of the three allocations for campus-based federal aid programs and the money runs out very fast. For this reason, your school's financial aid office probably has a policy of "first come, first served" when it comes to handing out SEOG dollars. This is why you need to pay attention to and meet your financial aid office's application deadlines.

Chapter 4

Federal Work-Study

The final campus-based federal aid program is interest free, but it requires work on the part of the student. Federal work-study is intended to help students earn money for educational expenses while gaining experience in their field or by serving the public interest. Just like the SEOG and the Perkins Loan, an annual allocation sets the maximum amount of federal work-study dollars available at each school. The demand for federal work-study is high, and the funds are limited, so your institution probably has a similar "first come, first served" award policy. Pay attention to your financial aid office application deadlines.

Why is the demand for federal work-study awards so high? In this case, the demand is not driven by the students as much as by employers. With Federal work-study awards, an on-campus employer pays 25 percent of a student's wages and the federal government pays the other 75 percent. The federal portion of the wages can go as high as 100 percent if the job is in a community service field such as working as a reading tutor. Although the student worker probably doesn't care who is paying his wages, employers are anxious to pay only a small portion of the student's earnings. For example, if the chemistry department hires a non-work-study student for $10 an hour, it pays the entire amount out of the Chemistry department budget. But if it can hire a work-study student for $10 an hour, it pays only $2.50 an hour because the federal aid program pays the other $7.50 an hour. For budget reasons, many campus employers will specify "work-study students only" in their job postings. That is how employers drive up demand for work-study awards.

Although it is in high demand, federal work-study is by far the most confusing aid program to students and their families when it comes to understanding their bill from the institution. Federal work-study dollars are not available to the student until they receive a check for hours worked. On the other hand, federal work-study usually appears on student award letters as part of the financial aid offered by the school. For example, if a student receives a $1,500 Pell Grant for the fall semester, this amount is applied directly to the student's educational expenses and deducted from the amount the family owes on the bill. However, if the same student receives a $1,500 federal work-study award for the fall, this amount is not usually deducted from the bill because the student has not yet earned the money.

www.petersons.com

Financial Aid 101

Federal Student Aid

Federal Student Aid Program	Type of Program	Repayment	2003-2004 Maximum Annual Amount	Interest Rate	Loan Fee
Pell Grant	grant	none	$4,050	none	none
SEOG	grant	none	$4,000	none	none
Work-Study	work	none	varies	none	none

Comparing Federal Student Aid Programs

The table above will help you understand the main differences between the primary federal Student Aid programs discussed in this chapter. Do not make any decisions on your financial aid package based on this table. Refer to the individual sections of this chapter for the details on each program.

Now that you have a general idea of the primary federal Student Aid programs, it's time to move forward into private (or outside) awards and institutional aid programs. But you need to take another break before you can absorb any more information. So close the book and give your eyes and brain a rest.

CHAPTER 5

Institutional Aid and Private Scholarships

The card game Go Fish! is a matching game that young children learn to play at an early age. At the end of the game, the player with the most matches wins. When it comes to searching for financial aid, you want to be the player who collects the most "matches" at the end of the scholarship search game.

Finding Scholarships

How do you "go fish" for scholarships? Unlike the game, there are a number of steps, and any one of them can turn up matches. Although there are no guarantees that any of these steps will turn up a match, the more effort you put into your search, the better your chances are of finding new sources of financial assistance. In the following examples, Web site addresses are included for electronic scholarship search tools only. Remember that the Web site addresses listed here are only a few examples of the many opportunities available.

Internet Scholarship Searches

Sign up for every *free* scholarship search you can find on the Internet. It's a good idea to create an e-mail account just for scholarship searches. That way, the scholarship search results won't clutter up your everyday e-mail account. Lycos and other Internet Service Providers offer free e-mail accounts. Search for "free e-mail" in your Web browser.

Here are a few examples of free scholarship search Web sites:

- *Free-4U* (www.free-4u.com/scholarships1.htm)
- *FastWeb.com* (www.fastweb.com)
- *FastAID.com* (www.fastaid.com/)
- *Brokescholar.com* (http://brokescholar.com)
- *CollegeXpress.com* (www.collegexpress.com)
- *WiredScholar.com* (www.wiredscholar.com/index.jsp)

Institutional Aid and Private Scholarships

- Scholarships.com (www.scholarships.com)
- StudentAwards.com (Canadian target audience option at www.studentawards.com)

Trade and Commerce Organizations

Ask your employer, your parents' employers, or any trade organizations associated with your job or your parents' jobs, about scholarship opportunities. Wal-Mart and McDonald's, for example, have strong reputations for scholarship assistance for their employees and the dependents of their employees. Other examples include:

- Association of Iron and Steel Engineers (AISE)
- American Dairy Association/Dairy Council of Nebraska (Nebraska dairy farmers' dependents)
- Burlington Northern Santa Fe Railway
- California Farm Bureau Federation
- Louisiana Farm Bureau Federation
- National Society of Black Engineers (NSBE)
- North Dakota State University Department of Agribusiness and Applied Economics

Religious, Cultural, Health, and Other Affiliations

Research foundations and organizations associated with your religious, cultural, or physical impairment affiliations are major sources of scholarship awards. Let your imagination wander, because you may be taking some of your connections for granted. Hopefully, this short list of examples will spark ideas of other groups that fit your own situation:

- Catholic Daughter Scholarship Fund®
- Children of Breast Cancer Scholarships
- Financial Support for Jewish College Students
- Indian American Scholarship Fund
- Jackie Robinson Foundation (minority students)
- Japanese American Citizens League

Chapter 5

- Kosciuszko Foundation (Polish descendants)
- Latino Money magazine
- Little People of America (dwarfism)
- League of United Latin American Citizens (LULAC) Scholarships
- Methodist Scholarships
- Minnie Pearl Scholarship (significant bilateral hearing loss, mainstreamed in education)
- National Federation of the Blind
- Office of Navajo Nation Scholarship and Financial Assistance

Talent and Club Connections

Don't stop now! Fourth on your list of resources for your "fishing expedition" is to research scholarships for the field you hope to enter, such as music scholarships, school club (debate, government, speech, etc.) scholarships, or visual and performing arts scholarships. Organizations for these include:

- American Institute of Certified Public Accountants (AICPA)
- American Dental Association
- American Harp Society Foundation
- American Kennel Club Veterinary Scholarships
- Arts Recognition and Talent Search® (www.ARTSawards.org)
- ASCAP Foundation
- DiscoverNursing.com
- Illinois Institute of Technology Armour Pre-Med Scholarship
- John M. Long School of Music (Texas Southern University) Scholarship Auditions
- ROTC programs
- Tylenol Scholarship

Institutional Aid and Private Scholarships

Printed Resources
Peterson's publishes several guides listing scholarships and scholarship donors. These can be found in your high school counselor's office, at your local library, or online at www.petersons.com. They include:

- *Getting Money for College: Scholarships for Asian-American Students*
- *Getting Money for College: Scholarships for African-American Students*
- *Getting Money for College: Scholarships for Hispanic Students*
- *Scholarships, Grants, & Prizes 2004*
- *College Money Handbook 2004*
- *Scholarship Almanac 2004*

Financial Aid Office
Finally, ask your college or university for advice. The financial aid officers at the schools nearest you are often the most knowledgeable about scholarship opportunities that pertain to your situation. For example, one of the best resources for tribal scholarships is the list put together by the Office of Student Financial Assistance at Coconino Community College in Flagstaff, Arizona. Visit www.coco.cc.az.us/finaid/tribal%20info.htm for the most recent list. In addition, your college or university receives announcements for scholarship competitions from various foundations and donors. Ask your college's financial aid office if it keeps the announcements so you can come to the office to review them.

Applying for Institutional Scholarships
Merit scholarships at the institutions you are considering may be open to everyone who is admitted to the institution. If that is the case, the application for institutional merit aid is essentially invisible. You cannot apply for specific institutional merit scholarships at colleges and universities that practice this "everyone is considered" philosophy. So how do you receive this aid? It's simple. When your admission application is reviewed, the committee notes your interests, awards, and other characteristics that might make you a desirable student. When admission offers are issued and you are one of the school's top choices, you will probably be offered some type of merit award as an incentive to accept the school's offer of admission. That is how everyone is considered for that particular school's

Chapter 5

institutional merit awards. It's true, everyone was considered, but only the most desirable students were offered scholarships.

Another school may follow a slightly different everyone is considered policy for its institutional need-based awards. In this case, everyone who applies for financial aid is reviewed during the "packaging" step of the aid process. If the applicant has any interests, hobbies, awards, or other distinctions (major, GPA, class rank, etc.) that fit a particular institutional need-based scholarship, then the student receives the scholarship as part of his total financial aid package. The information that is used to match up the students with the scholarship criteria comes from an external or institutional application that every student applying for financial aid (at this school) must complete. Like the merit award mentioned above, there is no separate application for institutional need-based scholarships at a school that follows the everyone is considered policy. The school's financial aid application serves as both the scholarship application and the overall financial aid application.

Some schools, such as the University of Chicago, Texas A&M University, Pennsylvania State University–Berks Campus, and New Mexico Highlands University, use institutional aid applications or supplemental applications for specific awards or aid programs. There's a specific application for the Michigan State University 4-H Rabbit and Cavy Scholarship (as opposed to the Michigan State University 4-H Scholarship). Central Washington University uses a separate institutional application for merit scholarships, and the University of Southern California uses a supplemental institutional application for all need-based financial aid and non-need-based loan applicants.

Athletic Scholarships

The NCAA has strict rules about the maximum number of years of aid offered and the types of aid an athlete can receive. There are *no four-year athletic scholarships*. An athletic scholarship is awarded for one academic year only. It may or may not be renewed each year. The maximum number of years a student may receive an athletic scholarship is five, and the five years must occur within a six-year period. According to the NCAA, a Division I or II college may offer financial aid that includes tuition, fees, room and board, and books. Personal expenses and transportation are certainly components of a school's COA (cost of attendance), but they are not

Institutional Aid and Private Scholarships

listed in the types of expenses that a school is allowed to cover with financial aid for athletes. On the other hand, Division III colleges have the flexibility of offering financial aid (up to the full cost of attendance) if the aid is based on financial need and not associated with athletic ability. As a result, student athletes with low EFCs (estimated family contributions) who attend Division III schools may actually receive *more* financial aid if they are *not* on an athletic scholarship because they can receive up to their entire COA in need-based financial aid. If these same students receive athletic scholarships, their scholarship dollars can cover only specific components of their COA, but not 100 percent of their COA. Regardless of your school's division, the NCAA is very specific about prohibiting grant-in-aid students (recipients of institutional athletic awards, no matter how large or small the amount) from receiving awards that cause the total dollar of aid to exceed the permissible amount of a full grant-in-aid for the student. There are a few exempted government grants that are not counted toward the total aid amount, including the Pell Grant, Veterans Educational Assistance Program (VEAP), and state or federal welfare benefits. There are additional programs that fall under the exempt category, and your financial aid officer will be able to address your specific concerns.

That is why the best resource for institutional athletic aid is your school's financial aid office. More than likely, your coach will not know all the answers to the questions you have about financial aid. If you're lucky, your school's athletic office may have an athletic scholarship specialist on staff. Very often this position is found in large programs where an athletic administrator has budget responsibilities. In addition, there should be at least one athletic scholarship specialist in your school's financial aid office, and some schools have several financial aid officers who are trained to deal with athletic scholarships.

Because of the strict NCAA rules that govern financial aid for athletes, students who receive any amount of athletic scholarship dollars must notify their financial aid officer of any additional awards or work opportunities they receive. For example, if your high school booster club awards you a scholarship, your financial aid officer must include it in your financial aid package and make sure that your total financial aid dollars do not exceed the NCAA cap. The same holds true for employment. Some athletes can't accept a work-study job because the amount of work-study earnings is counted toward the total aid for the award year and can cause them to

Chapter 5

lose their program eligibility. Further, some athletes are prohibited from accepting any type of employment if they wish to retain their eligibility to participate in their sport. Again, if you are on an athletic scholarship and receive any type of award or work opportunity, contact your financial aid officer immediately.

When it comes to general athletic aid information, the best resource available is the *NCAA Guide for the College-Bound Student Athlete*. This booklet is available free of charge to individuals. You may order by phone at 800-638-3731 or view a copy online at www.ncaa.org/library/general.html#cbsa.

Academic Scholarships

The competition to recruit top scholars has led to ingenious financial aid incentive programs at both public and private colleges and universities, and many of these incentives are called **merit awards**. To get an idea of the merit aid maze, imagine that you are the director of admissions at Tiny School, a small reputable university that receives $100,000 from an endowment each year for awards to meritorious first-year students. Tiny School has only 500 people applying for the freshman class next year. The school can accept 250 students in its freshman class. As director of admissions, how would you use your $100,000 this year? The easiest way is to rate all 500 applicants and award $4,000 to each of the top 50 percent of the ranked students. To hedge your bet, you may offer $4,000 to the top 60 percent because the school's history shows that not everyone who is offered admission to Tiny School actually matriculates.

To complicate matters, Tiny's president instructs you to enroll at least 5 National Merit Scholars and 10 "blue chip" students (highly desirable or competitive students). The president is particularly interested in attracting competitive students who are probably going to receive admission offers from your state's other large universities. You can identify all the National Merit Scholars in your applicant pool because the National Merit Scholarship® Corporation (NMSC) sends you names of students who listed Tiny as their first-choice school. Identifying and attracting 10 competitive students may be more difficult.

After some late-night number crunching, you identify about 20 students in the pool of 500 who are probably "highly desirable," and you have 15 National Merit

Scholars in the pool as well. In both cases, you decide to offer these target groups more merit dollars. But you still have only $100,000 to work with. Let's say you spend $35,000 of the $100,000 on these 35 students, awarding each of them $10,000 instead of $4,000. These students received an extra $6,000 of merit aid because they fit a profile that your president prefers. If you just spend the remaining $65,000 evenly among the rest of the students in the top 50 percent of the previous rankings, those kids will now get only about $300 each.

Okay, take off your director of admission hat and just be a parent or a college student again. Even if you receive an admission offer from your favorite school, you may not fit its highly desirable student profile and may not receive a merit award at all. Don't take it personally. Next week, a school you applied for on a whim may rate you in the top 3 percent of its prospective students for next year and offer you thousands of dollars in merit aid. The one thing you can't pin down is what is going to make a student highly desirable to a school. There are so many admissions committee members reading applications and contributing to the final ranking of each applicant that you simply can't know for sure what qualities will be in the school's highly desirable group of students from year to year.

National Merit® Scholarships

There is one merit-aid source that is consistently awarded year after year. The National Merit Scholarship® Corporation (NMSC) is an independent nonprofit organization that operates without government assistance. The NMSC conducts two privately financed annual competitions for recognition and college undergraduate scholarships: The National Merit® Scholarship Program and the National Achievement^{SM} Scholarship Program. Through the National Merit Program, NMSC also conducts competitions for special scholarships sponsored by corporate and business organizations.

NMSC cosponsors the PSAT/NMSQT® test for high school juniors with the College Board. More than 1.3 million students take this test each year, and the top 50,000 scorers are recognized as either Commended Students or semifinalists. About 34,000 are designated Commended Students. These students do not continue in the competition for the NMSC National Merit® Scholarship one-time award, but may be eligible for Special Scholarships sponsored by corporations and business organizations. The remaining 16,000 are designated on a "state-representational

Chapter 5

basis." Visit the NMSC Web site at www.nationalmerit.org/merit.htm for further details. The semifinalists are provided scholarship application materials that are distributed through their high schools. When all the materials have been reviewed, some of the semifinalists proceed to finalist designation. Semifinalists who do not proceed to the finalist level may be eligible to receive a corporate-sponsored Merit Scholarship (similar to Special Scholarships). Based on these tests, NMSC awards a small percentage of students a prestigious National Merit® Scholarship. This scholarship is a one-time award worth approximately $2,500.

Each year about 8,000 combined National Merit® Scholarships, NMSC special scholarships, corporate-sponsored Merit Scholarships, and college-sponsored Merit Scholarships are awarded through the NMSC process. College-sponsored Merit Scholarships are similar to the NMSC special scholarships, except that your institution—instead of mom or dad's company—purchases a Merit Scholarship for you through NMSC if you are a semifinalist and have selected that institution as your first-choice school. Although the one-time award from NMSC is limited to $2,500, Special Scholarships, college-sponsored Merit Scholarships, and corporate-sponsored Merit Scholarships do not have the same dollar or one-time limitation. Essentially, the amount of these scholarships depends on the purchaser of the scholarship. It's not as flexible as it sounds, though. Most organizations and institutions that purchase Special Scholarships or Merit Scholarships have a predetermined amount for the awards and the awards are usually renewable as long as you continue to meet the donor's criteria. If you receive a renewable Special Scholarship or Merit Scholarship from a college or corporate sponsor, you will be required to submit copies of your grades to NMSC each semester before the next semester's scholarship check is released to your school.

Start researching your parents' employee benefits now to determine whether or not you should submit a National Merit® Scholarship entry form to the employer. At the same time, start investigating your top-choice schools to find out if they participate in college-sponsored Merit Scholarships. Not all colleges have enough funding to purchase these scholarships. The colleges you are most interested in (if you feel that you have a good chance of making it to at least the semifinalist level) are the institutions that are proud of the number of National Merit® Scholars they enroll each year. If you find an institution that claims to "enroll the most National

Institutional Aid and Private Scholarships

Merit® Scholarship recipients" (for its size, type of institution, region of the U.S., etc.) then you have located a school that annually earmarks a relatively high percentage of institutional aid for purchasing these scholarships.

National Achievement℠ Scholarships

The National Achievement℠ Program was established in 1964 to provide recognition for outstanding Black American high school students. Although both the National Merit Scholarship Program and The National Achievement Scholarship Program are conducted simultaneously, their funding and operation are managed separately. Black American students can qualify for recognition and be honored as scholars in both programs, but can receive only one monetary award from NMSC.

After taking the PSAT/NMSQT® in high school, eligible students may request entry into the National Achievement Program by marking the specific space provided on the competition's answer sheet. Although more than 120,000 students enter the program each year, only about 4,600 are honored. Of these 4,600 students, about 3,000 are referred to colleges for their academic promise and 1,600 are named semifinalists. Semifinalists are the only students who have an opportunity to compete for the program's scholarship awards. Information is mailed to the semifinalists concerning the academic standards and other requirements, which must be met in order to be considered for the next level of the competition. From the group of semifinalists who meet these requirements, approximately 1,300 students are selected as finalists. About 775 scholarship winners are then selected from this group of finalists based on their abilities, skills, and accomplishments. Of the 775 or more scholarships, some are one-time awards of $2,500, some scholarships are awarded through corporate sponsors, and some are sponsored by colleges and universities. Although college- and university-sponsored scholarships are typically renewable for up to four years of undergraduate study, corporately sponsored scholarships are either renewable or one-time awards. The scholarship award amounts vary by sponsor. Examples of corporate sponsors of special scholarships or corporate-sponsored Merit or Achievement Scholarships include:

- Armstrong
- Ashland, Inc.
- Boeing

Financial Aid 101   www.petersons.com

Chapter 5

- ☑ Cargill
- ☑ Dun and Bradstreet
- ☑ Fujitsu
- ☑ Knight Ridder
- ☑ Lockheed Martin
- ☑ Scripps Howard
- ☑ Siemens

Examples of institutional sponsors of college-sponsored Merit or Achievement Scholarships include:

- ☑ Carleton College
- ☑ Case Western Reserve University
- ☑ Johns Hopkins University
- ☑ Marquette University
- ☑ Pennsylvania State University
- ☑ Texas A&M University
- ☑ University of Arizona
- ☑ University of Florida
- ☑ University of Iowa
- ☑ University of Kansas
- ☑ University of Kentucky
- ☑ University of Oregon
- ☑ University of Rochester
- ☑ University of Tennessee
- ☑ Wabash College

Institutional Aid and Private Scholarships

Other Scholarships

So what's left in the way of scholarship opportunities? Your free scholarship search has uncovered every connection you could think of for your family's situation. Now turn your focus to your high school and your community.

- What scholarships are offered to graduating seniors each year?
- If you can apply, what are the requirements for the scholarship?
- If you can't apply for the scholarship, what qualities or grades do the nominators look for?
- Who nominates (high school counselor, nominating committee, etc.)?
- Can or should you request a brief meeting to express your interest?

Don't forget to research scholarship opportunities offered by businesses and organizations in your community. Compare this part of your scholarship search to a job search. Prepare a resume of your achievements and a cover letter that you can customize for each group. Point out your accomplishments and explain why a college education is important to you. Close your letter with an inquiry as to the availability of scholarships and reiterate why you would be a good choice for their business or organization. If you can work summers or part-time during the school year, include that offer as well. You could end up with a part-time job opportunity that leads to a scholarship offer and then to full-time employment upon completion of your college degree.

Now you are ready to implement a widespread scholarship search. Give yourself enough time to jot down the first ideas that come to you, plus additional time to revise or increase the scope of your plan as more and more ideas come to you. So close the book, start taking notes, and wait awhile before starting chapter 6.

CHAPTER 6

State Aid Programs

If you live in one of the states or territories that make up the United States, you are probably paying state taxes whether you are a resident of that state or not. If you have moved recently, you may be considered a resident and invited to participate in jury duty, but still not be considered a resident for in-state tuition rates at the local college. If you moved to your current state to attend graduate school, your school may never consider you a state resident while you are completing your graduate courses. Depending on the agency you are dealing with, each one seems to have its own interpretation of what it takes to be a resident of a state.

State Residency

States raise funds to educate their residents in a number of ways, from taxes to lotteries. In addition to the aid dollars raised by individual states, there are three programs where federal dollars are channeled to states for administration at the local level. Each state's legislature determines how its state financial aid programs will be awarded to both residents and nonresidents. The legislature often appoints a state agency to manage the funds and to determine the reporting requirements for the schools that receive these funds. However, when it comes to individual interpretation of the legislature's definition of a state resident, that decision is usually made by the financial aid office at your school.

Financial aid directors have different views on the accuracy of self-reported residency status. (Remember the question on the FAFSA about the student's state of residency?) Some financial aid directors simply accept the student's self-reported status from the FAFSA, others take the student's permanent address as an accurate reflection of the student's home state, and still others require a signed statement. As a potential financial aid recipient, now is the time to contact your top choice schools to ask how they determine state residency. You should also ask which scholarships, grants, or work programs are based on state residency.

State Aid Programs

Federally Assisted State Aid Programs

Leveraging Educational Assistance Partnership

The three federal programs that direct aid funds to individual states for administration are the Leveraging Educational Assistance Partnership (LEAP) Program, the Robert C. Byrd Honors Scholarship Program, and Vocational Rehabilitation. Each state has its own name for LEAP, formerly known as the State Student Incentive Grant. States also have their own maximum award amounts and application procedures for this program, and each state probably matches federal dollars with state dollars. Many states award their individual colleges and universities a percentage of the fund based on the institution's enrollment figures as well as the level of need of the institution's students. Based on the amount of funding for LEAP that the colleges and universities receive from their state, these institutions then include the aid dollars in the financial aid packages of individual students. Obviously, the LEAP recipient must be enrolled in a college or university within the state. In addition, one of the common requirements is that the recipient is a state resident. So in most cases this award goes to state residents who *remain* in state for their education (regardless of whether or not their institution is public or private). This award is made based on funding and eligibility, but it is not renewable. Like many of the other limited dollars funds, LEAP is often awarded on a first-come, first-served basis. Once again, pay attention to your school's financial aid application deadlines. Usually there is a cap on the maximum dollars awarded to each student, and LEAP is often tied to a family's need.

Robert C. Byrd Honors Scholarship

Unlike LEAP, the Robert C. Byrd Honors Scholarship is not need-based. In fact, the student may apply for the award through his high school administrators even before his family's EFC is finalized. The Byrd scholarship was established to award and encourage the most able students who are graduating from high school each year, so the scholarship must be applied for during the student's senior year, and the student must be a resident of the state that is making the award. In this case, there are no requirements on the location of the college or university the student attends. To summarize, the Byrd Scholarship is awarded to state residents who can attend college in-state or out-of-state. The Byrd Scholarship is renewable, so a specific amount can be received by the student for each of his first four years of undergraduate study. Contact your state agency to find out if there are any requirements for renewing the award.

Financial Aid 101

www.petersons.com

Chapter 6

Vocational Rehabilitation

For individuals with disabilities, vocational rehabilitation (voc-rehab) provides opportunities to enter or reenter the workforce and live more independently. A person's vocation is her area of employment. To rehabilitate means to restore to health or usefulness. Voc-rehab is simply training or retraining a person for employment. Sometimes the individual is trained for a vocation that she has not tried before but where her disability will not undermine her quality of work. Sometimes she returns to her former vocation but is "retrained" so she can perform the job in ways that allow her to work around or with her disability. The Department of Education's Rehabilitation Services Administration provides grants to the state vocational rehabilitation agencies to assist in this training. Any type of disability can be considered for voc-rehab. The Americans with Disabilities Act specifically refrains from listing disabilities, so if you have any condition that could cause you difficulty in finding employment, contact your state's vocational rehabilitation agency to determine your eligibility for the program.

Students are most likely to receive the maximum assistance available if they begin to inquire about voc-rehab programs as early as possible, contacting both their state agency and the school they hope to attend. Like LEAP and the Byrd scholarship, vocational rehabilitation funds are awarded to state residents. If the training the student needs is offered at an institution within the state, the voc-rehab counselor for the state agency will probably encourage the student to remain in the state for his education. However, if the training is not offered in state, the voc-rehab counselor may be more flexible in accommodating the student's desire to attend an out-of-state institution.

Many states offer numerous scholarship, grant, work, and loan programs, and your options are not limited to only the three federally sponsored initiatives. A comprehensive state-by-state listing of grant, scholarship, and forgivable loan programs can be found in Appendix D.

The primary contact agency is listed first. The primary contact agency usually handles LEAP as well as other state programs. The Byrd Scholarship contact information is listed next, followed by the contact information for the state vocational rehabilitation agency. If there is not a separate listing for the Byrd Scholarship, then the state's primary contact office or agency manages the Byrd Scholarship program in addition to other state aid programs (such as LEAP). For voc-rehab, general contact information for the state agency is listed. However, participation in each state's voc-rehab program always begins with assessment at the local level, so search for the list of local offices and contact a representative

State Aid Programs

close to you. When available, pertinent Web site addresses are also listed for the state agencies.

Each of the following links has been carefully researched to give you the best information available with "one click." Some links may take you directly to a hard-to-find page instead of the home page for the agency. In two or three instances, no links for the state's scholarships or grants could be found at the time of publication. The absence of a link does not indicate a lack of state scholarship and grant opportunities, only a lack of electronic information about the state's scholarships. If your state is one of those with a minimal electronic presence on the Internet, suggestions are included for alternative ways to research state scholarships and grants.

State or Territory	Agency
Alabama	Alabama Commission on Higher Education Grants and Scholarships Department P.O. Box 302000 Montgomery, Alabama 36130-2000 Phone: 334-242-2273 www.ache.state.al.us/
Byrd Scholarship	State Department of Education Classroom Improvement Division Gordon Persons Office Building P.O. Box 302101 Montgomery, Alabama 36130-2101 Phone: 334-242-8059
Vocational Rehabilitation	Alabama Department of Rehabilitation Services 2129 E. South Boulevard Montgomery, Alabama 36116 Phone: 334-281-8780 Phone: 800-441-7607 www.rehab.state.al.us/

Financial Aid 101

Chapter 6

State or Territory	Agency
Alaska	Alaska Commission on Postsecondary Education 3030 Vintage Boulevard Juneau, Alaska 99801-7109 Phone: 907-465-6743 www.state.ak.us/acpe/
Byrd Scholarship	Alaska Department of Education and Early Development 801 West 10th Street, Suite 200 Juneau, Alaska 99801-1894 Phone: 907-465-8728
Vocational Rehabilitation	Division of Vocational Rehabilitation 801 W. 10th Street, Suite A Juneau, Alaska 99801-1894 Phone: 907-465-2814 or 800-478-2815 (toll-free) www.labor.state.ak.us/dvr/home.htm
Arizona	Arizona Commission for Postsecondary Education Suite 550 2020 North Central Avenue Phoenix, Arizona 85004-4503 Phone: 602-258-2435 Ext. 101 www.acpe.asu.edu/
Byrd Scholarship	State Department of Education Robert C. Byrd Scholarship Office 1535 West Jefferson Phoenix, Arizona 85007 Phone: 602-542-7469
Vocational Rehabilitation	Rehabilitation Services Administration 1789 West Jefferson, 2NW Phoenix, Arizona 85007 Phone: 602-542-3332 TTY: 602-542-6049 www.de.state.az.us/rsa/contact.asp

State Aid Programs

State or Territory	Agency
Arkansas	Arkansas Department of Higher Education 114 East Capitol Little Rock, Arkansas 72201-3818 Phone: 501-682-4396 www.arkansashighered.com/
Byrd Scholarship	Arkansas Department of Education Room 107A 4 State Capitol Mall Little Rock, Arkansas 72201-1071 Phone: 501-682-4396
Vocational Rehabilitation	Arkansas Rehabilitation Services Administrative Offices 1616 Brookwood Drive P.O. Box 3781 Little Rock, Arkansas 72203 Phone: 501-296-1600 TDD: 501-296-1669 www.arsinfo.org/directory.html
California	California Student Aid Commission P.O. Box 419027 Rancho Cordova, California 95741-9027 Phone: 916-526-7590 http://216.190.132.67/
Byrd Scholarship	California Student Aid Commission Attn: Specialized Programs P.O. Box 419029 Rancho Cordova, California 95741-9027 Phone: 888-224-7268 (toll-free)
Vocational Rehabilitation	California Department of Rehabilitation P.O. Box 944222 2000 Evergreen Street Sacramento, California 95815 Phone: 916-263-8981 TTY: 916-263-7477 www.rehab.cahwnet.gov/eps/default.htm

State or Territory	Agency
Colorado	Colorado Commission on Higher Education 1380 Lawrence Street, Suite 1200 Denver, Colorado 80204 Phone: 303-866-2723 www.state.co.us/cche/
Byrd Scholarship	Colorado Department of Education Robert Byrd Scholarships, Room 501 East Colfax Avenue Denver, Colorado 80203-1705 Phone: 303-866-6974
Vocational Rehabilitation	Colorado Division of Vocational Rehabilitation 2211 West Evans, Bldg. B Denver, Colorado 80223 Phone: 303-866-4150 TDD: 303-866-4150 www.cdhs.state.co.us/ods/dvr/ods_dvr1.html
Connecticut	Connecticut Department of Higher Education 61 Woodland Street Hartford, Connecticut 06105-2326 Phone: 860-947-1833 www.ctdhe.org/SFA/default.htm www.ctdhe.org/SFA/pdfs/ByrdScholarship.pdf
Vocational Rehabilitation	Bureau of Rehabilitation Services Department of Social Services 25 Sigourney Street 11th Floor Hartford, Connecticut 06106 Phone: 800-537-2549 TDD/TTY: 860-424-4839 www.brs.state.ct.us/

State Aid Programs

State or Territory	Agency
Delaware	Delaware Higher Education Commission Fifth Floor Carvel State Office Building 820 North French Street Wilmington, Delaware 19801 Phone: 302-577-3240 www.doe.state.de.us/high-ed/scholarships.htm
Vocational Rehabilitation	Delaware Division of Vocational Rehabilitation 4425 North Market Street P.O. Box 9969 Wilmington, Delaware 19089-0969 Phone: 302-761-8275 TTY/FAX: 302-761-6611 www.delawareworks.com/divisions/dvr/welcome.htm
District of Columbia	State Education Office (District of Columbia) Suite 350 North 441 Fourth Street, NW Washington, DC 20001 Phone: 202-727-2824 or 877-485-6751 (toll-free) http://seo.dc.gov/services/post_secondary_financial_assistance/index.shtm
Byrd Scholarship	District of Columbia Public Schools Student Affairs Branch 6th Floor 825 North Capitol Street, NE Washington, DC 20002 Phone: 202-442-5110
Vocational Rehabilitation	Rehabilitation Services Department of Human Services John A. Wilson Building 1350 Pennsylvania Avenue, NW Washington, DC 20004 Phone: 202-442-8400 TTY: 202-442-8600 http://dhs.dc.gov/info/rehabservices.shtm

Chapter 6

State or Territory	Agency
Florida	Florida Department of Education Office of Student Financial Assistance 1940 North Monroe Street, Suite 70 Tallahassee, Florida 32303 - 4759 Phone: 888-827-2004 www.firn.edu/doe/bin00065/splist.htm
Vocational Rehabilitation	Division of Vocational Rehabilitation 2002 Old Saint Augustine Road, Building A Tallahassee, Florida 32301-4862 Phone: 850-488-6210 www.rehabworks.org/
Georgia	Georgia Student Finance Commission 2082 East Exchange Place Tucker, Georgia 30084 Phone: 770-724-9000 or 800-776-6878 www.gsfc.org/GSFC/gsfc_index.cfm
Byrd Scholarship	Governor's Honors' Program Georgia Department of Education 1770 Twin Towers East 205 Butler Street Atlanta, Georgia 30334 Phone: 404-657-0183 www.doe.k12.ga.us/_documents/support/sss/scholarship_byrd.pdf
Vocational Rehabilitation	Rehabilitation Services 148 Andrew Young International Boulevard Suite 510, Sussex Place Atlanta, Georgia 30303 Phone: 404-235-0140 www.vocrehabga.org/

State Aid Programs

State or Territory	Agency
Hawaii	Hawaii State Postsecondary Education Commission Room 209 2444 Dole Street Honolulu, Hawaii 96822-2302 Phone: 808-956-8213 http://doe.k12.hi.us/bulletin15.pdf
Vocational Rehabilitation	Vocational Rehabilitation and Services for the Blind Division Department of Human Services 1390 Miller Street, Room 209 Honolulu, Hawaii 96813 www.state.hi.us/dhs/vr.pdf
Idaho	Idaho State Board of Education P.O. Box 83720 Boise, Idaho 83720-0027 Phone: 208-334-2270 www.idahoboardofed.org/scholarships.asp
Byrd Scholarship	Idaho State Department of Education 650 West State Street P.O. Box 83720 Boise, Idaho 83720-0027 Phone: 208-332-6800 www.sde.state.id.us/instruct/scholarships.htm
Vocational Rehabilitation	Idaho Vocational Rehabilitation P.O. Box 83720 650 West State Street, Room 150 Boise, Idaho 83720-0096 Phone: 208-334-3390

Financial Aid 101

State or Territory	Agency
Illinois	Illinois Student Assistance Commission 1755 Lake Cook Road Deerfield, Illinois 60015-5209 Phone: 847-948-8500 or 800-899-4722 www.isac1.org/ilaid/ilaid.html
Vocational Rehabilitation	ORS Vocational Rehabilitation (VR) Program Department of Human Services 100 South Grand Avenue, E Springfield, Illinois 62762 Phone: 800-843-6154 TTY: 800-447-6404 www.dhs.state.il.us/ors/vr/
Indiana	State Student Assistance Commission of Indiana 150 West Market Street, Suite 500 Indianapolis, Indiana 46204 Tel: 317-232-2350 www.in.gov/ssaci/
Vocational Rehabilitation	Vocational Rehabilitation Services Indiana Family and Social Services Administration Office of Communications P.O. Box 7083 Indianapolis, Indiana 46207-7083 www.ai.org/fssa/servicedisabl/vr/index.html
Iowa	Iowa College Student Aid Commission 200 10th Street, 4th Floor Des Moines, Iowa 50309-3609 Phone: 515-242-3344 www.iowacollegeaid.org/
Vocational Rehabilitation	Division of Vocational Rehabilitation Services 510 East 12th Street Des Moines, Iowa 50319-0240 Phone/TTY: 515-281-4211 www.dvrs.state.ia.us/index.html

State Aid Programs

State or Territory	Agency
Kansas	Kansas Board of Regents 1000 Southwest Jackson Street, Suite 520 Topeka, Kansas 66612-1368 Phone: 735-296-3421 www.kansasregents.org/financial_aid/index.html
Byrd Scholarship	Kansas Department of Education Robert C. Byrd Scholarship Program 120 Southeast 10th Avenue Topeka, Kansas 66612-1103 Phone: 785-296-4950 www.ksbe.state.ks.us/Welcome.html
Vocational Rehabilitation	Vocational Rehabilitation Services Kansas Department of Social and Rehabilitation Services 915 Southwest Harrison Street Topeka, Kansas 66612 Phone: 785-296-3959 TTY: 785-296-1491 www.srskansas.org/rehab/text/VR.htm
Kentucky	Kentucky Higher Education Assistance Authority P.O. Box 798 Frankfort, Kentucky 40602-0798 Phone: 800-928-8926 www.kheaa.com/prog_home.html
Byrd Scholarship	Kentucky Department of Education 500 Mero Street, 19th Floor Capitol Plaza Tower Frankfort, Kentucky 40601 Phone: 800-533-5372 (toll-free in Kentucky)
Vocational Rehabilitation	Kentucky Department of Vocational Rehabilitation 209 St. Clair Frankfort, Kentucky 40601 Phone: 502-564-4440 TTY: 888-420-9874 http://kydvr.state.ky.us/

Chapter 6

State or Territory	Agency
Louisiana	Louisiana Student Financial Assistance Commission P.O. Box 91202 Baton Rouge, Louisiana 70821-9202 Phone: 800-259-5626, extension 1012 www.osfa.state.la.us/
Byrd Scholarship	Louisiana Department of Education P.O. Box 94064 626 North 4th Street, 12th Floor Baton Rouge, Louisiana 70804-9064 Phone: 225-342-2098
Vocational Rehabilitation	Louisiana Rehabilitation Services—Vocational Rehabilitation Program 8225 Florida Boulevard Baton Rouge, Louisiana 70806 Phone: 800-737-2958 www.dss.state.la.us/offlrs/html/vocational_rehabilitation.html
Maine	Finance Authority of Maine 5 Community Drive P.O. Box 949 Augusta, Maine 04332-0949 Phone: 207-623-3263 www.famemaine.com/html/education/index.html
Vocational Rehabilitation	Maine Bureau of Rehabilitation Services 150 State House Station Augusta, Maine 04333-0150 Phone: 207-624-5950 TTY: 888 755-0023 www.state.me.us/rehab/

State Aid Programs

State or Territory	Agency
Maryland	Maryland Higher Education Commission 839 Bestgate Road, Suite 400 Annapolis, Maryland 21401-3013 Phone: 410-260-4565 or 800-974-1024 TTY: 800-735-2258 www.mhec.state.md.us/SSA/progdesc.htm
Byrd Scholarship	Maryland State Department of Education School and Community Outreach Office 200 West Baltimore Street Baltimore, Maryland 21201 Phone: 410-767-0483 www.msde.state.md.us/programs/ byrdscholarship.html
Vocational Rehabilitation	Division of Rehabilitation Services 2301 Argonne Drive Baltimore, Maryland 21218-1696 Phone: 410-554-9385 TTY: 410-554-9411 www.dors.state.md.us/
Massachusetts	Office of Student Financial Assistance 454 Broadway Suite 200 Revere, Massachusetts 02151-3034 Phone: 617-727-9420 www.osfa.mass.edu/
Byrd Scholarship	Robert C. Byrd Scholarship Coordinator Massachusetts Department of Education 350 Main Street Malden, Massachusetts 02148-5023 Phone: 781-338-3000
Vocational Rehabilitation	The Massachusetts Rehabilitation Commission Fort Point Place, Suite 600 27 Wormwood Street Boston, Massachusetts 02210-1616 Phone/TTY: 800-245-6543 www.state.ma.us/mrc/vr/vrmain.htm

Financial Aid 101

Chapter 6

State or Territory	Agency
Michigan	Bureau of Student Financial Aid Office of Information and Resources P.O. Box 30466 Lansing, Michigan 48909-7966 Phone: 877-323-2287 www.michigan.gov/mistudentaid
Vocational Rehabilitation	Michigan Department of Career Development 201 North Washington Square Victor Office Center, 7th Floor Lansing, Michigan 48913 Phone/TTY: 866-694-6257 www.michigan.gov/mdcd/ 0,1607,7-122-1681--,00.html
Minnesota	Minnesota Higher Education Services Office 1450 Energy Park Drive, Suite 350 Saint Paul, Minnesota 55108-5227 Phone: 651-642-0567 www.mheso.state.mn.us/
Byrd Scholarship	Minnesota Department of Children, Families, and Learning 1500 Highway 36 West Roseville, Minnesota 55113 Phone: 615-582-8255
Vocational Rehabilitation	Paul Bridges Department of Economic Security Rehabilitation Services Branch 390 North Robert Street St. Paul, Minnesota 55101 Phone: 651-296-9981 or 800-328-9095 TTY: 651-296-3900 or 800-657-3973 www.mnworkforcecenter.org/rehab/vr/ main_vr.htm

State Aid Programs

State or Territory	Agency
Mississippi	Mississippi Student Financial Aid 3825 Ridgewood Road Jackson, Mississippi 39211-6453 Phone: 800-327-2980 (toll-free in Mississippi) www.ihl.state.ms.us/financialaid/
Byrd Scholarship	Mississippi Department of Education Robert C. Byrd Honors Scholarship Program P.O. Box 771 Jackson, Mississippi 39205-0771 Phone: 601-359-4305
Vocational Rehabilitation	Mississippi Department of Rehabilitation Services P.O. Box 1698 Jackson, Mississippi 39215-1698 Phone: 601-853-5100 or 800-443-1000 www.mdrs.state.ms.us/vrpage.htm
Missouri	Missouri Department of Higher Education 3515 Amazonas Drive Jefferson City, Missouri 65109-5717 Phone: 573-751-2361 www.dhe.mo.gov/Mostars/scholar2b.htm
Byrd Scholarship	Missouri Department of Education Division of Teacher Quality and Urban Education Robert C. Byrd Honors Scholarship P.O. Box 480 Jefferson City, Missouri 65109 Phone: 573-751-1668
Vocational Rehabilitation	Missouri Division of Vocational Rehabilitation VR Central Office 3024 Dupont Circle Jefferson City, Missouri 65109-0525 Phone: 573-751-3251 or 877-222-8963 (toll-free) TDD: 573-751-0881 www.vr.dese.state.mo.us/

Financial Aid 101

Chapter 6

State or Territory	Agency
Montana	Office of Commissioner of Higher Education 2500 Broadway Street P.O. Box 203101 Helena, Montana 59620-3101 Phone: 406-444-6570 http://gearup.montana.edu/financingeducation.htm
Byrd Scholarship	The Montana Office of Public Instruction P.O. Box 202501 Helena, Montana 59620-2501 Phone: 406-444-3095 or 888-231-9393 (Toll free in-state) www.opi.state.mt.us/
Vocational Rehabilitation	Vocational Rehabilitation 111 Sanders Suite 307 P.O. Box 4210 Helena, Montana 59604-4210 Phone/TDD: 406-444-2590 www.dphhs.state.mt.us/dsd/govt_programs/vrp/index.htm

State Aid Programs

State or Territory	Agency
Nebraska	Nebraska Coordinating Commission for Postsecondary Education Suite 300 140 North Eighth Street P.O. Box 95005 Lincoln, Nebraska 68509-5005 Phone: 402-471-2847 Currently, none of the state of Nebraska Web sites include a list of scholarships for Nebraska residents; try checking the links for each of the individual institutions listed under the Colleges and Universities heading at www.nol.org/education/.
Byrd Scholarship	Nebraska Department of Education 301 Centennial Mall Lincoln, Nebraska 68509-4987 Phone: 402-471-3962 www.nde.state.ne.us/byrd/
Vocational Rehabilitation	Quality Employment Solutions® Department of Education State of Nebraska P.O. Box 94987 Lincoln, Nebraska 68509 Phone: 402-471-3644 877-637-3422 (toll-free in Nebraska only) www.vocrehab.state.ne.us/

Financial Aid 101 www.petersons.com

Chapter 6

State or Territory	Agency
Nevada	Nevada Department of Education 700 East Fifth Street Carson City, Nevada 89701-5096 Phone: 775-687-9228 Although the Nevada Department of Education does not publish a list of state scholarships on its current Web page, the Nevada State Treasurer's office thoroughly describes the Nevada Millennium Scholarship at http://nevadatreasurer.com/millennium/.
Vocational Rehabilitation	Department of Employment, Training and Rehabilitation Rehabilitation Division Bureau of Vocational Rehabilitation 505 East King Street, Room 501 Carson City, Nevada 89701-3704 Phone: 775-684-4070 http://detr.state.nv.us/es/es_cep.htm
New Hampshire	Postsecondary Education Commission 3 Barrell Court, Suite 300 Concord, New Hampshire 03301-8543 Phone: 603-271-2555 TDD: 800-735-2964 www.state.nh.us/postsecondary/fin.html
Byrd Scholarship	New Hampshire Department of Education 101 Pleasant Street Concord, New Hampshire 03301-3860 Phone: 603-271-3494
Vocational Rehabilitation	New Hampshire Department of Education Vocational Rehabilitation 78 Regional Drive, Building 2 Concord, New Hampshire 03301 Phone: 603-271-3471 www.ed.state.nh.us/VR/VocRehab/WhatisVocRehab.html

State Aid Programs

State or Territory	Agency
New Jersey	State of New Jersey Higher Education Student Assistance Authority P.O. Box 540 Trenton, New Jersey 08625 Phone: 800-792-8670 (toll-free) www.hesaa.org/students/index.asp
Byrd Scholarship	New Jersey Department of Education 100 Riverview Plaza, P.O. Box 500 Trenton, New Jersey 08625-0500 Phone: 609-777-0800
Vocational Rehabilitation	New Jersey Department of Labor 135 East State Street P.O. Box 398 Trenton, New Jersey 08625-0398 Phone: 609-292-5987 TTY: 609-292-2919 www.nj.gov/labor/dvrs/vrsindex.html
New Mexico	New Mexico Commission on Higher Education 1068 Cerrillos Road Santa Fe, New Mexico 87505 Phone: 505-476-6500 www.nmche.org/collegefinance/stateaid.html
Byrd Scholarship	Robert C. Byrd Honors Scholarship Program New Mexico Department of Education Title I & Title V-A Office 300 Don Gaspar Santa Fe, New Mexico 87501-2786 www.sde.state.nm.us/div/sipds/Title6/byrd.html
Vocational Rehabilitation	State of New Mexico Division of Vocational Rehabilitation Disability Determination Services P.O. Box 4588 Albuquerque, New Mexico 87196 www.dvrgetsjobs.com/Public/Index.asp

Financial Aid 101

Chapter 6

State or Territory	Agency
New York	New York State Higher Education Services Corporation 99 Washington Avenue Albany, New York 12255 Phone: 518-473-1574 or 888-697-4372 (toll-free) www.hesc.com/free_money.html
Byrd Scholarship	The University of the State of New York The State Education Department Office of K-16 Initiatives and Access Programs Scholarships and Grants Administration Unit Room 1078 EBA Albany, New York 12234 Phone: 518-486-1319 www.highered.nysed.gov/kiap/scholarships/rcb.htm
Vocational Rehabilitation	New York State Education Department Vocational and Educational Services for Individuals with Disabilities Special Education Services One Commerce Plaza, Room 1624 Albany, New York 12234 Phone: 800-222-5627 www.vesid.nysed.gov/all/services.htm

State Aid Programs

State or Territory	Agency
North Carolina	North Carolina State Education Assistance Authority P.O. Box 14103 Research Triangle Park, North Carolina 27709 Phone: 919-549-8614 www.ncseaa.edu/Paying_for_college.htm
Byrd Scholarship	North Carolina Department of Public Instruction Center for Recruitment and Retention Division of Human Resource Management Department of Public Instruction 301 North Wilmington Street Raleigh, North Carolina 27601 Phone: 919-807-3369 www.ncpublicschools.org/scholarships/robcbyrd.htm Another resource for scholarship information on the Department of Public Instruction Web pages is www.ncpublicschools.org/scholarships/.
Vocational Rehabilitation	North Carolina Department of Health and Human Services 2801 Mail Service Center Raleigh, North Carolina 27699-2801 Phone: 919-855-3500 http://dvr.dhhs.state.nc.us/DVR/VRS/vrshome.htm

Financial Aid 101

Chapter 6

State or Territory	Agency
North Dakota	North Dakota University System 10th Floor, State Capitol 600 East Boulevard Avenue, Dept. 215 Bismarck, North Dakota 58505-0230 Phone: 701-328-2960 www.ndus.edu/student_info/financial_aid/default.asp
Byrd Scholarship	North Dakota Department of Public Instruction 600 East Boulevard Avenue, Dept. 201 Bismarck, North Dakota 58505-0440 Phone: 701-328-2260 www.dpi.state.nd.us/resource/byrd.shtm
Vocational Rehabilitation	Vocational Rehabilitation 600 South 2nd Street, Suite 1B Bismarck, North Dakota 58504 Phone: 701-328-8950 or 800-755-2745 TDD: 701-328-8968 www.crisnd.com/cris/program.html?program=1046

State Aid Programs

State or Territory	Agency
Ohio	Ohio Board of Regents State Grants and Scholarships Department P.O. Box 182452 Columbus, Ohio 43218-2452 Phone: 614-466-7420 or 888-833-1133 (toll-free) www.regents.state.oh.us/sgs/
Byrd Scholarship	Ohio Department of Education Robert C. Byrd Honors Scholarship Program Information 25 South Front Street Columbus, Ohio 43215-4183 Phone: 614-466-4590 www.regents.state.oh.us/sgsinstitution/robert_information.htm
Vocational Rehabilitation	Ohio Rehabilitation Services Commission Bureau of Vocational Rehabilitation June K. Gutterman, Director 400 East Campus View Boulevard, SW3C Columbus, Ohio 43235-4604 Phone: 614-438-1250 TTY (in Ohio only): 800-282-4536, ext. 1250 www.state.oh.us/rsc/VR_Services/BVR/bvr.asp

Chapter 6

State or Territory	Agency
Oklahoma	Oklahoma State Regents for Higher Education 655 Research Parkway, Suite 200 Oklahoma City, Oklahoma 73104 Phone: 405-225-9100 www.okhighered.org/student-center/financial-aid/grants.shtml
Byrd Scholarship	Oklahoma State Department of Education Professional Services Division Oliver Hodge Building 2500 North Lincoln Boulevard Oklahoma City, Oklahoma 73105-4599 Phone: 405-521-2808 www.okhighered.org/student-center/financial-aid/byrd.shtml
Vocational Rehabilitation	Department of Rehabilitation Services 3535 Northwest 58th Street, Suite 500 Oklahoma City, Oklahoma 73112-4815 Phone: 405-951-3400 or 800-845-8476 (toll-free) www.okrehab.org/indexmanual.html (Scroll to the link for Education.)

State Aid Programs

State or Territory	Agency
Oregon	Grants and Scholarships Division Oregon Student Assistance Commission 1500 Valley River Drive, Suite 100 P.O. Box 40370 Eugene, Oregon 97404 Phone: 541-687-7395 or 800-452-8807, ext. 7395 (toll-free) www.getcollegefunds.org/ong.html www.osac.state.or.us/byrd_scholarships.pdf Additional information about private scholarships can be found at www.osac.state.or.us/private.html.
Vocational Rehabilitation	Oregon Department of Human Services 500 Summer Street, NE E25 Salem, Oregon 97301-1098 Phone: 503-945-5944 TTY: 503-947-5330 www.dhs.state.or.us/vr/
Pennsylvania	Pennsylvania Higher Education Assistance Agency Pennsylvania State Grants and Special Programs 1200 North 7th Street Harrisburg, Pennsylvania 17102-1444 Phone: 800-692-7392 TDD (in Pennsylvania): 717-720-2366 or 800-654-5988 (toll-free) www.pheaa.org/index.html www.pheaa.org/specialprograms/Robert_C_Byrd_Honors_Scholarship_Program.shtml
Vocational Rehabilitation	Pennsylvania Department of Labor and Industry Office of Vocational Rehabilitation 1521 North Sixth Street Harrisburg, Pennsylvania 17102 Phone: 800-442-6351 www.dli.state.pa.us/landi/cwp/browse.asp?a=128&bc=0&c=27855

Financial Aid 101

Chapter 6

State or Territory	Agency
Rhode Island	Rhode Island Higher Education Assistance Authority 560 Jefferson Boulevard Warwick, Rhode Island 02886 Phone: 401-736-1100 www.riheaa.org/borrowers/ (Scroll down left menu bar to Scholarships link and then to Grants link.) Rhode Island Office of Higher Education Academic and Student Affairs 301 Promenade Street Providence, Rhode Island 02908-5748 Phone: 401-222-6560 www.ribghe.org/fin-aid.htm
Byrd	Rhode Island Department of Education 255 Westminster Street Providence, RI 02903 Phone: 401-222-4600
Vocational Rehabilitation	Rhode Island Department of Human Services Office of Rehabilitation Services 40 Fountain Street Providence, Rhode Island 02903 Phone: 401-421-7005 TTY: 401-421-7016 www.ors.state.ri.us/

State Aid Programs

State or Territory	Agency
South Carolina	South Carolina Commission On Higher Education 1333 Main Street, Suite 200 Columbia, South Carolina 29201 Phone: 803-737-2260 www.sctuitiongrants.com/
Byrd Scholarship	South Carolina Department of Education 1100 Rutledge Building 1429 Senate Street Columbia, South Carolina 29201 Phone: 803-734-8116 www.sde.state.sc.us/superintendent/scholarships.cfm
Vocational Rehabilitation	South Carolina Rehabilitation Department (see list of local SCVRD offices for contact information) www.scvrd.net/welcome.htm

Financial Aid 101

State or Territory	Agency
South Dakota	South Dakota Board of Regents 306 East Capitol Ave Suite 200 Pierre, South Dakota 57501-2545 Phone: 605-773-3455 www.ris.sdbor.edu/paying_for_college.htm
Byrd Scholarship	South Dakota Department of Education and Cultural Affairs Davison of Education 700 Governors Drive Pierre, South Dakota 57501-2291 Phone: 605-773-3426 www.state.sd.us/deca/secretary/byrd/index.htm
Vocational Rehabilitation	Division of Rehabilitation Services Hillsview Plaza 3800 East Highway 34 c/o 500 East Capitol Pierre, South Dakota 57501-5070 Phone: 605-773-3195 www.state.sd.us/dhs/drs/vocrehab/vr.htm

State Aid Programs

State or Territory	Agency
Tennessee	Tennessee Higher Education Commission Suite 1900 Parkway Towers 404 James Robertson Parkway Nashville, Tennessee 37243 Phone: 615-741-3605 www.state.tn.us/thec/fin_grant_tuition.html
Byrd Scholarship	Tennessee Student Assistance Corporation 404 James Robertson Parkway, Suite 1950 Nashville, Tennessee 37243-0820 Phone: 615-741-1346 www.state.tn.us/tsac/finaidap.htm
Vocational Rehabilitation	Vocational Rehabilitation Department of Human Services 400 Deaderick Street, 15th Floor Nashville, Tennessee 37248-0001 Phone: 615-313-4700 www.state.tn.us/humanserv/VRServices.html

Financial Aid 101

Chapter 6

State or Territory	Agency
Texas	Texas Higher Education Coordinating Board P.O. Box 12788 1200 East Anderson Lane Austin, Texas 78711 Phone: 512-427-6101 www.collegefortexans.com/residency/finaid.cfm (Click on each award listed on this Web page for a link to a description page, which includes details on the program.)
Byrd Scholarship	Office of Education Services — Youth Services Attn: Gregory Travillion, CC: 350 Texas Education Agency 1701 North Congress Avenue Austin, Texas 78701 Phone: 512-475-0228 www.tea.state.tx.us/youth/byrd.html
Vocational Rehabilitation	Texas Rehabilitation Commission 4900 North Lamar Boulevard Austin, Texas 78751 Phone: 512-424-4000 www.rehab.state.tx.us/services.html

State Aid Programs

State or Territory	Agency
Utah	Utah System of Higher Education 60 South 400 West Salt Lake City, Utah 84101-1284 Phone: 801-321-7101 www.utahsbr.edu/html/financial_aid.html
Byrd Scholarship	Office of the Utah State Superintendent of Public Instruction 250 East 500 South P.O. Box 144200 Salt Lake City, Utah 84114-4200 Phone: 801-538-7741 www.usoe.k12.ut.us/cert/scholarships/BYRDSCHO.htm
Vocational Rehabilitation	Utah State Office of Rehabilitation 250 East 500 South Salt Lake City, Utah 84111 Phone: 801-538-7530 www.usor.utah.gov/public/vocrehab.htm
Vermont	Vermont Student Assistance Corporation P.O. Box 2000 Champlain Mill Winooski, Vermont 05404 Phone: 802-655-9602 www.vsac.org/paying/pw_pay1.htm
Vocational Rehabilitation	Agency of Human Services Department of Aging and Disabilities 103 South Main Street Waterbury, Vermont 05671 Phone: 802-241-2400 www.dad.state.vt.us/dvr/VRFAQ.htm

Chapter 6

State or Territory	Agency
Virginia	State Council of Higher Education for Virginia 101 North 14th Street James Monroe Building Richmond, Virginia 23219 Phone: 804-225-2600 www.schev.edu/Students/financialAidState.asp
Byrd Scholarship	Virginia Department of Education James Monroe Building P.O. Box 2120 101 North 14th Street Richmond, Virginia 23219 Phone: 800-292-3820 www.schev.edu/students/programdescriprcbyrdschprog.asp
Vocational Rehabilitation	Department of Rehabilitative Services P.O. Box K-300 8004 Franklin Farms Drive Richmond, Virginia 23288-0300 Phone: 800-552-5019 TTY: 800-464-9950 www.vadrs.org/vocrehab.htm

State Aid Programs

State or Territory	Agency
Washington	Student Financial Aid Office Washington Higher Education Coordinating Board 917 Lakeridge Way P.O. Box 43430 Olympia, Washington 98504-3430 Phone: 360-753-7850 www.hecb.wa.gov/paying/waaidprgm/waaidprgmindex.asp
Byrd Scholarship	Office of Superintendent of Public Instruction Old Capitol Building P.O. Box 47200 Olympia, WA 98504-7200 Phone: 360-725-6103 www.k12.wa.us/integratedcurr/Byrd/Byrd%20Info.asp
Vocational Rehabilitation	Washington State Department of Social and Health Services P.O. Box 45130 Olympia, Washington 98504-5130 Phone: 800-737-0617 (Washington State only) www1.dshs.wa.gov/dvr/aboutdvr/abilities.htm (Scroll to the bottom of this Web page to the Contact us for more information link, then use the first link on the new page to access a list of local offices.)

Financial Aid 101

Chapter 6

State or Territory	Agency
West Virginia	West Virginia Higher Education Policy Commission 1018 Kanawha Boulevard East Suite 700 Charleston, West Virginia 25301 Phone: 304-558-2101 www.hepc.wvnet.edu/students/index.html
Byrd Scholarship	Robert C. Byrd Honors Scholarship Program West Virginia Higher Education Policy Commission 1018 Kanawha Boulevard East, Suite 700 Charleston, West Virginia 25301 Phone: 304-558-4618 www.hepc.wvnet.edu/students/index.html
Vocational Rehabilitation	West Virginia Department of Education and the Arts Division of Rehabilitation Services P.O. Box 50890 Charleston, West Virginia 25305 Phone: 800-642-8207 www.wvdrs.org/Service_to_PWD.html

State Aid Programs

State or Territory	Agency
Wisconsin	Higher Educational Aids Board P.O. Box 7885 Madison, Wisconsin 53707-7885 Phone: 608-267-2206 http://heab.state.wi.us/programs.html
Byrd Scholarship	Federal Robert C. Byrd Honors Scholarship Program Wisconsin Department of Public Instruction 125 South Webster Street P.O. Box 7841 Madison, Wisconsin 53707-7841 Phone: 608-266-3706 www.dpi.state.wi.us/dpi/dlsis/cal/caltbyr.html
Vocational Rehabilitation	Vocational Rehabilitation Wisconsin Department of Workforce Development 201 East Washington Avenue P.O. Box 7852 Madison, Wisconsin 53707-7852 Phone: 608-261-0050 TTY: 888-877-5939 www.dwd.state.wi.us/dvr/jobseek.htm

Financial Aid 101

Chapter 6

State or Territory	Agency
Wyoming	Wyoming Department of Education 2300 Capitol Avenue Hathaway Building, 2nd Floor Cheyenne, Wyoming 82002-0050 Phone: 307-777-7675 www.k12.wy.us/ADMIN/awards/faq.html The University of Wyoming has created a thorough list of scholarships available at each of the Wyoming Colleges. Go to the Office of Student Financial Aid Web site at http://uwadmnweb.uwyo.edu/sfa/schlbook/schlbook.htm for additional details on state scholarships and grants.
Vocational Rehabilitation	Wyoming Department of Workforce Services Vocational Rehabilitation Services 1100 Herschler Building Cheyenne, Wyoming 82002 Phone: 307-777-7389 http://dwsweb.state.wy.us/vr.asp

CHAPTER 7

What a Deal!

How do you make decisions about major purchases? More than likely, you compare the costs of different brands, compare the features of different models, and review your comfort level as far as the total expenditure. Whether you are purchasing a car, a computer, a camera, a refrigerator, a dishwasher, a new roof, or a lawn irrigation system, these three components are probably going to play important roles in your decision-making process. And although all of the three components are probably equally important, their priorities may change from purchase to purchase.

For example, you may be loyal to Chevrolet for all your driving needs, and that brand is your number-one priority when it comes to purchasing a new car. No matter what price, model, or features you're looking for, Chevrolet is the only dealership you will consider. On the other hand, when it comes to buying a refrigerator, as long as the model has an icemaker, you don't care which brand you choose. You also may decide to spend no more than $1,000 including tax and delivery, making price your second-highest priority for the refrigerator purchase. However, when it comes to buying a computer, price might be your highest priority. Perhaps the computer is only going to be used to check your e-mail and shop on the Web, and you feel that all computers can deliver these basic functions. You don't care whether you work in Windows on a PC or in OS X on a Mac. You are just looking for the least expensive computer you can find. Now, your neighbor may not agree with your decision or your priorities. Your relatives may nag you constantly about why you bought that particular car, refrigerator, or computer. And you will definitely run into someone at work, at home, or in the neighborhood who "could have gotten you a better deal." Resist the urge to make a rude gesture; just smile and walk away. It's your purchase, and it's important that you are happy with your decision.

Don't be surprised then when I tell you that these same three components—brand, features, and price—are going to play important parts in your decision about which college to attend. You may be set on a University of California education, regardless of which campus you attend or the total cost of attendance. You may want a degree in biomedical engineering but don't care where you go as long as the college has a high placement rate for its bio-med undergraduates and costs less than $28,000 per year. Or, you may look at your finances and decide that your family can afford to pay $2,000 each year for your education and make a decision about your university and major based solely on cost of attendance and the financial aid package offered by the school.

More than likely, you will create a list or chart to compare your choices. For simple purchases, you might make the comparison in your head. But for complex decisions, such as which college to attend or which financial aid package is better, creating a chart is your best bet. If you want to set up this table in Excel or in another electronic format, go right ahead. If you think better with a pen or pencil and a piece of paper, make as many copies of the form as you need. The comparison can be started as early as you desire, but you will not be able to complete the chart until you have received your financial aid offer. Although some financial aid offers are made as early as January, most financial aid offices do not have their software or their tentative budgets ready until late February or March. A few financial aid offices are set up to make initial aid offers with generic award names, such as *loan, work-study, institutional grant*, etc. Later in the year, possibly as late as July, the generic names are replaced with the official award names. This allows the financial aid office to notify you of the dollar amount of your package, without having to commit to a specific award name. After their federal and state allocations and their institutional fund amounts are announced, the aid officers will use these awards to replace the estimated awards in the initial package. You may have to make a decision on whether or not to accept the school's offer of admission based on the estimated aid offer.

I know you have accumulated enough information to know that a grant is preferable to a loan or to work-study. However, most schools offer a combination of loan, work-study, and grants. When reviewing combination packages, many families become confused as to how to judge which package is most favorable. This chapter shows you three different ways to compare your aid offers. The most easy-to-use method is first. This is the **Checkbook Comparison** and simply totals your costs, subtracts your aid package, and leaves you to make a decision based

Chapter 7

on the results. The second method is the **Accountant Comparison**. More complex than the first method, this method compares your different schools' costs and financial aid and then backs out loans and work-study, which are types of aid that place the burden of payment back on the family. The most analytical method is shown last. Think of this method as the **Wall Street Comparison**. Not only does this method take into consideration your costs and financial aid package, it also incorporates your family's priorities as far as importance of aid awards versus institution reputation or other school features. Feel free to use the tool that suits you best and ignore the others. The more you manipulate the costs and aid packages to try to get the results you want, the more frustrated you will become. You are not going to make a college decision just because Aunt Sally said it's the best deal, so don't make your final decision based on the results of these comparison charts. A comparison chart is only one more tool to help you put your thoughts in order.

The Checkbook Comparison

Just as you balance your checkbook by noting the money that comes into your account and the money that flows out of your account, this method compares your educational costs and your anticipated aid package. The only award you do not count in your total aid package is work-study. This award typically shows up in your financial aid offer, but it cannot be deducted from your bill because the award is only a promise of dollars to be earned by the student. This award can be used—as it is earned—to help cover monthly expenses, so it is counted as a resource in the last section, "More Expenses."

www.petersons.com

Financial Aid 101

What a Deal!

	School 1	School 2	School 3	Notes
	Large University	Famous College	University of My Hometown	
Billed Institutional Costs				
Tuition	$16,000	$43,000	$28,600	
Fees	486	1,100	254	
Room and Board	8,000	8,200	8,600	Maybe I should live at home.
Total Cost of Attendance (on your school bill)	$24,486	$52,300	$37,454	
Net Financial Aid Awards (can be used for credit on bill)				
Loan (net amount you receive to put toward payment of the student's bill; estimated 3% deducted for processing fees for these examples)	2,546	1,940	4,486	Large U. offered me $2,625 in student loans, Famous College offered $2,500, and U. of My Hometown offered $2,625 in federal loans and $2,000 in institutional loans for a total of $4,625
Work-Study (counts zero toward paying your bill)	-0-	-0-	-0-	Large U. and Famous College both offered $1,500 in Federal Work-Study; U. of My Hometown offered $3,000 in institutional work-study.
Pell Grant	400	400	400	
SEOG Grant	1,000	1,000	-0-	
State Grant(s)	-0-	1,000	2,000	

Financial Aid 101

www.petersons.com

Chapter 7

	School 1 Large University	School 2 Famous College	School 3 University of My Hometown	Notes
Institutional Grant(s) or Scholarship(s)	2,000	2,500	5,000	
Outside Scholarship(s)	800	800	800	Lions Club and PTA Scholarships
Total Financial Aid Package (excluding work-study) that you can apply to your bill	$6,746	$7,640	$12,686	
Your Immediate Cost = COA on bill minus Total Aid. The lowest number is the best "deal."	$17,740	$44,660	$24,768	This is what we'd have to pay to each school out of our pocket.
More Expenses				
Personal Expenses	1,570	1,500	1,650	
Transportation (all forms of travel during school year)	400	580	300	Famous College is farther from home than the other two.
Books	600	600	650	
Parking (if not included in fees on your bill)	-0-	50	235	Parking is included in the fees for Large U.
One-time Freshman Orientation Expenses	65	135	215	

www.petersons.com

Financial Aid 101

What a Deal!

	School 1	School 2	School 3	Notes
	Large University	Famous College	University of My Hometown	
Additional Annual Fees (athletic events, college, dorm, club or fraternity dues, etc.)	45	163	465	Large U. has a general use fee; Famous College has fees for ID, lab, and GoTeam card; U. of My Hometown has newspaper, intramural, and communications fees.
Total Additional Expenses	2,680	3,028	3,515	
Work-Study or other earnings from school-year employment	1,500	1,500	3,000	See notes above on work-study awards.
Your Monthly Costs = Additional Expenses minus Work-Study. Although these expenses may seem minor compared to your bill, you still need to discuss how they will be covered.	$ 1,180	$ 1,528	$ 515	This is how much more I need for my extra expenses after I use my work-study earnings.

The Accountant Comparison

What do the different forms of aid mean to you in the long run? If your long-range concern is how much the total education is going to cost you, then you should deduct loans from the financial aid package. Instead, this method lumps student and parent educational loans in with the other resources families draw on to cover their anticipated expenses. This method gives you a more realistic idea of how much each institution is "giving" you in aid dollars that require neither repayment nor work. In this case, an institution that offers your student a few grant dollars and a great deal of loan dollars is not going to receive a favorable comparison regardless of the total dollars in the aid package. For example, what if Big State

Financial Aid 101   www.petersons.com

Chapter 7

University offers you a total aid package of $20,000 ($9,000 is in the form of loans, $1,000 is in work-study) and Rival Rural University offers you a total aid package of $16,000 ($2,000 in loans and no work-study requirement)? Which is the better package? Rival Rural University is offering you $14,000 in grants and scholarships. Big State University is offering you $10,000 in grants and scholarships. If their costs are similar, then Rival is offering you the best package. For the table below, the original three fictional schools reappear with the exact same costs and financial aid offers. As noted in the explanation above, loans have been removed from the financial aid package.

	School 1	School 2	School 3	Notes
	Large University	Famous College	University of My Hometown	
Billed Institutional Costs					
Tuition	$16,000	$43,000	$28,600	
Fees	486	1,100	254	
Room and Board	8,000	8,200	8,600	Maybe I should live at home.
Total Cost of Attendance (on your school bill)	$24,486	$52,300	$37,454	

What a Deal!

	School 1	School 2	School 3	Notes
	Large University	Famous College	University of My Hometown	
Net Financial Aid Awards (can be used for credit on bill)				
Loans (count as zero in this method)	-0-	-0-	-0-	Large U. offered me $2,625 in student loans, Famous College offered $2,500, and U. of My Hometown offered $2,625 in federal loans and $2,000 in institutional loans for a total of $4,625.
Work-Study (counts zero toward paying your bill)	-0-	-0-	-0-	Large U. and Famous College both offered $1,500 in Federal Work-Study. U. of MH offered $3,000 in institutional work-study.
Pell Grant	400	400	400	
SEOG Grant	1,000	1,000	-0-	
State Grant(s)	-0-	1,000	2,000	
Institutional Grant(s) or Scholarship(s)	2,000	2,500	5,000	
Outside Scholarship(s)	800	800	800	Lions Club and PTA Scholarships

Financial Aid 101

www.petersons.com

Chapter 7

	School 1	School 2	School 3	Notes
	Large University	Famous College	University of My Hometown	
Total Financial Aid Package (excluding loans and work-study) that you can apply to your bill. The highest number is the best "free money deal," but the institution's costs may also be much higher than competitors'. Watch the next line for your actual expenses.	$ 4,200	$ 5,700	$ 8,200	This is "free" money because I don't have to work to earn it and I don't have to pay it back in the future.
Your Immediate Cost = COA on bill minus Total Aid	$20,286	$46,600	$29,254	This is what we'd have to pay to each university. We need to decide if we want to use personal loans, a home equity loan, or education loans like those that the school offered us.
More Expenses					
Personal Expenses	1,570	1,500	1,650	
Transportation (all forms of travel during school year)	400	580	300	Famous College is farther from home than the other two.
Books	600	600	650	
Parking (if not included in fees on your bill)	-0-	50	235	Parking is included in the fees for Large U.

www.petersons.com

Financial Aid 101

What a Deal!

	School 1	School 2	School 3	Notes
	Large University	Famous College	University of My Hometown	
One-time freshman orientation expenses	65	135	215	
Additional Annual Fees (athletic events, college, dorm, club or fraternity dues, etc.)	45	163	465	Large U. has a general use fee; Famous College has fees for ID, lab, and GoTeam card; U. of My Hometown has newspaper, intramural, and communications fees.
Total Additional Expenses	2,680	3,028	3,515	
Work-Study or other earnings from school-year employment	1,500	1,500	3,000	See notes above on work-study awards.
Your Monthly Costs = Additional Expenses minus Work-Study. Although these expenses may seem minor compared to your bill, you still need to discuss how they will be covered.	$ 1,180	$ 1,528	$ 515	This is how much more I need for my extra expenses after I use my work-study earnings.

The Wall Street Comparison

If you are thinking about the big picture and the cost and value of the education for your college student that each institution provides, you have much more to consider than just the financial aid package. For example, some people don't consider loans to be financial aid because, in their minds, financial aid means a reduction in the cost of the student's education. Loans do not reduce the cost of education; they simply provide a way to postpone payment of those costs. If you include the interest you will pay on the loans over time, then you have just increased the cost of paying for your student's education. On the other hand, the majority of families in the U.S. cannot make any major purchases, including education, without loans.

For the Wall Street Comparison, set your priorities first. Rate each of the three components (reputation, features, and aid) from 0 to 100 and adjust your figures so that the total of the three components is 100 percent. You will probably have a different priority rating for each of the schools you compare. Before comparing costs and financial aid, determine the importance of this particular component to your overall decision.

When all your figures are in and all the logic says School 3 is the best choice, you may still choose a different college or university. If so, make your decision with the understanding that other priorities took precedence over the cost of the school or the gift aid offered. That does not mean you made a bad decision. It simply means you made the best decision for you.

	School 1	School 2	School 3	Notes
	Large University	Famous College	University of My Hometown	
Importance of College's or University's Reputation or Name (rate 0%-100%)	30%	40%	55%	
Importance of Features: Major(s), Dormitories, Athletics, Study Abroad Programs (rate 0%-100%)	30%	5%	10%	
Importance of Cost and Aid (rate 0%-100%)	40%	55%	35%	Famous College more expensive than just about anywhere. I'm going to have to have more aid there.
Total	100%	100%	100%	

What a Deal!

	School 1	School 2	School 3	Notes
	Large University	Famous College	University of My Hometown	
Billed Institutional Costs					
Tuition	$16,000	$43,000	$28,600	
Fees	486	1,100	254	
Room and Board	8,000	8,200	8,600	Maybe I should live at home.
Total Cost of Attendance (on your school bill)	$24,486	$52,300	$37,454	
Gift Aid Awards (can be used for credit on bill)					
Loan (counts as zero in this method; consider as a resource later)	-0-	-0-	-0-	Large U. offered me $2,625 in student loans, Famous College offered $2,500, and U. of My Hometown offered $2,625 in federal loans and $2,000 in institutional loans for a total of $4,625.
Work-Study (counts zero towards paying your bill)	-0-	-0-	-0-	Large U. and Famous College both offered $1,500 in Federal Work-Study; U. of My Hometown offered $3,000 in institutional work-study.
Pell Grant	400	400	400	
SEOG Grant	1,000	1,000	-0-	
State Grant(s)	-0-	1,000	2,000	

Financial Aid 101   www.petersons.com

Chapter 7

	School 1	School 2	School 3	Notes
	Large University	Famous College	University of My Hometown	
Institutional Grant(s) or Scholarship(s)	2,000	2,500	5,000	
Outside Scholarship(s)	800	800	800	Lions Club and PTA Scholarships
Total Gift Aid Package that you can apply to your bill	$ 4,200	$ 5,700	$ 8,200	(Work-study is applied to "other expenses" and loans are used to offset the remaining bill balance.)
Remaining Bill Balance or Immediate Cost = COA on bill minus Total Gift Aid	$20,286	$46,600	$29,254	This is what we'd have to pay to each school. We need to decide if we want to use personal loans, a home equity loan, or education loans like those that the school offered us. Which one has the best interest rate and repayment terms? The home equity loan could help on taxes, but is it the wisest choice?
The Ratings				
Gift Aid Rating (financial aid package—gift aid only—divided by cost)	17%	11%	22%	
Financial Aid Priority (noted above in Importance of Cost and Aid)	40%	55%	35%	

www.petersons.com

Financial Aid 101

What a Deal!

	School 1	School 2	School 3	Notes
	Large University	Famous College	University of My Hometown	
APPROVAL RATING: (Financial Aid Rating divided by Financial Aid Priority). The highest number is the best "deal," according to your priorities. Notice that although U of My Hometown has a higher remaining bill balance after gift aid has been applied, the percentage of the school's cost that is covered by gift aid is also higher.	0.43	0.20	0.63	
Reference Remaining Bill Balance: Amount of billed expenses remaining to be paid by family using cash, loans, or a payment plan	$20,286	$46,600	$29,254	
More Expenses					
Personal Expenses	1,570	1,500	1,650	
Transportation (all forms of travel during school year)	400	580	300	Famous College is farther from home than the other two.
Books	600	600	650	
Parking (if not included in Fees on your bill)	-0-	50	235	Parking is included in the fees for Large U.

Financial Aid 101   www.petersons.com

Chapter 7

	School 1	School 2	School 3	Notes
	Large University	Famous College	University of My Hometown	
One-time Freshman Orientation Expenses	65	135	215	
Additional Annual Fees (athletic events, college, dorm, club or fraternity dues, etc.)	45	163	465	Large U. has a general use fee; Famous College has fees for ID lab, and GoTeam card; U. of My Hometown has newspaper, intramural, and communications fees.
Total Additional Expenses	2,680	3,028	3,515	
Work-Study or other earnings from school-year employment	1,500	1,500	3,000	See notes above on work-study awards.
Your Monthly Costs = Additional Expenses minus Work-Study. Although these expenses may seem minor compared to the student's bill, you still need to discuss how they will be covered.	1,180	1,528	515	This is how much more I need for my extra expenses after I use my work-study earnings.

And the Winner Is . . .

Now that you have learned the three different ways to compare your aid packages, you should feel more confident about your final decision. It is difficult to turn down a $20,000 aid package to a prestigious school. However, if your family is going to have to pay $18,000 for the student to attend this school compared to $8000 or $11,000 at another university, the end result is that you and your family are going to have to bear significantly higher expenses if you accept this financial aid package. In some cases, you may decide that the reputation of the institution is worth the additional expense. Good luck with your decision! Now go get some ice cream and apply it directly to your brain. See you in chapter 8 after you get cleaned up.

CHAPTER 8

Can You Lend Me a Dollar?

Not counting money, what was the last thing you borrowed? Maybe you borrowed a lawnmower, a leaf blower, or a snowblower. Maybe you borrowed a cup of sugar or a vacuum cleaner. Perhaps you borrowed one of your parents' cars while yours was in the repair shop. Why did you borrow the item? Probably, because it was something you needed *right now* to complete a job, finish a meal, or get to work. Now step back and think again about borrowing money for college. You're required to pay for your or your child's college education *right now.* You may need to borrow more than a cup of sugar to help cover expenses.

In a perfect world, the cost of a college education could be deferred until the student's income caught up to the expense, and the student would simply go to college when she could afford to pay cash. Unfortunately, that is not possible in the real world. For one thing, a student's income may never catch up to the expense of a college education.

Although many families prefer to consider only scholarships and grants as viable financial aid options, more dollars are used in loans every year than any other type of financial aid. Although you can't defer the cost, you can defer payment if you use educational loans. By using educational loans to pay for a portion of your or your child's education, you receive the dollars necessary to pay for the expense *right now* and have the convenience of repaying the loan gradually over time.

Federal Perkins Loan

Compared to other federal loan programs, the Perkins Loan is a popular program because it carries a low interest rate (5 percent) and has a long grace period (9 months) before repayment begins. Also, the Perkins Loan does not incur an origination fee. So, if you borrow $2,000 in a Perkins Loan, $2,000 is available to apply toward your school costs. For this reason, many students prefer the Perkins Loan. Like other campus-based federal aid programs, each school has an established maximum amount of funds for the Perkins Loan each year. Regardless of the amount in the school's Perkins fund, the maximum undergraduate student award is $4000 each year.

Since the amount of Perkins Loan dollars each institution has for current year students is limited and the demand is high, a first-come, first-served policy may exist at your school for this campus-based federal aid program. If you are eligible for a loan and all the Perkins Loan dollars have already been exhausted, you will probably be offered a different student loan. That may not be a disadvantage. In previous years, the Perkins Loan's fixed 5 percent interest rate created a high demand for this award. More recently, the drop in interest rates has meant that Stafford Loan interest rates have become competitive with—or even better than—the Perkins Loan interest rate. We'll take a more detailed look at Stafford Loan interest rates later in this chapter.

Perkins Loan Repayment

Once you graduate, withdraw from school, or drop below half-time during the course of your education, your Perkins Loan repayment period begins. Fortunately, you have a 9-month grace period after your graduation, last day of class, or last day of at least half-time enrollment before interest accrues and payment begins. After this time of no interest and no payments, the student borrower begins to make payments on his Perkins Loan. During this grace period, you have a chance to collect yourself, get your finances in order, and prepare to make monthly payments on your Perkins Loan. Your monthly payments depend on the amount you borrowed and the number of years you have to repay the loan. For example, the payment on a $4000 Perkins Loan that will be repaid over 10 years would be about $42 per month. This may not seem like much, but don't forget that you may also have other loans to repay in addition to the Perkins Loan.

Perkins Loan Repayment Assistance

Your employer may offer to repay some or all of your Perkins Loan for you, depending on the career you choose. The U.S. Department of Defense might repay some of your Perkins Loan (as an enlistment incentive) if you serve as an enlisted person in some of the specialties of the Armed Forces. Contact your recruiting officer for details. However, if you're already in the service as you're reading this

Chapter 8

book and didn't negotiate a repayment deal when you enlisted, it may be too late to obtain that benefit now.

Another area of employment where borrowers may see Perkins Loan repayment offered as a hiring incentive is the nursing profession. The U.S. Department of Health and Human Services' Nursing Education Loan Repayment Program can help repay student loans for registered nurses in exchange for their service in eligible facilities (usually located in areas experiencing a shortage of nurses). For more information, go to www.bhpr.hrsa.gov/nursing/loanrepay.htm.

Perkins Loan Forgiveness

There are several ways to have your Perkins Loan "forgiven," which means you don't have to repay part (or sometimes all) of the loan. The first way is the least favorable to you. Death or permanent disability results in 100 percent forgiveness of your Perkins Loan. For details on permanent disability forgiveness, refer to *The Student Guide*, published by the U.S. Department of Education, available in print or on the Web at www.studentaid.ed.gov.

The other ways to have your Perkins Loan forgiven are much more advantageous. These programs encourage you to work in fields that provide community service or protection to your area. You may have up to 100 percent of your Perkins Loan forgiven if you choose any of the following careers:

- Full-time teacher in a designated elementary or secondary school serving students from low-income families

- Full-time special education teacher (includes teaching children with disabilities in a public or other nonprofit elementary or secondary school)

- Full-time qualified professional provider of early intervention services for the disabled

- Full-time teacher of math, science, foreign languages, bilingual education, or other fields designated as teacher shortage areas

- Full-time employee of a public or nonprofit child- or family-services agency providing services to high-risk children and their families from low-income communities

- Full-time nurse or medical technician
- Full-time law enforcement or corrections officer
- Full-time staff member in the education component of a Head Start Program

You may have up to 70 percent of your Perkins Loan forgiven if you work as a Vista or Peace Corps volunteer, and you may have up to 50 percent of your Perkins Loan forgiven for service in the U.S. Armed Forces if you are in an area of hostilities or imminent danger.

According to a September 2003 article published by **American Forces Press**, military personnel who have been deployed or mobilized are not required to make student loan payments during their absences.

Federal regulations require lenders to postpone the student loan program payments of active duty military personnel. This applies to members of the National Guard and Ready Reserves who have been called to active duty, as well as to active duty personnel whose duty station has been changed as a result of a military mobilization.

The regulations apply to student loans made under the Federal Family Education Loan, William D. Ford Federal Direct Loan, and the Federal Perkins Loan programs.

Colleges will not be required to collect financial aid funds that now-active duty students were given to pay for books and living expenses. Additionally, Education Department officials encourage colleges and universities to either fully refund tuition and other institutional charges or give comparable credit against future charges to students forced to withdraw from school to fulfill their military obligations. Additional information is available by calling 800-433-3243 or logging on to www.ifap.ed.gov/IFAPWebApp/index.jsp.

Chapter 8

Stafford Loans

Stafford Loans come in two flavors: **Subsidized** and **Unsubsidized**. With subsidized loans, the federal government will pay your interest for you, subsidizing the debt, while you are enrolled at least half-time. Subsidized Stafford Loans are a great deal for students because the borrower is not responsible for interest on the loan while she is enrolled at least half-time in school. Unsubsidized Stafford Loans are less favorable for students because while the borrower is enrolled in school, he must either make interest payments on the loan or allow the interest to capitalize (this month's interest accrues on the principal as well as the interest the student did not pay in the previous month) before his repayment period begins. Still, both types of Stafford Loans are beneficial to student borrowers because of the cap on the loan interest rates. For Stafford Loans, the interest rate has a cap of 8.25 percent. Although in recent years, the interest rate has dropped significantly to 4.06 percent in 2002–03 and 3.42 percent in 2003–04. The Stafford Loan interest rate applies to both subsidized and unsubsidized loans.

Example

Delia's estimated family contribution (EFC) is $29,000 and her school's cost of attendance (COA) is $30,000. The only financial aid she is awarded for this year, her first year in college, is a Subsidized Stafford Loan for $1,000, which is the amount of need that she has remaining when her EFC is subtracted from her COA. Delia asks her financial aid officer if she can borrow the rest of her first-year maximum ($2,625) in an Unsubsidized Stafford Loan and the financial aid officer certifies the unsubsidized portion of her loan for $1,625.

The maximum amount a student is eligible to borrow through the Stafford Loan program varies according to a student's dependency status, level in school, and whether or not the Stafford Loan is subsidized or unsubsidized. The following table may help you see the differences in the amounts available to students.

> *Note:* Do not make any decisions on your financial aid package based on this table. You must discuss your loan amounts, disbursements, and repayment terms with your financial aid officer.

Can You Lend Me a Dollar?

Type of Stafford Loan	Dependency Status	Year in School	Maximum Amount	Limitations	Maximum Total Stafford Debt upon Graduation
Subsidized	Dependent	1st	$2,625	Actual loan amount is based on COA minus other financial aid awards	$23,000 as a dependent undergraduate student
	Independent	1st	$2,625	Actual loan amount is based on COA minus other financial aid awards	
	Dependent	2nd	$3,500	Actual loan amount is based on COA minus other financial aid awards	
	Independent	2nd	$3,500	Actual loan amount is based on COA minus other financial aid awards	
	Dependent	3rd–4th	$5,500	Actual loan amount is based on COA minus other financial aid awards	
	Independent	3rd–4th	$5,500	Actual loan amount is based on COA minus other financial aid awards	
	Independent	Graduate	$8,500	Actual amount is based on COA minus other financial aid awards	
Unsubsidized	Dependent	1st	Varies	Not eligible unless parent's PLUS application was declined, then Independent student rules apply	$46,000 as an independent undergraduate student (only $23,000 of the independent student's maximum can be in subsidized loans)
	Independent	1st	$6,625	Less any Subsidized Stafford Loan amount this year	
	Dependent	2nd	Varies	Not eligible unless parent's PLUS application was declined, then Independent student rules apply	
	Independent	2nd	$7,500	Less any Subsidized Stafford Loan amount this year	
	Dependent	3rd–4th	Varies	Not eligible unless parent's PLUS application was declined, then Independent student rules apply	
	Independent	3rd–4th	$10,500	Less any Subsidized Stafford Loan amount this year	$138,500 as a graduate or professional student (only $65,500 of this amount may be in subsidized loans)
	Independent	Graduate	$18,500	less any Subsidized Stafford Loan amount this year	

Financial Aid 101

Chapter 8

Stafford Loan Repayment

The Subsidized Stafford Loan has a 6-month grace period for repayment. After the grace period ends, you begin making payments on the loan. Payments on Stafford Loans depend upon the total amount borrowed, the interest rate, and the number of payments. The payment on a $5,000 Stafford Loan that will be repaid over 10 years, for example, would be about $61 per month in a Standard Repayment Plan.

For the Unsubsidized Stafford Loan, there is no grace period for interest, but there is a 6-month grace period for the principal. This means that as soon as the loan is disbursed (money is sent to your school), your interest on the Unsubsidized Stafford Loan begins to accrue. Your best option is to pay the interest as it accrues each month, even if you are still enrolled in school. The reason that this option is best is that it means you repay a lower total amount for the loan and interest.

Example

David took out both Subsidized and Unsubsidized Stafford Loans. He didn't read all the information on his Unsubsidized Stafford Loan and has been ignoring the payment notices for the interest on his unsubsidized loan because he remembers hearing his financial aid officer say something about a 6-month grace period. If the first month's interest amount was $15 and went unpaid, this $15 would be added to the amount David borrowed and the second month's interest rate would be calculated on this new higher amount. Perhaps the second month's interest amount was $18 and David again ignored the payment notice. The third month's interest would now be calculated on the amount David borrowed plus $15 plus $18. So David would now be charged interest on his loan amount (the loan principal), plus interest on his interest! If David can make a fast payment to catch up his interest charges and continue making monthly payments as the interest accrues, he will pay less in the long run because the interest will only be charged against the principal of his loan each month. Repayment amounts for the Unsubsidized Stafford Loan are similar to the Subsidized Stafford Loan.

Stafford Loan Forgiveness

There are a few ways to have your Stafford Loan "forgiven." Your death or permanent disability can lead to 100 percent forgiveness of your Stafford Loan, so that your survivors do not bear responsibility for your debt. Full-time teachers for five consecutive years in a designated elementary or secondary school serving students from low-income families may be eligible for forgiveness of up to $5,000 of their aggregate Stafford loan debt *after* completing the fifth year of teaching. There are a few other means of forgiveness, but their occurrence is either rare or limited to a very small percentage of Stafford Loan borrowers. For full details, see *The Student Guide*, published by the Department of Education.

Parent Loans for Undergraduate Students (PLUS)

Although the Perkins and Stafford Loans are considered the best loans available for educational purposes, the total dollars available to students on an annual basis in these programs simply does not cover many students' total cost of attendance. There may still be a "gap" between the amount the student can borrow and his total COA. This gap can be bridged with a Parent Loan for Undergraduate Students, otherwise known as a Federal PLUS Loan, or PLUS. For families with high incomes or assets with high values but low to no liquidity, this news is often greeted with a huge sigh of relief.

PLUS was first established in 1980. This loan is not exactly a last resort for families, but it is the least favorable of all the federal student aid programs. You can apply for a PLUS loan through your student's financial aid office. A creditworthy parent may borrow up to the COA (minus any other aid awards) in a PLUS for their dependent student. An absence of credit or of a credit history is not the same as an adverse credit history. Parents can't be turned down because they don't have a credit history, only if they have a poor credit history. A credit check will be run on the parent who applies for a PLUS, but remember that "no credit" is very different from "poor credit." A parent who has not established a credit history is not penalized or rejected for a PLUS for his lack of a credit history. On the other hand, a parent with a poor credit history is more likely to be rejected for a PLUS. Parents should not be intimidated by the credit check, though. If a family needs assistance to bridge the gap between its undergraduate student's COA and the amount of financial aid the student is receiving, one of the parents should apply for a PLUS. If that parent's loan application is rejected, the student may be able to borrow additional dollars through an Unsubsidized Stafford Loan, but this possibility cannot be considered by a financial aid officer unless the parent borrower was first rejected

Chapter 8

for a PLUS. In some cases, one parent borrower may be rejected while the other parent is accepted. Parents do not have to be divorced or separated to apply for a PLUS individually. (Perhaps the house, car, or credit card history is in the father's name and the mother's name is not associated with a credit report.) A word of caution: if one of the married parents is rejected for a PLUS, the family should consider whether or not there are significant factors contributing to this rejection. Before worrying about how to get a PLUS after an initial rejection, parents should weigh their current debt ratio against their income and try to determine whether or not they can afford to take on additional debt.

Example

John's Whit's COA is $27,500 and he received a Mensa scholarship for $1,500 for the year. His remaining cost is $26,000 and his parents were approved to receive this amount in a PLUS loan. The PLUS loan lender retained the full 4 percent origination fee, and the remaining $24,960 was disbursed to his school in two equal payments of $12,480 for each of the fall and spring semesters. Notice that although John had $26,000 in remaining costs and John's parents borrowed $26,000, the amount disbursed was $24,960 and John's family is responsible for finding a way to make up the $1,040 difference between his cost and their total PLUS Loan disbursements ($26,000 minus $24,960).

What Is the Interest Rate?

For a PLUS loan, the variable interest rate is adjusted annually. The interest rate for PLUS loans has a cap of 9 percent, but the rates have dropped significantly in recent years, to 4.86 percent in 2002–03 and 4.22 percent in 2003–04. Interest begins accruing when the first disbursement of the loan is made, and parents are usually expected to begin repayment within 60 days after the last disbursement. There is no grace period for the PLUS, and parents begin paying both interest and principal on this loan while the student is in school.

In the above example, John's parents borrowed $26,000. The first half of the loan amount was disbursed ($13,000 minus a 4 percent origination fee for a net disbursement of $12,480) in August and interest began to accrue on this $13,000 portion of the loan immediately. John's parents were not required to begin repayment until their PLUS loan was fully disbursed, so their actual repayment period began 60 days after the January disbursement. Monthly loan payments are based upon the amount borrowed, the interest rate, and the number of months in the repayment period. For this same $26,000 loan, monthly payments could be $266 if the interest rate is 4.22 percent and the repayment period extends for 10 years.

PLUS Deferment

There are a few circumstances where a parent can ask for a deferment (postponement) of their PLUS payments. This does not stop the interest from accruing on the PLUS. If your parents are unable to find full-time employment or are experiencing economic hardship, they should contact their lender and ask for details about deferment. Deferment is easier to achieve if you have not missed any loan payments, so don't ignore your payment dates. As soon as you are uncertain about how you are going to make your monthly payments, you should contact your lender for guidance.

Alternative Loan Programs

After the student's financial aid awards have been totaled and subtracted from the student's total cost of attendance (COA), there may still be a gap. Even if the parent was approved for a PLUS loan and it was calculated in the total, there may still be a remaining balance on the student's bill. Independent students do not have the option of a PLUS loan. This is not the time to give up on college education goals. This is the time to consider other loan options, or alternative loans. An alternative loan is an educational loan that is made by a private lender to the student borrower and the loan is not guaranteed by either the federal or state government. Federal- and state-guaranteed student or parent loans are backed by the government, and the government has the option to draw upon the resources of its various branches to assist in collecting on loans should the borrower default in their repayment of the loan. Private lenders do not have the same resources when it comes to collecting loan repayments, so they may be more cautious in approving borrowers. Alternative loan applications may contain a few more questions or take a little longer to process than a federal loan application; some applications may require a co-borrower's information and signature. Although the interest rate for alternative loans may be slightly higher than the interest rate for Perkins or Stafford Loans, alternative loans can still provide the additional funding necessary for college education expenses.

Chapter 8

When you begin to explore alternative loans, shop around. Find the features that are most beneficial to you. Need an answer in a hurry? The Key Alternative Loan offers preapproval in just minutes, 24 hours a day, 7 days a week. Want no cost up front? CitiAssist boasts no loan fees, which means you receive every dollar you borrow. Need a tailored loan that favors a great credit history? ***Educaid Select Loan*®** offers various tiers of benefits based upon the creditworthiness of the borrower or co-borrower. Many lenders build money-saving benefits into their repayment plans. ***Sallie Mae's Cash Back*™** program can make 3.3 percent of your Federal Stafford Loan original amount borrowed available to you in the form of cash or a check after you have made 33 scheduled payments on time, enrolled in their ***Manage Your Loans*™** service, and agreed to receive account information from Sallie Mae at a valid e-mail address. These are just a few of the options available to you when you begin to research alternative loans. For a complete list of alternative lenders for your school, contact your financial aid officer.

How Much Do I Get?

Alternative loans require certification by a financial aid officer at your school and the maximum you can borrow is your total cost of education minus any other financial aid. Sounds like the PLUS loan maximum amount doesn't it? So can families or students get both? Yes, but the total amount of the student's alternative loan and the parent's loan cannot exceed the student's total COA minus any other financial aid. As far as how much the actual disbursement will be, subtract any fees that may be charged by the individual lender from the loan amount. Look for *zero-fee* alternative loans when shopping for alternative loans. Once again, the school's financial aid office is the place to begin researching alternative loans. Ask for their list of alternative loan lenders and begin comparing the lenders' fees, interest rates, and repayment terms.

How Much Do I Pay Back and When?

Although each individual lender sets the repayment terms, many alternative loans offer zero payments while the student is in school. The interest rate, amount borrowed, and repayment period are all components of the monthly repayment amount.

Example

Natalie borrows $10,000 for her first year of college through an alternative loan. Her lender adds a 4 percent origination fee to the loan amount, so that Natalie received $10,000 for her college expenses but immediately owed $10,400 instead of just $10,000. Natalie made no interest or principal payments while she was enrolled for four years in an undergraduate program. The interest rates for her enrollment period and her repayment period ranged between 4.6 percent and 4.9 percent. When Natalie pays back her loan over 10 years, she will pay about $130 per month.

How Much Is the Interest Rate?

The interest rates for alternative loans vary, and many are tied to the prime rate. Prime rate is a term for the interest rate that banks charge to their most creditworthy customers and is published by the Federal Reserve Board. Alternative loans lenders may advertise "Prime plus 1 percent" or "Prime plus 0 percent," which means that your interest rate is variable, depending upon the fluctuations of the prime rate.

State Loan Programs

Although there is no universal loan program used by individual states, the resources available for state scholarships, work-study, and vocational rehabilitation programs may also have links to state loan programs. Use the agencies listed in chapter 6 to begin research on educational loans available in the student's state of residency. For example, Georgia offers an alternative loan called the Georgia First Education Loans. Information about this loan program is available through the same agency and Web site listed for Georgia's LEAP and Byrd programs. In Texas, the *Hinson-Hazlewood College Access Loan Program* is outlined at the same Web site listed for state scholarships. Michigan's *MI-LOAN* program is outlined on the Web site listed for their Byrd and LEAP programs. Once again, the best resource for finding out about state loans programs is the student's college financial aid office.

Chapter 8

What Is the Best Program for Me?

What loan or combination of loans is best for the student or the family? Depending upon their need, the time they have to research different kinds of loans and lenders, and the student's future income expectations, the answer may change from year to year or even between one student and another within the same family. A future doctor's income, a future commercial artist's income, a future electrical engineer's income, and a future elementary school teacher's income are all very different. The student bound for the highest-paying job may not hesitate to borrow heavily to finance her educational costs because she feels confident that her income will bear the cost of debt repayment in addition to her other costs of living. A student who loves the work in a low-salary field may have a difficult time making a decision to borrow the entire cost of his education. Parents who find themselves in the middle of a job transition, but have confidence in their future employability and income, may not hesitate to use loans as a temporary means of paying for their student's education expenses for a year or more.

Both students and families should determine their priorities before making a loan decision. If the monthly repayment amount is the most important issue, the borrower will target the loans that offer the lowest monthly payment, regardless of the total amount they repay for the loan itself. If the borrower wants to keep the total repayment amount as low as possible, even at the risk of making higher monthly payments, they will be focused on the loans that offer rebates and variable interest rates to borrowers who make extra efforts to pay off their loans early. Possibly, students and parents will find themselves in a situation where they need another $6,000 or $8,000 to meet the cost of education not covered by the rest of the student's financial aid. If this happens, the financial aid officer may recommend a combination of loans, listing the most beneficial loans first.

Example

Theo's COA for his first year of college is $19,000 and his total financial aid package (without any loans) is $11,000. Theo's family needs to find another $8,000 to apply toward his educational expenses. Theo's financial aid officer suggests a Perkins Loan for $3,000. Now Theo's family only needs $5,000. Theo's parents are both rejected for a PLUS loan and Theo approaches his financial aid officer about an Unsubsidized Stafford Loan. Theo's financial aid officer suggests a combination of Subsidized Stafford Loan ($2,625) and Unsubsidized Stafford Loan ($2,375) to cover the $5,000 balance. In reality, the financial aid officer would probably have researched institutional and state funds before making this suggestion, because the student now has $8,000 in student loans for his first year of college ($3,000 in Perkins, $2,625 in Subsidized Stafford, and $2,375 in Unsubsidized Stafford), and a student who begins his college education with this amount of debt may feel overwhelmed by his responsibility to repay the debt. Another option the financial aid officer may have suggested after Theo's parents were rejected was an alternative loan with a creditworthy co-borrower or even another PLUS loan application with a creditworthy co-borrower.

Guilt, Dreams, and Bankruptcy

For parents, guilt plays heavily into the assumption of debt for their child's education. Many parents feel that they *have* to borrow a PLUS Loan or take out a personal loan to help their child get the education that they desire. However, guilt is a lousy reason for making a debt decision. If the parent's (or parents') current and future financial situation simply cannot tolerate a loan repayment amount, the parents should not take out an education loan for their college student. Regardless of the student's dreams of an expensive "famous" college or university, he or she probably doesn't want to walk across the graduation stage and receive a diploma that was paid for by selling the family home, depleting her parents' retirement savings, and/or seeing her parents file for bankruptcy. Parents should be honest with their college student from the beginning about the amount of money they can spend on college expenses, covering both monthly payments to the school as well as future payments on a loan. Armed with reality, families can and will make a decision that is best for both the student and the parents.

CHAPTER 9

Alternative Payment Plans

Most of the financial aid programs discussed in this book are "right now" proposals and quick fixes. Complete and submit financial aid forms early, work with your financial aid officer to explain unusual circumstances, research every private and state aid program, and apply for fast turn-around loans. Is there anything else you can do when it comes to covering educational expenses? Actually, there are still a few "outside the box" ideas left to consider.

Other Ways to Finance Higher Education

Save! Save! Save! The first—and best—way to cover your educational expenses is to start saving now. Some families use a 529 Plan (the common identifier for a *Qualified Tuition Program*) that allows them to lock in a price for a particular college or group of colleges with a pre-paid tuition plan or simply contribute to a college savings plan. One of the best reviews of 529 Plans is given by *The Motley Fool*® in its June 18, 2003 article, "*Pros and Cons of 529.*" You can access the article online at www.fool.com/news/commentary/2003/commentary030618bro.htm.

Retirement Plans

For families hesitant to place savings in an account that is limited to education-expense withdrawals, retirement plan savings plans are excellent ways to build a nest egg. Although traditional (noneducation) IRAs have a penalty for early or before-retirement withdrawals, exceptions are made for education expense–related withdrawals as long as the withdrawal doesn't exceed the amount of the educational expenses.

> *Note:* Don't try to pull a fast one on the IRS. The student's school will send a statement that shows the qualified educational expenses for the tax year, and if this sum is less than the amount withdrawn from the parent's IRA, a penalty on the excess amount will be assessed.

Alternative Payment Plans

In addition to traditional IRAs, employer 401(k) accounts are a sound way to build retirement savings with an education-expense caveat. Although contributors may not withdraw money from a 401(k) for educational expenses, they may borrow against their account. Acting as both the *borrower* and the *lender,* the owners of these savings plans pay themselves back, with interest. An excellent review of retirement savings versus college savings accounts is found in the *Business Week* article of June 26, 2003, "*A Lesson in Saving for College.*" You can access this article at: www.businessweek.com/bwdaily/dnflash/jun2003/nf20030626_4171_db026.htm.

Cut Costs

The second idea for bringing college student expenses closer to the family's financial resources (including any financial aid offered) is to cut the expenses. Room and board are often a significant expense for college. Can the student live at home and still get the education he desires? Obviously, two-hour commutes don't make sense. But are there any other options? Is there a relative or close family friend with whom the student could live during the school year?

Can you reduce educational expenses with Advanced Placement courses and tests before the student graduates from high school? If you get a qualifying grade on the AP Exam, there are thousands of colleges that will give credit or advanced placement for your efforts. This means that a student who can complete an AP course in high school and pass the test with a qualifying grade can get credit for this course at a large number of colleges and universities. Many institutions accept AP scores (in lieu of completion of the course at their campus) as a prerequisite for a subsequent course. By advancing on to a higher-level course, the student is not required to pay the college for the entry-level course. In addition, a large number of institutions give credit for AP courses with a specific score. In one case, a single parent was delighted to find out that her entering freshman student was awarded 46 credit hours (based on the student's AP scores) toward her undergraduate degree. A full-time enrollment course load is usually 12 or 15 credit hours per semester, so 46 credit hours translates into approximately three semesters of college that this student was not required to take or pay for.

Financial Aid 101 www.petersons.com

Assets

If grandmother left money for your education, use it. If there is a stock or investment that's been set aside for a rainy day, it's pouring now. If the family has multiple residences, it might be time to sell one. Many families try to "keep it all" and attempt to use only their current income to pay for college expenses. The federal methodology EFC already includes a certain percentage of the parent and student assets in the resulting family contribution. Perhaps it is time to actually use some of those assets to pay for college.

Borrow from Yourself

The fourth option is to borrow against a parent's life insurance policy. Also ask about the repayment schedule, penalties, and other components of this type of loan.

- Are there long-term savings in a credit union?
- Can the account holder borrow against these savings for education expenses?

Sell the House? Second Mortgages

Once parents make the leap and begin to creatively consider their various assets, it is time to take a deep breath and examine what may be the family's largest asset, its home. No, parents don't have to sell the family home. For most families, a house represents a large sacrifice of money and energy, and no financial aid counselor will suggest a family sells its home to pay for college expenses. On the other hand, if parents have acquired a large amount of equity in their home (equity is the amount or value of the house that is debt-free), they may have an asset that has not yet been considered.

Example 1

The Smithers family home is currently valued at $200,000, although Mr. and Mrs. Smithers purchased the house 20 years ago when it was valued at only $79,000. Their mortgage was finally paid off late last year. The Smithers now have a debt-free $200,000 asset. Selling their home is not a good idea because if the Smithers sell their current home, they'll just have to purchase another one and their income from the sale will not go very far in today's current housing market.

But the Smithers can ask for a home equity loan, stay in their house, and still receive some of the cash they need for education expenses. If the Smithers receive a $50,000 home equity loan, they have essentially refinanced a portion of their home (probably Junior's room!) worth $50,000. Even though the original mortgage was paid off late last year, they have taken out a subsequent or second mortgage. Depending on the types of education loans available, the Smithers may decide that a home equity loan is the best type of loan for their family because of its tax advantages for filers who itemize their deductions.

Example 2

Conversely, the Weston family's home equity situation is a bit different. The Weston house is currently worth $125,000 and was purchased 8 years ago for $100,000. The Westons applied Mr. Weston's unexpected performance bonus to their mortgage three years ago and their remaining house debt is now $50,000. Even though the Westons have not yet retired their mortgage, they currently have $75,000 in equity in their home. (Current value of $125,000 minus debt of $50,000 equals $75,000 in equity.) If the Westons choose to borrow against their home equity, they will continue to make their standard mortgage payment each month, and they will also have a second monthly payment for the home equity loan. Again, the tax advantages for filers who itemize their deductions may make this second mortgage (or home equity loan) the most attractive of the debt options when it comes to covering educational expenses.

Hope Credit and Lifetime Learning Credit Programs

If a home equity loan seems like a better choice than a PLUS loan or an alternative loan, then the Hope Credit and the Lifetime Learning Credit may also be an attractive option. Through the Hope Credit and the Lifetime Learning Credit programs, families can get a credit toward the taxes they owe, based upon the amount of educational expenses the family paid in the previous year. No, families do not receive a check from the government for a Hope Scholarship, nor do colleges and universities receive a voucher to apply toward the student's bill courtesy of the Lifetime Learning Program. Neither of these programs will be obvious when it comes time to pay the student's semester bill. The one time these two programs will be beneficial is at tax time. However, unless a professional prepares the family's returns, the family may not even realize the credit.

Financial Aid 101   www.petersons.com

Chapter 9

Unlike the itemized deduction of a home equity loan, which may reduce the amount of income upon which the filer's tax amount is based, the Hope Credit and the Lifetime Learning Credits are both directly applicable to the amount of tax owed for the year. If eligible for these credits, tax filers will complete IRS Form 8863 and attach it to their 1040A or 1040 tax return. Filers will also note the amount from line 18 of Form 8863 as a tax credit on line 31 of their 1040A or line 48 of their 1040. These amounts will be directly subtracted from the tax amount for the year.

Example 3

If Mr. and Mrs. Johnston are responsible for $9,980 in taxes for the year, but have a Hope Credit of $1,500 for each of their two college-age children, their amount of tax is reduced to $6,980 ($9,980 minus $3,000). The Hope Credit is available only for the first two years of each student's postsecondary education. The Lifetime Learning Credit is a lower amount ($1,000 total credit per return as opposed to the Hope Credit's maximum of $1,500 per eligible student per return) but does not have the two-year limitation.

For the complete details on these two tax credit programs, refer to the Internal Revenue Service publications for the specific tax year. One reference for current information on these programs is Publication 970, *Tax Benefits for Education.* The IRS has several easy ways to obtain these forms if the publications are not available at a local library. For Web surfers, the IRS site at www.irs.gov has a quick link to electronic forms.

Education Expenses as Income Reductions

Want more tax benefits? For tax years 2002, 2003, 2004, and 2005, qualified tuition and fees may be subtracted from your income before the tax assessment for the year is calculated. The qualified tuition and related expenses (fees) can reduce taxable income by up to $3,000, regardless of whether or not you itemize deductions. This particular income reduction program should be beneficial to filers whose income is too high to take advantage of the Hope and Lifetime Learning Credits. To claim the deduction, use the Form 1098-T supplied by your student's institution (due to families by January 31 of each year) and note the qualified tuition and fees on line 26 of the 1040 tax return or line 19 of the 1040A tax return.

Alternative Payment Plans

Student-loan interest payments and student-loan origination fees can also directly reduce the taxable income amount before the tax assessment is calculated. Student-loan interest deduction can reduce the amount of income subject to tax by up to $2,500. In fact, borrowers who pay $600 or more in interest for the year to a single lender receive a statement at the end of the year showing the amount paid. To calculate the deduction, use the *Student Loan Interest Deduction Worksheet* that is included in the instruction booklet for the 1040 tax return or the 1040A tax return. Upon completion of the form, you can claim the deduction amount on line 25 of your Form 1040 or line 18 of your Form 1040A.

For both income reduction tax benefits, details are available in IRS Publication 970, *Tax Benefits for Education*. In addition to the methods of accessing IRS publications discussed at the end of the section on Hope and Lifetime Learning Credits, Publication 970 is available at www.irs.gov/pub/irs-pdf/p970.pdf.

CHAPTER 10

What Do the New Higher Education Amendments Say?

The system of checks and balances in the federal government requires that U.S. spending on education programs, including postsecondary financial aid programs, be reviewed, re-approved, or revised. "Reauthorization" must be conducted for a number of federal programs, not just financial aid. Even the U.S. Department of Labor's Workforce Investment Act and the U.S. Department of Transportation's Transportation Equity Act must be reviewed through reauthorization. But this book is concerned with the ***Reauthorization of the Higher Education Act of 1965***, which was amended by the Higher Education Amendments of 1998.

Reauthorization for Fiscal Year 2004 (FY 2004 begins October 1) entered serious debate in the House and Senate in July 2003. Although significant increases were proposed for the ***Pell Grant***, ***FSEOG***, and ***federal state aid programs (such as LEAP)***, the early signs were not good for these increases. The initial bills approved on June 25 and 26 provided for no increase in the maximum ***Pell Grant*** award, and ***FSEOG***, ***Federal Work-Study***, ***Perkins Loans***, and ***LEAP*** were all funded at previous-year levels. Only TRIO received increases in both bills.

The ***Federal TRIO Programs*** are educational opportunity outreach programs designed to motivate and support students from disadvantaged backgrounds. For additional information on TRIO programs, contact the Department of Education or visit its Web site at www.ed.gov/about/offices/list/ope/trio/index.html. In addition, financial and educational publications—such as the ***Wall Street Journal*** and ***The Chronicle of Higher Education***—will carry several articles as well as editorial observations on the effects of the reauthorization decisions.

At present, the proposed revisions can be viewed here. Remember that the proposed revisions—which were due by the end of February 2003—were optimistic with regard to significant increases in federal student aid. However, the initial bills out of the House and Senate were disappointing for proponents of the February recommendations.

What Do the New Higher Education Amendments Say?

Pell Grant

Recommendations

1. Double the maximum Pell Grant award over the next 5 years, from $5,800 for award year 2004–05 to $8,000 for award year 2009–10.

2. Award additional Pell Grant funds, up to $750 in addition to previously proposed maximums for students with negative EFCs. Phase in an increased minimum Pell Grant award of $750.

Proposed Changes in Initial House and Senate Bills

1. No change; maximum Pell Grant award remains at $4,050.

Federal Supplemental Opportunity Education Grant (FSEOG)

Recommendations

1. Increase authorization levels for FSEOG.

2. Eliminate the lowest EFC order for awarding, permitting schools to direct no more than 10 percent in FSEOG funds to other exceptional (non-Pell Grant) recipients.

Proposed Changes in Initial House and Senate Bills

1. No change; fund FSEOG programs remain at existing levels.

Federal Perkins Loan

Recommendations

1. Increase the authorization level for the Federal Perkins Loan Program.

2. Increase the Federal Perkins Loan annual undergraduate maximum award to $7,000 and the maximum award for graduate/professional students to $10,000.

3. Maintain the current interest rate for the federal Perkins Loan program.

Chapter 10

Proposed Changes in Initial House and Senate Bills
1. No change; funding for Perkins Loan programs remains at existing levels; interest level remains at 5 percent.

Federal Work-Study (FWS)

Recommendations
1. Increase FWS authorization.
2. Expand definition of community service jobs to include child-care services provided only to campus employees and students.

Proposed Changes in Initial House and Senate Bills
1. No change; funding for FWS programs remains at existing levels.

Leveraging Educational Assistance Partnership (LEAP)

Recommendations
1. Continue and increase LEAP funding to prevent the elimination or severe reduction of some state need-based grant programs.

Proposed Changes in Initial House and Senate Bills
1. No change; funding for LEAP programs remains at existing levels.

Epilogue

The United States is full of pioneers who make their own future. Therefore, it is no surprise that American families are constantly taking financial matters into their own hands. From retirement savings to their children's education, more and more families are realizing that their preferred option is to "do-it-themselves."

Today, the barriers to elementary and secondary education that once existed are gone. Regardless of race, religion, or income, every child has the opportunity to attend postsecondary education. For most Americans, the question is not "Can I go to college" but "Which college should I attend?" Although many families find a way to pay for the majority of their college student's expenses, there are many families for whom financial aid means the difference between their child attending college or not.

My favorite analogy for the admission-and-financial-aid dance that partners families with institutions of higher education is the idea of getting a date for the prom. The senior prom is a big deal for most high school students. But just as the prom is not a prelude to marriage, college is not a prelude to a career. Rather, it's a prelude to a first job. Whatever job a potential employee pursues depends on his skills, not the name of the college or university he attends. Like the prom, partnering students and institutions should result in a comfortable match for both participants. If the most popular girl in the senior class accepts your son's invitation to the prom but expects him to buy a new suit, shirt, and shoes to match her lime-green dress and pick her up in a limousine, perhaps this girl is not the best partner for the prom after all. Conversely, if Mr. Tall-Dark-and-Handsome thrills your daughter with an all-expenses-paid invitation to the prom that even includes the cost of her dress, she may think she's found the perfect date but then decide that he's not really the right choice after spending an afternoon with him. The bottom line is that there is a good match for every student. Regardless of the thrill of a famous school's invitation, if the financial match isn't right, that school is not a good choice for the student. And if the financial aid offer of a school is overwhelming, but the institution doesn't feel right to the student, that school is probably not a good match either.

This book came about because families everywhere with college-bound students have questions. From friends and family, to friends of friends, to work colleagues of family members, everyone planning for college who hears about my experience in financial aid has questions for me. And, like all of my peers in financial aid offices across the country, I like to help people and answer questions. So, when Peterson's approached me with the idea of writing a basic "how to apply for financial aid" book, the opportunity to provide all the answers to the myriad questions in one easily accessible publication seemed like a no-brainer.

Hopefully, by the time my own children graduate from high school, they will receive about the same percentage of need-based aid that my parents received for my college expenses. Loans will probably comprise the bulk of the financial aid package my children are offered, and our family will determine if a PLUS loan, a home equity loan, or other arrangements will be the best choice for our family at that time. On the other hand, my financial situation could be much different from what it is now. A number of my friends have lost spouses through death or divorce. Some still have their original spouses but have lost their jobs or accepted as much as a 50 percent pay cut due to recent economic crises; sometimes they have lost the family home as well. They are now facing college expenses for their children as either a single parent with a limited income or as married parents with severely reduced incomes. If any of these types of situations become my reality, our family's biggest decision will not be whether or not to take out a home equity loan or a parent loan, but which college we can afford. I am confident, as you should be, that we will find a financial aid package and college combination that is a good match for our children and our family.

APPENDIX A

Key Terms

A

Academic year
The period of time during which classes are in session. The typical nine-month academic year typically begins in late August and concludes in May. Students who attend summer courses should find out from their school's financial aid office whether or not the summer semester is included at the beginning or end of the academic year.

Accrual date
For education loans, this is the date on which interest charges begin to be applied to the principal. For parent loans, interest may begin accruing on the portion of the loan that has been disbursed, even though the repayment period does not begin until after the final disbursement of the loan. Similarly, Unsubsidized Stafford Loans may enter repayment much later than the actual interest began accruing on the disbursed portions of the loan.

Accrue
Interest accrues in monthly increments. Students with unsubsidized loans may decide to pay the interest on their loan as it accumulates or accrues each month so that the their loan balance remains the same as the amount they borrowed. When the student enters repayment and begins making both principal and interest payments, the total loan balance is lower than it would have been if the student did not pay the interest on the loan as it accrued or accumulated each month.

Adjusted available income
The federal government uses a specific methodology to calculate a family's expected contribution to financing its student's education. In using this methodology, the adjusted available income is the amount of funds available to a family after certain allowances, such as taxes and a basic living allowance, have been subtracted from the family's gross income.

Key Terms

AGI (Adjusted Gross Income)
Drawn directly from the filer's income tax return, this is income before taxes and other deductions have been subtracted. The AGI is a component of the EFC calculation.

Amortization
A repayment option for loans, this process involves making payments to both the loan interest and principal over time in periodic installments.

Appeal
Should a family determine that the offered financial aid package is inadequate—especially in the case of a parent's or spouse's death, unemployment, or other factors that seriously alter a family's financial status—the family can appeal the circumstances that contributed to the family's EFC. A financial aid officer will review the components of the family's EFC and determine whether or not the family's special circumstances warrant a revision to one or more of the EFC components. Should the financial aid officer decide that the original EFC is not realistic due to the special circumstances, the financial aid officer may make adjustments that result in a lower EFC and then revise the offered financial aid package in accordance with the lower EFC.

Asset
This refers to any item of value, including a home, business, real estate, stocks, mutual funds, bank accounts, etc. When completing financial aid applications, read the instructions to determine which assets should be included in each of the questions. Current FAFSA asset questions exclude the family home and divide the remaining assets into categories according to liquidity, with cash, savings, and checking account balances in one category and investments such as stock, bonds, certificates of deposit, and real estate in a second category. The final category of assets covered in the FAFSA is the worth of the student's or parents' business or investment farm.

Financial Aid 101

Appendix A

Award Letter

After the student's financial aid application is complete and has been reviewed and processed by a financial aid officer, the student will be packaged (financial aid awards will be assigned to the student). Most institutions advise students of their aid awards by issuing an award letter. This letter contains the details of the student's various financial awards for the academic year. Historically, award letters were printed and mailed to students as their aid application was processed. However, more and more colleges and universities are applying Web technologies to their student information systems, and award notices may be issued via e-mail or simply presented in a secure Web page. Students and families may bear the responsibility of checking the Web site periodically for the presence of, or revisions to, their financial awards for the year instead of waiting for a printed award letter to be delivered by the U.S. Postal Service.

Award Year

This is the period of time when financial assistance is received, usually falling between July 1 and June 30. Many institutions have similar award and academic years (both run August through May), but there are a number of institutions with overlapping award and academic years. For example, a school on a quarter system may consider three consecutive quarters to be an academic year. A student might begin classes in April so that her first academic year runs April through December, but this time period spans two different award years. The student's federal (and possibly state) grants and work-study awards for her first quarter (April through June) will be based on her FAFSA for the current award year, and these same awards for the next two quarters (July through September and October through December) will be based on her FAFSA for the forthcoming award year. Then the student begins her second academic year in January, once again spanning two different award years in her next nine-month or three-quarter academic year. The first two quarters (January through March and April through June) of the student's federal financial aid will be based on remaining eligibility in the current award year, and the federal grants and work-study awards for the student's final quarter of the academic year (July through September) will be based on the next award year's FAFSA.

B

Balloon payment
This refers to a loan payment that is larger than the previous monthly payments, used to pay off the balance of a loan. Most, but not all, education loan lenders offer a balloon repayment option. The advantage of a balloon repayment program is the typical low monthly payments for the first several years of repayment and then a significant increase in the amount of the payments in order to pay off the loan in a shorter amount of time than continued lower payments would attain.

Base year
This refers to the tax year used to determine financial eligibility. For example, for first-year freshmen, the base year is the tax year that begins January 1 of their junior year in high school and ends December 31 of their senior year.

C

Campus-based aid
This refers to financial aid dollars provided by the federal government, but managed by the institution. Each institution determines student eligibility and award amounts for these campus-based funds, including the Perkins Loan, the Federal Supplemental Educational Opportunity Grant (FSEOG), and the Federal Work-Study Program.

Capitalization
This term refers to the interest that builds on previously unpaid interest, as in the case of a loan. If a student receives an unsubsidized loan, the interest on his loan begins to accrue with the first disbursement. If the student decides to capitalize the interest instead of paying the interest as it accrues, his unpaid interest is charged additional interest.

COA (Cost of Attendance)
This refers to the total direct and indirect costs of a student's educational expenses for an award year. Tuition, mandatory fees, room and board, books and supplies, transportation expenses, and personal expenses make up the traditional components of a student's COA. Some institutions may include other institution-specific expenses in a student's COA budget.

Financial Aid 101   www.petersons.com

Appendix A

Commuter student
This term refers to a student who does not live on campus or in a student apartment. Typically, commuter students live with parents or other family members to minimize their room and board expenses. A commuter student's COA budget reflects this low or zero room and board expense but usually includes a higher transportation factor due to the increased expense of frequent trips to campus.

Compounded interest
This refers to the interest paid on both the principal and any previously accrued, unpaid interest during the process of capitalization on a loan. Also see
Simple interest.

Cosigner
This refers to a person who will take responsibility for the loan should the primary borrower default. Cosigners often include a parent, spouse, close friend, or family member. Stafford Loans do not require cosigners. PLUS Loans do not initially require a cosigner, but if the application is rejected due to a poor credit history, the parent may reapply with a credit-worthy cosigner. Some alternative loans require a creditworthy cosigner on the initial application.

Custodial parent
This term refers to an unmarried parent who has financially supported the student most in the previous twelve months. The custodial parent is the parent who will complete the financial aid applications and upon whose assets and income the Federal Methodology EFC will be calculated. If the custodial parent remarries, his or her spouse's income and assets are included in the student's EFC calculation. There are no exceptions to this rule.

D

Debt load
This is a student's repayment obligation, or the amount of loans included in a student's financial aid package. A $20,000 financial aid package that includes $15,000 in student loans is not as favorable as a $10,000 financial aid package that includes only $2,000 in student loans.

Key Terms

Default
This is a failure to pay financial debts. If loan payments are neglected or the borrower otherwise violates the terms of a loan, the loan will enter default and legal action may be taken to enforce the conditions of the loan. Borrowers who find themselves unable to make a scheduled loan payment should contact their lender immediately because there are a number of precautionary steps that can be taken to avoid default, and educational lenders are anxious to guide their customers through these steps. In many cases, a request for temporary deferment can be granted.

Deferment
This is the time period during which payments on a loan are legally postponed. Loans that are already in default cannot be deferred. Subsidized Stafford Loans have an automatic deferment for student borrowers, during which time the federal government makes interest payments on the student's loan. The deferment ends six months after a student's last day of at least half-time enrollment. Repayment begins when deferment ends. Unsubsidized Stafford Loan principal payments are automatically deferred, but interest begins to accrue with the first loan disbursement. Unsubsidized loan borrowers may either pay the interest as it accrues or allow the lender to capitalize the interest until the borrower enters repayment.

Delinquent
This is a borrower who fails to make a loan payment. Usually, late fees are assessed on the unpaid amount, increasing the total payment amount owed by the borrower.

Dependency status
For educational expenses, this refers to the determination of a student's financial dependency on their parents or guardians. Students are automatically dependent on their family for the cost their education unless the student is:

- Age 24 before January 1 preceding the award
- Working on a master's or doctorate program
- Married (including separated but not yet divorced)

Financial Aid 101

Appendix A

- ☑ Providing more than half of the financial support for his or her own children

- ☑ Providing more than half of the financial support for other dependents (not a spouse or child)

- ☑ An orphan as a result of the death of both parents, or is or was a ward/dependent of the state until age 18

- ☑ A veteran of the U.S. Armed Forces

E

Early decision

This refers to an admissions option for prospective freshmen, and is not available at all colleges and universities. Early decision applicants have earlier application deadlines as well as earlier decision notification dates. If offered admission, early decision applicants usually receive an estimated financial aid package to help them decide whether or not to attend the institution.

EFC (Expected Family Contribution)

This is the dollar amount families are expected to contribute to their child's COA for the award year. The EFC is determined by a complex formula developed to draw upon a number of components such as family size, number in college, income, and assets. Financial aid packages are usually created to provide financial assistance for the difference between the COA and the EFC.

Eligible noncitizen

This term refers to a U.S. permanent resident in possession of an Alien Registration Receipt Card (I-551), a conditional permanent resident (I-551C), or an eligible noncitizen with an Arrival-Departure Record (I-94) from the U.S. Immigration and Naturalization Service showing one of the following designations: *"Refugee," "Asylum Granted," "Indefinite Parole," "Humanitarian Parole,"* or *"Cuban-Haitian Entrant."*

Key Terms

Enrollment status
This is the designation of course load attempted by student. A student who is completing 12 or more undergraduate credit hours is usually considered a full-time student. Other designations include three-quarter-time, half-time, and less-than-half-time.

External awards
These refer to financial assistance awards such as scholarships and grants not provided by the federal government, state government, or by the institution.

F

FAFSA (Free Application for Federal Student Aid)
This is the required application for federal student aid. The FAFSA is used to determine eligibility for basic federal aid programs. Most institutions require that federal aid be applied for before students are considered for need-based institutional aid.

Federal methodology
This is the formula used by the government to determine financial need and to arrive at the EFC. The formula takes into account factors such as the number of family members in college, income (both taxable and nontaxable), and other assets.

Fellowship
This refers to financial aid without repayment obligations for graduate students. Fellowships typically include tuition waivers and may include a living stipend.

Fixed interest
With regard to loans, this is an interest rate that does not change during the life of a loan. Variable interest is the opposite of fixed interest.

Forbearance
This is the time period during which payments on the principal of a loan are postponed. Interest continues to accrue and the borrower must pay the interest as it accrues monthly.

Appendix A

G

Gift aid
This refers to financial aid that does not include a repayment or work obligation. Scholarships and grants are two forms of gift aid. A $15,000 financial aid package with $10,000 in gift aid is more favorable than a $20,000 financial aid package with only $7,000 in gift aid.

Grace period
Following graduation, the grace period is a fixed length of time during which a borrower need not begin loan payments. If a borrower leaves school for a given amount of time or fails to meet the status requirements, the grace period may begin prematurely. Should the student once again return to school, he or she would lose the grace period (or part of it) after graduation.

Grade point average (GPA)
This refers to the average of a student's grades or grade points. On a 4.0 scale: A = 4 points, B = 3 points, C = 2 points, D = 1 point, and F = 0 points.

Graduate student
This is a student who already posses a bachelor's degree and is currently working toward an advanced degree, such as a master's or doctorate.

Graduated repayment
This is a repayment plan where the payment amount increases over the life of the loan.

Grant
This is gift aid and does not require either work or repayment.

H

Holder
This refers to the lender or institution that holds the title to a loan.

Hope Credit
This is a tax credit for families who pay postsecondary educational expenses for undergraduate degree related courses or coursework for other recognized education credentials. The Hope Credit is only applicable for the first two years of postsecondary education. Tax filers get a credit towards the tax they owe, based on the amount of educational expenses the family paid in the previous year. Also see **LIFETIME LEARNING CREDIT.**

Key Terms

I

In-state student or resident student
This is a student who is a legal resident of the state. Resident students often receive reduced tuition at state universities and colleges. Private institutions usually apply the same tuition rate to both state and non-state residents.

Income contingent repayment
This is a loan repayment option where the amount of the loan payment is based on a borrower's yearly income, family size, interest rate, and amount borrowed.

Income sensitive repayment
This is a loan repayment option where the amount of the loan payment is based on a borrower's yearly income and amount borrowed. If a borrower's income increases, so does the loan payment amount. If a borrower's income decreases, so does the amount of the loan payment. Each monthly payment must equal at least the amount of interest that has accrued on the loan.

Interest
This refers to the cost of or charge for borrowing money; usually a percentage of the amount to be repaid.

Interim admissions decision
This is an admissions application option that provides an earlier decision notification than regular decision, but later then early decision. Not all institutions offer an interim admission decision.

L

LEAP (Leveraging Educational Assistance Partnership)
Formerly known as the State Student Incentive Grant, or SSIG, this federal grant administered program is often supplemented by the state. Each state has its own name for the program as well as award amounts and application procedures.

Financial Aid 101   www.petersons.com

Appendix A

Lifetime Learning Credit
This is a tax credit for families who pay postsecondary educational expenses that is not limited to degree related courses. Tax filers get a credit toward the tax they owe, based on the amount of educational expenses the family paid in the previous year. The Lifetime Learning Credit is a lower amount than the Hope Credit ($1,000 total credit per return as opposed to the Hope Credit's maximum of $1,500 per eligible student per return) but does not have the two-year limitation. Also see **HOPE CREDIT.**

This is a financial assistance award that carries a repayment obligation. Most lenders of education loans charge interest. Some colleges and universities offer no-interest short-term loans.

Loan entrance counseling
This refers to a loan requirement that must be met before disbursement can be made. Loan entrance counseling usually takes the form of a short presentation of borrowers' rights and responsibilities followed by a quiz. The counseling session provides an opportunity to review the loan process and vocabulary with the borrower. Many institutions offer this type of loan counseling online.

Loan forgiveness
This refers to the cancellation of a portion—or all—of an education loan in exchange for the borrower's service in a designated area.

M

Maturity date
With regard to educational loans, this is the date on which loan payments begin.

Merit-based aid
This is financial assistance awarded based on scholastic or other individual achievement. Student and family income and assets are not relevant, and standard need-based aid applications such as the FAFSA are not required.

N

Need
This represents the difference between the educational expenses and a family's ability to pay. (COA − EFC = Need)

Need-based aid
This refers to financial assistance awarded based on a family's ability to pay for educational expenses. Even if a family receives additional aid from external sources after a financial aid package has been offered, the sum of all forms of aid cannot exceed a family's need if any need-based aid is included in the package.

Need-blind
This refers to an admission policy used to admit students without considering the financial circumstances of their families.

Net income
This is gross income after taxes and other deductions.

O

Out-of-state student
This refers to a student who is not a legal resident of the state where the school is located. At state colleges and universities, these students may be required to pay a higher tuition. Private institutions usually have a standard tuition plan for all students, regardless of residency.

Outside awards
This refers to financial assistance such as scholarships and grants that are not provided by the federal government, state government, or the institution.

Overawards
This refers to the amount of financial aid that exceeds a student's need. If a student receives any type of federal aid award, his total aid plus EFC may not exceed his COA by more than $300. Note: Pell Grants are never adjusted due to overawards. If an overaward exists, other forms of financial aid must be revised. Because Unsubsidized Stafford Loans, PLUS loans, and non-federal loans may be used to cover a portion of a family's EFC, the financial aid officer may adjust the financial aid package to reflect this use of loan funds, thereby reducing the overaward to an acceptable level or eliminating it completely.

P

Pell Grant
This is a federal financial aid award without repayment or work obligations. To date, the maximum annual Pell Grant award is $4,050.

Financial Aid 101

Appendix A

Perkins Loan
This is a federal loan program that allows students to borrow for their educational expenses at a 5 percent fixed interest rate with a 9-month grace period following a student's last day of at least half-time enrollment.

PLUS (Parent Loan for Undergraduate Students)
This is a loan program for parents who wish to borrow money as a way to cover a portion—or all—of their child's undergraduate education expenses. Parents can borrow up to the child's COA minus any other financial aid each year. The loan has a variable interest rate, but will never exceed 9 percent on the unpaid balance of the loan. PLUS loans are not need-based, but most institutions recommend completion of a FAFSA as a means of determining whether or not the student is eligible for any additional types of financial aid.

Prepayment
This term refers to the payment of all or part of a loan prior to its due date.

Principal
This is the amount of money borrowed on a loan, or the amount of the loan that remains unpaid.

Promissory note
This is a legally binding document that contains the terms of the loan, including the loan amount, conditions of the loan, interest rate, and repayment schedule.

R

Regular decision
This is the standard admissions application option. This option has the latest application and notification deadlines of all application options, but most schools can provide a financial aid offer for regular decision applicants who have been offered admission before the student is required to accept or decline the school's admissions offer.

Renewable scholarship
This is a scholarship awarded for more than one year. Most renewable scholarships are contingent on satisfactory academic progress and may require a student to submit an official copy of her grades each semester or once a year.

Repayment schedule
This refers to the outlining of a payment plan for a borrower, which sets out the repayment terms of a loan, including the loan amount, payment amount, interest rate, and number of payments.

S

SAR (Student Aid Report)
This is a notification received from the U.S. Department of Education after successful completion of the FAFSA. This notification may be issued via e-mail or sent through the U.S. Postal Service. The SAR provides a summary of the answers submitted on the FAFSA as well as a family's EFC.

SAP (Satisfactory Academic Progress)
This refers to the completion of courses in a manner consistent with the pursuit of a specific degree and with grades indicative of student's attentiveness to course completion requirements. SAP is required for all financial aid recipients. Each school must provide students with details on their SAP requirements.

Scholarship
This is a form of gift aid awarded without repayment or work obligations. Scholarships may be need-based or merit-based.

Selective Service
The United States requires that all males between the ages of 18 and 25 must have registered with the Selective Service in order to receive federal aid. Call 847-688-6888 or visit www.sss.gov for more information.

SEOG (FSEOG or Federal Supplemental Educational Opportunity Grant)
The maximum award for the FSEOG (commonly called SEOG) is $4,000, and the minimum is $100. Each institution is awarded a limited amount of funding, and awards are often made on a first-come, first-served basis.

Simple interest
This refers to the interest paid only on the principal of a loan and not on accrued interest.

Stafford Loans
Subsidized Stafford Loans are for students demonstrating financial need, with a $23,000 limit for undergraduates and a $65,500 limit for graduates. These sums cannot be borrowed all at once, however. They must be spread over a period of years. The government pays the interest on these loans while the student is in school and throughout the grace period. Unsubsidized loans are for students without financial need who can use the unsubsidized loan to cover their EFC. These loans are available to independent students, graduate/professional students, and dependent students whose parents could not acquire a PLUS loan for the EFC.

Standard Repayment Plan
This refers to a repayment option in which the payments (on interest and principal) are paid in regular installments of equal size each month.

Statement of Educational Purpose
This is a statement included in the FAFSA certifying that the student will use all financial awards for educational purposes only.

Subsidized loan
This is a loan in which the federal government pays the interest while the borrower is in school at least half-time as well as the interest which accrues during the 6-month grace period following the borrower's last day of at least half-time enrollment.

T

Term
With regard to education loans, term is the number of years or months over which a loan is to be paid.

U

Unsubsidized loan
This is a loan in which the borrower is responsible for all interest payments, even while he or she is in school and during the grace period.

Key Terms

V

Variable interest
With regard to education loans, this is an interest rate that changes over time, according to market fluctuations.

W

W-2 form
This is a summary of wages earned for the previous tax year. The W-2 is essential for filing taxes and completing the FAFSA. The government requires that a W-2 form be completed for and delivered to every employee of every business.

Work-study
This is a form of self-help aid that carries the obligation of work in order to receive the award. Students earn money for tuition and expenses by working either on campus or in pre-approved community service jobs.

APPENDIX 5

Financial Aid Calendar

Keeping on top of financial aid deadlines, dates, and things to do is one of the toughest parts of the financial aid process. Calendars and checklists work best when you check them in advance to see what's ahead.

Junior Year

September

- Make sure that PSAT/NMSQT® registration is handled by your guidance staff so you do not miss an opportunity to qualify for a National Merit Scholarship.

- If you have not already done so, obtain a social security number.

October

- Make sure the PSAT/NMSQT test date is on the family calendar.

December

- Take an introductory look at financial aid forms (see **Appendix C**).

- Buy a copy of this book as a holiday gift for every parent and college-bound student on your shopping list.

January

- Begin thinking about worthwhile summer plans (job, study, camp, volunteer work, travel, etc.), since many financial aid awards are targeted toward students with a diverse background.

- Mark projected SAT test dates on your calendar. Also mark registration deadlines.

March

- Consider and plan spring vacation college visits.
- Visit college Web sites. Begin calling, writing, or e-mailing target colleges to request information.
- Look ahead to SAT registration deadlines. Mark the appropriate test and registration dates on your calendar.

April

- Again, look ahead to SAT registration deadlines. Are you about to miss one? Mark the appropriate dates on your calendar.

June

- Set up an e-mail account for scholarship searches. Take advantage of the summer slow-down by visiting scholarship search and financial aid Web sites.

Senior Year

September

- Collect prior year tax return and W-2s (for example, 2003 tax return and W-2s in fall 2004).
- Complete CSS/PROFILE® Pre-Application Worksheet, if applicable, using prior year tax information and current year income estimates.
- Complete CSS/PROFILE®, if applicable.

October

- Take the SAT, if you haven't already.
- Attend admission and financial aid presentations. If top-choice schools are not presenting locally, attend another school's presentation for general information.

Appendix B

- Inquire about merit-based scholarships and applications at each school in which you are interested.

December

- Review last paycheck stubs for previous year and compare income to previous tax year.

- List documentation required for completing tax return (itemized expenses, charitable contributions, etc.) Be prepared to estimate tax return information in order to complete FAFSA to meet institutional deadlines (often one month or more before tax return filing date of April 15).

January

- Complete FAFSA Pre-Application Worksheet if FAFSA will be completed online. If tax return will not be completed before mid-February, use estimates to file the FAFSA.

- Complete and submit FAFSA. Gather all required signatures before submission to prevent processing delays

February

- Complete additional supplemental institutional aid applications.

- Complete tax return as soon as possible. Some institutions will not process financial aid applications until the school receives a completed tax return.

- Submit supplemental institutional aid documentation (tax return, W-2s, other forms as required by each institution).

- Contact financial aid office to determine status of financial aid application materials.

March

- Contact financial aid office to follow up on status of aid application materials.

- Ask financial aid office if financial aid offers are included in admission offer packets.

April

- Review financial aid offers. Ask financial aid officer to review your COA, EFC, and awards in your financial aid package. Are there special circumstances that were omitted from the calculation? Do not ask the financial aid officer to "meet or beat" another school's financial aid offer. Do ask if there are any other options for minimizing the family's contribution. If there appear to be significant differences in the family's EFC contribution for various schools, ask the financial aid officer what components contributed to his school's higher EFC calculation. Is an appeal warranted?

- Review family contribution. What resources will the family use to meet this obligation?

- Contact the **Student Accounting** or **Cashier's Office** and inquire about payment plans for balances not covered by financial aid.

May

- Make a final decision on the school you will attend. Contact your top-choice school to accept admission offer. Ask again about additional financial aid awards before accepting.

June

- Inquire about **Loan Entrance Counseling** or any final requirements to process disbursements of financial aid awards.

- Complete PLUS loan application, if applicable.

APPENDIX C

Forms Bank

Use the FAFSA Pre-Application Worksheet if you plan to complete your FAFSA online. Although the 2004–05 Pre-Application Worksheet was not available at the time of publication of this book, the 2003–04 worksheet provides valuable insight as to the type of information students and their families are asked to provide on their financial aid application.

2003-2004 FAFSA on the Web
Pre-Application Worksheet

www.fafsa.ed.gov

Complete this worksheet only if you plan to use **FAFSA on the Web** to apply for financial aid.
Please **DO NOT** mail in this worksheet.

Instructions:

1. Use this worksheet to collect your (and your parents') information before beginning your 2003-2004 online Free Application for Federal Student Aid (FAFSA). The worksheet does not include all questions asked on the online FAFSA, just the ones that you might not know off the top of your head.
2. Questions on this worksheet are in the same order as they appear on the online FAFSA; however, because the online FAFSA allows you to skip some questions based on your answers to earlier questions, you may not have to answer all of the questions on this worksheet.
3. The numbers in parentheses to the right of each question correspond to the question numbers on the paper FAFSA.
4. In addition to completing the Pre-Application Worksheet, you might want to complete student (and parent) Worksheets A, B, and C before beginning your online FAFSA. To print Worksheets A, B, and C, go to www.fafsa.ed.gov/worksheet.htm.
5. Do not use this worksheet if you plan to fill out a paper FAFSA.

Question	Answer
The first part of the online FAFSA will ask you some basic questions about you, the student, such as your name, address, and Social Security Number (SSN).	
Student's Citizenship Status (13)	☐ U.S. Citizen ☐ Eligible Noncitizen ☐ Neither See notes on page 4
Student's Alien Registration Number (14)	A _ _ _ _ _ _ _ _ _ See notes on page 4
Student's Marital Status (15)	☐ Single, Divorced or Widowed ☐ Married/Remarried ☐ Separated
Student's Date of Marital Status (16)	(Month and Year; e.g., 05/1995)
Student's Enrollment Summer 2003 (17)	☐ Full time/Not sure ☐ ¾ time ☐ Half time ☐ Less than half ☐ Not attending
Student's Enrollment Fall 2003 (18)	☐ Full time/Not sure ☐ ¾ time ☐ Half time ☐ Less than half ☐ Not attending
Student's Enrollment Winter 2003-2004 (19)	☐ Full time/Not sure ☐ ¾ time ☐ Half time ☐ Less than half ☐ Not attending
Student's Enrollment Spring 2004 (20)	☐ Full time/Not sure ☐ ¾ time ☐ Half time ☐ Less than half ☐ Not attending
Student's Enrollment Summer 2004 (21)	☐ Full time/Not sure ☐ ¾ time ☐ Half time ☐ Less than half ☐ Not attending
Student's Father's Educational Level (22)	☐ Middle school/Jr. High ☐ High school ☐ College or beyond ☐ Other/unknown
Student's Mother's Educational Level (23)	☐ Middle school/Jr. High ☐ High school ☐ College or beyond ☐ Other/unknown
What is the student's state of legal residence? (24)	
Did you, the student, become a legal resident of this state before January 1, 1998? (25)	☐ Yes ☐ No
If no, what date did you become a legal resident of your state? (26)	(Month and Year; e.g., 05/1995)
If you, the student, are male, age 18-25, and not already registered with the Selective Service, if you answer "Yes" to this question on the online FAFSA, the Selective Service will register you. (28)	☐ Yes ☐ No
Student's type of degree or certificate (29)	☐ 1 (1st Bachelor's degree) ☐ 2 (2nd Bachelor's degree) ☐ 3 (Associate degree - occupational/technical program) ☐ 4 (Associate degree - general education or transfer program) ☐ 5 (Certificate or diploma for completing an occupational, technical, or educational program of less than two years) ☐ 6 (Certificate or diploma for completing an occupational, technical, or educational program of at least two years) ☐ 7 (Teaching credential program nondegree) ☐ 8 (Graduate or professional degree) ☐ 9 (Other/Undecided)

Page 1 of 4

Financial Aid 101   www.petersons.com

Appendix C

Question		Answer	
Student's grade level in college in 2003-2004 (30)	☐ 0 (1st yr, Never Attended) ☐ 1 (1st yr, Previously Attended) ☐ 2 (2nd yr/Sophomore) ☐ 3 (3rd yr/Junior)	☐ 4 (4th yr/Senior) ☐ 5 (5th yr or More) ☐ 6 (1st Year Graduate/Professional) ☐ 7 (Continuing Graduate/Professional)	
Will you, the student, have a high school diploma or GED before you enroll? (31)		☐ Yes	☐ No
Will you, the student, have your first bachelor's degree by July 1, 2003? (32)		☐ Yes	☐ No
Are you, the student, interested in student loans? (33)		☐ Yes	☐ No
Are you, the student, interested in work-study? (34)		☐ Yes	☐ No
Does the student have a drug conviction that will affect eligibility for aid? (35)		See notes on page 4	
Were you, the student, born before January 1, 1980? (52)		☐ Yes	☐ No
In 2003-2004, will you, the student, be working on a master's or doctorate program? (53)		☐ Yes	☐ No
As of today, are you, the student, married? (54)		☐ Yes	☐ No
Do you, the student, have children who receive more than half of their support from you? (55)		☐ Yes	☐ No
Do you, the student, have dependents other than your children/spouse? (56)		☐ Yes	☐ No
Is the student an orphan, or are you or were you (until age 18) a ward/dependent of the court? (57)		☐ Yes	☐ No
Are you, the student, a veteran of the U.S. Armed Forces? (58)		☐ Yes ☐ No See notes on page 4	
Has the student completed a 2002 IRS or other income tax return? (36)		☐ Have already completed ☐ Will file, have not yet completed ☐ Not going to file	
What income tax return did you, the student, file or will you file for 2002? (37)	☐ 1 – IRS 1040 ☐ 2 – IRS 1040A, 1040EZ, or 1040 Telefile ☐ 3 – A Foreign tax return	☐ 4 – A tax return for Puerto Rico, Guam, American Samoa, the U.S. Virgin Islands, the Marshall Islands, the Federated States of Micronesia, or Palau	
If you, the student, filed a 1040, were you eligible to file a 1040A or 1040EZ? (38)		☐ Yes ☐ No See notes on page 4	
What was the student's (and spouse's) 2002 adjusted gross income from IRS form? (39) (Adjusted Gross Income is on IRS form 1040-line 35; 1040A-line 21; 1040EZ-line 4; or Telefile-line I.)		$	
What was the amount of the student's (and spouse's) income tax for 2002? (40) (Income tax amount is on IRS form 1040-line 55; 1040A-line 36; 1040EZ-line 10; or Telefile-line K(2).)		$	
Enter the student's (and spouse's) exemptions for 2002. (41) (Exemptions are on IRS form 1040-line 6d or 1040A-line 6d. For Form 1040EZ, if a person answered "Yes" on line 5, use EZ worksheet line F to determine the number of exemptions ($3,000 equals one exemption). If a person answered "No" on line 5, enter 01 if he or she is single, or 02 if he or she is married. For Form Telefile, use line J(2) to determine the number of exemptions ($3,000 equals one exemption).			
How much did you the student (and spouse) earn from working (wages, salaries, tips, etc.) in 2002? (42 and 43) (Answer these questions whether or not you, the student, filed a tax return. This information may be on your W-2 forms, or on IRS Form 1040-lines 7+12+18; 1040A-line 7; or 1040EZ-line 1. Telefilers should use their W-2 forms.)		Student (42) $ Spouse (43) $	
Student's household size (85)		See notes on page 4	
Student's number in college (86)		See notes on page 4	
Who is considered a Parent? Read the notes listed on page 4 to determine who is considered a parent for the purpose of the form. You **must** answer questions about your parent(s) if you answered "No" to all dependency questions (questions 52-58 on the paper FAFSA) listed on page 2 of this worksheet, even if you did not live with them. Please note: all questions related to your parent(s) are shaded. (Note that grandparents and legal guardians are not parents.)			
What is your parents' marital status as of today? (59)	☐ Married/Remarried ☐ Single	☐ Divorced/Separated ☐ Widowed	
Month and year your parents were married, separated, divorced, or widowed (60)		(Month and Year, e.g., 05/1995)	
Have your parents completed a 2002 IRS or other income tax return? (71)		☐ Have already completed ☐ Will file, have not yet completed ☐ Not going to file	

Question	Answer	
What type of tax return did your parents file, or will they file in 2002? (72)	☐ 1 – IRS 1040 ☐ 2 – IRS 1040A, 1040EZ, or 1040 Telefile ☐ 3 – A Foreign tax return	☐ 4 – A tax return for Puerto Rico, Guam, American Samoa, the U.S. Virgin Islands, the Marshall Islands, the Federated States of Micronesia, or Palau
If your parent filed a 1040, were they eligible to file a 1040A or 1040EZ? (73)	☐ Yes ☐ No	See notes on page 4
What was your parents' adjusted gross income from IRS form? (74) (Adjusted Gross Income is on IRS form 1040-line 35; 1040A-line 21; 1040EZ-line 4; or Telefile-line I.)	$	
How much did your parents earn from working (wages, salaries, tips, etc.) in 2002? (77 and 78) (Answer these questions whether or not your parents filed a tax return. This information may be on their W-2 forms, or on IRS Form 1040-lines 7+12+18; 1040A-line 7; or 1040EZ-line 1. Telefilers should use their W-2 forms.)	Father (77) $ Mother (78) $	
Student's amount from FAFSA Worksheet A (44)	$	See notes on page 4
Student's amount from FAFSA Worksheet B (45)	$	See notes on page 4
Student's amount from FAFSA Worksheet C (46)	$	See notes on page 4
As of today, student's (and spouse's) amount for net worth of current investments, including real estate (not your home) (47)	$	Net Worth means current value minus debt
As of today, student's (and spouse's) amount for net worth of current business and/or investment farms (48)	$	Net Worth means current value minus debt
As of today, student's (and spouse's) amount of cash, savings, and checking accounts (49)	$	
Number of months student will receive veterans' education (VA) benefits (50)		Use 01 to 12
Student's monthly VA benefits amount (51)	$	
Student's father's (or stepfather's) Social Security Number (61)		
Students father's (or stepfather's) last name (62)		
Student's mother's (or stepmother's) Social Security Number (63)		
Student's mother's (or stepmother's) last name (64)		
Student's parents' household size (65)		See notes on page 4
Student's parents' number in college (66)		See notes on page 4
Student's parents' state of legal residence (67)		
Did the student's parents become legal residents of the state before January 1, 1998? (68)	☐ Yes ☐ No	
If "No," date the student's parent became a legal resident of this state (69)		(Month and Year; e.g., 05/1995)
What is the age of the student's older parent? (70)		
What was the amount the student's parents paid in income tax for 2002? (75) (Income tax amount is on IRS form 1040-line 55; 1040A-line 36; 1040EZ-line 10; or Telefile-line K(2).)	$	
Enter the student's parents' exemptions for 2002 (76) (Exemptions are on IRS form 1040-line 6d or 1040A-line 6d. For Form 1040EZ, if a person answered "Yes" on line 5, use EZ worksheet line f to determine the number of exemptions ($3,000 equals one exemption). If a person answered "No" on line 5 enter 01 if he or she is single, or 02 if he or she is married. For Form Telefile, use line J(2) to determine the number of exemptions ($3,000 equals one exemption).		
Student's parents' amount from FAFSA Worksheet A (79)	$	See notes on page 4
Student's parents' amount from FAFSA Worksheet B (80)	$	See notes on page 4
Student's parents' amount from FAFSA Worksheet C (81)	$	See notes on page 4
As of today, student's parent's amount for net worth of current investments, including real estate (not your home) (82)	$	Net Worth means current value minus debt
As of today, student's parent's amount for net worth of current business and/or investment farms (83)	$	Net Worth means current value minus debt
As of today, student's parent's amount in cash, savings, and checking accounts (84)	$	

Near the end of the application, the online FAFSA will help you to list the schools you would like to receive your FAFSA information. In addition, if someone other than you, your spouse, or your parents completed the online FAFSA for you, you will be asked to report information about that person.

Appendix C

Notes Section:

Notes for Student's Citizenship Status and Alien Registration Number:

Generally you are an eligible noncitizen if you are: (1) a U.S. permanent resident and you have an Alien Registration Receipt card (I-551); (2) a conditional permanent resident (I-551C); or (3) an other eligible noncitizen with an Arrival-Department Record (I-94) from the U.S. Immigration and Naturalization Service showing any of the following designations: "Refugee", "Asylum Granted", "Indefinite Parole", "Humanitarian Parole", or "Cuban-Haitian Entrant". If you're not sure how to answer, FAFSA on the Web (www.fafsa.ed.gov/help.htm) provides additional information to help you answer these questions.

If you are an eligible noncitizen, enter your eight or nine digit Alien Registration Number.

Notes for Student's Drug Conviction Affecting Eligibility:

If you have a conviction for possessing or selling illegal drugs go to FAFSA on the Web (www.fafsa.ed.gov/worksheet.htm). The worksheet will walk you through a series of questions to help you figure out if your conviction affects your eligibility.

Notes for Was Student Eligible to File a 1040A or 1040EZ:

In general, a person is eligible to file a 1040A or 1040EZ if he or she makes less than $50,000, does not itemize deductions, doesn't receive income from his or her business farm, does not receive alimony, and is not required to file Schedule D for capital gains. If you filed a 1040 only to claim Hope and Lifetime Learning credits, and you would have otherwise been eligible to file a 1040A or 1040EZ, you should answer "Yes."

Notes for Are You, the Student, a Veteran of the U.S. Armed Forces:

Answer "No" (you are not a veteran) if you (1) have never engaged in active duty in the U.S. Armed Forces, (2) are currently an ROTC student or cadet or midshipman at a service academy, or (3) are a National Guard or Reserves enlistee activated only for training. Also answer "No" if you are currently serving in the U.S. Armed Forces and will continue to serve through June 30, 2004.

Answer "Yes" (you are a veteran) if you (1) have engaged in active duty in the U.S. Armed Forces (Army, Navy, Air Force, Marines, or Coast Guard) or as a member National Guard or Reserves who was called to active duty for purposes other than training, or were a cadet or midshipman at one of the service academies, **and** (2) were released under a condition other than dishonorable. Also answer "Yes" if you are not a veteran now but will be one by June 30, 2004.

Notes for Student's Household Size:

Include in your (and your spouse's) household: (1) Yourself (and your spouse, if you have one), and (2) your children if you will provide more than half of their support from July 1, 2003 through June 30, 2004, and (3) other people if they now live with you, and you provide more than half of their support, and you will continue to provide more than half of their support from July 1, 2003 through June 30, 2004.

Notes for Student's Number in College:

Always count yourself as a college student. **Don't include your parents.** Include others only if they will attend at least half time in a 2003-2004 program that leads to a college degree or certificate.

Notes for Who is Considered a Parent:

If your parents are both living and married to each other, answer the questions about them.

If your parent is widowed or single, answer the questions about that parent. If your widowed parent is remarried as of today, answer the questions about that parent **and** the person to whom your parent is married (your stepparent).

If your parents are divorced or separated, answer the questions about the parent you lived with during the past 12 months. (If you did not live with one parent more than the other, give answers about the parent who provided more financial support during the past 12 months, or during the most recent year that you actually received support from that parent.) If this parent is remarried as of today, answer the questions on the rest of this form about that parent **and** the person to whom your parent is married (your stepparent).

Notes for Were Your Parents Eligible to File a 1040A or 1040EZ:

In general, a person is eligible to file a 1040A or 1040EZ if he or she makes less than $50,000, does not itemize deductions, doesn't receive income from his or her business farm, does not receive alimony, and is not required to file Schedule D for capital gains. If your parents filed a 1040 only to claim Hope and Lifetime Learning credits, and would have otherwise been eligible to file a 1040A or 1040EZ, they should answer "Yes" to this question.

Notes for Student's Worksheets A, B and C:

For help with answering these questions, go to www.fafsa.ed.gov/worksheet.htm. Print out copies of all Worksheets and complete them prior to filling out the online FAFSA.

Notes for Parents' Household Size:

Include in your parents' household: (1) Your parents and yourself, even if you don't live with parents, and (2) your parents' other children if (a) your parents will provide more than half of their support from July 1, 2003 through June 30, 2004, or (b) the children could answer "No" to all of the dependency questions listed on page 2 of this Worksheet (questions 52-58 on the paper FAFSA), and (3) other people if they live with your parents, and your parents provide more than half of their support, and your parents will continue to provide more than half of their support from July 1, 2003 through June 30, 2004.

Notes for Parent's Number in College:

Always count yourself as a college student. **Don't include your parents.** Include others only if they will attend at least half time in a 2003-2004 program that leads to a college degree or certificate.

Notes for Parent's Worksheets A, B and C:

For help with answering these questions, go to www.fafsa.ed.gov/worksheet.htm. Print out copies of all Worksheets and complete them prior to filling out the online FAFSA.

The anticipated changes in the 2004–05 FAFSA include a redesigned layout, so that information contained on each page is more easily identified; the addition of questions or clarification of existing questions, for increased accuracy of answers; and the consolidation of five enrollment questions (full-time, half-time, etc., for each semester of the school year) into one enrollment question (full-time, half-time, etc. for academic year in general) and the repositioning of this information at the end of form.

Appendix C

FAFSA
We Help Put America Through School

July 1, 2004 — June 30, 2005
FREE APPLICATION FOR FEDERAL STUDENT AID
OMB # 1845-0001

Apply free for federal and state student grants, work-study, and loans using this form!

Or apply free over the internet at www.fafsa.ed.gov

Applying by the Deadlines

For federal aid, submit your application as early as possible, but no earlier than January 1, 2004. We must receive your application no later than June 30, 2005. Your college must have your correct, complete information by your last day of enrollment in the 2004-2005 school year.

For state or college aid, the deadline may be as early as January 2004. See the table to the right for state deadlines. You may also need to complete additional forms. Check with your high school guidance counselor or a financial aid administrator at your college about state and college sources of student aid and deadlines.

If you are filing close to one of these deadlines, we recommend you file over the internet at **www.fafsa.ed.gov**. This is the fastest way to apply for aid.

Using Your Tax Return

If you are filing a 2003 federal income tax return, we recommend that you complete it before filling out this form. If you have not filed your return, you can still submit your FAFSA. Once you file your tax return, you must correct any income or tax data that changed on your FAFSA.

Filling Out the FAFSA

Your answers on this form will be read electronically. Therefore:

- use black ink and fill in ovals completely;
- print clearly in CAPITAL letters and skip a box between words;
- report dollar amounts (such as $12,356.41) like this:

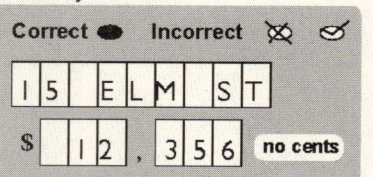

Correct ● Incorrect ⊗ ☑

`1 5   E L M   S T`

`$    1 2 , 3 5 6` no cents

Pink is for student information and purple is for parent information.

If you or your family has unusual circumstances not shown on this form (such as loss of employment) that might affect your need for student financial aid, submit this form and then consult with the financial aid office at the college you plan to attend.

If you have questions about this application, or for more information on eligibility requirements and the U.S. Department of Education's student aid programs, look on the internet at **www.studentaid.ed.gov**. You can also call 1-800-4-FED-AID (1-800-433-3243). TTY users may call 1-800-730-8913.

Mailing Your FAFSA

After you complete this application, make a copy of pages 3 through 6 for your records. Then mail the original of only pages 3 through 6 in the attached envelope or send it to: Federal Student Aid Programs, P.O. Box 4691, Mt. Vernon, IL 62864-0059. Be sure to keep the worksheets on page 8.

You should hear from us within four weeks. If you do not, please check online at **www.fafsa.ed.gov** or call 1-800-433-3243. If you provided your e-mail address in question 13, you will receive information about your application within a few days after we process it.

Let's Get Started!

Now go to page 3, detach the application form, and begin filling it out. Refer to the notes as instructed.

STATE AID DEADLINES
File On-Line and File On-Time
www.fafsa.ed.gov

	AR	For State Grant - April 1, 2004 For Workforce Grant - July 1, 2004 *(date received)*
	AZ	June 30, 2005 *(date received)*
*^	CA	For initial awards - March 2, 2004 For additional community college awards - September 2, 2004 *(date postmarked)*
*	DC	June 28, 2004 *(date received by state)*
	DE	April 15, 2004 *(date received)*
	FL	May 15, 2004 *(date processed)*
^	IA	July 1, 2004 *(date received)*
#	IL	First-time applicants - September 30, 2004 Continuing applicants - August 15, 2004 *(date received)*
	IN	March 10, 2004 *(date received)*
#*	KS	April 1, 2004 *(date received)*
#	KY	March 15, 2004 *(date received)*
#^	LA	May 1, 2004 Final deadline - July 1, 2004 *(date received)*
#*	MA	May 1, 2004 *(date received)*
	MD	March 1, 2004 *(date postmarked)*
	ME	May 1, 2004 *(date received)*
	MI	March 1, 2004 *(date received)*
	MN	14 days after term starts *(date received)*
	MO	April 1, 2004 *(date received)*
#	MT	March 1, 2004 *(date processed)*
	NC	March 15, 2004 *(date received)*
	ND	March 15, 2004 *(date received)*
	NH	May 1, 2004 *(date received)*
^	NJ	June 1, 2004 if you received a Tuition Aid Grant in 2003-2004 All other applicants - October 1, 2004, fall & spring term - March 1, 2005, spring term only *(date received)*
*^	NY	May 1, 2005 *(date postmarked)*
	OH	October 1, 2004 *(date received)*
#	OK	April 30, 2004 Final deadline - June 30, 2004 *(date received)*
*	PA	All 2003-2004 State Grant recipients & all non-2003-2004 State Grant recipients in degree programs - May 1, 2004 All other applicants - August 1, 2004
	PR	May 2, 2005 *(date application signed)*
#	RI	March 1, 2004 *(date received)*
	SC	June 30, 2004 *(date received)*
	TN	May 1, 2004 *(date processed)*
*^	WV	March 1, 2004 *(date received)*

Check with your financial aid administrator for these states: AK, AL, *AS, *CT, CO, *FM, GA, *GU, *HI, ID, *MH, *MP, MS, *NE, *NM, *NV, OR, *PW, *SD, *TX, UT, *VA, *VI, *VT, WA, WI, and WY.

\# For priority consideration, submit application by date specified.

^ Applicants encouraged to obtain proof of mailing.

* Additional form may be required.

Notes for questions 14 – 15 (page 3)

If you are an eligible noncitizen, write in your eight- or nine-digit Alien Registration Number. Generally, you are an eligible noncitizen if you are: (1) a U.S. permanent resident and you have an Alien Registration Receipt Card (I-551); (2) a conditional permanent resident (I-551C); or (3) an other eligible noncitizen with an Arrival-Departure Record (I-94) from the Department of Homeland Security showing any one of the following designations: "Refugee," "Asylum Granted," "Parolee" (I-94 confirms paroled for a minimum of one year and status has not expired), or "Cuban-Haitian Entrant." If you are in the U.S. on an F1 or F2 student visa, or a J1 or J2 exchange visitor visa, or a G series visa (pertaining to international organizations), you must fill in oval c. If you are neither a citizen nor an eligible noncitizen, you are not eligible for federal student aid. However, you may be eligible for state or college aid.

Notes for question 23 (page 3) — Enter the correct number in the box in question 23.

Enter 1 for 1st bachelor's degree
Enter 2 for 2nd bachelor's degree
Enter 3 for associate degree (occupational or technical program)
Enter 4 for associate degree (general education or transfer program)
Enter 5 for certificate or diploma for completing an occupational, technical, or educational program of less than two years
Enter 6 for certificate or diploma for completing an occupational, technical, or educational program of at least two years
Enter 7 for teaching credential program (nondegree program)
Enter 8 for graduate or professional degree
Enter 9 for other/undecided

Notes for question 24 (page 3) — Enter the correct number in the box in question 24.

Enter 0 for never attended college & 1st year undergraduate
Enter 1 for attended college before & 1st year undergraduate
Enter 2 for 2nd year undergraduate/sophomore
Enter 3 for 3rd year undergraduate/junior
Enter 4 for 4th year undergraduate/senior
Enter 5 for 5th year/other undergraduate
Enter 6 for 1st year graduate/professional
Enter 7 for continuing graduate/professional or beyond

Notes for questions 29 – 30 (page 3)

Some states and colleges offer aid based on the level of schooling your parents completed.

Notes for questions 33 c. and d. (page 4) and 71 c. and d. (page 5)

If you filed or will file a foreign tax return, or a tax return with Puerto Rico, Guam, American Samoa, the U.S. Virgin Islands, the Marshall Islands, the Federated States of Micronesia, or Palau, use the information from that return to fill out this form. If you filed a foreign return, convert all figures to U.S. dollars, using the exchange rate that is in effect today. Go to **www.federalreserve.gov/releases/h10/update** to view the daily exchange rate.

Notes for questions 34 (page 4) and 72 (page 5)

In general, a person is eligible to file a 1040A or 1040EZ if he or she makes less than $50,000, does not itemize deductions, does not receive income from his or her own business or farm, and does not receive alimony. A person is not eligible if he or she itemizes deductions, receives self-employment income or alimony, or is required to file Schedule D for capital gains. If you filed a 1040 only to claim Hope or Lifetime Learning credits, and you would have otherwise been eligible for a 1040A or 1040EZ, you should answer "Yes" to this question.

Notes for questions 37 (page 4) and 75 (page 5) — only for people who filed a 1040EZ or Telefile

On the 1040EZ, if a person answered "Yes" on line 5, use EZ worksheet line F to determine the number of exemptions ($3,050 equals one exemption). If a person answered "No" on line 5, enter 01 if he or she is single, or 02 if he or she is married.

On the Telefile, use line J(2) to determine the number of exemptions ($3,050 equals one exemption).

Notes for questions 43 – 45 (page 4) and 81 – 83 (page 5)

By applying over the internet at **www.fafsa.ed.gov**, you may be eligible to skip some questions. If you do not have internet access, completing questions 43–45 will not penalize you.

Net worth means current value minus debt. If net worth is one million or more, enter $999,999. If net worth is negative, enter 0.

Investments include real estate (do not include the home you live in), trust funds, money market funds, mutual funds, certificates of deposit, stocks, stock options, bonds, other securities, Coverdell savings accounts, college savings plans, installment and land sale contracts (including mortgages held), commodities, etc. Investment value includes the market value of these investments as of today. Investment debt means only those debts that are related to the investments.

Investments do not include the home you live in, the value of life insurance, retirement plans (pension funds, annuities, noneducation IRAs, Keogh plans, etc.), and prepaid tuition plans, or cash, savings, and checking accounts already reported in 43 and 81.

Business and/or investment farm value includes the market value of land, buildings, machinery, equipment, inventory, etc. Business and/or investment farm debt means only those debts for which the business or investment farm was used as collateral.

Notes for question 54 (page 4)

Answer **"No"** (you are not a veteran) if you (1) have never engaged in active duty in the U.S. Armed Forces, (2) are currently an ROTC student or a cadet or midshipman at a service academy, or (3) are a National Guard or Reserves enlistee activated only for training. Also answer "No" if you are currently serving in the U.S. Armed Forces and will continue to serve through June 30, 2005.

Answer **"Yes"** (you are a veteran) if you (1) have engaged in active duty in the U.S. Armed Forces (Army, Navy, Air Force, Marines, or Coast Guard) or are a National Guard or Reserve enlistee, who was called to active duty for purposes other than training, or were a cadet or midshipman at one of the service academies, **and** (2) were released under a condition other than dishonorable. Also answer "Yes" if you are not a veteran now but will be one by June 30, 2005.

Financial Aid 101

Appendix C

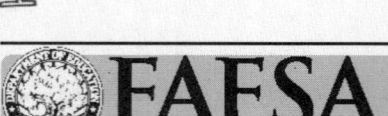

FAFSA
JULY 1, 2004 — JUNE 30, 2005
FREE APPLICATION FOR FEDERAL STUDENT AID
We Help Put America Through School

OMB # 1845-0001

Step One: For questions 1–30, leave blank any questions that do not apply to you (the student).

1-3. Your full name (as it appears on your Social Security card)
1. LAST NAME: FOR INFORMATION ONLY
2. FIRST NAME: DO NOT SUBMIT
3. MIDDLE INITIAL

4-7. Your permanent mailing address
4. NUMBER AND STREET (INCLUDE APT. NUMBER)
5. CITY (AND COUNTRY IF NOT U.S.)
6. STATE
7. ZIP CODE

8. Your Social Security Number: XXX-XX-XXXX
9. Your date of birth: __ / __ / 19__
10. Your permanent telephone number

11-12. Your driver's license number and state (if any)
11. LICENSE NUMBER
12. STATE

13. Your e-mail address — WE WILL USE THIS E-MAIL ADDRESS TO CORRESPOND WITH YOU. YOU WILL RECEIVE YOUR FAFSA INFORMATION THROUGH A SECURE LINK ON THE INTERNET, SENT TO THE E-MAIL ADDRESS YOU PROVIDE. LEAVE BLANK TO RECEIVE INFORMATION THROUGH REGULAR MAIL. WE WILL ONLY SHARE THIS ADDRESS WITH THE SCHOOLS YOU LIST ON THE FORM AND YOUR STATE. THEY MAY USE THE E-MAIL ADDRESS TO COMMUNICATE WITH YOU.

14. Are you a U.S. Citizen? Pick one. See page 2.
a. Yes, I am a U.S. citizen. **Skip to question 16.** ○ 1
b. No, but I am an eligible noncitizen. **Fill in question 15.** ○ 2
c. No, I am not a citizen or eligible noncitizen. ○ 3

15. ALIEN REGISTRATION NUMBER: A_____

16. What is your marital status as of today?
I am single, divorced, or widowed ○ 1
I am married/remarried ○ 2
I am separated ○ 3

17. Month and year you were married, separated, divorced, or widowed — MONTH / YEAR

18. What is your state of legal residence? STATE
19. Did you become a legal resident of this state before January 1, 1999? Yes ○ 1 No ○ 2

20. If the answer to question 19 is "No," give month and year you became a legal resident. MONTH / YEAR

21. Are you male? (Most male students must register with Selective Service to get federal aid.) Yes ○ 1 No ○ 2
22. If you are male (age 18–25) and not registered, answer "Yes" and Selective Service will register you. Yes ○ 1 No ○ 2

23. What degree or certificate will you be working on during 2004–2005? See page 2 and enter the correct number in the box.
24. What will be your grade level when you begin the 2004–2005 school year? See page 2 and enter the correct number in the box.

25. Will you have a high school diploma or GED before you begin the 2004–2005 school year? Yes ○ 1 No ○ 2
26. Will you have your first bachelor's degree before July 1, 2004? Yes ○ 1 No ○ 2
27. In addition to grants, are you interested in student loans (which you must pay back)? Yes ○ 1 No ○ 2
28. In addition to grants, are you interested in "work-study" (which you earn through work)? Yes ○ 1 No ○ 2

29. Highest school your father completed — Middle school/Jr. High ○ 1   High School ○ 2   College or beyond ○ 3   Other/unknown ○ 4
30. Highest school your mother completed — Middle school/Jr. High ○ 1   High School ○ 2   College or beyond ○ 3   Other/unknown ○ 4

31. Do not leave this question blank. Have you ever been convicted of possessing or selling illegal drugs? If you have, answer "Yes," complete and submit this application, and we will send you a worksheet in the mail for you to determine if your conviction affects your eligibility for aid.
No ○ 1   Yes ○ 5

DO NOT LEAVE QUESTION 31 BLANK

Page 3

For Help -- www.studentaid.ed.gov/completefafsa

www.petersons.com

Financial Aid 101

Forms Bank

Step Two: For questions 32–45, report your (the student's) income and assets. If you are married as of today, report your and your spouse's income and assets, even if you were not married in 2003. Ignore references to "spouse" if you are currently single, separated, divorced, or widowed.

32. For 2003, have you (the student) completed your IRS income tax return or another tax return listed in question 33?
    - a. I have already completed my return. ○₁
    - b. I will file, but I have not yet completed my return. ○₂
    - c. I'm not going to file. (Skip to question 38.) ○₃

33. What income tax return did you file or will you file for 2003?
    - a. IRS 1040 ○₁
    - b. IRS 1040A, 1040 EZ, 1040 Telefile ○₂
    - c. A foreign tax return. **See page 2.** ○₃
    - d. A tax return for Puerto Rico, Guam, American Samoa, the U.S. Virgin Islands, the Marshall Islands, the Federated States of Micronesia, or Palau. **See page 2** ○₄

34. If you have filed or will file a 1040, were you eligible to file a 1040A or 1040 EZ? **See page 2.** Yes ○₁ No ○₂ Don't Know ○₃

For questions 35–47, if the answer is zero or the question does not apply to you, enter 0.

35. What was your (and spouse's) adjusted gross income for 2003? Adjusted gross income is on IRS Form 1040—line 34; 1040A—line 21; 1040EZ—line 4; or Telefile—line I. $ ⬚

36. Enter the total amount of your (and spouse's) income tax for 2003. Income tax amount is on IRS Form 1040—line 54; 1040A—line 36; 1040EZ—line 10; or Telefile—line K(2). $ ⬚

37. Enter your (and spouse's) exemptions for 2003. Exemptions are on IRS Form 1040—line 6d or on Form 1040A—line 6d. For Form 1040EZ or Telefile, **see page 2.** ⬚

38-39. How much did you (and spouse) earn from working (wages, salaries, tips, etc.) in 2003? Answer this question whether or not you filed a tax return. This information may be on your W-2 forms, or on IRS Form 1040—lines 7 + 12 + 18; 1040A—line 7; or 1040EZ—line 1. Telefilers should use their W-2 forms.
    - You (38) $ ⬚
    - Your Spouse (39) $ ⬚

Student (and Spouse) Worksheets (40–42)

40–42. Go to page 8 and complete the columns on the left of Worksheets A, B, and C. Enter the student (and spouse) totals in questions 40, 41, and 42, respectively. Even though you may have few of the Worksheet items, check each line carefully.
    - Worksheet A (40) $ ⬚
    - Worksheet B (41) $ ⬚
    - Worksheet C (42) $ ⬚

43. As of today, what is your (and spouse's) total current balance of **cash, savings, and checking accounts**? Do not include student financial aid. $ ⬚

44. As of today, what is the net worth of your (and spouse's) **investments**, including real estate (not your home)? **See page 2.** $ ⬚

45. As of today, what is the net worth of your (and spouse's) current **businesses and/or investment farms**? Do not include a farm that you live on and operate. **See page 2.** $ ⬚

46-47. If you receive veterans' education benefits, for how many months from July 1, 2004, through June 30, 2005, will you receive these benefits, and what amount will you receive per month? Do not include your spouse's veterans' education benefits.
    - Months (46) ⬚
    - Amount (47) $ ⬚

Step Three: Answer all seven questions in this step.

48. Were you born before January 1, 1981? .... Yes ○₁ No ○₂
49. At the beginning of the 2004–2005 school year, will you be working on a master's or doctorate program (such as an MA, MBA, MD, JD, PhD, EdD, or graduate certificate, etc.)? .... Yes ○₁ No ○₂
50. As of today, are you married? (Answer "Yes" if you are separated but not divorced.) .... Yes ○₁ No ○₂
51. Do you have children who receive more than half of their support from you? .... Yes ○₁ No ○₂
52. Do you have dependents (other than your children or spouse) who live with you and who receive more than half of their support from you, now and through June 30, 2005? .... Yes ○₁ No ○₂
53. Are both of your parents deceased, or are you or were you (until age 18) a ward/dependent of the court? .... Yes ○₁ No ○₂
54. Are you a veteran of the U.S. Armed Forces? **See page 2.** .... Yes ○₁ No ○₂

If you (the student) answer "No" to every question in Step Three, go to Step Four.
If you answer "Yes" to any question in Step Three, skip Step Four and go to Step Five on page 6.

(**Health Profession Students**: Your school may require you to complete Step Four even if you answered "Yes" to any Step Three question.)

Page 4

For Help —1-800-433-3243

Financial Aid 101

www.petersons.com

Appendix C

Step Four: Complete this step if you (the student) answered "No" to all questions in Step Three. Go to page 7 to determine who is a parent for this step.

55. What is your parents' marital status as of today?
- Married/Remarried ○₁
- Single ○₂
- Divorced/Separated ○₃
- Widowed ○₄

56. Month and year they were married, separated, divorced, or widowed
MONTH / YEAR

57–64. What are the Social Security Numbers, names, and dates of birth of the parents reporting information on this form? If your parent does not have a Social Security Number, you must enter 000-00-0000.

57. FATHER'S/STEPFATHER'S SOCIAL SECURITY NUMBER
58. FATHER'S/STEPFATHER'S LAST NAME, AND
59. FIRST INITIAL
60. FATHER'S/STEPFATHER'S DATE OF BIRTH

61. MOTHER'S/STEPMOTHER'S SOCIAL SECURITY NUMBER
62. MOTHER'S/STEPMOTHER'S LAST NAME, AND
63. FIRST INITIAL
64. MOTHER'S/STEPMOTHER'S DATE OF BIRTH

65. Go to page 7 to determine how many people are in your parents' household.

66. Go to page 7 to determine how many in question 65 (exclude your parents) will be college students between July 1, 2004, and June 30, 2005.

67. What is your parents' state of legal residence? STATE

68. Did your parents become legal residents of this state before January 1, 1999? Yes ○₁ No ○₂

69. If the answer to question 68 is "**No**," give month and year legal residency began for the parent who has lived in the state the longest.
MONTH / YEAR

70. For 2003, have your parents completed their IRS income tax return or another tax return listed in question 71?
- **a.** My parents have already completed their return. ○₁
- **b.** My parents will file, but they have not yet completed their return. ○₂
- **c.** My parents are not going to file. **(Skip to question 76.)** ○₃

71. What income tax return did your parents file or will they file for 2003?
- a. IRS 1040 ○₁
- b. IRS 1040A, 1040 EZ, 1040 Telefile ○₂
- c. A foreign tax return. **See page 2.** ○₃
- d. A tax return for Puerto Rico, Guam, American Samoa, the U.S. Virgin Islands, the Marshall Islands, the Federated States of Micronesia, or Palau. **See page 2.** ○₄

72. If your parents have filed or will file a 1040, were they eligible to file a 1040A or 1040EZ? **See page 2.**
Yes ○₁ No ○₂ Don't Know ○₃

For questions 73–83, if the answer is zero or the question does not apply, enter 0.

73. What was your parents' adjusted gross income for 2003? Adjusted gross income is on IRS Form 1040—line 34; 1040A—line 21; 1040EZ—line 4; or Telefile—line I. $

74. Enter the total amount of your parents' income tax for 2003. Income tax amount is on IRS Form 1040—line 54; 1040A—line 36; 1040EZ—line 10; or Telefile—line K(2). $

75. Enter your parents' exemptions for 2003. Exemptions are on IRS Form 1040—line 6d or on Form 1040A—line 6d. For Form 1040EZ or Telefile, **see page 2.**

76–77. How much did your parents earn from working (wages, salaries, tips, etc.) in 2003? Answer this question whether or not your parents filed a tax return. This information may be on their W-2 forms, or on IRS Form 1040—lines 7 + 12 + 18; 1040A—line 7; or 1040EZ—line 1. Telefilers should use their W-2 forms.
- Father/Stepfather (76) $
- Mother/Stepmother (77) $

Parent Worksheets (78–80)

78–80. Go to page 8 and complete the columns on the right of Worksheets A, B, and C. Enter the parents totals in questions 78, 79, and 80, respectively. Even though your parents may have few of the Worksheet items, check each line carefully.
- Worksheet A (78) $
- Worksheet B (79) $
- Worksheet C (80) $

81. As of today, what is your parents' total current balance of **cash, savings, and checking accounts**? $

82. As of today, what is the net worth of your parents' **investments**, including real estate (not your home)? **See page 2.** $

83. As of today, what is the net worth of your parents' current **businesses and/or investment farms**? Do not include a farm that your parents live on and operate. **See page 2.** $

Now go to Step Six.

Page 5

For Help — www.studentaid.ed.gov/completefafsa

www.petersons.com — Financial Aid 101

Forms Bank

Step Five: Complete this step only if you (the student) answered "Yes" to any Step Three question.

84. Go to **page** 7 to determine how many people in your (and your spouse's) household.

85. Go to **page** 7 to determine how many in question 84 will be college students, attending at least half time between July 1, 2004, and June 30, 2005.

Step Six: Please tell us which schools may request your information, and your enrollment level.

Enter the 6-digit federal school code and your housing plans. Look for the federal school codes at **www.fafsa.ed.gov**, at your college financial aid office, at your public library, or by asking your high school guidance counselor. If you cannot get the federal school code, write in the complete name, address, city, and state of the college. For state aid, you may wish to list your preferred school first.

86. 1ST FEDERAL SCHOOL CODE OR NAME OF COLLEGE / ADDRESS AND CITY STATE **87.** HOUSING PLANS: on campus ○1, off campus ○2, with parent ○3

88. 2ND FEDERAL SCHOOL CODE OR NAME OF COLLEGE / ADDRESS AND CITY STATE **89.** on campus ○1, off campus ○2, with parent ○3

90. 3RD FEDERAL SCHOOL CODE OR NAME OF COLLEGE / ADDRESS AND CITY STATE **91.** on campus ○1, off campus ○2, with parent ○3

92. 4TH FEDERAL SCHOOL CODE OR NAME OF COLLEGE / ADDRESS AND CITY STATE **93.** on campus ○1, off campus ○2, with parent ○3

94. 5TH FEDERAL SCHOOL CODE OR NAME OF COLLEGE / ADDRESS AND CITY STATE **95.** on campus ○1, off campus ○2, with parent ○3

96. 6TH FEDERAL SCHOOL CODE OR NAME OF COLLEGE / ADDRESS AND CITY STATE **97.** on campus ○1, off campus ○2, with parent ○3

98. See page 7. At the start of the 2004–2005 academic year, please mark if you will be: Full time ○1 3/4 time ○2 Half time ○3 Less than half time ○4 Not sure ○5

Step Seven: Read, sign, and date.

If you are the student, by signing this application you certify that you (1) will use federal and/or state student financial aid only to pay the cost of attending an institution of higher education, (2) are not in default on a federal student loan or have made satisfactory arrangements to repay it, (3) do not owe money back on a federal student grant or have made satisfactory arrangements to repay it, (4) will notify your school if you default on a federal student loan, and (5) will not receive a Federal Pell Grant for more than one school for the same period of time.

If you are the parent or the student, by signing this application you agree, if asked, to provide information that will verify the accuracy of your completed form. This information may include your U.S. or state income tax forms. Also, you certify that you understand that **the Secretary of Education has the authority to verify information reported on this application with the Internal Revenue Service and other federal agencies.** If you purposely give false or misleading information, you may be fined $20,000, sent to prison, or both.

99. Date this form was completed.
MONTH / DAY / 2004 ○ or 2005 ○

100. Student (Sign below)

1 **FOR INFORMATION ONLY.**

Parent (A parent from Step Four sign below)

2 **DO NOT SUBMIT.**

If this form was filled out by someone other than you, your spouse, or your parent(s), that person must complete this part.
Preparer's name, firm, and address

101. Preparer's Social Security Number (or 102)

102. Employer ID number (or 101)

103. Preparer's signature and date

SCHOOL USE ONLY:
D/O ○1
FAA SIGNATURE

Federal School Code

DATA ENTRY USE ONLY: ○P ○* ○L ○E

Page 6

For Help —1-800-433-3243

Financial Aid 101 www.petersons.com

Appendix C

Notes for questions 55–83 (page 5) Step Four: Who is considered a parent in this step?

Read these notes to determine who is considered a parent on this form. **Answer all questions in Step Four about them**, even if you do not live with them. (Note that grandparents and legal guardians are not parents.)

If your parents are both living and married to each other, answer the questions about them.

If your parent is widowed or single, answer the questions about that parent. If your widowed parent is remarried as of today, answer the questions about that parent and the person whom your parent married (your stepparent).

If your parents are divorced or separated, answer the questions about the parent you lived with more during the past 12 months. (If you did not live with one parent more than the other, give answers about the parent who provided more financial support during the past 12 months, or during the most recent year that you actually received support from a parent.) If this parent is remarried as of today, answer the questions on the rest of this form about that parent and the person whom your parent married (your stepparent).

Notes for question 65 (page 5)

Include in your parents' household (see notes, above, for who is considered a parent):
- your parents and yourself, even if you don't live with your parents, and
- your parents' other children if (a) your parents will provide more than half of their support from July 1, 2004 through June 30, 2005 or (b) the children could answer "no" to every question in Step Three on page 4 of this form, and
- other people if they now live with your parents, your parents provide more than half of their support, and your parents will continue to provide more than half of their support from July 1, 2004, through June 30, 2005.

Notes for questions 66 (page 5) and 85 (page 6)

Always count yourself as a college student. Do not include your parents. Include others only if they will attend, at least half time in 2004-2005, a program that leads to a college degree or certificate.

Notes for question 84 (page 6)

Include in your (and your spouse's) household:
- yourself (and your spouse, if you have one), and
- your children, if you will provide more than half of their support from July 1, 2004, through June 30, 2005, and
- other people if they now live with you, and you provide more than half of their support, and you will continue to provide more than half of their support from July 1, 2004, through June 30, 2005.

Notes for question 98 (page 6)

For undergraduates, full time generally means taking at least 12 credit hours in a term or 24 clock hours per week. 3/4 time generally means taking at least 9 credit hours in a term or 18 clock hours per week. Half time generally means taking at least 6 credit hours in a term or 12 clock hours per week. Provide this information about the college you are most likely to attend.

Information on the Privacy Act and use of your Social Security Number

We use the information that you provide on this form to determine if you are eligible to receive federal student financial aid and the amount that you are eligible to receive. Sections 483 and 484 of the Higher Education Act of 1965, as amended, give us the authority to ask you and your parents these questions, and to collect the Social Security Numbers of you and your parents. We use your Social Security Number to verify your identity and retrieve your records, and we may request your Social Security Number again for those purposes.

State and institutional student financial aid programs may also use the information that you provide on this form to determine if you are eligible to receive state and institutional aid and the need that you have for such aid. Therefore, we will disclose the information that you provide on this form to each institution you list in questions 86–96, state agencies in your state of legal residence, and the state agencies of the states in which the colleges that you list in questions 86–96 are located.

If you are applying solely for federal aid, you must answer all of the following questions that apply to you: 1–9, 14–16, 18, 21–22, 25–26, 31–36, 38–45, 48–67, 70–74, 76–85, and 99–100. If you do not answer these questions, you will not receive federal aid.

Without your consent, we may disclose information that you provide to entities under a published "routine use." Under such a routine use, we may disclose information to third parties that we have authorized to assist us in administering the above programs; to other federal agencies under computer matching programs, such as those with the Internal Revenue Service, Social Security Administration, Selective Service System, Department of Homeland Security, and Veterans Affairs; to your parents or spouse; and to members of Congress if you ask them to help you with student aid questions.

If the federal government, the U.S. Department of Education, or an employee of the U.S. Department of Education is involved in litigation, we may send information to the Department of Justice, or a court or adjudicative body, if the disclosure is related to financial aid and certain conditions are met. In addition, we may send your information to a foreign, federal, state, or local enforcement agency if the information that you submitted indicates a violation or potential violation of law, for which that agency has jurisdiction for investigation or prosecution. Finally, we may send information regarding a claim that is determined to be valid and overdue to a consumer reporting agency. This information includes identifiers from the record; the amount, status, and history of the claim; and the program under which the claim arose.

State Certification

By submitting this application, you are giving your state financial aid agency permission to verify any statement on this form and to obtain income tax information for all persons required to report income on this form.

The Paperwork Reduction Act of 1995

The Paperwork Reduction Act of 1995 says that no one is required to respond to a collection of information unless it displays a valid OMB control number, which for this form is 1845-0001. The time required to complete this form is estimated to be one hour, including time to review instructions, search data resources, gather the data needed, and complete and review the information collection. If you have comments about this estimate or suggestions for improving this form, please write to: U.S. Department of Education, Washington DC 20202-4651.

We may request additional information from you to process your application more efficiently. We will collect this additional information only as needed and on a voluntary basis.

Page 7

For Help — www.studentaid.ed.gov/completefafsa

Forms Bank 187

Worksheets
Calendar Year 2003

Do not mail these worksheets in with your application.
Keep these worksheets; your school may ask to see them.

Worksheet A
Report Annual Amounts

Student/Spouse For question 40		Parent(s) For question 78
$	Earned income credit from IRS Form 1040—line 63; 1040A—line 41, 1040EZ—line 8, or Telefile—line L	$
$	Additional child tax credit from IRS Form 1040—line 65 or 1040A—line 42	$
$	Welfare benefits, including Temporary Assistance for Needy Families (TANF). Don't include food stamps or subsidized housing.	$
$	Social Security benefits received, for all household members as reported in question 84 (or 65 for your parents), that were not taxed (such as SSI)	$
$ — Enter in question 40.		Enter in question 78. — $

Worksheet B
Report Annual Amounts

For question 41		For question 79
$	Payments to tax-deferred pension and savings plans (paid directly or withheld from earnings), including, but not limited to, amounts reported on the W-2 Form in Boxes 12a through 12d, codes D, E, F, G, H, and S	$
$	IRA deductions and payments to self-employed SEP, SIMPLE, and Keogh and other qualified plans from IRS Form 1040—total of lines 24 + 30 or 1040A—line 17	$
$	Child support you received for all children. Don't include foster care or adoption payments.	$
$	Tax exempt interest income from IRS Form 1040—line 8b or 1040A—line 8b	$
$	Foreign income exclusion from IRS Form 2555—line 43 or 2555EZ—line 18	$
$	Untaxed portions of IRA distributions from IRS Form 1040—lines (15a minus 15b) or 1040A—lines (11a minus 11b). Exclude rollovers. If negative, enter a zero here.	$
$	Untaxed portions of pensions from IRS Form 1040—lines (16a minus 16b) or 1040A—lines (12a minus 12b). Exclude rollovers. If negative, enter a zero here.	$
$	Credit for federal tax on special fuels from IRS Form 4136—line 10 — nonfarmers only	$
$	Housing, food, and other living allowances paid to members of the military, clergy, and others (including cash payments and cash value of benefits)	$
$	Veterans' noneducation benefits such as Disability, Death Pension, or Dependency & Indemnity Compensation (DIC), and/or VA Educational Work-Study allowances	$
$	Any other untaxed income or benefits not reported elsewhere on Worksheets A and B, such as workers' compensation, untaxed portions of railroad retirement benefits, Black Lung Benefits, disability, etc. Don't include student aid, Workforce Investment Act educational benefits, or benefits from flexible spending arrangements, e.g., cafeteria plans.	$
$	Money received, or paid on your behalf (e.g., bills), not reported elsewhere on this form	XXXXXXXXX
$ — Enter in question 41.		Enter in question 79. — $

Worksheet C
Report Annual Amounts

For question 42		For question 80
$	Education credits (Hope and Lifetime Learning tax credits) from IRS Form 1040—line 47 or 1040A—line 31	$
$	Child support you paid because of divorce or separation or as a result of a legal requirement. Don't include support for children in your (or your parents') household, as reported in question 84 (or question 65 for your parents).	$
$	Taxable earnings from need-based employment programs, such as Federal Work-Study and need-based employment portions of fellowships and assistantships	$
$	Student grant and scholarship aid reported to the IRS in your (or your parents') adjusted gross income. Includes AmeriCorps benefits (awards, living allowances, and interest accrual payments), as well as grant or scholarship portions of fellowships and assistantships.	$
$ — Enter in question 42.		Enter in question 80. — $

Page 8

For Help —1-800-433-3243

Financial Aid 101

www.petersons.com

Using the CSS/Profile Pre-Application Worksheet is a useful tool for collecting the family's financial information. The CSS/Profile Application is usually available on the College Board Web site by the middle of September, and the Pre-Application Worksheet should also be available at that time.

Pre-Application Worksheet

You can use this worksheet to help you collect your family's financial information before you begin your online PROFILE Application. You can print instructions by returning to the previous screen and clicking on "application instructions/help". As you are completing your online application, you will find more detailed online help.

The worksheet contains questions found in Sections A through P of the PROFILE Application. In general, these are standard questions that all families must complete.

- When you complete your online application, you may find additional questions in Section Q that are not found on the pre-application worksheet. These are questions required by one or more of the colleges or scholarship programs to which you are applying. If your customized application does not contain a Section Q, it means that none of the colleges and programs to which you are applying require questions beyond those collected in Sections A through P.

- Based on your dependency status, you may not be required to complete all of the questions in Sections A through O. When you complete your online PROFILE Application, these questions will not be presented to you for completion. For example, if you are a dependent student, you will not be asked to complete Questions 1 and 2, or Questions 24 and 25.

Do not mail this form to the College Board. It is a Pre-Application Worksheet and cannot be processed. Any worksheets received for processing will be destroyed.

Pre-Application Worksheet

Section A - Student's Information
(If you are a dependent student, skip Questions 1 and 2.)

1. How many people are in the student's (and spouse's) household? <u>Always include the student (and spouse)</u>. List their names and give information about them in Section M. ☐

2. Of the number in 1, how many will be college students enrolled at least half-time between July 1, 2003 and June 30, 2004? Include yourself. ☐

3. What is the student's state of legal residence? ☐

4 a What is the student's citizenship status?
   - ○ U.S. citizen (Skip to question 5.)
   - ○ Eligible non-citizen (Skip to Question 5.)
   - ○ Neither of the above (Answer 'b' and 'c' below.)

   b Country of citizenship? ☐

   c Visa classification? ○ F1 ○ F2 ○ J ○ J2 ○ G ○ Other

Section B - Student's 2002 Income & Benefits
Questions 5-14 ask for information about the student's (and spouse's) income and benefits. If married, include spouse's information in Sections B, C, D, E and F.

5. The following 2002 U.S. Income Tax return figures are: (Fill in only one oval.)
   - ○ estimated. Will file IRS Form 1040EZ, 1040A, or Telefile. Go to 6.
   - ○ estimated. Will file IRS Form 1040. Go to 6.
   - ○ from a completed IRS Form 1040EZ, 1040A, or Telefile. Go to 6.
   - ○ from a completed IRS Form 1040. Go to 6.
   - ○ a tax return will not be filed. Skip to 10.

6. 2002 total number of exemptions (IRS Form 1040, line 6d or 1040A, line 6d or 1040EZ or Telefile) ☐

7. 2002 Adjusted Gross Income from IRS Form 1040, line 35 or 1040A, line 21 or 1040EZ, line 4 or Telefile, line I $ ____

8 a 2002 U.S. income tax paid (IRS Form 1040, line 55 or 1040A, line 33 or 1040EZ, line 10 or Telefile, line K) $ ____
   b 2002 Education Credits - Hope and Lifetime Learning (IRS Form 1040, line 48 or 1040a, line 31) $ ____

9. 2002 itemized deductions (IRS Form 1040, Schedule A, line 28. Fill in "0" if deductions were not itemized.) $ ____

10. 2002 income earned from work by student $ ____

11. 2002 income earned from work by student's spouse $ ____

12. 2002 dividend and interest income $ ____

13. 2002 untaxed income and benefits (Give total amount for year.)
    a Social security benefits (untaxed portion only) $ ____
    b Welfare benefits, including TANF $ ____
    c Child support received for all children $ ____
    d Earned Income Credit (IRS Form 1040, line 64 or 1040A, line 41 or 1040EZ, line 8 or Telefile, line L) $ ____
    e Other - write total from instruction worksheet at the end of this document. $ ____

14. 2002 earnings from Federal Work-Study or other need-based work programs plus any grant, fellowship, scholarship, and assistantship aid reported to the IRS in your adjusted gross income $ ____

Section C - Student's Assets
Questions 15-22 ask for information about the student's (and spouse's) assets. Include trust accounts in Section D.

15. Cash, savings, and checking accounts (as of today) $ ____

16. Total value of IRA, Keogh, 401k, 403b, etc. accounts as of December 31, 2002 $ ____

17. Investments (Including Uniform Gifts to Minors)
    What is it worth today? $ ____
    What is owed on it? $ ____

18. Home
What is it worth today? (Renters write in "0") $ ____
What is owed on it? $ ____

19. Other real estate
What is it worth today? $ ____
What is owed on it? $ ____

20. Business and farm
What is it worth today? $ ____
What is owed on it? $ ____

21. If a farm is included in 20, is the student living on the farm? ○ Yes ○ No

22. If student owns home, give
  a year purchased ____
  b purchase price $ ____

Section D - Student's Trust Information

23. a Total value of all trust(s) $ ____
  b Is any income or part of the principal currently available? ○ Yes ○ No
  c Who established the trust(s)? ○ Student's parents ○ Other

Section E - Student's 2002 Expenses
(If you are a dependent student, skip Questions 24 and 25.)

24. 2002 child support paid because of divorce or separation $ ____

25. 2002 medical and dental expenses not covered by insurance $ ____

Section F - Student's Expected Summer/School-Year Resources for 2003-2004

26. Student's veterans benefits (July 1, 2003 - June 30, 2004)
  Amount per month $ ____
  Number of months ____

27. Student's (and spouse's) resources (Don't enter monthly amounts.)
  a Student's wages, salaries, tips, etc.
    Summer 2003 (3 months) $ ____
    School year 2003-2004 (9 months) $ ____
  b Spouse's wages, salaries, tips, etc.
    Summer 2003 (3 months) $ ____
    School year 2003-2004 (9 months) $ ____
  c Other taxable income
    Summer 2003 (3 months) $ ____
    School year 2003-2004 (9 months) $ ____
  d Untaxed income and benefits
    Summer 2003 (3 months) $ ____
    School year 2003-2004 (9 months) $ ____
  e Grants, scholarships, fellowships, etc. from sources other than the colleges or universities
    to which the student is applying (List sources in Section P) $ ____
  f Tuition benefits from the parents' and/or the student's or spouse's employer $ ____
  g Amount the student's parent(s) think they will be able to pay for 2003-2004 college expenses $ ____
  h Amounts expected from prepaid tuition plan withdrawals, other relatives, spouse's parents, and all
    other sources (List sources and amounts in Section P.)

Section G - Parents' Household Information

28. How many people are in your parents' household? <u>Always include the student and parents</u>. List their names and give information about them in Section M. ____

Financial Aid 101   www.petersons.com

Appendix C

29. Of the number in 28, how many will be college students enrolled at least half-time between July 1, 2003 and June 30, 2004? Do not include parents. Include the student. ☐

30. How many parents will be in college at least half-time in 2003-2004?   ○ Neither Parent   ○ One Parent   ○ Both Parent

31. What is the current marital status of your parents?   ○ Single   ○ Separated   ○ Widowed
    (Fill in only one oval.)   ○ Married/Remarried   ○ Divorced

32. What is your parents' state of legal residence? ☐☐

Section H - Parents' Expenses

33. Child support paid because of divorce or separation
    2002 $ _____
    Expected 2003 $ _____

34. Repayment of parents' educational loans
    2002 $ _____
    Expected 2003 $ _____

35. Medical and dental expenses not covered by insurance
    2002 $ _____
    Expected 2003 $ _____

36. Total elementary, junior high school, and high school tuition paid for dependent children
    a Amount paid (Don't include tuition paid for the student)
    2002 $ _____
    Expected 2003 $ _____
    b For how many dependent children? (Don't include the student.)
    2002 _____
    Expected 2003 _____

Section I - Parents' Assets

If parents own all or part of a business or farm, enter its name and the percent of ownership in Section P.

37. Cash, savings, and checking accounts (as of today) _____

38. a Total value of assets held in the names of the student's brothers
       and sisters who are under age 19 and not college students $ _____
    b Total value of assets held in Section 529 prepaid tuition plans
       for the student's brothers and sisters $ _____
    c Total value of assets held in Section 529 prepaid tuition plans
       for the student $ _____

39. Investments
    What is it worth today? $ _____
    What is owed on it? $ _____

40. Home
    a What is it worth today? (Renters fill in "0" and skip to 40d.) $ _____
      What is owed on it? $ _____
    b Year purchased ☐☐☐☐
    c Purchase price $ _____
    d Monthly home mortgage or rental payment (If none, explain in Section P) $ _____

41. Business
    What is it worth today? $ _____
    What is owed on it? $ _____

42. Farm
    a What is it worth today? $ _____
      What is owed on it? $ _____
    b Does family live on the farm?   ○ Yes   ○ No

Forms Bank

43. Other real estate
   a What is it worth today? $
      What is owed on it? $
   b Year purchased
   c Purchase price $

Section J - Parents' 2001 Income & Benefits

44. 2001 Adjusted Gross Income (IRS Form 1040, line 33 or 1040A, line 19 or 1040EZ, line 4 or Telefile, line I) $

45. 2001 U.S. income tax paid (IRS Form 1040, line 52 or, 1040A, line 34 or 1040EZ, line 11 or Telefile, line K) $

46. 2001 itemized deductions (IRS Form 1040, Schedule A, line 28. Enter "0" if deductions were not itemized.) $

47. 2001 untaxed income and benefits (Include the same types of income that are listed in 55 a-k.) $

Section K - Parents' 2002 Income & Benefits

48. The following 2002 U.S. income tax return figures are (Fill in only one oval.)
    ○ estimated. Will file IRS Form 1040EZ, 1040A, or Telefile. Go to 49.
    ○ estimated. Will file IRS Form 1040. Go to 49.
    ○ from a completed IRS Form 1040EZ, 1040A, or Telefile. Go to 49.
    ○ from a completed IRS Form 1040. Go to 49.
    ○ a tax return will not be filed. Skip to 53.

49. 2002 total number of exemptions (IRS Form 1040, line 6d or 1040A, line 6d or 1040EZ or Telefile.)

50. a Wages, salaries, tips (IRS Form 1040, line 7 or 1040A, line 7 or 1040EZ, line 1) $
   b Interest income (IRS Form 1040, line 8a or 1040A, line 8a or 1040EZ, line 2 or Telefile, line C) $
   c Dividend income (IRS Form 1040, line 9 or 1040A, line 9) $
   d Net income (or loss) from business, farm, rents, royalties, partnerships, estates,
      trusts, etc. (IRS Form 1040, lines 12, 17, and 18) (If a loss, enter the amount in (parentheses). $
   e Other taxable income such as alimony received, capital gains (or losses), pensions,
      annuities, etc. (IRS Form 1040, lines 10, 11, 13, 14, 15b, 16b, 19, 20b and 21 or 1040A,
      lines 10, 11b, 12b, 13, and 14b or 1040EZ, line 3 or Telefile, line D) $
   f Adjustments to income (IRS Form 1040, line 34 or 1040A, line 20) $
   g 2002 Adjusted Gross Income (IRS Form 1040, line 35 or 1040A, line 21 or 1040EZ, line 4 or
      Telefile line I). This entry is the sum of 50a to 50e, minus 50f. $

51. a 2002 U.S. income tax paid (IRS Form 1040, line 55, 1040A, line 36 or 1040EZ, line 10 or Telefile, line K) $
   b 2002 Education Credits - Hope and Lifetime Learning (IRS Form 1040, line 48 or 1040A, line 31) $

52. 2002 itemized deductions (IRS Form 1040, Schedule A, line 28. Fill in "0" if deductions were not itemized.) $

53. 2002 income earned from work by father/stepfather $

54. 2002 income earned from work by mother/stepmother $

55. 2002 untaxed income and benefits (Give total amount for the year. Do not give monthly amounts.)
   a Social security benefits received (untaxed portion only) $
   b Welfare benefits, including TANF $
   c Child support received for all children $
   d Deductible IRA and/or SEP, SIMPLE, or Keogh payments $
   e Payments to tax-deferred pension and savings plans $
   f Amounts withheld from wages for dependent care and medical spending accounts $
   g Earned Income Credit (IRS Form 1040, line 64 or 1040A, line 41 or 1040EZ, line 8 or Telefile, line L) $
   h Housing, food, and other living allowances received by military, clergy, and others $
   i Tax-exempt interest income (IRS Form 1040, line 8b or 1040A, line 8b) $
   j Foreign income exclusion (IRS Form 2555, line 43 or Form 2555EZ, line 18) $
   k Other - write in the total from the worksheet in the instructions at the end of this document. $

Financial Aid 101   www.petersons.com

Appendix C

Section L - Parents' 2003 Expected Income & Benefits
If the expected total income and benefits will differ from the 2002 total income by $3,000 or more, explain in Section P.

56. 2003 income earned from work by father $ _____

57. 2003 income earned from work by mother $ _____

58. 2003 other taxable income $ _____

59. 2003 untaxed income and benefits (See 55a-k.) $ _____

Section M - Family Member Listing
Give information for all family members entered in question 1 or 28. Only six family members are shown here but you will be able to enter up to seven family members in addition to the student on our website. **Failure to complete all information could reduce your aid eligibility.** *If there are more than seven, list first those who will be in school or college at least half-time. List the others in Section P.*

Question 60.

Student - Family Member 1
Full name of family member _____   Claimed by parents as tax exemption in 2002? ○ Yes ○ No

2002-2003 school year
Name of school or college _____   Year in school _____
Scholarships and grants $ _____   Parents' contribution $ _____

Family Member 2
Full name of family member _____   Claimed by parents as tax exemption in 2002? ○ Yes ○ No

Relationship to student: ○ Student's parent   ○ Student's stepparent   ○ Student's brother or sister
Age: ____   ○ Student's husband or wife   ○ Student's son or daughter   ○ Student's grandparent
           ○ Student's stepbrother/stepsister   ○ Other (explain in Section P)

2002-2003 school year
Name of school or college _____   Year in school _____
Scholarships and grants _____   Parents' contribution $ _____

2003-2004 school year
Attend college at least one term   ○ Full-time   ○ Half-time   ○ Does not apply
College or university name _____
Type: ○ 2-year public college   ○ 2-year private college   ○ 4-year public college/university
       ○ 4-year private college/university   ○ graduate/professional school   ○ proprietary school

Family Member 3
Full name of family member _____   Claimed by parents as tax exemption in 2002? ○ Yes ○ No

Relationship to student: ○ Student's parent   ○ Student's stepparent   ○ Student's brother or sister
Age: ____   ○ Student's husband or wife   ○ Student's son or daughter   ○ Student's grandparent
           ○ Student's stepbrother/stepsister   ○ Other (explain in Section P)

2002-2003 school year
Name of school or college _____   Year in school _____
Scholarships and grants $ _____   Parents' contribution $ _____

2003-2004 school year
Attend college at least one term   ○ Full-time   ○ Half-time   ○ Does not apply
College or university name _____
Type: ○ 2-year public college   ○ 2-year private college   ○ 4-year public college/university
       ○ 4-year private college/university   ○ graduate/professional school   ○ proprietary school

www.petersons.com   Financial Aid 101

Forms Bank

Family Member 4

Full name of family member [_____] Claimed by parents as tax exemption in 2002? ○ Yes ○ No

Relationship to student: ○ Student's parent ○ Student's stepparent ○ Student's brother or sister
Age: [__] ○ Student's husband or wife ○ Student's son or daughter ○ Student's grandparent
○ Student's stepbrother/stepsister ○ Other (explain in Section P)

<u>2002-2003 school year</u>
Name of school or college [_____] Year in school [_____]
Scholarships and grants $[_____] Parents' contribution $[_____]

<u>2003-2004 school year</u>
Attend college at least one term ○ Full-time ○ Half-time ○ Does not apply
College or university name [_____]
Type: ○ 2-year public college ○ 2-year private college ○ 4-year public college/university
○ 4-year private college/university ○ graduate/professional school ○ proprietary school

Family Member 5

Full name of family member [_____] Claimed by parents as tax exemption in 2002? ○ Yes ○ No

Relationship to student: ○ Student's parent ○ Student's stepparent ○ Student's brother or sister
Age: [__] ○ Student's husband or wife ○ Student's son or daughter ○ Student's grandparent
○ Student's stepbrother/stepsister ○ Other (explain in Section P)

<u>2002-2003 school year</u>
Name of school or college [_____] Year in school [_____]
Scholarships and grants $[_____] Parents' contribution $[_____]

<u>2003-2004 school year</u>
Attend college at least one term ○ Full-time ○ Half-time ○ Does not apply
College or university name [_____]
Type: ○ 2-year public college ○ 2-year private college ○ 4-year public college/university
○ 4-year private college/university ○ graduate/professional school ○ proprietary school

Family Member 6

Full name of family member [_____] Claimed by parents as tax exemption in 2002? ○ Yes ○ No

Relationship to student: ○ Student's parent ○ Student's stepparent ○ Student's brother or sister
Age: [__] ○ Student's husband or wife ○ Student's son or daughter ○ Student's grandparent
○ Student's stepbrother/stepsister ○ Other (explain in Section P)

<u>2002-2003 school year</u>
Name of school or college [_____] Year in school [_____]
Scholarships and grants $[_____] Parents' contribution $[_____]

<u>2003-2004 school year</u>
Attend college at least one term ○ Full-time ○ Half-time ○ Does not apply
College or university name [_____]
Type: ○ 2-year public college ○ 2-year private college ○ 4-year public college/university
○ 4-year private college/university ○ graduate/professional school ○ proprietary school

Financial Aid 101 www.petersons.com

Appendix C

Section N - Parents' Information
(to be answered by the parent(s) completing this form)

61. a Select one: ○ Father   ○ Stepfather   ○ Legal guardian   ○ Other (Explain in Section P)
    b Name
    c Age
    d Select if: ○ Self-employed   ○ Unemployed
    e If unemployed enter date unemployment began:
    f Occupation
    g Employer
    h Number of years employed by employer listed above
    i Work telephone
    j Retirement plans available (Check all that apply.)
       ○ Social security   ○ Civil service/state   ○ Military
       ○ Union/employer   ○ IRA/Keogh/tax-deferred   ○ Other

62. a Select one: ○ Mother   ○ Stepmother   ○ Legal guardian   ○ Other (Explain in Section P)
    b Name
    c Age
    d Select if: ○ Self-employed   ○ Unemployed
    e If unemployed enter date unemployment began:
    f Occupation
    g Employer
    h Number of years employed by employer listed above
    i Work telephone
    j Retirement plans available (Check all that apply.)
       ○ Social security   ○ Civil service/state   ○ Military
       ○ Union/employer   ○ IRA/Keogh/tax-deferred   ○ Other

Parent Loan Information

The questions that follow are intended to provide the student's family with options for financing the parents' share of the student's college costs. Many families choose to borrow through the Federal Parent Loan for Undergraduate Students (PLUS) Program to supplement the financial aid offer. This program, as well as most private loan programs, requires a check of parent credit worthiness to qualify.

Families that answer the questions on this page will:

- get information about their eligibility to borrow through the PLUS program.
- learn what their monthly payment responsibilities would be, should they decide to borrow (a valid email address is required to receive financing guidance).
- learn about loan programs sponsored by the College Board.

By answering Questions B-G below, you are authorizing the College Board (or its agent), to use the information you provide below and the student's name to evaluate the parents' credit record and report the results of the credit evaluation to the parent whose information is provided below. A positive credit rating will mean that the parent is pre-approved to borrow a PLUS Loan from most lenders, including the College Board's CollegeCredit PLUS Loan program, should additional financial assistance be necessary. (Most other lenders use the same criteria in approving families' applications for PLUS Loans.) The College Board will not share this information with the student, the student's colleges, or anyone else. Reporting of credit worthiness results will begin in February 2003 to ensure that your credit results remain valid when you are ready to apply for a PLUS loan. (The results are valid for only 180 days.)

You may skip the questions below if you are not interested in learning about your eligibility for the Federal PLUS program.

A. Does the parent want to be considered for an educational loan to cover college costs?   ○ Yes   ○ No

If you answered "Yes", complete Questions B-G.

Forms Bank 197

B. Parent's name: _____ _____ ___
   Last name   First name   M.I.

C. Parent's home address: _____
   Number, street, and apartment number
   _____ _____ _____
   City   State   Zip code

D. Telephone number: ___ ___ ___
   Area code

E. Parent's social security number: ___ ___ ___

F. Parent's date of birth: ___ ___ ___
   Month   Day   Year

G. Parent's e-mail address: _____

Section O - Information About Noncustodial Parent
(to be answered by the parent who completes this form if the student's biological or adoptive parents are divorced, separated, or were never married to each other)

63 a Noncustodial parent's name: _____
   b Home address- street _____
   c Home address- city, state, zip _____
   d Occupation/Employer _____
   e Year of separation ____
   f Year of divorce ____
   g According to court order, when will support for the student end? (MM/YYYY) _____
   h Who last claimed the student as a tax exemption? _____
   i Year last claimed? ____
   j How much does the noncustodial parent plan to contribute to the student's education for the 2003-2004 school year? (Do not include this amount in 27g.) _____
   k Is there an agreement specifying this contribution for the student's education?   ○ Yes   ○ No

Section P - Explanations/Special Circumstances
Use this space to explain any unusual expenses such as high medical or dental expenses, educational and other debts, child care, elder care, or special circumstances. Also give information for any outside scholarships you have been awarded. If more space is needed, use sheets of paper and send them directly to your schools and programs. When online, please limit your responses to no more than 27 lines of information.

Financial Aid 101   www.petersons.com

Appendix C

PROFILE Online 2003-2004 Worksheet

Question 13e

Complete the worksheet below and calculate the total at the end of the questions. Enter the total in question 13e. **Don't include:** any income reported elsewhere on the PROFILE Application, money from student financial aid, food stamps, "rollover" pensions, Workforce Investments Act educational benefits, or gifts and support, other than money, received from friends or relatives.

Deductible IRA and/or SEP, SIMPLE, or Keogh payments from IRS Form 1040, total of lines 24 and 31 or 1040A, line 17	$
Tax exempt interest income from IRS Form 1040, line 8b or 1040A, line 8b	+
Payments to tax-deferred pension and savings plans (paid directly or withheld from earnings), including but not limited to, amounts reported on the W-2 Form in Boxes 12a-12d, codes D, E, F, G, H, and S on the W-2 Form. Include untaxed payments to 401(k) and 403(b) plans.	+
Additional child tax credit from IRS Form 1040, line 66 or 1040A, line 42	+
Workers' Compensation	+
Veterans non-educational benefits such as Death Pension, Disability, etc.	+
Housing, food, and other living allowances paid to members of the military, clergy, and others (including cash payments and cash value of benefits)	+
Cash received or any money paid on the student's behalf, not reported elsewhere on this form	+
VA educational work-study allowances	+
Any other untaxed income and benefits	+
TOTAL =	$

Question 55k

Complete the worksheet below and calculate the total at the end of the questions. Enter the total in question 55k. **Don't include:** any income reported elsewhere on the PROFILE Application, money from student financial aid, Workforce Investments Act educational benefits, or gifts and support, other than money, received from friends or relatives.

Untaxed portions of IRA distributions from IRS forms (excluding "rollovers")	$
Untaxed portions of pensions from IRS forms (excluding "rollovers")	+
Additional child tax credit from IRS Form 1040, line 66 or 1040A, line 42	+
Veterans non-educational benefits such as Disability, Death Pension, Dependency & Indemnity Compensation	+
Workers' Compensation	+
Cash received or any money paid on your behalf (Don't include child support.)	+
Black Lung Benefits, Refugee Assistance	+
Credit for federal tax on special fuels	+
Untaxed portions of Railroad Retirement benefits	+
Any other untaxed income and benefits	+
TOTAL =	$

www.petersons.com

Financial Aid 101

APPENDIX D

Additional State Aid Programs

Each state government has established one or more state-administered financial aid programs for qualified students. In many instances, these state programs are restricted to legal residents of the state. However, they often are available to out-of-state students who will be or are attending colleges or universities within the state. In addition to residential status, other qualifications frequently exist.

Gift aid and forgivable loan programs open to undergraduate students for all states and the District of Columbia are described on the following pages. They are arranged in alphabetical order, first by state name, then by program name. The annotation for each program provides information about the program, eligibility, and the contact addresses for applications or further information. Unless otherwise stated, this information refers to awards for 2003–2004. Information is provided by the state-sponsoring agency in response to Peterson's ***Annual Survey of Non-institutional Aid***, which was conducted between November 2002 and March 2003. Information is accurate when Peterson's receives it. However, it is always advisable to check with the sponsor to ascertain that the information remains correct.

You should write to the address given for each program to request that award details for 2004–2005 be sent to them as soon as they are available. Descriptive information brochures and application forms for state scholarship programs are usually available from the financial aid offices of public colleges or universities within the specific state. High school guidance offices often have information and relevant forms for awards for which high school seniors may be eligible. Increasingly, state government agencies are putting state scholarship information on state government agency Web sites. In searching state government Web sites, however, you should be aware that the higher education agency in many states is separate from the state's general education office, which is often responsible only for elementary and secondary education. Also, the page at public university Web sites that provides information about student financial aid frequently has a list of

Additional State Aid Programs

state-sponsored scholarships and financial aid programs. College and university Web sites can be easily accessed through Peterson's (www.petersons.com/ugchannel).

Names of scholarship programs are frequently used inconsistently or become abbreviated in popular usage. Many programs have variant names by which they are known. The program's sponsor has approved the title of the program that Peterson's uses in this guide, yet this name may differ from the program's official name or from its most commonly used name.

In addition to the grant aid and forgivable loan programs listed on the following pages, states may also offer internship or work-study programs, graduate fellowships and grants, or low-interest loans. If you are interested in learning more about these other kinds of programs, the state education office that supplies information or applications for the undergraduate scholarship programs listed here should be able to provide information about other kinds of higher education financial aid programs that are sponsored by the state.

Appendix D

Alabama

Alabama G.I. Dependents Scholarship Program. Full scholarship for dependents of Alabama disabled, prisoner of war, or missing-in-action veterans. Child or stepchild must initiate training before 26th birthday; age 30 deadline may apply in certain situations. No age deadline for spouses or widows. Contact for application procedures and deadline. *Award:* Scholarship for use in freshman, sophomore, junior, senior, or graduate year; renewable. *Award amount:* up to $7000. *Eligibility Requirements:* Applicant must be enrolled or expecting to enroll full or part-time at a two-year, four-year, or technical institution or university; resident of Alabama and studying in Alabama. Available to U.S. and non-U.S. citizens. Applicant or parent must meet one or more of the following requirements: general military experience; retired from active duty; disabled or killed as a result of military service; prisoner of war; or missing in action. *Application Requirements:* Application.

Contact Willie E. Moore, Scholarship Administrator, Alabama Department of Veterans Affairs, PO Box 1509, Montgomery, AL 36102-1509. *E-mail:* wmoore@va.state.al.us. *Phone:* 334-242-5077. *Fax:* 334-242-5102. *Web site:* www.va.state.al.us/scholarship.htm.

Alabama National Guard Educational Assistance Program. Renewable award aids Alabama residents who are members of the Alabama National Guard and are enrolled in an accredited college in Alabama. Forms must be signed by a representative of the Alabama Military Department and financial aid officer. Recipient must be in a degree-seeking program. *Award:* Grant for use in freshman, sophomore, junior, senior, or graduate year; renewable. *Award amount:* up to $1000. *Eligibility Requirements:* Applicant must be enrolled or expecting to enroll full or part-time at a two-year, four-year, or technical institution or university; resident of Alabama and studying in Alabama. Available to U.S. citizens. Applicant must have served in the Air Force National Guard or Army National Guard. *Application Requirements:* Application. **Deadline:** continuous.

Contact Dr. William Wall, Associate Executive Director for Student Assistance, Alabama Commission on Higher Education, PO Box 302000, Montgomery, AL 36130-2000. *Web site:* www.ache.state.al.us.

Alabama Scholarship for Dependents of Blind Parents. Scholarship given to defray the cost of books and fees for children of blind parents. Must be accepted or enrolled in a Alabama state supported school. Must be Alabama resident. Financial need is considered. Family income must be less than 1.5 times the federal poverty guideline for size of family unit. *Award:* Scholarship for use in freshman, sophomore, junior, or senior year; renewable. *Number of awards:* 10–15. *Eligibility Requirements:* Applicant must be age 28 or under; enrolled or expecting to enroll full-time at a two-year, four-year, or technical institution or university; resident of Alabama and studying in Alabama. Available to U.S. citizens. *Application Requirements:* Application, financial need analysis. **Deadline:** continuous.

Contact Don Sims, Rehabilitation Specialist for the Blind, Alabama Department of Rehabilitation Services, Alabama Scholarship for Dependents of Blind Parents, 2129 East South Boulevard, Montgomery, AL 36111. *Phone:* 800-441-7607.

Alabama Student Grant Program. Renewable awards available to Alabama residents for undergraduate study at certain independent colleges within the state. Both full-time and half-time students are eligible. Deadlines: September 15, January 15, and February 15. *Award:* Grant for use in freshman, sophomore, junior, or senior year; renewable. *Award amount:* up to $1200. *Eligibility Requirements:* Applicant must be enrolled or expecting to enroll full or part-time at a four-year institution; resident of Alabama and studying in Alabama. Available to U.S. citizens. *Application Requirements:* Application.

Contact Dr. William Wall, Associate Executive Director for Student Assistance, ACHE, Alabama Commission on Higher Education, PO Box 302000, Montgomery, AL 36130-2000. *Web site:* www.ache.state.al.us.

American Legion Department of Alabama Scholarship Program. Renewable award for Alabama residents directly related to any war veteran. Parents must be legal residents of Alabama. Send self-addressed stamped envelope to receive scholarship application, list of available schools, and instructions. *Award:* Scholarship for use in freshman, sophomore, junior, or senior year; renewable. *Award amount:* $850. *Number of awards:* 150. *Eligibility Requirements:* Applicant must be enrolled or expecting to enroll full or part-time at a four-year institution or university; resident of Alabama and studying in Alabama. Available to U.S. citizens. Applicant or parent must meet one or more of the following requirements: general military experience; retired from active duty; disabled or killed as a result of military service; prisoner of war; or missing in action. *Application Requirements:* Application, photo, references, self-addressed stamped envelope, test scores, transcript. **Deadline:** May 1.

Contact Braxton Bridgers, Department Adjutant, American Legion, Department of Alabama, PO Box 1069, Montgomery, AL 36101-1069. *E-mail:* allegion@bellsouth.net. *Phone:* 334-285-2225. *Web site:* www.alabamalegion.org.

Math and Science Scholarship Program for Alabama Teachers. For full-time students pursuing teaching certificates in mathematics, general science, biology, or physics. Applicants must agree to teach for five years (if a position is offered) in a targeted system with critical needs. Renewable if recipient continues to

Additional State Aid Programs

meet the requirements. Minimum 3.0 GPA required. Must be resident of Alabama and attend school in Alabama. *Academic/Career Areas:* Biology; Earth Science; Meteorology/Atmospheric Science; Natural Sciences; Physical Sciences and Math. *Award:* Forgivable loan for use in junior or senior year; renewable. *Award amount:* $2000–$12,000. *Eligibility Requirements:* Applicant must be enrolled or expecting to enroll full-time at an institution or university; resident of Alabama and studying in Alabama. Applicant must have 3.0 GPA or higher. Available to U.S. citizens. *Application Requirements:* Application.

Contact Dr. Jayne Meyer, Assistant Superintendent, Alabama State Department of Education, Special Education Services, PO Box 302101, Montgomery, AL 36130-2101. *Phone:* 334-242-9560.

Police Officers and Firefighters Survivors Education Assistance Program—Alabama. Provides tuition, fees, books, and supplies to dependents of full-time police officers and firefighters killed in the line of duty. Must attend any Alabama public college as an undergraduate. Must be Alabama resident. Renewable. *Award:* Grant for use in freshman, sophomore, junior, or senior year; renewable. *Award amount:* $2000–$5000. *Number of awards:* 15–30. *Eligibility Requirements:* Applicant must be enrolled or expecting to enroll full or part-time at a two-year, four-year, or technical institution or university; single; resident of Alabama and studying in Alabama. Applicant or parent of applicant must have employment or volunteer experience in police/firefighting. Available to U.S. citizens. *Application Requirements:* Application, transcript. **Deadline:** continuous.

Contact Dr. William Wall, Associate Executive Director for Student Assistance, ACHE, Alabama Commission on Higher Education, PO Box 302000, Montgomery, AL 36130-2000. *Web site:* www.ache.state.al.us.

Alaska

A.W. "Winn" Brindle Memorial Scholarship Loans. Renewable loan for study of approved curriculum in fisheries, seafood processing, food technology or related fields for Alaska residents. Must maintain good standing at institution. Eligible for up to 50% forgiveness if recipient returns to Alaska for employment in fisheries-related field. *Academic/Career Areas:* Agribusiness; Animal/Veterinary Sciences; Biology; Food Science/Nutrition; Natural Resources. *Award:* Forgivable loan for use in freshman, sophomore, junior, senior, or graduate year; renewable. *Eligibility Requirements:* Applicant must be enrolled or expecting to enroll full-time at a two-year, four-year, or technical institution or university and resident of Alaska. Available to U.S. citizens. *Application Requirements:* Application, essay. **Deadline:** May 15.

Contact Lori Stedman, Administrative Assistant, Special Programs, Alaska Commission on Postsecondary Education, 3030 Vintage Boulevard, Juneau, AK 99801-7100. *Phone:* 907-465-6741. *Fax:* 907-465-5316. *Web site:* www.state.ak.us/acpe/.

Alaska Commission on Postsecondary Education Teacher Education Loan. Renewable loans for graduates of an Alaskan high school pursuing teaching careers in rural elementary and secondary schools in Alaska. Must be nominated by rural school district. Eligible for 100% forgiveness if loan recipient teaches in rural Alaska upon graduation. Several awards of up to $7500 each. Must maintain good standing at institution. *Academic/Career Areas:* Education. *Award:* Forgivable loan for use in freshman, sophomore, junior, or senior year; renewable. *Award amount:* up to $7500. *Number of awards:* 100. *Eligibility Requirements:* Applicant must be enrolled or expecting to enroll full-time at a four-year institution or university. Available to U.S. citizens. *Application Requirements:* Application, transcript. **Deadline:** July 1.

Contact Lori Stedman, Administrative Assistant, Special Programs, Alaska Commission on Postsecondary Education, 3030 Vintage Boulevard, Juneau, AK 99801-7100. *Phone:* 907-465-6741. *Fax:* 907-465-5316. *Web site:* www.state.ak.us/acpe/.

Western Undergraduate Exchange (WUE) Program. Program allowing Alaska residents to enroll at two-or four-year institutions in participating states at a reduced tuition level, which is the in-state tuition plus a percentage of that amount. To be used for full-time undergraduate studies. See Web site at www.state.ak.us/acpe for further information, a list of eligible institutions, and deadlines. *Award:* Grant for use in freshman, sophomore, junior, or senior year; renewable. *Eligibility Requirements:* Applicant must be enrolled or expecting to enroll full-time at a two-year or four-year institution or university; resident of Alaska and studying in Arizona, Colorado, Hawaii, Idaho, Montana, Nevada, New Mexico, North Dakota, Oregon, South Dakota, Utah, or Washington. Available to U.S. citizens.

Contact college admissions office, for further information, Alaska Commission on Postsecondary Education. *Web site:* www.state.ak.us/acpe/.

Arizona

Arizona Private Postsecondary Education Student Financial Assistance Program. Provides grants to financially needy Arizona Community College graduates to attend a private postsecondary baccalaureate degree-granting institution. *Award:* Forgivable loan for use in junior or senior year; renewable. *Award amount:* $750–$1500. *Eligibility Requirements:* Applicant must be enrolled or expecting to enroll full-time at a four-year institution or university; resident of Arizona and studying in Arizona. Available to U.S. and non-Canadian citizens. *Application Requirements:* Application, promissory note. **Deadline:** continuous.

Contact Danny Lee, PFAP Program Manager, Arizona Commission for Postsecondary Education, 2020 North Central Avenue, Suite 550, Phoenix, AZ 85004-4503. *E-mail:* danny_lee@azhighered.org. *Phone:* 602-258-2435 Ext. 103. *Fax:* 602-258-2483. *Web site:* www.acpe.asu.edu.

Leveraging Educational Assistance Partnership. LEAP provides grants to financially needy students who enroll in and attend postsecondary education or training in Arizona schools. LEAP Program was formerly known as the State Student Incentive Grant or SSIG Program. *Award:* Grant for use in freshman, sophomore, junior, senior, or graduate year; not renewable. *Award amount:* $100–$2500. *Eligibility Requirements:* Applicant must be enrolled or expecting to enroll full or part-time at a two-year, four-year, or technical institution or university; resident of Arizona and studying in Arizona. Available to U.S. and non-Canadian citizens. *Application Requirements:* Application. **Deadline:** continuous.

Contact Mila A. Zaporteza, Business Manager/LEAP Financial Aid Management, Arizona Commission for Postsecondary Education, 2020 North Central Avenue, Suite 550, Phoenix, AZ 85004-4503. *E-mail:* mila@azhighered.org. *Phone:* 602-258-2435 Ext. 102. *Fax:* 602-258-2483. *Web site:* www.acpe.asu.edu.

Arkansas

Arkansas Academic Challenge Scholarship Program. Awards for Arkansas residents who are graduating high school seniors to study at an Arkansas institution. Must have at least a 2.75 GPA, meet minimum ACT composite score standards, and have financial need. Renewable up to three additional years. *Award:* Scholarship for use in freshman, sophomore, junior, or senior year; renewable. *Award amount:* up to $2500. *Eligibility Requirements:* Applicant must be high school student; planning to enroll or expecting to enroll full-time at a two-year or four-year institution or university; resident of Arkansas and studying in Arkansas. Available to U.S. citizens. *Application Requirements:* Application, financial need analysis, test scores, transcript. **Deadline:** June 1.

Contact Assistant Coordinator, Arkansas Department of Higher Education, 114 East Capitol, Little Rock, AR 72201. *Phone:* 501-371-2050. *Fax:* 501-371-2001. *Web site:* www.arscholarships.com.

Arkansas Health Education Grant Program (ARHEG). Award provides assistance to Arkansas residents pursuing professional degrees in dentistry, optometry, veterinary medicine, podiatry, chiropractic medicine, or osteopathic medicine at out-of-state, accredited institutions (programs that are unavailable in Arkansas). *Academic/Career Areas:* Animal/Veterinary Sciences; Dental Health/Services; Health and Medical Sciences. *Award:* Grant for use in sophomore, junior, senior, or graduate year; renewable. *Award amount:* $5000–$14,600. *Number of awards:* 258–288. *Eligibility Requirements:* Applicant must be enrolled or expecting to enroll full-time at a four-year institution or university and resident of Arkansas. Available to U.S. citizens. *Application Requirements:* Application, affidavit of Arkansas residency. **Deadline:** continuous.

Contact Ms. Judy McAinsh, Coordinator, Arkansas Health Education Grant Program, Arkansas Department of Higher Education, 114 East Capitol, Little Rock, AR 72201-3818. *E-mail:* judym@adhe.arknet.edu. *Phone:* 501-371-2013. *Fax:* 501-371-2002. *Web site:* www.arscholarships.com.

Arkansas Minority Teacher Scholars Program. Renewable award for Native-Americans, African-American, Hispanic and Asian-American students who have completed at least 60 semester hours and are enrolled full-time in a teacher education program in Arkansas. Award may be renewed for one year. Must be Arkansas resident with minimum 2.5 GPA. Must teach for three to five years in Arkansas to repay scholarship funds received. Must pass PPST exam. *Academic/Career Areas:* Education. *Award:* Forgivable loan for use in junior or senior year; renewable. *Award amount:* up to $5000. *Number of awards:* up to 100. *Eligibility Requirements:* Applicant must be American Indian/Alaska Native, Asian/Pacific Islander, Black (non-Hispanic), or Hispanic; enrolled or expecting to enroll full-time at a four-year institution or university; resident of Arkansas and studying in Arkansas. Applicant must have 2.5 GPA or higher. Available to U.S. citizens. *Application Requirements:* Application, transcript. **Deadline:** June 1.

Contact Lillian Williams, Assistant Coordinator, Arkansas Department of Higher Education, 114 East Capitol, Little Rock, AR 72201. *Phone:* 501-371-2050. *Fax:* 501-371-2001. *Web site:* www.arscholarships.com.

Arkansas Student Assistance Grant Program. Award for Arkansas residents attending a college within the state. Must be enrolled full-time, have financial need, and maintain satisfactory progress. One-time award for undergraduate use only. Application is the FAFSA. *Award:* Grant for use in freshman, sophomore, junior, or senior year; not renewable. *Award amount:* $600. *Number of awards:* 600–5500. *Eligibility Requirements:* Applicant must be enrolled or expecting to enroll full-time at a two-year, four-year, or technical institution or university; resident of Arkansas and studying in Arkansas. Available to U.S. citizens. *Application Requirements:* Application, financial need analysis, FAFSA. **Deadline:** April 1.

Additional State Aid Programs

Contact Assistant Coordinator, Arkansas Department of Higher Education, 114 East Capitol, Little Rock, AR 72201. *Phone:* 501-371-2050. *Fax:* 501-371-2001. *Web site:* www.arscholarships.com.

Emergency Secondary Education Loan Program. Must be Arkansas resident enrolled full-time in approved Arkansas institution. Renewable award for students majoring in secondary math, chemistry, physics, biology, physical science, general science, special education, or foreign language. Must teach in Arkansas at least five years. Must rank in upper half of class or have a minimum 2.5 GPA. *Academic/Career Areas:* Biology; Education; Foreign Language; Physical Sciences and Math; Special Education. *Award:* Forgivable loan for use in sophomore, junior, senior, or graduate year; renewable. *Award amount:* up to $2500. *Number of awards:* up to 50. *Eligibility Requirements:* Applicant must be enrolled or expecting to enroll full-time at a two-year or four-year institution or university; resident of Arkansas and studying in Arkansas. Applicant must have 2.5 GPA or higher. Available to U.S. citizens. *Application Requirements:* Application, transcript. **Deadline:** April 1.

Contact Lillian K. Williams, Assistant Coordinator, Arkansas Department of Higher Education, 114 East Capitol, Little Rock, AR 72201. *Phone:* 501-371-2050. *Fax:* 501-371-2001. *Web site:* www.arscholarships.com.

Governor's Scholars—Arkansas. Awards for outstanding Arkansas high school seniors. Must be an Arkansas resident and have a high school GPA of at least 3.5 or have scored at least 27 on the ACT. Award is $4000 per year for four years of full-time undergraduate study. Applicants who attain 32 or above on ACT, 1410 or above on SAT and have an academic 3.50 GPA, or are selected as National Merit or National Achievement finalists may receive an award equal to tuition, mandatory fees, room, and board up to $10,000 per year at any Arkansas institution. *Award:* Scholarship for use in freshman, sophomore, junior, or senior year; renewable. *Award amount:* $4000–$10,000. *Number of awards:* 75–250. *Eligibility Requirements:* Applicant must be high school student; planning to enroll or expecting to enroll full-time at a two-year or four-year institution or university; resident of Arkansas and studying in Arkansas. Applicant must have 3.5 GPA or higher. Available to U.S. citizens. *Application Requirements:* Application, test scores, transcript. **Deadline:** February 1.

Contact Philip Axelroth, Assistant Coordinator of Financial Aid, Arkansas Department of Higher Education, 114 East Capitol, Little Rock, AR 72201. *E-mail:* phila@adhe.arknet.edu. *Phone:* 501-371-2050. *Fax:* 501-371-2001. *Web site:* www.arscholarships.com.

Law Enforcement Officers' Dependents Scholarship-Arkansas. For dependents, under 23 years old, of Arkansas law-enforcement officers killed or permanently disabled in the line of duty. Renewable award is a waiver of tuition, fees, and room at two- or four-year Arkansas institution. Submit birth certificate, death certificate, and claims commission report of findings of fact. Proof of disability from State Claims Commission may also be submitted. *Award:* Scholarship for use in freshman, sophomore, junior, or senior year; renewable. *Award amount:* $2000–$2500. *Number of awards:* 27–32. *Eligibility Requirements:* Applicant must be age 23 or under; enrolled or expecting to enroll full or part-time at a two-year or four-year institution or university; resident of Arkansas and studying in Arkansas. Applicant or parent of applicant must have employment or volunteer experience in police/firefighting. Available to U.S. citizens. *Application Requirements:* Application. **Deadline:** continuous.

Contact Lillian Williams, Assistant Coordinator, Arkansas Department of Higher Education, 114 East Capitol, Little Rock, AR 72201. *E-mail:* lillianw@adhe.arknet.edu. *Phone:* 501-371-2050. *Fax:* 501-371-2001. *Web site:* www.arscholarships.com.

Missing in Action/Killed in Action Dependent's Scholarship—Arkansas. Available to Arkansas residents whose parent or spouse was classified either as missing in action, killed in action or a prisoner-of-war. Must attend state-supported institution in Arkansas. Renewable waiver of tuition, fees, room and board. Submit proof of casualty. *Award:* Scholarship for use in freshman, sophomore, junior, or senior year; renewable. *Award amount:* up to $2500. *Eligibility Requirements:* Applicant must be enrolled or expecting to enroll full-time at a two-year, four-year, or technical institution or university; resident of Arkansas and studying in Arkansas. Available to U.S. citizens. Applicant or parent must meet one or more of the following requirements: general military experience; retired from active duty; disabled or killed as a result of military service; prisoner of war; or missing in action. *Application Requirements:* Application, report of casualty. **Deadline:** continuous.

Contact Lillian K. Williams, Assistant Coordinator, Arkansas Department of Higher Education, 114 East Capitol, Little Rock, AR 72201. *Phone:* 501-371-2050. *Fax:* 501-371-2001. *Web site:* www.arscholarships.com.

Second Effort Scholarship. Awarded to those scholars who achieved one of the 10 highest scores on the Arkansas High School Diploma Test (GED). Must be at least age 18 and not have graduated from high school. Students do not apply for this award, they are contacted by the Arkansas Department of Higher Education. *Award:* Scholarship for use in freshman, sophomore, junior, or senior year; renewable. *Award amount:* up to $1000. *Number of awards:* 10. *Eligibility Requirements:* Applicant must be age 18; enrolled or expecting to enroll full or part-time at a two-year or

Financial Aid 101

Appendix D

four-year institution or university; resident of Arkansas and studying in Arkansas. Applicant must have 2.5 GPA or higher. *Application Requirements:* Application.

Contact Arkansas Department of Higher Education. *Phone:* 501-371-2050. *Fax:* 501-371-2001. *Web site:* www.arscholarships.com.

California

Assumption Programs of Loans for Education. The APLE is a competitive teacher loan assumption program designed to encourage outstanding students and out-of-state teachers to become California teachers with in subject areas where a teacher shortage has been identified or in schools meeting specific criteria identified annually. Participants may receive up to $19,000 towards outstanding student loans. *Award:* Forgivable loan for use in junior, senior, or graduate year; renewable. *Award amount:* up to $19,000. *Number of awards:* up to 6500. *Eligibility Requirements:* Applicant must be enrolled or expecting to enroll full or part-time at a four-year institution or university; resident of California and studying in California. Available to U.S. citizens. *Application Requirements:* Application, references. **Deadline:** June 30.

Contact California Student Aid Commission, P O Box 419027, Rancho Cordova, CA 95741-9027. *E-mail:* custsvcs@csac.ca.gov. *Phone:* 916-526-7590. *Fax:* 916-526-8002. *Web site:* www.csac.ca.gov.

Cal Grant C. Award for California residents who are enrolled in a short-term vocational training program. Program must lead to a recognized degree or certificate. Course length must be a minimum of 4 months and no longer than 24 months. Students must be attending an approved California institution and show financial need. *Award:* Grant for use in freshman, sophomore, junior, or senior year; renewable. *Award amount:* $576–$3168. *Number of awards:* up to 7761. *Eligibility Requirements:* Applicant must be enrolled or expecting to enroll full or part-time at a two-year or technical institution; resident of California and studying in California. Available to U.S. citizens. *Application Requirements:* Application, financial need analysis. **Deadline:** March 2.

Contact California Student Aid Commission, P O Box 419027, Rancho Cordova, CA 95741-9027. *E-mail:* custsvs@csac.ca.gov. *Phone:* 916-526-7590. *Fax:* 916-526-8002. *Web site:* www.csac.ca.gov.

Child Development Teacher and Supervisor Grant Program. Award is for those students pursuing an approved course of study leading to a Child Development Permit issued by the California Commission on Teacher Credentialing. In exchange for each year funding is received, recipients agree to provide one year of service in a licensed childcare center. *Award:* Grant for use in freshman, sophomore, junior, or senior year; renewable. *Award amount:* $1000–$2000. *Number of awards:* 100–200. *Eligibility Requirements:* Applicant must be enrolled or expecting to enroll full or part-time at a two-year, four-year, or technical institution or university; resident of California and studying in California. Available to U.S. citizens. *Application Requirements:* Application, financial need analysis, references, FAFSA. **Deadline:** June 1.

Contact California Student Aid Commission, PO Box 419027, Rancho Cordova, CA 95741-9027. *E-mail:* custsvcs@csac.ca.gov. *Phone:* 916-526-7590. *Fax:* 916-526-8002. *Web site:* www.csac.ca.gov.

Competitive Cal Grant A. Award for California residents who are not recent high school graduates attending an approved college or university within the state. Must show financial need and meet minimum 3.0 GPA requirements. *Award:* Grant for use in freshman, sophomore, junior, or senior year; renewable. *Award amount:* $1572–$9708. *Number of awards:* up to 22,500. *Eligibility Requirements:* Applicant must be enrolled or expecting to enroll full or part-time at a two-year, four-year, or technical institution or university; resident of California and studying in California. Applicant must have 3.0 GPA or higher. Available to U.S. citizens. *Application Requirements:* Application, financial need analysis. **Deadline:** March 2.

Contact California Student Aid Commission, P O Box 41907, Rancho Cordova, CA 95741-9027. *E-mail:* custsvcs@csac.ca.gov. *Phone:* 916-526-7590. *Fax:* 916-526-8002. *Web site:* www.csac.ca.gov.

Competitive Cal Grant B. Award is for California residents who are not recent high school graduates attending an approved college or university within the state. Must show financial need and meet the minimum 2.0 GPA requirements. *Award:* Grant for use in freshman, sophomore, or junior year; renewable. *Award amount:* $700–$11,259. *Number of awards:* up to 22,500. *Eligibility Requirements:* Applicant must be enrolled or expecting to enroll full or part-time at a two-year, four-year, or technical institution or university; resident of California and studying in California. Available to U.S. citizens. *Application Requirements:* Application, financial need analysis, GPA Verification. **Deadline:** March 2.

Contact California Student Aid Commission, PO Box 419027, Rancho Cordova, CA 95741-9027. *E-mail:* custsvcs@gsac.ca.gov. *Phone:* 916-526-7590. *Fax:* 916-526-8002. *Web site:* www.csac.ca.gov.

Cooperative Agencies Resources for Education Program. Renewable award available to California resident attending a two-year California community college. Must have no more than 70 degree-applicable units, currently receive CALWORKS/TANF, and have at least one child under 14 years of age. Must be in EOPS, single head of household, and 18 or older. Contact local college EOPS-CARE office. *Award:* Grant for use in freshman or sophomore year; renewable. *Number of awards:* 11,000. *Eligibility Requirements:* Applicant must be age 18; enrolled or expecting to enroll full-time at a two-year institution; single; resident of California and studying in California. Applicant or parent of applicant must be member of Extended Opportunity Program Service. Available to U.S. citizens. *Application Requirements:* Application, financial need analysis, test scores, transcript. **Deadline:** continuous.

Contact Local Community College EOPS/CARE Program, California Community Colleges, 1102 Q Street, Sacramento, CA 95814-6511. *Web site:* www.cccco.edu.

Entitlement Cal Grant A. Award is for California residents who are recent high school graduates attending an approved college or university within the state. Must show financial need and meet the minimum 3.0 GPA requirements. *Award:* Grant for use in freshman, sophomore, junior, or senior year; renewable. *Award amount:* $1572–$9708. *Eligibility Requirements:* Applicant must be enrolled or expecting to enroll full or part-time at a two-year, four-year, or technical institution or university; resident of California and studying in California. Applicant must have 3.0 GPA or higher. Available to U.S. citizens. *Application Requirements:* Application, financial need analysis, GPA Verification. **Deadline:** March 2.

Contact California Student Aid Commission, PO Box 419027, Rancho Cordova, CA 95741-9027. *E-mail:* custsvcs@csac.ca.gov. *Phone:* 916-526-7590. *Fax:* 916-526-8002. *Web site:* www.csac.ca.gov.

Entitlement Cal Grant B. Award for California residents who are high school graduates attending an approved college or university within the state. Must show financial need and meet the minimum 2.0 GPA requirements. *Award:* Grant for use in freshman, sophomore, junior, or senior year; renewable. *Award amount:* $700–$11,259. *Eligibility Requirements:* Applicant must be enrolled or expecting to enroll full or part-time at a two-year, four-year, or technical institution or university; resident of California and studying in California. Available to U.S. citizens. *Application Requirements:* Application, financial need analysis. **Deadline:** March 2.

Contact California Student Aid Commission, P O Box 419027, Rancho Cordova, CA 95741-9027. *E-mail:* custsvcs@csac.ca.gov. *Phone:* 916-526-7590. *Fax:* 916-526-8002. *Web site:* www.csac.ca.gov.

Governor's Distinguished Mathematics and Science Scholars Award. One-time scholarship for California public high school students who, in addition to receiving the Governor's Scholars Award, attain required scores on certain Advanced Placement exams, International Baccalaureate exams, or Golden State exams. See Web site at www.scholarshare.com for further details. *Award:* Scholarship for use in freshman, sophomore, junior, senior, or graduate year; not renewable. *Award amount:* $2500. *Eligibility Requirements:* Applicant must be high school student; planning to enroll or expecting to enroll at a two-year, four-year, or technical institution or university and resident of California. *Application Requirements:* Test scores.

Contact application available at Web site, ScholarShare Investment Board. *Web site:* www.scholarshare.com/gsp/index.html.

Governor's Scholars Award. Award to California students who demonstrate high academic achievement on certain exams in the Standardized Testing and Reporting program in the 9th, 10th, or 11th grades. For use at any postsecondary institution eligible to participate in federal Title IV financial aid programs, including schools outside the country. See Web site at www.scholarshare.com for further details. *Award:* Scholarship for use in freshman, sophomore, junior, senior, or graduate year; not renewable. *Award amount:* $1000. *Eligibility Requirements:* Applicant must be high school student; planning to enroll or expecting to enroll at a two-year, four-year, or technical institution or university and resident of California. *Application Requirements:* Test scores.

Contact application available at Web site, ScholarShare Investment Board. *Web site:* www.scholarshare.com/gsp/index.html.

Law Enforcement Personnel Development Scholarship. The Law Enforcement Personnel Dependents Scholarship Program provides college grants to needy dependents of California law enforcement officers, officers and employees of the Department of Corrections and Department of Youth Authority, and firefighters killed or disabled in the line of duty. *Award:* Grant for use in freshman, sophomore, junior, or senior year; renewable. *Award amount:* $100–$11,259. *Eligibility Requirements:* Applicant must be enrolled or expecting to enroll full or part-time at a two-year, four-year, or technical institution or university; resident of California and studying in California. Applicant or parent of applicant must have employment or volunteer experience in police/firefighting. Available to U.S. citizens. *Application Requirements:* Application, financial need analysis. **Deadline:** continuous.

Contact California Student Aid Commission, PO Box 419027, Rancho Cordova, CA 95741-9027. *E-mail:* custsvcs@csac.ca.gov. *Phone:* 916-526-7590. *Fax:* 916-526-8002. *Web site:* www.csac.ca.gov.

Appendix D

Colorado

Colorado Leveraging Educational Assistance Partnership (CLEAP) and SLEAP. Renewable awards for Colorado residents who are attending Colorado state-supported postsecondary institutions at the undergraduate level. Must document financial need. Contact colleges for complete information and deadlines. *Award:* Grant for use in freshman, sophomore, junior, or senior year; not renewable. *Award amount:* $50–$900. *Number of awards:* 5000. *Eligibility Requirements:* Applicant must be enrolled or expecting to enroll full or part-time at a two-year, four-year, or technical institution or university; resident of Colorado and studying in Colorado. Available to U.S. citizens. *Application Requirements:* Application, financial need analysis.

Contact Financial Aid Office at college/institution, Colorado Commission on Higher Education, 1380 Lawrence Street, Suite 1200, Denver, CO 80204-2059. *Web site:* www.state.co.us/cche.

Colorado Nursing Scholarships. Renewable awards for Colorado residents pursuing nursing education programs at Colorado state-supported institutions. Applicant must agree to practice nursing in Colorado upon graduation. Contact colleges for complete information and deadlines. *Academic/Career Areas:* Nursing. *Award:* Scholarship for use in freshman, sophomore, junior, or senior year; not renewable. *Number of awards:* 100. *Eligibility Requirements:* Applicant must be enrolled or expecting to enroll full or part-time at a two-year, four-year, or technical institution or university; resident of Colorado and studying in Colorado. *Application Requirements:* Application, financial need analysis. **Deadline:** April 1.

Contact Financial Aid Office at college/institution, Colorado Commission on Higher Education, 1380 Lawrence Street, Suite 1200, Denver, CO 80204-2059. *Web site:* www.state.co.us/cche.

Colorado Student Grant. Assists Colorado residents attending eligible public, private, or vocational institutions within the state. Application deadlines vary by institution. Renewable award for undergraduates. Contact the financial aid office at the college/institution for more information and an application. *Award:* Grant for use in freshman, sophomore, junior, or senior year; renewable. *Award amount:* $500–$5000. *Eligibility Requirements:* Applicant must be enrolled or expecting to enroll full or part-time at a two-year, four-year, or technical institution or university; resident of Colorado and studying in Colorado. *Application Requirements:* Application, financial need analysis.

Contact Financial Aid Office at college/institution, Colorado Commission on Higher Education, 1380 Lawrence Street, Suite 1200, Denver, CO 80204-2059. *Web site:* www.state.co.us/cche.

Colorado Undergraduate Merit Scholarships. Renewable awards for students attending Colorado state-supported institutions at the undergraduate level. Must demonstrate superior scholarship or talent. Contact college financial aid office for complete information and deadlines. *Award:* Scholarship for use in freshman, sophomore, junior, or senior year; renewable. *Award amount:* $1230. *Number of awards:* 10,823. *Eligibility Requirements:* Applicant must be enrolled or expecting to enroll full or part-time at a two-year, four-year, or technical institution or university; resident of Colorado and studying in Colorado. Applicant must have 3.0 GPA or higher. *Application Requirements:* Application, test scores, transcript.

Contact Financial Aid Office at college/institution, Colorado Commission on Higher Education, 1380 Lawrence Street, Suite 1200, Denver, CO 80204-2059. *Web site:* www.state.co.us/cche.

Governor's Opportunity Scholarship. Scholarship available for the most needy first-time freshmen whose parents' adjusted gross income is less than $26,000. Must be U.S. citizen for permanent legal resident. Work-study is part of the program. *Award:* Scholarship for use in freshman, sophomore, junior, or senior year; renewable. *Award amount:* $5665. *Number of awards:* up to 1052. *Eligibility Requirements:* Applicant must be high school student; planning to enroll or expecting to enroll full-time at a two-year, four-year, or technical institution or university; resident of Colorado and studying in Colorado. Available to U.S. citizens. *Application Requirements:* Application, financial need analysis, test scores, transcript. **Deadline:** continuous.

Contact Financial Aid Office at college/institution, Colorado Commission on Higher Education, 1380 Lawrence Street, Suite 1200, Denver, CO 80204-2059. *Web site:* www.state.co.us/cche.

Law Enforcement/POW/MIA Dependents Scholarship—Colorado. Aid available for dependents of Colorado law enforcement officers, fire or national guard personnel killed or disabled in the line of duty, and for dependents of prisoner-of-war or service personnel listed as missing in action. Award covers tuition and room and board. *Award:* Scholarship for use in freshman, sophomore, junior, or senior year; renewable. *Eligibility Requirements:* Applicant must be enrolled or expecting to enroll full or part-time at a two-year, four-year, or technical institution or university. Applicant must have 2.5 GPA or higher. *Application Requirements:* Application, financial need analysis, transcript. **Deadline:** continuous.

Contact Dianne Lindner, Financial Director, Colorado Commission on Higher Education, 1380 Lawrence Street, Suite 1200, Denver, CO 80204. *Phone:* 303-866-2723. *Fax:* 303-866-4266. *Web site:* www.state.co.us/cche.

Western Undergraduate Exchange Program. Residents of Alaska, Arizona, Colorado, Hawaii, Idaho, Montana, Nevada, New Mexico, North Dakota, Oregon, South Dakota, Utah, Washington and Wyoming can enroll in designated two- and four-year undergraduate programs at public institutions in participating states at reduced tuition level (resident tuition plus half). Contact Western Interstate Commission for Higher Education for list and deadlines. *Award:* Scholarship for use in freshman, sophomore, junior, or senior year; renewable. *Eligibility Requirements:* Applicant must be enrolled or expecting to enroll full or part-time at a two-year or four-year institution; resident of Alaska, Arizona, Colorado, Hawaii, Idaho, Montana, Nevada, New Mexico, North Dakota, Oregon, South Dakota, Utah, Washington, or Wyoming and studying in Alaska, Colorado, Hawaii, Idaho, Montana, Nevada, New Mexico, North Dakota, Oregon, South Dakota, Utah, or Wyoming. Available to U.S. citizens. *Application Requirements:* Application.

Contact Ms. Sandy Jackson, Program Coordinator, Western Interstate Commission for Higher Education, PO Box 9752, Boulder, CO 80301-9752. *E-mail:* info-sep@wiche.edu. *Phone:* 303-541-0214. *Fax:* 303-541-0291. *Web site:* www.wiche.edu/sep.

Connecticut

Aid for Public College Students Grant Program/Connecticut. Award for students at Connecticut public college or university. Must be state residents and enrolled at least half-time. Renewable award based on financial need and academic progress. Application deadlines vary by institution. Apply at college financial aid office. *Award:* Grant for use in freshman, sophomore, junior, or senior year; renewable. *Eligibility Requirements:* Applicant must be enrolled or expecting to enroll full or part-time at a two-year or four-year institution or university; resident of Connecticut and studying in Connecticut. *Application Requirements:* Application, financial need analysis, transcript.

Contact John Siegrist, Financial Aid Office, Connecticut Department of Higher Education, 61 Woodland Street, Hartford, CT 06105-2326. *Phone:* 860-947-1855. *Fax:* 860-947-1311. *Web site:* www.ctdhe.org.

Capitol Scholarship Program. Award for Connecticut residents attending eligible institutions in Connecticut or in a state with reciprocity with Connecticut (Delaware, Maine, Massachusetts, New Hampshire, Pennsylvania, Rhode Island, Vermont), or in Washington, D.C. Must be U.S. citizen or permanent resident alien who is a high school senior or graduate with rank in top 20% of class or score at least 1200 on SAT and show financial need. *Award:* Scholarship for use in freshman, sophomore, junior, or senior year; renewable. *Award amount:* up to $2000. *Eligibility Requirements:* Applicant must be enrolled or expecting to enroll at a two-year or four-year institution or university; resident of Connecticut and studying in Connecticut, Delaware, District of Columbia, Maine, Massachusetts, New Hampshire, Pennsylvania, Rhode Island, or Vermont. Applicant must have 3.5 GPA or higher. Available to U.S. citizens. *Application Requirements:* Application, financial need analysis, test scores. **Deadline:** February 15.

Contact John Siegrist, Financial Aid Office, Connecticut Department of Higher Education, 61 Woodland Street, Hartford, CT 06105-2326. *Phone:* 860-947-1855. *Fax:* 860-947-1311. *Web site:* www.ctdhe.org.

Connecticut Army National Guard 100% Tuition Waiver. 100% Tuition Waiver Program is for any active member of the Connecticut Army National Guard in good standing. Must be a resident of Connecticut attending any Connecticut state (public) university, community-technical college or regional vocational-technical school. *Award:* Scholarship for use in freshman, sophomore, junior, or senior year; not renewable. *Award amount:* $2000–$8000. *Eligibility Requirements:* Applicant must be age 17-65; enrolled or expecting to enroll full or part-time at a two-year, four-year, or technical institution or university; resident of Connecticut and studying in Connecticut. Available to U.S. and non-U.S. citizens. Applicant must have served in the Army National Guard. *Application Requirements:* Application. **Deadline:** continuous.

Contact Education Services Officer, Connecticut Army National Guard. *E-mail:* education@ct.ngb.army.mil. *Phone:* 860-524-4816. *Web site:* www.ct.ngb.army.mil/armyguard/join/tuition.asp.

Connecticut Independent College Student Grants. Award for Connecticut residents attending an independent college or university within the state on at least a half-time basis. Renewable awards based on financial need. Application deadline varies by institution. Apply at college financial aid office. *Award:* Grant for use in freshman, sophomore, junior, or senior year; renewable. *Award amount:* up to $8600. *Eligibility Requirements:* Applicant must be enrolled or expecting to enroll full or part-time at a two-year or four-year institution or university; resident of Connecticut and studying in Connecticut. *Application Requirements:* Application, financial need analysis, transcript.

Contact John Siegrist, Financial Aid Office, Connecticut Department of Higher Education, 61 Woodland Street, Hartford, CT 06105-2326. *Phone:* 860-947-1855. *Fax:* 860-947-1311. *Web site:* www.ctdhe.org.

Connecticut Special Education Teacher Incentive Grant. Renewable award for upper-level undergraduates or graduate students in special education programs. Must be in a program at a Connecticut college or university, or be a Connecticut resident enrolled in an approved out-of-state program. Priority is placed on minority and bilingual candidates. Application deadline is October 1. Must be nominated by the education dean of institution attended. *Academic/Career Areas:* Special Education. *Award:* Grant for use in junior, senior, or graduate year; renewable. *Award amount:* $2000–$5000. *Eligibility Requirements:* Applicant must be enrolled or expecting to enroll full or part-time at a four-year institution or university. *Application Requirements:* Application. **Deadline:** October 1.

Contact John Siegrist, Financial Aid Office, Connecticut Department of Higher Education, 61 Woodland Street, Hartford, CT 06105-2326. *Phone:* 860-947-1855. *Fax:* 860-947-1311. *Web site:* www.ctdhe.org.

Connecticut Tuition Waiver for Senior Citizens. Renewable tuition waiver for a Connecticut senior citizen age 62 or older to use at an accredited two- or four-year public institution in Connecticut. Must show financial need and prove senior citizen status. Award for undergraduate study only. Must be enrolled in credit courses. *Award:* Grant for use in freshman, sophomore, junior, or senior year; renewable. *Eligibility Requirements:* Applicant must be age 62; enrolled or expecting to enroll at a two-year or four-year institution; resident of Connecticut and studying in Connecticut. *Application Requirements:* Application, financial need analysis. **Deadline:** continuous.

Contact John Siegrist, Financial Aid Office, Connecticut Department of Higher Education, 61 Woodland Street, Hartford, CT 06105-2326. *Phone:* 860-947-1855. *Fax:* 860-947-1311. *Web site:* www.ctdhe.org.

Connecticut Tuition Waiver for Veterans. Renewable tuition waiver for a Connecticut veteran to use at an accredited two-or four-year public institution in Connecticut. Military separation papers are required; see application for qualifications of service. *Award:* Grant for use in freshman, sophomore, junior, or senior year; renewable. *Eligibility Requirements:* Applicant must be enrolled or expecting to enroll at a two-year or four-year institution; resident of Connecticut and studying in Connecticut. Applicant or parent must meet one or more of the following requirements: general military experience; retired from active duty; disabled or killed as a result of military service; prisoner of war; or missing in action. *Application Requirements:* Application, financial need analysis, military discharge papers. **Deadline:** continuous.

Contact John Siegrist, Financial Aid Office, Connecticut Department of Higher Education, 61 Woodland Street, Hartford, CT 06105-2326. *Phone:* 860-947-1855. *Fax:* 860-947-1311. *Web site:* www.ctdhe.org.

Tuition Set-Aside Aid—Connecticut. Need-based program that assists Connecticut residents who are enrolled at state-supported colleges and universities in Connecticut. Award amounts are variable but do not exceed student's financial need. Deadlines vary by institution. Apply at college financial aid office. *Award:* Grant for use in freshman, sophomore, junior, or senior year; not renewable. *Eligibility Requirements:* Applicant must be enrolled or expecting to enroll at a two-year or four-year institution or university; resident of Connecticut and studying in Connecticut. *Application Requirements:* Application, financial need analysis.

Contact John Siegrist, Financial Aid Office, Connecticut Department of Higher Education, 61 Woodland Street, Hartford, CT 06105-2326. *Phone:* 860-947-1855. *Fax:* 860-947-1311. *Web site:* www.ctdhe.org.

Delaware

Christa McAuliffe Teacher Scholarship Loan—Delaware. Award for Delaware residents who are pursuing teaching careers. Must agree to teach in Delaware public schools as repayment of loan. Minimum award is $1000 and is renewable for up to four years. Available only at Delaware colleges. Based on academic merit. Must be ranked in upper half of class, and have a score of 1050 on SAT or 25 on the ACT. *Academic/Career Areas:* Education. *Award:* Forgivable loan for use in freshman, sophomore, junior, or senior year; renewable. *Award amount:* $1000–$5000. *Number of awards:* 1–60. *Eligibility Requirements:* Applicant must be enrolled or expecting to enroll full-time at a four-year institution or university; resident of Delaware and studying in Delaware. Applicant must have 2.5 GPA or higher. Available to U.S. citizens. *Application Requirements:* Application, essay, test scores, transcript. **Deadline:** March 31.

Contact Donna Myers, Higher Education Analyst, Delaware Higher Education Commission, 820 North French Street, 5th Floor, Wilmington, DE 19711-3509. *E-mail:* dhec@doe.k12.de.us *Phone:* 302-577-3240. *Fax:* 302-577-6765. *Web site:* www.doe.state.de.us/high-ed.

Delaware Nursing Incentive Scholarship Loan. Award for Delaware residents pursuing a nursing career. Must be repaid with nursing practice at a Delaware state-owned hospital. Based on academic merit. Must have minimum 2.5 GPA. Renewable for up to four years. *Academic/Career Areas:* Nursing. *Award:* Forgivable loan for use in freshman, sophomore, junior, or senior year; renewable. *Award amount:* $1000–$5000. *Number of awards:* 1–40. *Eligibility Requirements:* Applicant must be enrolled or expecting to enroll full-time at a two-year or four-year institution or university and resident of Delaware. Applicant must have 2.5 GPA or higher. Available to U.S. citizens. *Application Requirements:* Application, essay, test scores, transcript. **Deadline:** March 31.

Contact Donna Myers, Higher Education Analyst, Delaware Higher Education Commission, 820 North French Street, 5th Floor, Wilmington, DE 19711-3509. *E-mail:* dhec@doe.k12.de.us *Phone:*

Additional State Aid Programs

302-577-3240. *Fax:* 302-577-6765. *Web site:* www.doe.state.de.us/high-ed.

Delaware Solid Waste Authority Scholarship. Scholarships given to residents of Delaware who are high school seniors or freshmen or sophomores in college. Must be majoring in either environmental engineering or environmental sciences in a Delaware college. Must file the Free Application for Federal Student Aid (FAFSA). Scholarships are automatically renewed for three years if a 3.0 GPA is maintained. Deadline: March 15. *Award:* Scholarship for use in freshman or sophomore year; renewable. *Award amount:* $2000. *Eligibility Requirements:* Applicant must be enrolled or expecting to enroll full-time at a two-year or four-year institution or university; resident of Delaware and studying in Delaware. Applicant must have 3.0 GPA or higher. *Application Requirements:* Financial need analysis, FAFSA. **Deadline:** March 15.

Contact Donna Myers, Higher Education Analyst, Delaware Higher Education Commission, 820 North French Street, 5th Floor, Wilmington, DE 19711-3509. *E-mail:* dhec@doe.k12.de.us. *Phone:* 302-577-3240. *Fax:* 302-577-6765. *Web site:* www.doe.state.de.us/high-ed.

Diamond State Scholarship. Renewable award for Delaware high school seniors enrolling full-time at an accredited college or university. Must be ranked in upper quarter of class and score 1200 on SAT or 27 on the ACT. *Award:* Scholarship for use in freshman year; renewable. *Award amount:* $1250. *Number of awards:* 50–200. *Eligibility Requirements:* Applicant must be high school student; planning to enroll or expecting to enroll full-time at a four-year institution or university and resident of Delaware. Applicant must have 3.5 GPA or higher. Available to U.S. citizens. *Application Requirements:* Application, essay, test scores, transcript. **Deadline:** March 31.

Contact Donna Myers, Higher Education Analyst, Delaware Higher Education Commission, 820 North French Street, 5th Floor, Wilmington, DE 19711-3509. *E-mail:* dhec@doe.k12.de.us. *Phone:* 302-577-3240. *Fax:* 302-577-6765. *Web site:* www.doe.state.de.us/high-ed.

Educational Benefits for Children of Deceased Military and State Police. Renewable award for Delaware residents who are children of state or military police who were killed in the line of duty. Must attend a Delaware institution unless program of study is not available. Funds cover tuition and fees at Delaware institutions. The amount varies at non-Delaware institutions. Must submit proof of service and related death. Must be ages 16-24 at time of application. Deadline is three weeks before classes begin. *Award:* Grant for use in freshman, sophomore, junior, or senior year; renewable. *Award amount:* $6255. *Number of awards:* 1–10. *Eligibility Requirements:* Applicant must be age 16-24; enrolled or expecting to enroll full-time at a two-year or four-year institution or university and resident of Delaware. Applicant or parent of applicant must have employment or volunteer experience in police/firefighting. Available to U.S. citizens. Applicant or parent must meet one or more of the following requirements: general military experience; retired from active duty; disabled or killed as a result of military service; prisoner of war; or missing in action. *Application Requirements:* Application, verification of service-related death. **Deadline:** continuous.

Contact Donna Myers, Higher Education Analyst, Delaware Higher Education Commission, 820 North French Street, 5th Floor, Wilmington, DE 19711-3509. *E-mail:* dhec@doe.k12.de.us. *Phone:* 302-577-3240. *Fax:* 302-577-6765. *Web site:* www.doe.state.de.us/high-ed.

Legislative Essay Scholarship. Must be a senior in high school and Delaware resident. Submit an essay of 500 to 2000 words on a designated historical topic (changes annually). Deadline: November 16. For more information visit: www.doe.state.de.us/high-ed. *Award:* Scholarship for use in freshman year; not renewable. *Award amount:* $500–$5500. *Number of awards:* 62. *Eligibility Requirements:* Applicant must be high school student; planning to enroll or expecting to enroll full or part-time at a two-year, four-year, or technical institution or university and resident of Delaware. Available to U.S. citizens. *Application Requirements:* Application, applicant must enter a contest, essay. **Deadline:** November 16.

Contact Donna Myers, Higher Education Analyst, Delaware Higher Education Commission, 820 North French Street, 5th Floor, Wilmington, DE 19711-3509. *E-mail:* dhec@doe.k12.de.us. *Phone:* 302-577-3240. *Fax:* 302-577-6765. *Web site:* www.doe.state.de.us/high-ed.

Scholarship Incentive Program-Delaware. One-time award for Delaware residents with financial need. May be used at an institution in Delaware or Pennsylvania, or at another out-of-state institution if a program is not available at a publicly supported school in Delaware. Must have minimum 2.5 GPA. *Award:* Grant for use in freshman, sophomore, junior, or senior year; not renewable. *Award amount:* $700–$2200. *Number of awards:* 1000–1300. *Eligibility Requirements:* Applicant must be enrolled or expecting to enroll full-time at a two-year or four-year institution or university; resident of Delaware and studying in Delaware or Pennsylvania. Applicant must have 2.5 GPA or higher. Available to U.S. citizens. *Application Requirements:* Application, financial need analysis, transcript. **Deadline:** April 15.

Contact Donna Myers, Higher Education Analyst, Delaware Higher Education Commission, 820 North French Street, 5th Floor, Wilmington, DE 19711-3509. *E-mail:* dhec@doe.k12.de.us. *Phone:* 302-577-3240. *Fax:* 302-577-6765. *Web site:* www.doe.state.de.us/high-ed.

Appendix D

State Tuition Assistance. Award providing tuition assistance for any member of the Air or Army National Guard attending a Delaware two-year or four-year college. Awards are renewable. Applicant's minimum GPA must be 2.0. For full- or part-time study. Amount of award varies. *Award:* Scholarship for use in freshman, sophomore, junior, or senior year; renewable. *Eligibility Requirements:* Applicant must be enrolled or expecting to enroll full or part-time at a two-year or four-year institution and studying in Delaware. Available to U.S. citizens. Applicant must have served in the Air Force National Guard or Army National Guard. *Application Requirements:* **Deadline:** continuous.

Contact TSgt. Robert L. Csizmadia, State Tuition Assistance Manager, Delaware National Guard, First Regiment Road, Wilmington, DE 19808-2191. *E-mail:* robert.csizmadi@de.ngb.army.mil. *Phone:* 302-326-7012. *Fax:* 302-326-7055. *Web site:* www.delawarenationalguard/home.htm.

District of Columbia

American Council of the Blind Scholarships. Merit-based award available to undergraduate, graduate, vocational or technical students who are legally blind in both eyes. Submit certificate of legal blindness and proof of acceptance at an accredited postsecondary institution. *Award:* Scholarship for use in freshman, sophomore, junior, senior, or graduate year; not renewable. *Award amount:* $500–$5000. *Number of awards:* 30. *Eligibility Requirements:* Applicant must be enrolled or expecting to enroll full-time at a two-year, four-year, or technical institution or university. Applicant must be visually impaired. Applicant must have 3.5 GPA or higher. *Application Requirements:* Application, autobiography, essay, references, transcript. **Deadline:** March 1.

Contact Terry Pacheco, Affiliate and Membership Services, American Council of the Blind, 1155 15th Street, NW, Suite 1004, Washington, DC 20005. *E-mail:* info@acb.org. *Phone:* 202-467-5081. *Fax:* 202-467-5085. *Web site:* www.acb.org.

DC Leveraging Educational Assistance Partnership Program (LEAP). Available to Washington, D.C. residents who have financial need. Must also apply for the Federal Pell Grant. Must attend an eligible college at least half-time. Contact financial aid office or local library for more information. Proof of residency may be required. Deadline is last Friday in June. *Award:* Scholarship for use in freshman, sophomore, junior, or senior year; not renewable. *Award amount:* $500–$1500. *Number of awards:* 1200–1500. *Eligibility Requirements:* Applicant must be enrolled or expecting to enroll full or part-time at a two-year, four-year, or technical institution or university and resident of District of Columbia. Available to U.S. citizens. *Application Requirements:* Application, financial need analysis, Student Aid Report (SAR). **Deadline:** June 28.

Contact Angela M. March, Program Manager, District of Columbia State Education Office, 441 4th Street NW, Suite 350 North, Washington, DC 20001. *E-mail:* angela.march@dc.gov. *Phone:* 202-727-6436. *Fax:* 202-727-2019. *Web site:* www.seo.dc.gov.

Florida

Critical Teacher Shortage Student Loan Forgiveness Program—Florida. Eligible Florida teachers may receive up to $5,000 for repayment of undergraduate and graduate educational loans which led to certification in critical teacher shortage subject area. Must teach full-time at a Florida public school in a critical area for a minimum of ninety days to be eligible. Visit Web site for further information. *Award:* Forgivable loan for use in freshman, sophomore, junior, senior, or graduate year; not renewable. *Award amount:* up to $5000. *Eligibility Requirements:* Applicant must be enrolled or expecting to enroll at a two-year or four-year institution or university; resident of Florida and studying in Florida. Applicant or parent of applicant must have employment or volunteer experience in teaching. Available to U.S. citizens. *Application Requirements:* Application. **Deadline:** July 15.

Contact Scholarship Information, Florida Department of Education, Office of Student Financial Assistance, 1940 North Monroe, Suite 70, Tallahassee, FL 32303-4759. *E-mail:* osfa@fldoe.org. *Phone:* 888-827-2004. *Web site:* www.floridastudentfinancialaid.org.

Critical Teacher Shortage Tuition Reimbursement-Florida. One-time awards for full-time Florida public school employees who are certified to teach in Florida and are teaching or preparing to teach in critical teacher shortage subject areas. Must earn minimum grade of 3.0 in approved courses. May receive tuition reimbursement up to 9 semester hours or equivalent per academic year, not to exceed $78 per semester hour, for maximum 36 hours. Must be resident of Florida. *Academic/Career Areas:* Education. *Award:* Scholarship for use in freshman, sophomore, junior, senior, or graduate year; not renewable. *Award amount:* up to $234. *Number of awards:* 1000–1200. *Eligibility Requirements:* Applicant must be enrolled or expecting to enroll part-time at a two-year or four-year institution or university; resident of Florida and studying in Florida. Applicant or parent of applicant must have employment or volunteer experience in teaching. Applicant must have 3.0 GPA or higher. Available to U.S. citizens. *Application Requirements:* Application, financial need analysis. **Deadline:** September 15.

Contact Scholarship Information, Florida Department of Education, Office of Student Financial Assistance, 1940 North Monroe, Suite 70, Tallahassee, FL 32303-4759. *E-mail:* osfa@fldoe.org. *Phone:*

888-827-2004. *Web site:* www.floridastudentfinancialaid.org.

Excellence in Service Award. This award program recognizes Florida College students who have a distinguished community service record in Florida. See Web site (www.floridacompact.org) for application form and further requirements. **Award:** Scholarship for use in freshman, sophomore, or junior year; not renewable. *Award amount:* $1000. *Number of awards:* 3. *Eligibility Requirements:* Applicant must be enrolled or expecting to enroll full-time at a four-year institution or university; resident of Florida and studying in Florida. Available to U.S. and non-U.S. citizens. *Application Requirements:* Application, essay, photo, resume, references, transcript. **Deadline:** April 3.

Contact Saul A. Magana, Associate Director, Florida Campus Compact, 325 John Knox Road Building F, Suite 210, Tallahassee, FL 32303. *E-mail:* saul@floridacompact.org. *Phone:* 850-488-7782. *Fax:* 850-922-2928. *Web site:* www.floridacompact.org.

Florida Bright Futures Scholarship Program. Reward for Florida high school graduates who demonstrate high academic achievement, participate in community service projects and enroll in eligible Florida postsecondary institutions. There are three award levels. Each has different academic criteria and awards a different amount. Top ranked scholars from each county will receive additional $1500. Web site at www.firn.edu/doe contains complete information and application which must be completed and submitted to high school guidance counselor prior to graduation. **Award:** Scholarship for use in freshman, sophomore, junior, or senior year; renewable. *Eligibility Requirements:* Applicant must be high school student; planning to enroll or expecting to enroll full or part-time at a two-year, four-year, or technical institution or university; resident of Florida and studying in Florida. Available to U.S. citizens. *Application Requirements:* Application, financial need analysis, test scores, transcript.

Contact Scholarship Information, Florida Department of Education, Office of Student Financial Assistance, 1940 North Monroe, Suite 70, Tallahassee, FL 32303-4759. *E-mail:* osfa@fldoe.org. *Phone:* 888-827-2004. *Web site:* www.floridastudentfinancialaid.org.

Florida Space Research and Education Grant Program. One-time award for aerospace and technology research. Must be U.S. citizen. Grant is for research in Florida only. Submit research proposal with budget. Application deadline is March 1. **Award:** Grant for use in freshman, sophomore, junior, senior, graduate, or postgraduate years; not renewable. *Award amount:* $10,000–$30,000. *Number of awards:* 9–12. *Eligibility Requirements:* Applicant must be enrolled or expecting to enroll full or part-time at a four-year institution or university and studying in Florida. Available to U.S. citizens. *Application Requirements:* Proposal with budget. **Deadline:** March 1.

Contact Dr. Jaydeep Mukherjee, Administrator, NASA Florida Space Grant Consortium, Mail Stop: FSGC, Kennedy Space Center, FL 32899. *E-mail:* jmukherj@mail.ucf.edu. *Phone:* 321-452-4301. *Fax:* 321-449-0739. *Web site:* fsgc.engr.ucf.edu.

Jose Marti Scholarship Challenge Grant. Must apply as a senior in high school or as graduate student. Must be resident of Florida and study in Florida. Need-based, merit scholarship. Must be U.S. citizen or eligible non-citizen. Applicant must certify minimum 3.0 GPA and Hispanic origin. **Award:** Scholarship for use in freshman, sophomore, junior, senior, or graduate year; renewable. *Award amount:* $2000. *Number of awards:* 50. *Eligibility Requirements:* Applicant must be of Hispanic heritage; enrolled or expecting to enroll full-time at a two-year or four-year institution or university; resident of Florida and studying in Florida. Applicant must have 3.0 GPA or higher. Available to U.S. citizens. *Application Requirements:* Application, financial need analysis. **Deadline:** April 1.

Contact Jose Marti Scholarship Challenge Grant Fund, 1940 North Monroe Street, Suite 70, Tallahassee, FL 32303-4759. *Phone:* 888-827-2004. *Web site:* www.floridastudentfinancialaid.org.

Nursing Scholarship Program. Provides financial assistance for Florida residents who are full- or part-time nursing students enrolled in an approved nursing program in Florida. Awards are for a maximum of two years and must be repaid through full-time service. *Academic/Career Areas:* Nursing. **Award:** Scholarship for use in junior, senior, or graduate year; renewable. *Award amount:* $8000–$12,000. *Number of awards:* 15–30. *Eligibility Requirements:* Applicant must be enrolled or expecting to enroll full or part-time at a two-year or four-year institution or university; resident of Florida and studying in Florida. Available to U.S. and non-U.S. citizens. *Application Requirements:* Application. **Deadline:** continuous.

Contact Florida Department of Health, Division of EMS and Community Health Resources, 4052 Bald Cypress Way, Mail Bin C-15, Tallahassee, FL 32399-1735.

Nursing Student Loan Forgiveness Program. Forgivable loan available to LPNs, RNs, and ARNPs who are out of school and working full time at a designated facility. Program assists with repaying principal only of loans taken to subsidize nursing education. Pays $4,000 per year of outstanding debt for a maximum of four years. Contact for information. Deadlines: March 1, June 1, September 1, and December 1. *Academic/Career Areas:* Nursing. **Award:** Forgivable loan for use in freshman, sophomore, junior, or senior year; renewable. *Award amount:* up to $4000. *Eligibility Require-*

ments: Applicant must be enrolled or expecting to enroll at an institution or university; resident of Florida and studying in Florida. Available to U.S. and non-U.S. citizens. *Application Requirements:* Application, Nurse Diploma and Florida License (copy of each with application).

Contact Florida Department of Health, Division of EMS and Community Health Resources, 4052 Bald Cypress Way, Mail Bin C-15, Tallahassee, FL 32399-1735.

Rosewood Family Scholarship Fund. Renewable award for eligible minority students to attend a Florida public postsecondary institution on a full-time basis. Preference given to direct descendants of African-American Rosewood families affected by the incidents of January 1923. Must be Black, Hispanic, Asian, Pacific Islander, American-Indian, or Alaska Native. Free Application for Federal Student Aid (and Student Aid Report for nonresidents of Florida) must be processed by May 15. *Award:* Scholarship for use in freshman, sophomore, junior, or senior year; renewable. *Award amount:* up to $4000. *Number of awards:* up to 25. *Eligibility Requirements:* Applicant must be American Indian/Alaska Native, Asian/Pacific Islander, Black (non-Hispanic), or Hispanic; enrolled or expecting to enroll full-time at a two-year, four-year, or technical institution or university and studying in Florida. Available to U.S. citizens. *Application Requirements:* Application, financial need analysis. **Deadline:** April 1.

Contact Scholarship Information, Florida Department of Education, Office of Student Financial Assistance, 1940 North Monroe, Suite 70, Tallahassee, FL 32303-4759. *E-mail:* osfa@fldoe.org. *Phone:* 888-827-2004. *Web site:* www.floridastudentfinancialaid.org.

Scholarships for Children of Deceased or Disabled Veterans or Children of Servicemen Classified as POW or MIA. Scholarship provides full tuition assistance for children of deceased or disabled veterans or of servicemen classified as POW or MIA who are in full-time attendance at eligible public or non-public Florida institutions. Service connection must be as specified under Florida statute. Amount of payment to non-public institutions is equal to cost at public institutions at the comparable level. Must be between 16 and 22. Qualified veteran and applicant must meet residency requirements. *Award:* Scholarship for use in freshman, sophomore, junior, or senior year; renewable. *Number of awards:* 160. *Eligibility Requirements:* Applicant must be age 16-22; enrolled or expecting to enroll full-time at a two-year, four-year, or technical institution or university; resident of Florida and studying in Florida. Available to U.S. citizens. Applicant or parent must meet one or more of the following requirements: general military experience; retired from active duty; disabled or killed as a result of military service; prisoner of war; or missing in action. *Application Requirements:* Application, financial need analysis. **Deadline:** May 1.

Contact Scholarship Information, Florida Department of Education, Office of Student Financial Assistance, 1940 North Monroe, Suite 70, Tallahassee, FL 32303-4759. *E-mail:* osfa@fldoe.org. *Phone:* 888-827-2004. *Web site:* www.floridastudentfinancialaid.org.

William L. Boyd IV Florida Resident Access Grant. Awards given to Florida residents attending an independent nonprofit college or university in Florida for undergraduate study. Cannot have previously received bachelor's degree. Must enroll minimum 12 credit hours. Deadline set by eligible postsecondary financial aid offices. Contact financial aid administrator for application information. Reapply for renewal. *Award:* Grant for use in freshman, sophomore, junior, or senior year; not renewable. *Award amount:* up to $2686. *Eligibility Requirements:* Applicant must be enrolled or expecting to enroll full-time at a four-year institution or university; resident of Florida and studying in Florida. Available to U.S. citizens. *Application Requirements:* Application.

Contact Scholarship Information, Florida Department of Education, Office of Student Financial Assistance, 1940 North Monroe, Suite 70, Tallahassee, FL 32303-4759. *E-mail:* osfa@fldoe.org. *Phone:* 888-827-2004. *Web site:* www.floridastudentfinancialaid.org.

Georgia

Department of Human Resources Federal Stafford Loan with the Service Cancelable Loan Option. Forgivable loans of $4000 are awarded to current Department of Human Resources employees who will be enrolled in a baccalaureate or advanced nursing degree program at an eligible participating school in Georgia. Loans are cancelled upon two calendar years of service as a registered nurse for the Georgia DHR or any Georgia county board of health. *Academic/Career Areas:* Nursing. *Award:* Forgivable loan for use in freshman, sophomore, junior, senior, or graduate year; not renewable. *Award amount:* $4000. *Eligibility Requirements:* Applicant must be enrolled or expecting to enroll full or part-time at a four-year institution or university; resident of Georgia and studying in Georgia. Available to U.S. citizens. *Application Requirements:* Application, financial need analysis. **Deadline:** continuous.

Contact Peggy Matthews, Manager/GSFA Originations, State of Georgia, 2082 East Exchange Place, Suite 230, Tucker, GA 30084-5305. *E-mail:* peggy@mail.gsfc.state.ga.us. *Phone:* 770-724-9230. *Fax:* 770-724-9263. *Web site:* www.gsfc.org.

GAE GFIE Scholarship for Aspiring Teachers. Up to ten $1000 scholarships will be awarded to graduating seniors who currently attend a fully accredited public Georgia high school and will attend a fully accredited

Georgia college or university within the next 12 months. Must have a 3.0 GPA. Must submit three letters of recommendation. Must have plans to enter the teaching profession. *Academic/Career Areas:* Education. *Award:* Scholarship for use in freshman year; not renewable. *Award amount:* $1000. *Number of awards:* up to 10. *Eligibility Requirements:* Applicant must be high school student; planning to enroll or expecting to enroll at a two-year or four-year institution or university; resident of Georgia and studying in Georgia. Applicant must have 3.0 GPA or higher. Available to U.S. citizens. *Application Requirements:* Application, transcript. **Deadline:** March 15.

Contact Sally Bennett, Professional Development Specialist, Georgia Association of Educators, 100 Crescent Centre Parkway, Suite 500, Tucker, GA 30084-7049. *E-mail:* sally.bennett@gae.org. *Phone:* 678-837-1103. *Web site:* www.gae.org.

Georgia Leveraging Educational Assistance Partnership Grant Program. Based on financial need. Recipients must be eligible for the Federal Pell Grant. Renewable award for Georgia residents enrolled in a state postsecondary institution. Must be U.S. citizen. *Award:* Grant for use in freshman, sophomore, junior, or senior year; renewable. *Award amount:* $370. *Number of awards:* 3000–3500. *Eligibility Requirements:* Applicant must be enrolled or expecting to enroll full or part-time at a two-year, four-year, or technical institution or university; resident of Georgia and studying in Georgia. Available to U.S. citizens. *Application Requirements:* Application, financial need analysis. **Deadline:** continuous.

Contact William Flook, Director of Scholarships and Grants, Georgia Student Finance Commission, 2082 East Exchange Place, Suite 100, Tucker, GA 30084. *Phone:* 770-724-9050. *Fax:* 770-724-9031. *Web site:* www.gsfc.org.

Georgia National Guard Service Cancelable Loan Program. Forgivable loans will be awarded to residents of Georgia maintaining good military standing as an eligible member of the Georgia National Guard who are enrolled at least half-time in an undergraduate degree program at an eligible college, university or technical school within the state of Georgia. *Award:* Forgivable loan for use in freshman, sophomore, junior, or senior year; not renewable. *Award amount:* $150–$1395. *Number of awards:* 200–250. *Eligibility Requirements:* Applicant must be enrolled or expecting to enroll full or part-time at a two-year, four-year, or technical institution or university; resident of Georgia and studying in Georgia. Available to U.S. citizens. Applicant must have served in the Air Force National Guard or Army National Guard. *Application Requirements:* Application, financial need analysis. **Deadline:** continuous.

Contact Peggy Matthews, Manager/GSFA Originations, State of Georgia, 2082 East Exchange Place, Suite 230, Tucker, GA 30084-5305. *E-mail:* peggy@mail.gsfc.state.ga.us. *Phone:* 770-724-9230. *Fax:* 770-724-9263. *Web site:* www.gsfc.org.

Georgia PROMISE Teacher Scholarship Program. Renewable, forgivable loans for junior undergraduates at Georgia colleges who have been accepted for enrollment into a teacher education program leading to initial certification. Minimum cumulative 3.0 GPA required. Recipient must teach at a Georgia public school for one year for each $1500 awarded. Available to seniors for renewal only. Write for deadlines. *Academic/Career Areas:* Education. *Award:* Forgivable loan for use in junior or senior year; renewable. *Award amount:* $3000–$6000. *Number of awards:* 700–1400. *Eligibility Requirements:* Applicant must be enrolled or expecting to enroll full or part-time at a four-year institution or university and studying in Georgia. Applicant must have 3.0 GPA or higher. Available to U.S. citizens. *Application Requirements:* Application, transcript. **Deadline:** continuous.

Contact Stan DeWitt, Manager of Teacher Scholarships, Georgia Student Finance Commission, 2082 East Exchange Place, Suite 100, Tucker, GA 30084. *Phone:* 770-724-9060. *Fax:* 770-724-9031. *Web site:* www.gsfc.org.

Georgia Public Safety Memorial Grant/Law Enforcement Personnel Department Grant. Award for children of Georgia law enforcement officers, prison guards, or fire fighters killed or permanently disabled in the line of duty. Must attend an accredited postsecondary Georgia school. Complete the Law Enforcement Personnel Dependents application. *Award:* Grant for use in freshman, sophomore, junior, or senior year; renewable. *Award amount:* $2000. *Number of awards:* 20–40. *Eligibility Requirements:* Applicant must be enrolled or expecting to enroll full-time at a two-year, four-year, or technical institution or university; resident of Georgia and studying in Georgia. Applicant or parent of applicant must have employment or volunteer experience in police/firefighting. Available to U.S. citizens. *Application Requirements:* Application. **Deadline:** continuous.

Contact William Flook, Director of Scholarships and Grants Division, Georgia Student Finance Commission, 2082 East Exchange Place, Suite 100, Tucker, GA 30084. *Phone:* 770-724-9050. *Fax:* 770-724-9031. *Web site:* www.gsfc.org.

Georgia Tuition Equalization Grant (GTEG). Award for Georgia residents pursuing undergraduate study at an accredited two- or four-year Georgia private institution. Complete the Georgia Student Grant Application. Award is $1045 per academic year. Deadlines vary. *Award:* Grant for use in freshman, sophomore, junior, or senior year; renewable. *Award amount:* $1045. *Number of awards:* 25,000–32,000. *Eligibility Requirements:* Applicant must be enrolled or expecting to enroll full-time at a two-year or four-year institution or university; resident of Georgia and studying in Georgia.

Appendix D

Available to U.S. citizens. *Application Requirements:* Application. **Deadline:** continuous.

Contact William Flook, Director of Scholarships and Grants Division, Georgia Student Finance Commission, 2082 East Exchange Place, Suite 100, Tucker, GA 30084. *Phone:* 770-724-9050. *Fax:* 770-724-9031. *Web site:* www.gsfc.org.

Governor's Scholarship—Georgia. Award to assist students selected as Georgia scholars, STAR students, valedictorians, and salutatorians. For use at two- and four-year colleges and universities in Georgia. Recipients are selected as entering freshmen. Renewable award of up to $1575. Minimum 3.5 GPA required. *Award:* Scholarship for use in freshman, sophomore, junior, or senior year; renewable. *Award amount:* up to $1575. *Number of awards:* 2000–3000. *Eligibility Requirements:* Applicant must be high school student; planning to enroll or expecting to enroll full-time at a two-year or four-year institution or university; resident of Georgia and studying in Georgia. Applicant must have 3.5 GPA or higher. Available to U.S. citizens. *Application Requirements:* Application, transcript. **Deadline:** continuous.

Contact William Flook, Director of Scholarships and Grants Division, Georgia Student Finance Commission, 2082 East Exchange Place, Suite 100, Tucker, GA 30084. *Phone:* 770-724-9050. *Fax:* 770-724-9031. *Web site:* www.gsfc.org.

HOPE—Helping Outstanding Pupils Educationally. Grant program for Georgia residents who are college undergraduates to attend an accredited two- or four-year Georgia institution. Tuition and fees may be covered by the grant. Minimum 3.0 GPA required. Renewable if student maintains grades and reapplies. Write for deadlines. *Award:* Scholarship for use in freshman, sophomore, junior, or senior year; renewable. *Award amount:* $300–$3000. *Number of awards:* 140,000–170,000. *Eligibility Requirements:* Applicant must be enrolled or expecting to enroll full or part-time at a two-year or four-year institution or university; resident of Georgia and studying in Georgia. Applicant must have 3.0 GPA or higher. Available to U.S. citizens. *Application Requirements:* Application. **Deadline:** continuous.

Contact William Flook, Director of Scholarships and Grants Division, Georgia Student Finance Commission, 2082 East Exchange Place, Suite 100, Tucker, GA 30084. *Phone:* 770-724-9050. *Fax:* 770-724-9031. *Web site:* www.gsfc.org.

Intellectual Capital Partnership Program, ICAPP. Forgivable loans will be awarded to undergraduate students who are residents of Georgia studying high-tech related fields at a Georgia institution. Repayment for every $2500 that is awarded is one-year service in a high-tech field in Georgia. Can be enrolled in a certificate or degree program. *Academic/Career Areas:* Trade/Technical Specialties. *Award:* Forgivable loan for use in freshman, sophomore, junior, or senior year; not renewable. *Award amount:* $7000–$10,000. *Number of awards:* up to 328. *Eligibility Requirements:* Applicant must be enrolled or expecting to enroll full or part-time at a two-year or four-year institution or university; resident of Georgia and studying in Georgia. Available to U.S. citizens. *Application Requirements:* Application, financial need analysis. **Deadline:** continuous.

Contact Peggy Matthews, Manager/GSFA Originations, State of Georgia, 2082 East Exchange Place, Suite 230, Tucker, GA 30084-5305. *E-mail:* peggy@mail.gsfc.state.ga.us. *Phone:* 770-724-9230. *Fax:* 770-724-9263. *Web site:* www.gsfc.org.

Ladders in Nursing Career Service Cancelable Loan Program. Forgivable loans of $3,000 are awarded to students who agree to serve for one calendar year at an approved site within the state of Georgia. Eligible applicants will be residents of Georgia who are studying nursing at a Georgia institution. *Academic/Career Areas:* Nursing. *Award:* Forgivable loan for use in freshman, sophomore, junior, senior, or graduate year; not renewable. *Award amount:* $3000. *Eligibility Requirements:* Applicant must be enrolled or expecting to enroll full or part-time at a two-year, four-year, or technical institution or university; resident of Georgia and studying in Georgia. Available to U.S. citizens. *Application Requirements:* Application, financial need analysis. **Deadline:** continuous.

Contact Peggy Matthews, Manager/GSFA Originations, State of Georgia, 2082 East Exchange Place, Suite 230, Tucker, GA 30084-5305. *E-mail:* peggy@mail.gsfc.state.ga.us. *Phone:* 770-724-9230. *Fax:* 770-724-9263. *Web site:* www.gsfc.org.

Northeast Georgia Pilot Nurse Service Cancelable Loan. Up to 100 forgivable loans between $2,500 and $4,500 will be awarded to undergraduate students who are residents of Georgia studying nursing at a four-year school in Georgia. Loans can be repaid by working as a nurse in northeast Georgia. *Academic/Career Areas:* Nursing. *Award:* Forgivable loan for use in freshman, sophomore, junior, or senior year; not renewable. *Award amount:* $2500–$4500. *Number of awards:* up to 100. *Eligibility Requirements:* Applicant must be enrolled or expecting to enroll full or part-time at a four-year institution; resident of Georgia and studying in Georgia. Available to U.S. citizens. *Application Requirements:* Application, financial need analysis. **Deadline:** continuous.

Contact Peggy Matthews, Manager/GSFA Originations, State of Georgia, 2082 East Exchange Place, Suite 230, Tucker, GA 30084-5305. *E-mail:* peggy@mail.gsfc.state.ga.us. *Phone:* 770-724-9230. *Fax:* 770-724-9263. *Web site:* www.gsfc.org.

Additional State Aid Programs

Registered Nurse Service Cancelable Loan Program. Forgivable loans will be awarded to undergraduate students who are residents of Georgia studying nursing in a two-year or four-year school in Georgia. Loans can be repaid by working as a registered nurse in the state of Georgia. *Academic/Career Areas:* Nursing. *Award:* Forgivable loan for use in freshman, sophomore, junior, or senior year; not renewable. *Award amount:* $200–$4500. *Eligibility Requirements:* Applicant must be enrolled or expecting to enroll full or part-time at a two-year or four-year institution; resident of Georgia and studying in Georgia. Available to U.S. citizens. *Application Requirements:* Application, financial need analysis. **Deadline:** continuous.

Contact Peggy Matthews, Manager/GSFA Originations, State of Georgia, 2082 East Exchange Place, Suite 230, Tucker, GA 30084-5305. *E-mail:* peggy@mail.gsfc.state.ga.us. *Phone:* 770-724-9230. *Fax:* 770-724-9263. *Web site:* www.gsfc.org.

Robert C. Byrd Honors Scholarship-Georgia. Complete the application provided by the Georgia Department of Education. Renewable awards for outstanding graduating Georgia high school seniors to be used for full-time undergraduate study at eligible U.S. institution. *Award:* Scholarship for use in freshman, sophomore, junior, or senior year; renewable. *Award amount:* $1500. *Number of awards:* 600–700. *Eligibility Requirements:* Applicant must be high school student; planning to enroll or expecting to enroll full-time at a two-year or four-year institution or university and resident of Georgia. Available to U.S. citizens. *Application Requirements:* Application, transcript. **Deadline:** April 1.

Contact William Flook, Director of Scholarships and Grants Division, Georgia Student Finance Commission, 2082 East Exchange Place, Suite 100, Tucker, GA 30084. *Phone:* 770-724-9050. *Fax:* 770-724-9031. *Web site:* www.gsfc.org.

Service-Cancelable Stafford Loan-Georgia. To assist Georgia students enrolled in critical fields of study in allied health (e.g., nursing, physical therapy). For use at GSFA-approved schools. $3500 forgivable loan for dentistry students only. Contact school financial aid officer for more details. *Academic/Career Areas:* Dental Health/Services; Health and Medical Sciences; Nursing. *Award:* Forgivable loan for use in freshman, sophomore, junior, senior, or graduate year; not renewable. *Award amount:* $2000–$4500. *Number of awards:* 500–1200. *Eligibility Requirements:* Applicant must be enrolled or expecting to enroll full or part-time at a two-year, four-year, or technical institution or university; resident of Georgia and studying in Georgia. Available to U.S. citizens. *Application Requirements:* Application, financial need analysis. **Deadline:** continuous.

Contact Peggy Matthews, Manager/GSFA Originations, State of Georgia, 2082 East Exchange Place, Suite 230, Tucker, GA 30084-5305. *E-mail:* peggy@mail.gsfc.state.ga.us. *Phone:* 770-724-9230. *Fax:* 770-724-9263. *Web site:* www.gsfc.org.

Hawaii

Hawaii State Student Incentive Grant. Grants are given to residents of Hawaii who are enrolled in a Hawaiian state school. Funds are for undergraduate tuition only. Applicants must submit a financial need analysis. *Award:* Grant for use in freshman, sophomore, junior, or senior year; renewable. *Eligibility Requirements:* Applicant must be enrolled or expecting to enroll full or part-time at a two-year or four-year institution or university; resident of Hawaii and studying in Hawaii. Available to U.S. citizens. *Application Requirements:* Financial need analysis.

Contact Jo Ann Yoshida, Financial Aid Specialist, Hawaii State Postsecondary Education Commission, University of Hawaii at Manoa, Honolulu, HI 96822. *E-mail:* iha@hawaii.edu. *Phone:* 808-956-6066. *Web site:* www.hern.hawaii.edu.

Idaho

Education Incentive Loan Forgiveness Contract-Idaho. Renewable award assists Idaho residents enrolling in teacher education or nursing programs within state. Must rank in top 15% of high school graduating class, have a 3.0 GPA or above, and agree to work in Idaho for two years. Deadlines vary. Contact financial aid office at institution of choice. *Academic/Career Areas:* Education; Nursing. *Award:* Forgivable loan for use in freshman, sophomore, junior, or senior year; renewable. *Number of awards:* 29. *Eligibility Requirements:* Applicant must be enrolled or expecting to enroll full-time at a four-year institution or university; resident of Idaho and studying in Idaho. Applicant must have 3.0 GPA or higher. Available to U.S. citizens. *Application Requirements:* Application, test scores, transcript.

Contact Financial Aid Office, Idaho State Board of Education. *Web site:* www.idahoboardofed.org.

Idaho Minority and "At Risk" Student Scholarship. Renewable award for Idaho residents who are disabled or members of a minority group and have financial need. Must attend one of eight postsecondary institutions in the state for undergraduate study. Deadlines vary by institution. Must be a U.S. citizen and be a graduate of an Idaho high school. Contact college financial aid office. *Award:* Scholarship for use in freshman, sophomore, junior, or senior year; renewable. *Award amount:* $3000. *Number of awards:* 38–40. *Eligibility Requirements:* Applicant must be enrolled or expecting to enroll full-time at a two-year or four-year institution or university; resident of Idaho and studying

Appendix D

in Idaho. Available to U.S. citizens. *Application Requirements:* Application, financial need analysis.

Contact Financial Aid Office, Idaho State Board of Education. *Web site:* www.idahoboardofed.org.

Idaho Promise Category A Scholarship Program. Renewable award available to Idaho residents who are graduating high school seniors. Must attend an approved Idaho college full-time. Based on class rank (must be verified by school official), GPA, and ACT scores. Professional-technical student applicants must take COMPASS. *Award:* Scholarship for use in freshman, sophomore, junior, or senior year; renewable. *Award amount:* $3000. *Number of awards:* 25–30. *Eligibility Requirements:* Applicant must be high school student; planning to enroll or expecting to enroll full-time at a two-year, four-year, or technical institution or university; resident of Idaho and studying in Idaho. Applicant must have 3.5 GPA or higher. Available to U.S. citizens. *Application Requirements:* Application, test scores. **Deadline:** December 15.

Contact Lynn Humphrey, Scholarship Assistant, Idaho State Board of Education, PO Box 83720, Boise, ID 83720-0037. *E-mail:* lhumphre@osbe.state.id.us. *Phone:* 208-332-1574. *Fax:* 208-334-2632. *Web site:* www.idahoboardofed.org.

Idaho Promise Category B Scholarship Program. Available to Idaho residents entering college for the first time prior to the age of 22. Must have completed high school or its equivalent in Idaho and have a minimum GPA of 3.0 or an ACT score of 20 or higher. Renewable one time only. *Award:* Scholarship for use in freshman or sophomore year; renewable. *Award amount:* $500. *Eligibility Requirements:* Applicant must be age 22 or under; enrolled or expecting to enroll full-time at a two-year, four-year, or technical institution or university; resident of Idaho and studying in Idaho. Applicant must have 3.0 GPA or higher. Available to U.S. citizens. *Application Requirements:* Application. **Deadline:** continuous.

Contact Lynn Humphrey, Academic Program Coordinator, Idaho State Board of Education, PO Box 83720, Boise, ID 83720-0037. *Phone:* 208-332-1574. *Fax:* 208-334-2632. *Web site:* www.idahoboardofed.org.

Leveraging Educational Assistance State Partnership Program (LEAP). One-time award assists students attending participating Idaho colleges and universities majoring in any field except theology or divinity. Idaho residence is not required, but must be U.S. citizen or permanent resident. Must show financial need. Application deadlines vary by institution. *Award:* Grant for use in freshman, sophomore, junior, or senior year; not renewable. *Award amount:* up to $5000. *Eligibility Requirements:* Applicant must be enrolled or expecting to enroll full or part-time at a two-year or four-year institution or university and studying in Idaho. Available to U.S. citizens. *Application Requirements:* Application, financial need analysis, self-addressed stamped envelope.

Contact Lynn Humphrey, Academic Program Coordinator, Idaho State Board of Education, PO Box 83720, Boise, ID 83720-0037. *Phone:* 208-332-1574. *Fax:* 208-334-2632. *Web site:* www.idahoboardofed.org.

Illinois

Golden Apple Scholars of Illinois. Between 75 and 100 forgivable loans are given to undergraduate students. Loans are $7,000 a year for 4 years. Applicants must be between 17 and 21 and carry a minimum GPA of 2.5. Eligible applicants will be residents of Illinois who are studying in Illinois. The deadline is December 1. Recipients must agree to teach in high-need Illinois schools. *Academic/Career Areas:* Education. *Award:* Forgivable loan for use in freshman, sophomore, junior, or senior year; renewable. *Award amount:* $7000. *Number of awards:* 75–100. *Eligibility Requirements:* Applicant must be age 17-21; enrolled or expecting to enroll full-time at a four-year institution or university; resident of Illinois and studying in Illinois. Applicant must have 2.5 GPA or higher. Available to U.S. citizens. *Application Requirements:* Application, autobiography, essay, interview, photo, references, test scores, transcript. **Deadline:** December 1.

Contact Pat Kilduff, Director of Recruitment and Placement, Golden Apple Foundation, 8 South Michigan Avenue, Suite 700, Chicago, IL 60603-3318. *E-mail:* patnk@goldenapple.org. *Phone:* 312-407-0006 Ext. 105. *Fax:* 312-407-0344. *Web site:* www.goldenapple.org.

Grant Program for Dependents of Police, Fire, or Correctional Officers. Award for dependents of police, fire, and corrections officers killed or disabled in line of duty. Provides for tuition and fees at approved Illinois institutions. Must be resident of Illinois. Continuous deadline. Provide proof of status. *Award:* Grant for use in freshman, sophomore, junior, senior, graduate, or postgraduate years; renewable. *Award amount:* $3000–$4000. *Number of awards:* 50–55. *Eligibility Requirements:* Applicant must be enrolled or expecting to enroll at a two-year, four-year, or technical institution or university; resident of Illinois and studying in Illinois. Applicant or parent of applicant must have employment or volunteer experience in police/firefighting. Available to U.S. and non-U.S. citizens. *Application Requirements:* Application, proof of status. **Deadline:** continuous.

Contact David Barinholtz, Client Information, Illinois Student Assistance Commission (ISAC), 1755 Lake Cook Road, Deerfield, IL 60015-5209.

Additional State Aid Programs

E-mail: cssupport@isac.org. Phone: 847-948-8500 Ext. 2385. Web site: www.isac-online.org.

Higher Education License Plate Program—HELP. Need-based grants for students at institutions participating in program whose funds are raised by sale of special license plates commemorating the institutions. Deadline: June 30. Must be Illinois resident. *Award:* Grant for use in freshman, sophomore, junior, or senior year; not renewable. *Award amount:* up to $2000. *Number of awards:* 175–200. *Eligibility Requirements:* Applicant must be enrolled or expecting to enroll full or part-time at a two-year or four-year institution or university; resident of Illinois and studying in Illinois. Available to U.S. and non-U.S. citizens. *Application Requirements:* Financial need analysis. **Deadline:** June 30.

Contact David Barinholtz, Client Information, Illinois Student Assistance Commission (ISAC), 1755 Lake Cook Road, Deerfield, IL 60015-5209. E-mail: cssupport@isac.org. Phone: 847-948-8500 Ext. 2385. Web site: www.isac-online.org.

Illinois College Savings Bond Bonus Incentive Grant Program. Program offers holders of Illinois College Savings Bonds a $20 grant for each year of bond maturity payable upon bond redemption if at least 70% of proceeds are used to attend college in Illinois. May not be used by students attending religious or divinity schools. *Award:* Grant for use in freshman, sophomore, junior, senior, graduate, or postgraduate years; not renewable. *Award amount:* $40–$220. *Number of awards:* 1200–1400. *Eligibility Requirements:* Applicant must be enrolled or expecting to enroll full or part-time at a two-year, four-year, or technical institution or university and studying in Illinois. Available to U.S. and non-U.S. citizens. *Application Requirements:* Application. **Deadline:** continuous.

Contact David Barinholtz, Client Information, Illinois Student Assistance Commission (ISAC), 1755 Lake Cook Road, Deerfield, IL 60015-5209. E-mail: cssupport@isac.org. Phone: 847-948-8500 Ext. 2385. Web site: www.isac-online.org.

Illinois Incentive for Access Program. Award for eligible first-time freshmen enrolling in approved Illinois institutions. One-time grant of up to $500 may be used for any educational expense. Deadline: October 1. *Award:* Grant for use in freshman year; not renewable. *Award amount:* $300–$500. *Number of awards:* 19,000–22,000. *Eligibility Requirements:* Applicant must be enrolled or expecting to enroll full or part-time at a two-year, four-year, or technical institution or university; resident of Illinois and studying in Illinois. Available to U.S. and non-U.S. citizens. *Application Requirements:* Financial need analysis. **Deadline:** October 1.

Contact David Barinholtz, Client Information, Illinois Student Assistance Commission (ISAC), 1755 Lake Cook Road, Deerfield, IL 60015-5209.

E-mail: cssupport@isac.org. Phone: 847-948-8500 Ext. 2385. Web site: www.isac-online.org.

Illinois Monetary Award Program. Award for eligible students attending Illinois public universities, private colleges and universities, community colleges, and some proprietary institutions. Applicable only to tuition and fees. Based on financial need. Deadline: October 1. *Award:* Grant for use in freshman, sophomore, junior, or senior year; not renewable. *Award amount:* $300–$4320. *Number of awards:* 135,000–145,000. *Eligibility Requirements:* Applicant must be enrolled or expecting to enroll full or part-time at a two-year, four-year, or technical institution or university; resident of Illinois and studying in Illinois. Available to U.S. and non-U.S. citizens. *Application Requirements:* Financial need analysis. **Deadline:** October 1.

Contact David Barinholtz, Client Information, Illinois Student Assistance Commission (ISAC), 1755 Lake Cook Road, Deerfield, IL 60015-5209. E-mail: cssupport@isac.org. Phone: 847-948-8500 Ext. 2385. Web site: www.isac-online.org.

Illinois National Guard Grant Program. Award for qualified National Guard personnel which pays tuition and fees at Illinois public universities and community colleges. Must provide documentation of service. Deadline: September 15. *Award:* Grant for use in freshman, sophomore, junior, or senior year; renewable. *Award amount:* $1300–$1700. *Number of awards:* 2000–3000. *Eligibility Requirements:* Applicant must be enrolled or expecting to enroll full or part-time at a two-year or four-year institution or university; resident of Illinois and studying in Illinois. Available to U.S. and non-U.S. citizens. Applicant must have served in the Air Force National Guard or Army National Guard. *Application Requirements:* Application, documentation of service. **Deadline:** September 15.

Contact David Barinholtz, Client Information, Illinois Student Assistance Commission (ISAC), 1755 Lake Cook Road, Deerfield, IL 60015-5209. E-mail: cssupport@isac.org. Phone: 847-948-8500 Ext. 2385. Web site: www.isac-online.org.

Illinois Student-to-Student Program of Matching Grants. Award provides matching funds for need-based grants at participating Illinois public universities and community colleges. Deadline: October 1. *Award:* Grant for use in freshman, sophomore, junior, or senior year; not renewable. *Award amount:* $300–$500. *Number of awards:* 2000–4000. *Eligibility Requirements:* Applicant must be enrolled or expecting to enroll full or part-time at a two-year or four-year institution or university; resident of Illinois and studying in Illinois. Available to U.S. and non-U.S. citizens. *Application Requirements:* Financial need analysis. **Deadline:** October 1.

Contact David Barinholtz, Client Information, Illinois Student Assistance Commission (ISAC),

1755 Lake Cook Road, Deerfield, IL 60015-5209. *E-mail:* cssupport@isac.org. *Phone:* 847-948-8500 Ext. 2385. *Web site:* www.isac-online.org.

Illinois Veteran Grant Program—IVG. Award for qualified veterans for tuition and fees at Illinois public universities and community colleges. Must provide documentation of service (DD214). Deadline is continuous. *Award:* Grant for use in freshman, sophomore, junior, or senior year; renewable. *Award amount:* $1400–$1600. *Number of awards:* 11,000–13,000. *Eligibility Requirements:* Applicant must be enrolled or expecting to enroll full or part-time at a two-year or four-year institution or university; resident of Illinois and studying in Illinois. Available to U.S. and non-U.S. citizens. Applicant must have general military experience. *Application Requirements:* Application, documentation of service. **Deadline:** continuous.

Contact David Barinholtz, Client Information, Illinois Student Assistance Commission (ISAC), 1755 Lake Cook Road, Deerfield, IL 60015-5209. *E-mail:* cssupport@isac.org. *Phone:* 847-948-8500 Ext. 2385. *Web site:* www.isac-online.org.

ITEACH Teacher Shortage Scholarship Program. Award to assist Illinois students planning to teach at an Illinois pre-school, elementary school, or high school in a teacher shortage discipline. Must agree to teach one year in teacher shortage area for each year of award assistance received. Deadline: May 1. *Academic/Career Areas:* Education; Special Education. *Award:* Forgivable loan for use in freshman, sophomore, junior, senior, or graduate year; not renewable. *Award amount:* $4000–$5000. *Number of awards:* 500–600. *Eligibility Requirements:* Applicant must be enrolled or expecting to enroll full or part-time at a two-year or four-year institution or university; resident of Illinois and studying in Illinois. Applicant must have 2.5 GPA or higher. Available to U.S. and non-U.S. citizens. *Application Requirements:* Application, transcript. **Deadline:** May 1.

Contact Dave Barinholtz, Client Information, Illinois Student Assistance Commission (ISAC), 1755 Lake Cook Road, Deerfield, IL 60015-5209. *E-mail:* cssupport@isac.org. *Phone:* 847-948-8500 Ext. 2385. *Web site:* www.isac-online.org.

Merit Recognition Scholarship (MRS) Program. Award for Illinois high school seniors graduating in the top 5% of their class and attending Illinois postsecondary institution. Deadline: June 15. Contact for application procedures. *Award:* Scholarship for use in freshman year; not renewable. *Award amount:* $900–$1000. *Number of awards:* 5000–6000. *Eligibility Requirements:* Applicant must be high school student; planning to enroll or expecting to enroll full or part-time at a two-year or four-year institution or university; resident of Illinois and studying in Illinois. Applicant must have 3.5 GPA or higher. Available to U.S. and non-U.S. citizens. *Application Requirements:* Application. **Deadline:** June 15.

Contact David Barinholtz, Client Information, Illinois Student Assistance Commission (ISAC), 1755 Lake Cook Road, Deerfield, IL 60015-5209. *E-mail:* cssupport@isac.org. *Phone:* 847-948-8500 Ext. 2385. *Web site:* www.isac-online.org.

MIA/POW Scholarships. One-time award for spouse, child, or step-child of veterans who are missing in action or were a prisoner of war. Must be enrolled at a state-supported school in Illinois. Candidate must be U.S. citizen. Must apply and be accepted before beginning of school. Also for children and spouses of veterans who are determined to be 100% disabled as established by the Veterans Administration. *Award:* Scholarship for use in freshman, sophomore, junior, senior, or graduate year; renewable. *Eligibility Requirements:* Applicant must be enrolled or expecting to enroll full or part-time at a two-year or four-year institution or university; resident of Illinois and studying in Illinois. Available to U.S. citizens. Applicant or parent must meet one or more of the following requirements: general military experience; retired from active duty; disabled or killed as a result of military service; prisoner of war; or missing in action. *Application Requirements:* Application. **Deadline:** continuous.

Contact Ms. Tracy Mahan, Grants Section, Illinois Department of Veterans' Affairs, 833 South Spring Street, Springfield, IL 62794-9432. *Phone:* 217-782-3564. *Fax:* 217-782-4161.

Minority Teachers of Illinois Scholarship Program. Award for minority students planning to teach at an approved Illinois preschool, elementary, or secondary school. Deadline: May 1. Must be Illinois resident. *Academic/Career Areas:* Education; Special Education. *Award:* Forgivable loan for use in freshman, sophomore, junior, senior, graduate, or postgraduate years; renewable. *Award amount:* $4000–$5000. *Number of awards:* 450–550. *Eligibility Requirements:* Applicant must be American Indian/Alaska Native, Asian/Pacific Islander, Black (non-Hispanic), or Hispanic; enrolled or expecting to enroll full-time at a two-year or four-year institution or university; resident of Illinois and studying in Illinois. Applicant must have 2.5 GPA or higher. Available to U.S. and non-U.S. citizens. *Application Requirements:* Application. **Deadline:** May 1.

Contact David Barinholtz, Client Information, Illinois Student Assistance Commission (ISAC), 1755 Lake Cook Road, Deerfield, IL 60015-5209. *E-mail:* cssupport@isac.org. *Phone:* 847-948-8500 Ext. 2385. *Web site:* www.isac-online.org.

Veterans' Children Educational Opportunities. Award is provided to each child age 18 or younger of a veteran who died or became totally disabled as a result of service during World War I, World War II, Korean, or Vietnam War. Must be an Illinois resident and studying in Illinois. Death must be service-connected. Disability must be rated 100% for two or more years. *Award:* Grant for use in freshman year; not renewable. Award

Additional State Aid Programs

amount: up to $250. *Eligibility Requirements:* Applicant must be age 10-18; enrolled or expecting to enroll at an institution or university; resident of Illinois and studying in Illinois. Available to U.S. citizens. Applicant or parent must meet one or more of the following requirements: general military experience; retired from active duty; disabled or killed as a result of military service; prisoner of war; or missing in action. *Application Requirements:* Application. **Deadline:** June 30.

Contact Ms. Tracy Mahan, Grants Section, Illinois Department of Veterans' Affairs, 833 South Spring Street, Springfield, IL 62794-9432. *Phone:* 217-782-3564. *Fax:* 217-782-4161.

Indiana

Child of Disabled Veteran Grant or Purple Heart Recipient Grant. Free tuition at Indiana state-supported colleges or universities for children of disabled veterans or Purple Heart recipients. Must submit Form DD214 or service record. *Award:* Grant for use in freshman, sophomore, junior, or senior year; renewable. *Eligibility Requirements:* Applicant must be enrolled or expecting to enroll full or part-time at a two-year or four-year institution or university; resident of Indiana and studying in Indiana. Available to U.S. citizens. Applicant or parent must meet one or more of the following requirements: general military experience; retired from active duty; disabled or killed as a result of military service; prisoner of war; or missing in action. *Application Requirements:* Application. **Deadline:** continuous.

Contact Jon Brinkley, State Service Officer, Indiana Department of Veterans' Affairs, 302 West Washington Street, Room E-120, Indianapolis, IN 46204-2738. *E-mail:* jbrinkley@dva.state.in.us. *Phone:* 317-232-3910. *Fax:* 317-232-7721. *Web site:* www.ai.org/veteran/index.html.

Department of Veterans Affairs Free Tuition for Children of POW/MIA's in Vietnam. Renewable award for residents of Indiana who are the children of veterans declared missing in action or prisoner-of-war after January 1, 1960. Provides tuition at Indiana state-supported institutions for undergraduate study. *Award:* Grant for use in freshman, sophomore, junior, or senior year; renewable. *Eligibility Requirements:* Applicant must be enrolled or expecting to enroll at a two-year or four-year institution or university; resident of Indiana and studying in Indiana. Available to U.S. citizens. Applicant or parent must meet one or more of the following requirements: general military experience; retired from active duty; disabled or killed as a result of military service; prisoner of war; or missing in action. *Application Requirements:* Application. **Deadline:** continuous.

Contact Jon Brinkley, State Service Officer, Indiana Department of Veterans' Affairs, 302 West Washington Street, Room E-120, Indianapolis, IN 46204-2738. *E-mail:* jbrinkley@dva.state.in.us. *Phone:* 317-232-3910. *Fax:* 317-232-7721. *Web site:* www.ai.org/veteran/index.html.

Hoosier Scholar Award. The Hoosier Scholar Award is a $500 nonrenewable award. Based on the size of the senior class, one to three scholars are selected by the guidance counselor(s). The award is based on academic merit and may be used for any educational expense at an eligible Indiana institution of higher education. *Award:* Scholarship for use in freshman year; not renewable. *Award amount:* $500. *Number of awards:* 790–840. *Eligibility Requirements:* Applicant must be high school student; planning to enroll or expecting to enroll full-time at a two-year or four-year institution or university; resident of Indiana and studying in Indiana. Applicant must have 3.5 GPA or higher. Available to U.S. citizens. *Application Requirements:* **Deadline:** March 1.

Contact Ms. Ada Sparkman, Program Coordinator, State Student Assistance Commission of Indiana (SSACI), 150 West Market Street, Suite 500, Indianapolis, IN 46204-2805. *Phone:* 317-232-2350. *Fax:* 317-232-3260. *Web site:* www.ssaci.in.gov.

Indiana Freedom of Choice Grant. The Freedom of Choice Grant is a need-based, tuition-restricted program for students attending Indiana private institutions seeking a first undergraduate degree. It is awarded in addition to the Higher Education Award. Students (and parents of dependent students) who are U.S. citizens and Indiana residents must file the FAFSA yearly by the March 10 deadline. *Award:* Grant for use in freshman, sophomore, junior, or senior year; not renewable. *Award amount:* $200–$3906. *Number of awards:* 10,000–11,830. *Eligibility Requirements:* Applicant must be enrolled or expecting to enroll full-time at a four-year institution or university; resident of Indiana and studying in Indiana. Available to U.S. citizens. *Application Requirements:* Application, financial need analysis, FAFSA. **Deadline:** March 10.

Contact Grant Counselor, State Student Assistance Commission of Indiana (SSACI), 150 West Market Street, Suite 500, Indianapolis, IN 46204-2805. *E-mail:* grants@ssaci.state.in.us. *Phone:* 317-232-2350. *Fax:* 317-232-3260. *Web site:* www.ssaci.in.gov.

Indiana Higher Education Award. The Higher Education Award is a need-based, tuition-restricted program for students attending Indiana public, private or proprietary institutions seeking a first undergraduate degree. Students (and parents of dependent students) who are U.S. citizens and Indiana residents must file the FAFSA yearly by the March 10 deadline. *Award:* Grant for use in freshman, sophomore, junior, or senior year; not renewable. *Award amount:* $200–$4734. *Number of awards:* 38,000–43,660. *Eligibility Requirements:* Applicant must be enrolled or expecting to enroll full-time at a two-year, four-year, or technical institution or university; resident of Indiana and studying in Indiana.

Available to U.S. citizens. *Application Requirements*: Application, financial need analysis, FAFSA. **Deadline:** March 10.

Contact Grant Counselors, State Student Assistance Commission of Indiana (SSACI), 150 West Market Street, Suite 500, Indianapolis, IN 46204-2805. *E-mail:* grants@ssaci.state.in.us. *Phone:* 317-232-2350. *Fax:* 317-232-3260. *Web site:* www.ssaci.in.gov.

Indiana Minority Teacher and Special Education Services Scholarship Program. For Black or Hispanic students seeking teaching certification or for students seeking special education teaching certification or occupational or physical therapy certification. Must be a U.S. citizen and Indiana resident enrolled full-time at an eligible Indiana institution. Must teach in an Indiana-accredited elementary or secondary school after graduation. Contact institution for application and deadline. Minimum 2.0 GPA required. *Academic/Career Areas:* Education; Special Education; Therapy/Rehabilitation. *Award:* Scholarship for use in freshman, sophomore, junior, or senior year; not renewable. *Award amount:* $1000–$4000. *Number of awards:* 330–370. *Eligibility Requirements:* Applicant must be Black (non-Hispanic) or Hispanic; enrolled or expecting to enroll full-time at a four-year institution or university; resident of Indiana and studying in Indiana. Available to U.S. citizens. *Application Requirements:* Application, financial need analysis. **Deadline:** continuous.

Contact Ms. Yvonne Heflin, Director, Special Programs, State Student Assistance Commission of Indiana (SSACI), 150 West Market Street, Suite 500, Indianapolis, IN 46204-2805. *E-mail:* grants@ssaci.state.un.is. *Phone:* 317-232-2350. *Fax:* 317-232-3260. *Web site:* www.ssaci.in.gov.

Indiana National Guard Supplemental Grant. One-time award, which is a supplement to the Indiana Higher Education Grant program. Applicants must be members of the Indiana National Guard. All Guard paperwork must be completed prior to the start of each semester. The FAFSA must be received by March 10. Award covers tuition and fees at select public colleges. *Award:* Grant for use in freshman, sophomore, junior, or senior year; not renewable. *Award amount:* $200–$5314. *Number of awards:* 350–870. *Eligibility Requirements:* Applicant must be enrolled or expecting to enroll full or part-time at a two-year or four-year institution or university; resident of Indiana and studying in Indiana. Available to U.S. citizens. Applicant must have served in the Air Force National Guard or Army National Guard. *Application Requirements:* Application, financial need analysis. **Deadline:** March 10.

Contact Grants Counselor, State Student Assistance Commission of Indiana (SSACI), 150 West Market Street, Suite 500, Indianapolis, IN 46204-2805. *E-mail:* grants@ssaci.state.in.us. *Phone:* 317-232-2350. *Fax:* 317-232-2360. *Web site:* www.ssaci.in.gov.

Indiana Nursing Scholarship Fund. Need-based tuition funding for nursing students enrolled full- or part-time at an eligible Indiana institution. Must be an Indiana resident and have a minimum 2.0 GPA or meet the minimum requirements for the nursing program. Upon graduation, recipients must practice as a nurse in an Indiana health care setting for two years. *Academic/Career Areas:* Nursing. *Award:* Scholarship for use in freshman, sophomore, junior, or senior year; not renewable. *Award amount:* $200–$5000. *Number of awards:* 510–690. *Eligibility Requirements:* Applicant must be enrolled or expecting to enroll full or part-time at a two-year or four-year institution or university; resident of Indiana and studying in Indiana. Available to U.S. citizens. *Application Requirements:* Application, financial need analysis. **Deadline:** continuous.

Contact Ms. Yvonne Heflin, Director, Special Programs, State Student Assistance Commission of Indiana (SSACI), 150 West Market Street, Suite 500, Indianapolis, IN 46204-2805. *Phone:* 317-232-2350. *Fax:* 317-232-3260. *Web site:* www.ssaci.in.gov.

Indiana Wildlife Federation Scholarship. A $1000 scholarship will be awarded to an Indiana resident accepted for the study or already enrolled for the study of resource conservation or environmental education at the undergraduate level. For more details see Web site: www.indianawildlife.org. *Academic/Career Areas:* Natural Resources. *Award:* Scholarship for use in sophomore, junior, or senior year; not renewable. *Award amount:* $1000. *Eligibility Requirements:* Applicant must be enrolled or expecting to enroll at an institution or university and resident of Indiana. Available to U.S. citizens. *Application Requirements:* Application. **Deadline:** April 30.

Contact application available at Web site, Indiana Wildlife Federation Endowment. *Web site:* indianawildlife.org.

Part-time Grant Program. Program is designed to encourage part-time undergraduates to start and complete their associate or baccalaureate degrees or certificates by subsidizing part-time tuition costs. It is a term-based award that is based on need. State residency requirements must be met and a FAFSA must be filed. Eligibility is determined at the institutional level subject to approval by SSACI. *Award:* Grant for use in freshman, sophomore, junior, or senior year; not renewable. *Award amount:* $50–$4000. *Number of awards:* 4000–6366. *Eligibility Requirements:* Applicant must be enrolled or expecting to enroll part-time at a two-year, four-year, or technical institution or university; resident of Indiana and studying in Indiana. Available to U.S. citizens. *Application Requirements:* Application, financial need analysis. **Deadline:** continuous.

Additional State Aid Programs

Contact Grant Division, State Student Assistance Commission of Indiana (SSACI), 150 West Market Street, Suite 500, Indianapolis, IN 46204-2805. *E-mail:* grants@ssaci.state.in.us. *Phone:* 317-232-2350. *Fax:* 317-232-3260. *Web site:* www.ssaci.in.gov.

Police Corps Incentive Scholarship. Forgivable loans are available to highly qualified men and women entering the Police Corps. Up to $7500 a year can be used to cover the expenses of study toward a baccalaureate or graduate degree. For more details and an application see Web site: www.in.gov/cji.policecorps. *Academic/Career Areas:* Criminal Justice/Criminology. *Award:* Forgivable loan for use in freshman, sophomore, junior, senior, or graduate year; renewable. *Award amount:* up to $7500. *Eligibility Requirements:* Applicant must be enrolled or expecting to enroll at an institution or university. Available to U.S. citizens. *Application Requirements:* Application, driver's license, references, transcript. **Deadline:** continuous.

Contact application available at Web site, Indiana Police Corps. *Web site:* www.state.in.us/cji/policecorps.

Scholarships for Dependents of Fallen Officers. Scholarships are available to the dependents of officers who have been killed in the line of duty. For more details and an application see Web site: www.in.gov/cji/policecorps. **Award:** Scholarship for use in freshman, sophomore, junior, or senior year; renewable. *Award amount:* up to $30,000. *Eligibility Requirements:* Applicant must be enrolled or expecting to enroll at an institution or university. Applicant or parent of applicant must have employment or volunteer experience in police/firefighting. Available to U.S. citizens. *Application Requirements:* Application. **Deadline:** continuous.

Contact application available at Web site, Indiana Police Corps. *Web site:* www.state.in.us/cji/policecorps.

Twenty-first Century Scholars Award. Income-eligible 7th graders who enroll in the program fulfill a pledge of good citizenship and complete the Affirmation Form are guaranteed tuition for four years at any participating public institution. If the student attends a private institution, the state will award an amount comparable to that of a public institution. If the student attends a participating proprietary school, the state will award a tuition scholarship equal to that of Ivy Tech State College. FAFSA and affirmation form must be filed yearly by March 10. Applicant must be resident of Indiana. *Award:* Scholarship for use in freshman, sophomore, junior, or senior year; not renewable. *Award amount:* $1000–$5314. *Number of awards:* 2800–8100. *Eligibility Requirements:* Applicant must be enrolled or expecting to enroll full-time at a two-year, four-year, or technical institution or university; resident of Indiana and studying in Indiana. Applicant must have 2.5 GPA or higher. Available to U.S. citizens. *Application Requirements:* Application, financial need analysis, affirmation form. **Deadline:** March 10.

Contact Twenty-first Century Scholars Program Counselors, State Student Assistance Commission of Indiana (SSACI), 150 West Market Street, Suite 500, Indianapolis, IN 46204-2805. *Phone:* 317-233-2100. *Fax:* 317-232-3260. *Web site:* www.ssaci.in.gov.

Iowa

Governor Terry E. Branstad Iowa State Fair Scholarship. Up to four scholarships ranging from $500 to $1000 will be awarded to students graduating from an Iowa high school. Must actively participate at the Iowa State Fair. For more details see Web site: www.iowacollegeaid.org. **Award:** Scholarship for use in freshman year; not renewable. *Award amount:* $500–$1000. *Number of awards:* up to 4. *Eligibility Requirements:* Applicant must be high school student; planning to enroll or expecting to enroll at an institution or university; resident of Iowa and studying in Iowa. Available to U.S. citizens. *Application Requirements:* Application, essay, financial need analysis, references, transcript. **Deadline:** May 1.

Contact Julie Leeper, Director, State Student Aid Programs, Iowa College Student Aid Commission, 200 10th Street, 4th Floor, Des Moines, IA 50309-3609. *E-mail:* icsac@max.state.ia.us. *Phone:* 515-242-3370. *Fax:* 515-242-3388. *Web site:* www.iowacollegeaid.org.

Iowa Foster Child Grants. Grants renewable up to four years will be awarded to students graduating from an Iowa high school who are in Iowa foster care under the care and custody of the Iowa Department of Human Service. Must have a minimum GPA of 2.25 and have applied to an accredited Iowa college or university. For more details see Web site: www.iowacollegeaid.org. **Award:** Grant for use in freshman year; renewable. *Award amount:* $2000–$4200. *Eligibility Requirements:* Applicant must be high school student; planning to enroll or expecting to enroll at a two-year or four-year institution or university; resident of Iowa and studying in Iowa. Available to U.S. citizens. *Application Requirements:* Application. **Deadline:** April 15.

Contact Julie Leeper, Director, State Student Aid Programs, Iowa College Student Aid Commission, 200 10th Street, 4th Floor, Des Moines, IA 50309-3609. *E-mail:* icsac@max.state.ia.us. *Phone:* 515-242-3370. *Fax:* 515-242-3388. *Web site:* www.iowacollegeaid.org.

Iowa Grants. Statewide need-based program to assist high-need Iowa residents. Recipients must demonstrate a high level of financial need to receive awards ranging from $100 to $1,000. Awards are prorated for students enrolled for less than full-time. Awards must be used at

Financial Aid 101

Iowa postsecondary institutions. *Award:* Grant for use in freshman, sophomore, junior, or senior year; not renewable. *Award amount:* $100–$1000. *Eligibility Requirements:* Applicant must be enrolled or expecting to enroll full or part-time at a two-year, four-year, or technical institution or university; resident of Iowa and studying in Iowa. Available to U.S. citizens. *Application Requirements:* Application, financial need analysis. **Deadline:** continuous.

Contact Julie Leeper, Director, State Student Aid Programs, Iowa College Student Aid Commission, 200 10th Street, 4th Floor, Des Moines, IA 50309-3609. *E-mail:* icsac@max.state.ia.us. *Phone:* 515-242-3370. *Fax:* 515-242-3388. *Web site:* www.iowacollegeaid.org.

Iowa National Guard Education Assistance Program. Program provides postsecondary tuition assistance to members of Iowa National Guard Units. Must study at a postsecondary institution in Iowa. Contact for additional information. *Award:* Grant for use in freshman, sophomore, junior, or senior year; not renewable. *Award amount:* up to $1200. *Eligibility Requirements:* Applicant must be enrolled or expecting to enroll full or part-time at a two-year, four-year, or technical institution or university; resident of Iowa and studying in Iowa. Available to U.S. citizens. Applicant must have served in the Air Force National Guard or Army National Guard. *Application Requirements:* Application. **Deadline:** continuous.

Contact Julie Leeper, Director, State Student Aid Programs, Iowa College Student Aid Commission, 200 10th Street, 4th Floor, Des Moines, IA 50309-3609. *E-mail:* icsac@max.state.ia.us. *Phone:* 515-242-3370. *Fax:* 515-242-3388. *Web site:* www.iowacollegeaid.org.

Iowa Teacher Forgivable Loan Program. Forgivable loan assists students who will teach in Iowa secondary schools. Must be an Iowa resident attending an Iowa postsecondary institution. Contact for additional information. *Academic/Career Areas:* Education. *Award:* Forgivable loan for use in freshman, sophomore, junior, or senior year; not renewable. *Award amount:* $2686. *Eligibility Requirements:* Applicant must be enrolled or expecting to enroll full or part-time at a four-year institution or university; resident of Iowa and studying in Iowa. Applicant or parent of applicant must have employment or volunteer experience in teaching. Available to U.S. citizens. *Application Requirements:* Application, financial need analysis. **Deadline:** continuous.

Contact Brenda Easter, Special Programs Administrator, Iowa College Student Aid Commission, 200 10th Street, 4th Floor, Des Moines, IA 50309-3609. *E-mail:* icsac@max.state.ia.us. *Phone:* 515-242-3380. *Fax:* 515-242-3388. *Web site:* www.iowacollegeaid.org.

Iowa Tuition Grant Program. Program assists students who attend independent postsecondary institutions in Iowa. Iowa residents currently enrolled, or planning to enroll, for at least three semester hours at one of the eligible Iowa postsecondary institutions may apply. Awards currently range from $100 to $4000. Grants may not exceed the difference between independent college and university tuition and fees and the average tuition and fees at the three public Regent universities. *Award:* Grant for use in freshman, sophomore, junior, or senior year; not renewable. *Award amount:* $100–$4000. *Eligibility Requirements:* Applicant must be enrolled or expecting to enroll full or part-time at a two-year or four-year institution; resident of Iowa and studying in Iowa. Available to U.S. citizens. *Application Requirements:* Application, financial need analysis. **Deadline:** July 1.

Contact Julie Leeper, Director, State Student Aid Programs, Iowa College Student Aid Commission, 200 10th Street, 4th Floor, Des Moines, IA 50309-3609. *E-mail:* icsac@max.state.ia.us. *Phone:* 515-242-3370. *Fax:* 515-242-3388. *Web site:* www.iowacollegeaid.org.

Iowa Vocational Rehabilitation. Provides vocational rehabilitation services to individuals with disabilities who need these services in order to maintain, retain, or obtain employment compatible with their disabilities. Must be Iowa resident. *Award:* Grant for use in freshman, sophomore, junior, senior, graduate, or postgraduate years; renewable. *Award amount:* $500–$4000. *Number of awards:* up to 5000. *Eligibility Requirements:* Applicant must be enrolled or expecting to enroll full or part-time at a two-year, four-year, or technical institution or university and resident of Iowa. Applicant must be hearing impaired, learning disabled, physically disabled, or visually impaired. Available to U.S. and non-U.S. citizens. *Application Requirements:* Application, interview. **Deadline:** continuous.

Contact Ralph Childers, Policy and Workforce Initiatives Coordinator, Iowa Division of Vocational Rehabilitation Services, Division of Vocational Rehabilitation Services, 510 East 12th Street, Des Moines, IA 50319. *E-mail:* rchilders@dvrs.state.ia.us. *Phone:* 515-281-4151. *Fax:* 515-281-4703. *Web site:* www.dvrs.state.ia.us.

Iowa Vocational-Technical Tuition Grant Program. Program provides need-based financial assistance to Iowa residents enrolled in career education (vocational-technical), and career option programs at Iowa area community colleges. Grants range from $150 to $650, depending on the length of program, financial need, and available funds. *Award:* Grant for use in freshman or sophomore year; not renewable. *Award amount:* $150–$650. *Eligibility Requirements:* Applicant must be enrolled or expecting to enroll full or part-time at a technical institution; resident of Iowa and

Additional State Aid Programs

studying in Iowa. Available to U.S. citizens. *Application Requirements:* Application, financial need analysis. **Deadline:** July 1.

> **Contact** Julie Leeper, Director, State Student Aid Programs, Iowa College Student Aid Commission, 200 10th Street, 4th Floor, Des Moines, IA 50309-3609. *E-mail:* icsac@max.state.ia.us. *Phone:* 515-242-3370. *Fax:* 515-242-3388. *Web site:* www.iowacollegeaid.org.

State of Iowa Scholarship Program. Program provides recognition and financial honorarium to Iowa's academically talented high school seniors. Honorary scholarships are presented to all qualified candidates. Approximately 1700 top-ranking candidates are designated State of Iowa Scholars every March, from an applicant pool of nearly 5000 high school seniors. Must be used at an Iowa postsecondary institution. Minimum 3.5 GPA required. *Award:* Scholarship for use in freshman year; not renewable. *Award amount:* up to $400. *Number of awards:* up to 1700. *Eligibility Requirements:* Applicant must be high school student; planning to enroll or expecting to enroll full-time at a two-year, four-year, or technical institution or university; resident of Iowa and studying in Iowa. Applicant must have 3.5 GPA or higher. Available to U.S. citizens. *Application Requirements:* Application, test scores. **Deadline:** November 1.

> **Contact** Julie Leeper, Director, State Student Aid Programs, Iowa College Student Aid Commission, 200 10th Street, 4th Floor, Des Moines, IA 50309-3609. *E-mail:* icsac@max.state.ia.us. *Phone:* 515-242-3370. *Fax:* 515-242-3388. *Web site:* www.iowacollegeaid.org.

Kansas

Ethnic Minority Scholarship Program. This program is designed to assist financially needy, academically competitive students who are identified as members of the following ethnic/racial groups: African-American; American-Indian or Alaskan Native; Asian or Pacific Islander; or Hispanic. Must be resident of Kansas and attend college in Kansas. Application fee is $10. Deadline: May 1. Minimum 3.0 GPA required. Must be U.S. citizen. *Award:* Scholarship for use in freshman, sophomore, junior, or senior year; renewable. *Award amount:* $1850. *Number of awards:* 200–250. *Eligibility Requirements:* Applicant must be American Indian/Alaska Native, Asian/Pacific Islander, Black (non-Hispanic), or Hispanic; enrolled or expecting to enroll full-time at a two-year or four-year institution or university; resident of Kansas and studying in Kansas. Applicant must have 3.0 GPA or higher. Available to U.S. citizens. *Application Requirements:* Application, financial need analysis, test scores, transcript. *Fee:* $10. **Deadline:** May 1.

> **Contact** Diane Lindeman, Director of Student Financial Assistance, Kansas Board of Regents, 1000 Southwest Jackson, Suite 520, Topeka, KS 66612-1368. *E-mail:* dlindeman@ksbor.org. *Phone:* 785-296-3517. *Fax:* 785-296-0983. *Web site:* www.kansasregents.org.

Kansas Comprehensive Grant Program. Grants available for Kansas residents attending public or private baccalaureate colleges or universities in Kansas. Based on financial need. Must file Free Application for Federal Student Aid to apply. Renewable award based on continuing eligibility. Up to $3000 for undergraduate use. Deadline: April 1. *Award:* Grant for use in freshman, sophomore, junior, or senior year; renewable. *Award amount:* $1100–$3000. *Number of awards:* 7000–8200. *Eligibility Requirements:* Applicant must be enrolled or expecting to enroll full-time at a four-year institution or university; resident of Kansas and studying in Kansas. Available to U.S. citizens. *Application Requirements:* Financial need analysis. **Deadline:** April 1.

> **Contact** Diane Lindeman, Director of Student Financial Assistance, Kansas Board of Regents, 1000 Southwest Jackson, Suite 520, Topeka, KS 66612-1368. *E-mail:* dlindeman@ksbor.org. *Phone:* 785-296-3517. *Fax:* 785-296-0983. *Web site:* www.kansasregents.org.

Kansas Educational Benefits for Children of MIA, POW, and Deceased Veterans of the Vietnam War. Full-tuition scholarship awarded to students who are children of veterans. Must show proof of parent's status as missing in action, prisoner of war, or killed in action in the Vietnam War. Kansas residence required of veteran at time of entry to service. Must attend a state-supported postsecondary school. *Award:* Scholarship for use in freshman, sophomore, junior, or senior year; not renewable. *Eligibility Requirements:* Applicant must be enrolled or expecting to enroll at a two-year, four-year, or technical institution or university and studying in Kansas. Available to U.S. citizens. Applicant or parent must meet one or more of the following requirements: general military experience; retired from active duty; disabled or killed as a result of military service; prisoner of war; or missing in action. *Application Requirements:* Application, report of casualty, birth certificate, school acceptance letter. **Deadline:** continuous.

> Contact Dave DePue, Program Director, Kansas Commission on Veterans Affairs, 700 Southwest Jackson, Jayhawk Tower, #701, Topeka, KS 66603. *E-mail:* kcva004@ink.org. *Phone:* 785-291-3422. *Fax:* 785-296-1462. *Web site:* www.kcva.org.

Kansas National Guard Educational Assistance Award Program. Service scholarship for enlisted soldiers in the Kansas National Guard. Pays up to 100% of tuition and fees based on funding. Must attend a state-supported institution. Recipients will be required to serve in the KNG for four years after the last payment of state tuition assistance. Must not have over 15 years of service at time of application. Deadlines are January

Financial Aid 101

Appendix D

15 and August 20. Contact KNG Education Services Specialist for further information. Must be Kansas resident. *Award:* Scholarship for use in freshman, sophomore, junior, or senior year; not renewable. *Award amount:* $250–$3500. *Number of awards:* up to 400. *Eligibility Requirements:* Applicant must be enrolled or expecting to enroll full or part-time at a two-year, four-year, or technical institution or university; resident of Kansas and studying in Kansas. Available to U.S. citizens. Applicant must have served in the Air Force National Guard or Army National Guard. *Application Requirements:* Application.

Contact Steve Finch, Education Services Specialist, Kansas National Guard Educational Assistance Program, Attn: AGKS-DOP-ESO, The Adjutant General of Kansas, 2800 South West Topeka Boulevard, Topeka, KS 66611-1287. *E-mail:* steve.finch@ks.ngb.army.mil. *Phone:* 785-274-1060. *Fax:* 785-274-1617.

Kansas Nursing Service Scholarship Program. This program is designed to encourage Kansans to enroll in nursing programs and commit to practicing in Kansas. Recipients sign agreements to practice nursing at specific facilities one year for each year of support. Application fee is $10. Deadline: May 1. *Academic/Career Areas:* Nursing. *Award:* Forgivable loan for use in freshman, sophomore, junior, or senior year; renewable. *Award amount:* $2500–$3500. *Number of awards:* 100–200. *Eligibility Requirements:* Applicant must be enrolled or expecting to enroll full-time at a two-year or four-year institution or university; resident of Kansas and studying in Kansas. Available to U.S. citizens. *Application Requirements:* Application, financial need analysis, sponsor agreement form. *Fee:* $10. **Deadline:** May 1.

Contact Diane Lindeman, Director of Student Financial Assistance, Kansas Board of Regents, 1000 Southwest Jackson, Suite 520, Topeka, KS 66612-1368. *E-mail:* dlindeman@ksbor.org. *Phone:* 785-296-3517. *Fax:* 785-296-0983. *Web site:* www.kansasregents.org.

Kansas State Scholarship Program. The Kansas State Scholarship Program provides assistance to financially needy, academically outstanding students who attend Kansas postsecondary institutions. Must be Kansas resident. Minimum 3.0 GPA required for renewal. Application fee is $10. Deadline: May 1. *Award:* Scholarship for use in freshman, sophomore, junior, or senior year; renewable. *Award amount:* $1000. *Number of awards:* 1000–1500. *Eligibility Requirements:* Applicant must be enrolled or expecting to enroll full-time at a two-year or four-year institution or university; resident of Kansas and studying in Kansas. Applicant must have 3.0 GPA or higher. Available to U.S. citizens. *Application Requirements:* Application, financial need analysis, test scores, transcript. *Fee:* $10. **Deadline:** May 1.

Contact Diane Lindeman, Director of Student Financial Assistance, Kansas Board of Regents, 1000 Southwest Jackson, Suite 520, Topeka, KS 66612-1368. *E-mail:* dlindeman@ksbor.org. *Phone:* 785-296-3517. *Fax:* 785-296-0983. *Web site:* www.kansasregents.org.

Kansas Teacher Service Scholarship. Several scholarships for Kansas residents pursuing teaching careers. Must teach in a hard-to-fill discipline or underserved area of the state of Kansas for one year for each award received. Renewable award of $5000. Application fee is $10. Deadline: May 1. Must be U.S. citizen. *Academic/Career Areas:* Education. *Award:* Forgivable loan for use in freshman, sophomore, junior, or senior year; renewable. *Award amount:* $5000. *Number of awards:* 60–80. *Eligibility Requirements:* Applicant must be enrolled or expecting to enroll full-time at a two-year or four-year institution or university; resident of Kansas and studying in Kansas. Applicant must have 3.0 GPA or higher. Available to U.S. citizens. *Application Requirements:* Application, references, test scores, transcript. *Fee:* $10. **Deadline:** May 1.

Contact Diane Lindeman, Director of Student Financial Assistance, Kansas Board of Regents, 1000 Southwest Jackson, Suite 520, Topeka, KS 66612-1368. *E-mail:* dlindeman@ksbor.org. *Phone:* 785-296-3517. *Fax:* 785-296-0983. *Web site:* www.kansasregents.org.

Vocational Education Scholarship Program—Kansas. Several scholarships for Kansas residents who graduated from a Kansas accredited high school. Must be enrolled in a vocational education program at an eligible Kansas institution. Based on ability and aptitude. Deadline is July 1. Renewable award of $500. Must be U.S. citizen. *Academic/Career Areas:* Trade/Technical Specialties. *Award:* Scholarship for use in freshman or sophomore year; renewable. *Award amount:* $500. *Number of awards:* 100–200. *Eligibility Requirements:* Applicant must be enrolled or expecting to enroll full-time at a two-year or technical institution; resident of Kansas and studying in Kansas. Available to U.S. citizens. *Application Requirements:* Application, test scores. **Deadline:** July 1.

Contact Diane Lindeman, Director of Student Financial Assistance, Kansas Board of Regents, 1000 Southwest Jackson, Suite 520, Topeka, KS 66612-1368. *E-mail:* dlindeman@ksbor.org. *Phone:* 785-296-3517. *Fax:* 785-296-0983. *Web site:* www.kansasregents.org.

Kentucky

College Access Program (CAP) Grant. Award for U.S. citizen and Kentucky resident with no previous college degree. Provides $53 per semester hour for a minimum of six hours per semester. Applicants seeking degrees in religion are not eligible. Must demonstrate financial need and submit Free Application for Federal Student Aid. Priority deadline is March 15. *Award:* Grant for use in freshman, sophomore, junior, or senior year; not renewable. *Award amount:* up to $1260. *Number of awards:* 30,000–35,000. *Eligibility Requirements:* Applicant must be enrolled or expecting to enroll full or part-time at a two-year, four-year, or technical institution or university; resident of Kentucky and studying in Kentucky. Available to U.S. citizens. *Application Requirements:* Financial need analysis. **Deadline:** continuous.

Contact Allan Osborne, Program Coordinator, Kentucky Higher Education Assistance Authority (KHEAA), PO Box 798, Frankfort, KY 40602-0798. *E-mail:* aosborne@kheaa.com. *Phone:* 502-696-7394. *Fax:* 502-696-7373. *Web site:* www.kheaa.com.

Department of VA Tuition Waiver—KY KRS 164-515. Award provides exemption from tuition for spouse or child of permanently disabled member of the National Guard, war veteran, prisoner of war, or member of the Armed Services missing in action. Disability must have been sustained while in service; if not, time of service must have been during wartime. Applicant is eligible for 36 months of training, training until receipt of degree, or training until 23rd birthday, whichever comes first. There is no age limit for spouse. Must attend a school funded by the KY Dept. of Ed. *Award:* Scholarship for use in freshman, sophomore, junior, or senior year; renewable. *Eligibility Requirements:* Applicant must be enrolled or expecting to enroll at an institution or university; resident of Kentucky and studying in Kentucky. Available to U.S. citizens. Applicant or parent must meet one or more of the following requirements: general military experience; retired from active duty; disabled or killed as a result of military service; prisoner of war; or missing in action. *Application Requirements:* Application. **Deadline:** continuous.

Contact John Kramer, Coordinator, Kentucky Department of Veterans Affairs, 545 South Third Street, Room 123, Louisville, KY 40202-9095. *E-mail:* john.kramer@mail.state.ky.us. *Phone:* 502-595-4447. *Fax:* 502-595-4448. *Web site:* www.lrc.state.ky.us.

Department of Veterans Affairs Tuition Waiver—Kentucky KRS 164-505. Award provides exemption from matriculation or tuition fees for dependents, widows or widowers of members of the armed forces or members of the National Guard killed while in service or having died as a result of a service-connected disability incurred while serving during a wartime period. Veteran's home of record upon entry into the Armed Forces must have been KY. Applicant is eligible to get undergraduate/graduate degrees. Must attend a state-supported postsecondary institution. *Award:* Scholarship for use in freshman, sophomore, junior, senior, or graduate year; renewable. *Eligibility Requirements:* Applicant must be enrolled or expecting to enroll full or part-time at an institution or university; resident of Kentucky and studying in Kentucky. Available to U.S. citizens. Applicant or parent must meet one or more of the following requirements: general military experience; retired from active duty; disabled or killed as a result of military service; prisoner of war; or missing in action. *Application Requirements:* Application, proof of relationship. **Deadline:** continuous.

Contact John Kramer, Coordinator, Kentucky Department of Veterans Affairs, 545 South Third Street, Room 123, Louisville, KY 40202-9095. *E-mail:* john.kramer@mail.state.ky.us. *Phone:* 502-595-4447. *Fax:* 502-595-4448. *Web site:* www.lrc.state.ky.us.

Department of Veterans Affairs Tuition Waiver—KY 164-512. Award provides waiver of tuition for child of a veteran, regardless of age, who has acquired a disability as a direct result of service, as a member of the National Guard or Reserve Component. Must have served on state active duty, active duty for training, or inactive duty training or active duty with the Armed Forces. Veteran must have been a resident of Kentucky. *Award:* Scholarship for use in freshman, sophomore, junior, or senior year; renewable. *Eligibility Requirements:* Applicant must be enrolled or expecting to enroll full-time at a two-year, four-year, or technical institution or university; resident of Kentucky and studying in Kentucky. Available to U.S. citizens. Applicant or parent must meet one or more of the following requirements: general military experience; retired from active duty; disabled or killed as a result of military service; prisoner of war; or missing in action. *Application Requirements:* Application, proof of relationship. **Deadline:** continuous.

Contact John Kramer, Coordinator, Kentucky Department of Veterans Affairs, 545 South Third Street, Room 123, Louisville, KY 40202-9095. *E-mail:* john.kramer@mail.state.ky.us. *Phone:* 502-595-4447. *Fax:* 502-595-4448. *Web site:* www.lrc.state.ky.us.

Department of Veterans Affairs Tuition Waiver—KY KRS 164-507. Award provides exemption from matriculation or tuition fee for spouse or child of deceased veteran who served during wartime. Applicant is eligible for 36 months of training, or training until they receive a degree, or training until their 23rd birthday, whichever comes first. There is no age limit for spouse. Must attend a Kentucky state-supported university, junior college or vocational training institution. Must be a Kentucky resident. *Award:* Scholarship for use in freshman, sophomore, junior, or senior year; renewable. *Eligibility Requirements:* Applicant must be enrolled or expecting to enroll full or part-time at a two-year, four-year, or technical institution or university; resident of Kentucky and studying in Kentucky. Available to U.S. citizens. Applicant or parent must meet one or more of the following requirements: general military experience; retired from active duty; disabled or killed

Appendix D

as a result of military service; prisoner of war; or missing in action. *Application Requirements:* Application. **Deadline:** continuous.

Contact John Kramer, Coordinator, Kentucky Department of Veterans Affairs, 545 South Third Street, Room 123, Louisville, KY 40202-9095. *E-mail:* john.kramer@mail.state.ky.us. *Phone:* 502-595-4447. *Fax:* 502-595-4448. *Web site:* www.lrc.state.ky.us.

Environmental Protection Scholarships. Renewable awards for college juniors, seniors, and graduate students for tuition, fees, and room and board at a Kentucky state university. Awards of $3500 to $4500 per semester for up to four semesters. Minimum 2.5 GPA required. Must agree to work full-time for the Kentucky Natural Resources and Environmental Protection Cabinet upon graduation. Interview is required. *Academic/Career Areas:* Chemical Engineering; Civil Engineering; Earth Science; Materials Science, Engineering and Metallurgy. *Award:* Forgivable loan for use in junior, senior, or graduate year; renewable. *Award amount:* $3500–$4500. *Number of awards:* 3–5. *Eligibility Requirements:* Applicant must be enrolled or expecting to enroll full-time at a four-year institution or university and studying in Kentucky. Applicant must have 2.5 GPA or higher. Available to U.S. and non-U.S. citizens. *Application Requirements:* Application, essay, interview, references, transcript, non-U.S. citizens must have valid work permit. **Deadline:** February 15.

Contact James Kipp, Scholarship Program Coordinator, Kentucky Natural Resources and Environmental Protection Cabinet, 233 Mining/Mineral Resources Building, Lexington, KY 40506-0107. *E-mail:* kipp@uky.edu. *Phone:* 859-257-1299. *Fax:* 859-323-1049. *Web site:* www.uky.edu/waterresources.

Kentucky Department of Vocational Rehabilitation. Kentucky Department of Vocational Rehabilitation provides services necessary to secure employment. Eligible individual must possess physical or mental impairment that results in a substantial impediment to employment; benefit from vocational rehabilitation services in terms of an employment outcome; and require vocational rehabilitation services to prepare for, enter, or retain employment. *Award:* Grant for use in freshman, sophomore, junior, senior, graduate, or postgraduate years; renewable. *Eligibility Requirements:* Applicant must be enrolled or expecting to enroll full or part-time at a two-year, four-year, or technical institution or university and resident of Kentucky. Applicant must be learning disabled or physically disabled. *Application Requirements:* Application, financial need analysis, interview, test scores, transcript. **Deadline:** continuous.

Contact Ms. Marian Spencer, Program Administrator, Kentucky Department of Vocational Rehabilitation, 209 St. Clair Street, Frankfort, KY 40601. *E-mail:* marianu.spencer@mail.state.ky.us. *Phone:* 502-564-4440. *Fax:* 502-564-6745. *Web site:* www.ihdi.uky.edu/.

Kentucky Educational Excellence Scholarship (KEES). Annual award based on GPA and highest ACT or SAT score received by high school graduation. Awards are renewable if required cumulative GPA maintained at a Kentucky postsecondary school. Must be a Kentucky resident. *Award:* Scholarship for use in freshman, sophomore, junior, or senior year; renewable. *Award amount:* $125–$2000. *Number of awards:* 40,000–50,000. *Eligibility Requirements:* Applicant must be high school student; planning to enroll or expecting to enroll full or part-time at a two-year, four-year, or technical institution or university; resident of Kentucky and studying in Kentucky. Applicant must have 2.5 GPA or higher. Available to U.S. citizens. *Application Requirements:* Test scores, transcript.

Contact Tim Phelps, KEES Program Coordinator, Kentucky Higher Education Assistance Authority (KHEAA), PO Box 798, Frankfort, KY 40602-0798. *E-mail:* tphelps@kheaa.com. *Phone:* 502-696-7397. *Fax:* 502-696-7373. *Web site:* www.kheaa.com.

Kentucky National Guard Tuition Award Program. Tuition award available to all members of the Kentucky National Guard. Award is for study at state institutions. Members must be in good standing to be eligible for awards. Applications deadlines are April 1 and October 1. Completed AGO-18-7 required. Undergraduate study given priority. *Award:* Scholarship for use in freshman, sophomore, junior, or senior year; not renewable. *Eligibility Requirements:* Applicant must be enrolled or expecting to enroll full or part-time at a two-year, four-year, or technical institution or university and studying in Kentucky. Available to U.S. citizens. Applicant must have served in the Air Force National Guard or Army National Guard. *Application Requirements:* AGO-18-7.

Contact Annette Michelle Kelley, Administration Specialist, Kentucky National Guard, Education Office, 100 Minuteman Parkway, Frankfort, KY 40601. *Phone:* 502-607-1039. *Fax:* 502-607-1264. *Web site:* www.dma.state.ky.us.

Kentucky Teacher Scholarship Program. Award for Kentucky resident attending Kentucky institutions and pursuing initial teacher certification. Must teach one semester for each semester of award received. In critical shortage areas, must teach one semester for every two semesters of award received. Repayment obligation if teaching requirement not met. Submit Free Application for Federal Student Aid and Teacher Scholarship Application by May 1. *Academic/Career Areas:* Education; Special Education. *Award:* Forgivable loan for use in freshman, sophomore, junior, senior, or graduate year; not renewable. *Award amount:* $100–$5000. *Number of awards:* 600–700. *Eligibility Require-*

Additional State Aid Programs

ments: Applicant must be enrolled or expecting to enroll full-time at a two-year or four-year institution or university; resident of Kentucky and studying in Kentucky. Available to U.S. citizens. *Application Requirements:* Application, financial need analysis. **Deadline:** May 1.

> **Contact** Pam Polly, Program Coordinator, Kentucky Higher Education Assistance Authority (KHEAA), PO Box 798, Frankfort, KY 40602-0798. *E-mail:* ppolly@kheaa.com. *Phone:* 502-696-7392. *Fax:* 502-696-7373. *Web site:* www.kheaa.com.

Kentucky Transportation Cabinet Civil Engineering Scholarship Program. Scholarships are available to eligible applicants at 4 ABET-accredited universities in Kentucky. Our mission is to continually pursue statewide recruitment and retention of bright, motivated civil engineers in the Kentucky Transportation Cabinet. *Academic/Career Areas:* Civil Engineering. *Award:* Scholarship for use in freshman, sophomore, junior, senior, or graduate year; renewable. *Award amount:* $7200–$8000. *Number of awards:* 15–20. *Eligibility Requirements:* Applicant must be enrolled or expecting to enroll full-time at an institution or university; resident of Kentucky and studying in Kentucky. Available to U.S. citizens. *Application Requirements:* Application, essay, interview, references, test scores, transcript. **Deadline:** March 1.

> **Contact** Jo Anne Tingle, Scholarship Program Manager, Kentucky Transportation Cabinet, Attn: Scholarship Coordinator, State Office Building, 501 High Street, Room 913, Frankfort, KY 40622. *E-mail:* jo.tingle@mail.state.ky.us. *Phone:* 877-273-5222. *Fax:* 502-564-6683. *Web site:* www.kytc.state.ky.us/person/ScholarshipProgram.htm.

Kentucky Tuition Grant (KTG). Available to Kentucky residents who are full-time undergraduates at an independent college within the state. Must not be enrolled in a religion program. Based on financial need. Submit Free Application for Federal Student Aid. Priority deadline is March 15. *Award:* Grant for use in freshman, sophomore, junior, or senior year; not renewable. *Award amount:* $50–$1800. *Number of awards:* 9000–10,000. *Eligibility Requirements:* Applicant must be enrolled or expecting to enroll full-time at a two-year or four-year institution or university; resident of Kentucky and studying in Kentucky. Available to U.S. citizens. *Application Requirements:* Financial need analysis. **Deadline:** continuous.

> **Contact** Allan Osborne, Program Coordinator, Kentucky Higher Education Assistance Authority (KHEAA), PO Box 798, Frankfort, KY 40602-0798. *E-mail:* aosborne@kheaa.com. *Phone:* 502-696-7394. *Fax:* 502-696-7373. *Web site:* www.kheaa.com.

Related Service Occupational Therapy/Physical Therapy Scholarship. Must be a Kentucky resident who is seeking related service licensure and enrolled or accepted for enrollment at a participating institution as a full-time student. Recipients who do not fulfill requirements must repay the scholarship with interest. Application deadline is in the spring. *Academic/Career Areas:* Therapy/Rehabilitation. *Award:* Scholarship for use in freshman, sophomore, junior, senior, or graduate year. *Award amount:* up to $6250. *Eligibility Requirements:* Applicant must be enrolled or expecting to enroll full-time at an institution or university; resident of Kentucky and studying in Kentucky. Available to U.S. citizens. *Application Requirements:* Application.

> **Contact** Mike Miller, Kentucky Department of Veterans Affairs, 500 Mero Street, Capital Plaza Tower, Frankfort, KY 40601. *Phone:* 502-564-4970. *Web site:* www.lrc.state.ky.us.

Louisiana

Leveraging Educational Assistance Program (LEAP). LEAP program provides federal and state funds to provide need-based grants to academically qualified students. Individual award determined by Financial Aid Office and governed by number of applicants and availability of funds. File Free Application for Federal Student aid by school deadline to apply each year. For Louisiana students attending Louisiana postsecondary institutions. *Award:* Grant for use in freshman, sophomore, junior, or senior year; not renewable. *Award amount:* $200–$2000. *Number of awards:* 3000. *Eligibility Requirements:* Applicant must be enrolled or expecting to enroll full or part-time at a two-year, four-year, or technical institution or university; resident of Louisiana and studying in Louisiana. Available to U.S. citizens. *Application Requirements:* Application, financial need analysis.

> **Contact** Public Information, Louisiana Office of Student Financial Assistance, PO Box 91202, Baton Rouge, LA 70821-9202. *E-mail:* custserv@osfa.state.la.us. *Phone:* 800-259-5626 Ext. 1012. *Web site:* www.osfa.state.la.us.

Louisiana Department of Veterans Affairs State Aid Program. Tuition exemption at any state-supported college, university or technical institute for children of veterans that are rated 90% or above service-connected disabled by the U.S. Department of Veterans Affairs and surviving spouse and children of veterans that died on active duty, in line of duty or where death was the result of a disability incurred in or aggravated by military service. Applicant must be between the ages of 18-25. For residents of Louisiana that are attending a Louisiana institution. *Award:* Grant for use in freshman, sophomore, junior, senior, graduate, or postgraduate years; renewable. *Eligibility Requirements:* Applicant must be age 18-25; enrolled or expecting to enroll full-time at a two-year, four-year, or technical institution or university; resident of Louisiana and studying in Louisiana. Available to U.S. citizens.

Applicant or parent must meet one or more of the following requirements: general military experience; retired from active duty; disabled or killed as a result of military service; prisoner of war; or missing in action. *Application Requirements:* Application. **Deadline:** continuous.

Contact Richard Blackwell, Veterans Affairs Regional Manager, Louisiana Department of Veteran Affairs, PO Box 94095, Capitol Station, Baton Rouge, LA 70804-4095. *E-mail:* rblackwell@vetaffairs.com. *Phone:* 225-922-0500 Ext. 203. *Fax:* 225-922-0511.

Louisiana National Guard State Tuition Exemption Program. Renewable award for college undergraduates to receive tuition exemption upon satisfactory performance in the Louisiana National Guard. Must attend a state-funded institution in Louisiana. Must be a resident and registered voter in Louisiana. Must meet the academic and residency requirements of the university attended. Must provide documentation of Louisiana National Guard enlistment. The exemption can be used for up to 15 semesters. Minimum 2.5 GPA required. *Award:* Scholarship for use in freshman, sophomore, junior, or senior year; renewable. *Eligibility Requirements:* Applicant must be enrolled or expecting to enroll full- or part-time at a two-year, four-year, or technical institution or university; resident of Louisiana and studying in Louisiana. Applicant must have 2.5 GPA or higher. Available to U.S. citizens. Applicant must have served in the Air Force National Guard or Army National Guard. *Application Requirements:* **Deadline:** continuous.

Contact Maj. Jona M. Hughes, Education Services Officers, Louisiana National Guard—State of Louisiana, Military Department, Building 35, Jackson Barracks, DHR-MD, New Orleans, LA 70146-0330. *E-mail:* hughesj@la-arng.ngb.army.mil. *Phone:* 504-278-8531 Ext. 8304. *Fax:* 504-278-8025. *Web site:* www.la.ngb.army.mil.

Rockefeller State Wildlife Scholarship. For Louisiana residents attending a public college within the state studying wildlife, forestry, or marine sciences full-time. Renewable up to five years as an undergraduate and two years as a graduate. Must have at least a 2.5 GPA and have taken the ACT or SAT. *Academic/Career Areas:* Animal/Veterinary Sciences; Applied Sciences; Natural Resources. *Award:* Scholarship for use in freshman, sophomore, junior, senior, or graduate year; renewable. *Award amount:* $1000. *Number of awards:* 60. *Eligibility Requirements:* Applicant must be enrolled or expecting to enroll full-time at a four-year institution or university; resident of Louisiana and studying in Louisiana. Applicant must have 2.5 GPA or higher. Available to U.S. citizens. *Application Requirements:* Application, test scores, transcript. **Deadline:** July 1.

Contact Public Information, Louisiana Office of Student Financial Assistance, PO Box 91202, Baton Rouge, LA 70821-9202. *E-mail:* custserv@osfa.state.la.us. *Phone:* 800-259-5626 Ext. 1012. *Fax:* 225-922-0790. *Web site:* www.osfa.state.la.us.

TOPS Alternate Performance Award. Program awards an amount equal to tuition plus a $400 annual stipend to students attending a Louisiana public institution, or an amount equal to the weighted average public tuition plus a $400 annual stipend to students attending a LAICU private institution. Must have a minimum high school GPA of 3.0 based on TOPS core curriculum, ACT score of 24, completion of 10 honors courses graded on a 5.0 scale, and completion of a 16.5 unit core curriculum. Must be a resident of Louisiana. *Award:* Scholarship for use in freshman, sophomore, junior, or senior year; renewable. *Eligibility Requirements:* Applicant must be high school student; planning to enroll or expecting to enroll full-time at a two-year, four-year, or technical institution or university; resident of Louisiana and studying in Louisiana. Applicant must have 3.0 GPA or higher. Available to U.S. citizens. *Application Requirements:* Application, test scores. **Deadline:** July 1.

Contact Public Information Officer, Louisiana Office of Student Financial Assistance, PO Box 91202, Baton Rouge, LA 70821-9202. *E-mail:* custserv@osfa.state.la.us. *Phone:* 800-259-5626 Ext. 1012. *Fax:* 225-922-0790. *Web site:* www.osfa.state.la.us.

TOPS Honors Award. Program awards an amount equal to tuition plus an $800 per year stipend to students attending a Louisiana public institution, or an amount equal to the weighted average public tuition plus an $800 per year stipend to students attending a LAICU private institution. Must have a minimum high school GPA of 3.5 based on TOPS core curriculum, ACT score of 27, and complete a 16.5 unit core curriculum. Must be resident of Louisiana. *Award:* Scholarship for use in freshman, sophomore, junior, or senior year; renewable. *Award amount:* $1294–$3894. *Eligibility Requirements:* Applicant must be high school student; planning to enroll or expecting to enroll full-time at a two-year, four-year, or technical institution or university; resident of Louisiana and studying in Louisiana. Applicant must have 3.5 GPA or higher. Available to U.S. citizens. *Application Requirements:* Application, test scores. **Deadline:** July 1.

Contact Public Information, Louisiana Office of Student Financial Assistance, PO Box 91202, Baton Rouge, LA 70821-9202. *E-mail:* custserv@osfa.state.la.us. *Phone:* 800-259-5626 Ext. 1012. *Fax:* 225-922-0790. *Web site:* www.osfa.state.la.us.

TOPS Opportunity Award. Program awards an amount equal to tuition to students attending a Louisiana public institution, or an amount equal to the weighted average public tuition to students attending a

LAICU private institution. Must have a minimum high school GPA of 2.5 based on the TOPS core curriculum, the prior year's state average ACT score, and complete a 16.5 unit core curriculum. Must be a Louisiana resident. *Award:* Scholarship for use in freshman, sophomore, junior, or senior year; renewable. *Award amount:* $494–$3094. *Eligibility Requirements:* Applicant must be high school student; planning to enroll or expecting to enroll full-time at a two-year, four-year, or technical institution or university; resident of Louisiana and studying in Louisiana. Applicant must have 2.5 GPA or higher. Available to U.S. citizens. *Application Requirements:* Application, test scores. **Deadline:** July 1.

> **Contact** Public Information, Louisiana Office of Student Financial Assistance, PO Box 91202, Baton Rouge, LA 70821-9202. *E-mail:* custserv@osfa.state.la.us. *Phone:* 800-259-5626 Ext. 1012. *Fax:* 225-922-0790. *Web site:* www.osfa.state.la.us.

TOPS Performance Award. Program awards an amount equal to tuition plus a $400 annual stipend to students attending a Louisiana public institution, or an amount equal to the weighted average public tuition plus a $400 annual stipend to students attending a LAICU private institution. Must have a minimum high school GPA of 3.5 based on the TOPS core curriculum, an ACT score of 23 and completion of a 16.5 unit core curriculum. Must be a Louisiana resident. *Award:* Scholarship for use in freshman, sophomore, junior, or senior year; renewable. *Award amount:* $894–$3494. *Eligibility Requirements:* Applicant must be high school student; planning to enroll or expecting to enroll full-time at a two-year, four-year, or technical institution or university; resident of Louisiana and studying in Louisiana. Applicant must have 3.5 GPA or higher. Available to U.S. citizens. *Application Requirements:* Application, test scores. **Deadline:** July 1.

> **Contact** Public Information, Louisiana Office of Student Financial Assistance, PO Box 91202, Baton Rouge, LA 70821-9202. *E-mail:* custserv@osfa.state.la.us. *Phone:* 800-259-5626 Ext. 1012. *Fax:* 225-922-0790. *Web site:* www.osfa.state.la.us.

TOPS Tech Award. Program awards an amount equal to tuition for up to two years of technical training at a Louisiana postsecondary institution that offers a vocational or technical education certificate or diploma program, or a non-academic degree program. Must have a 2.5 high school GPA based on TOPS Tech core curriculum, an ACT score of 17 and complete the TOPS-Tech core curriculum. Must be a Louisiana resident. *Award:* Scholarship for use in freshman or sophomore year; renewable. *Award amount:* $494. *Eligibility Requirements:* Applicant must be high school student; planning to enroll or expecting to enroll full-time at a technical institution; resident of Louisiana and studying in Louisiana. Applicant must have 2.5 GPA or higher. Available to U.S. citizens. *Application Requirements:* Application, test scores. **Deadline:** July 1.

> **Contact** Public Information, Louisiana Office of Student Financial Assistance, PO Box 91202, Baton Rouge, LA 70821-9202. *E-mail:* custserv@osfa.state.la.us. *Phone:* 800-259-5626 Ext. 1012. *Fax:* 225-922-0790. *Web site:* www.osfa.state.la.us.

Maine

Educators for Maine Program. Loans for residents of Maine who are high school seniors, college students, or college graduates with a minimum 3.0 GPA, studying or preparing to study teacher education. Loan is forgivable if student teaches in Maine upon graduation. Awards are based on merit. *Academic/Career Areas:* Education. *Award:* Forgivable loan for use in freshman, sophomore, junior, senior, or graduate year; not renewable. *Award amount:* $1500–$3000. *Eligibility Requirements:* Applicant must be enrolled or expecting to enroll full-time at a two-year or four-year institution or university and resident of Maine. Applicant must have 3.0 GPA or higher. Available to U.S. citizens. *Application Requirements:* Application, essay, test scores, transcript. **Deadline:** April 1.

> **Contact** Trisha Malloy, Program Officer, Finance Authority of Maine, 5 Community Drive, Augusta, ME 04332-0949. *E-mail:* trisha@famemaine.com. *Phone:* 800-228-3734. *Fax:* 207-623-0095. *Web site:* www.famemaine.com.

Maine State Grant. Scholarships for residents of Maine attending an eligible school, full time, in Connecticut, Maine, Massachusetts, New Hampshire, Pennsylvania, Rhode Island, Washington, D.C., or Vermont. Award based on need. Must apply annually. Complete Free Application for Federal Student Aid to apply. One-time award of $500-$1250 for undergraduate study. *Award:* Grant for use in freshman, sophomore, junior, or senior year; not renewable. *Award amount:* $500–$1250. *Number of awards:* 8900–12,500. *Eligibility Requirements:* Applicant must be enrolled or expecting to enroll full-time at a two-year, four-year, or technical institution or university; resident of Maine and studying in Connecticut, District of Columbia, Maine, Massachusetts, New Hampshire, Pennsylvania, Rhode Island, or Vermont. *Application Requirements:* Application, financial need analysis, FAFSA. **Deadline:** May 1.

> **Contact** Claude Roy, Program Officer, Finance Authority of Maine, 5 Community Drive, Augusta, ME 04332-0949. *E-mail:* claude@famemaine.com. *Phone:* 800-228-3734. *Fax:* 207-623-0095. *Web site:* www.famemaine.com.

Quality Child Care Program Education Scholarship Program. Open to residents of Maine who are taking a minimum of one childhood education course or are pursuing a child development associate certificate, associate's degree, baccalaureate degree or post-baccalaureate teacher certification in child care-related fields. Scholarships of up to $500 per course or $2,000 per year available. See Web site for information (www.famemaine.com). *Academic/Career Areas:* Education. *Award:* Scholarship for use in sophomore, junior, senior, or graduate year; not renewable. *Award amount:* $500–$2000. *Eligibility Requirements:* Applicant must be enrolled or expecting to enroll at a two-year or four-year institution or university and resident of Maine. Available to U.S. citizens. *Application Requirements:* Application, financial need analysis. **Deadline:** continuous.

Contact Trisha Malloy, Program Officer, Finance Authority of Maine, 5 Community Drive, Augusta, ME 04332-0949. *E-mail:* trisha@famemaine.com. *Phone:* 800-228-3734. *Fax:* 207-623-0095. *Web site:* www.famemaine.com.

Tuition Waiver Programs. Provides tuition waivers for children and spouses of EMS personnel, firefighters, and law enforcement officers who have been killed in the line of duty and for students who were foster children under the custody of the Department of Human Services when they graduated from high school. Waivers valid at the University of Maine System, the Maine Technical College System, and Maine Maritime Academy. *Award:* Grant for use in freshman, sophomore, junior, or senior year; not renewable. *Eligibility Requirements:* Applicant must be enrolled or expecting to enroll at an institution or university; resident of Maine and studying in Maine. Applicant or parent of applicant must have employment or volunteer experience in designated career field or police/firefighting. Available to U.S. citizens. *Application Requirements:* Application. **Deadline:** continuous.

Contact Trisha Malloy, Program Officer, Finance Authority of Maine, 5 Community Drive, Augusta, ME 04332. *E-mail:* trisha@famemaine.com. *Phone:* 207-623-3263. *Fax:* 207-623-0095. *Web site:* www.famemaine.com.

Veterans Dependents Educational Benefits-Maine. Tuition waiver award for dependents or spouses of veterans who were prisoner-of-war, missing in action, or permanently disabled as a result of service. Veteran must have been Maine resident at service entry for five years preceding application. For use at Maine University system, technical colleges and Maine Maritime. Must be high school graduate. Must submit birth certificate and proof of VA disability of veteran. Award renewable for eight semesters for those under 22 years of age. *Award:* Scholarship for use in freshman, sophomore, junior, or senior year; renewable. *Eligibility Requirements:* Applicant must be age 21 or under; enrolled or expecting to enroll full or part-time at a technical institution or university; resident of Maine and studying in Maine. Available to U.S. citizens. Applicant or parent must meet one or more of the following requirements: general military experience; retired from active duty; disabled or killed as a result of military service; prisoner of war; or missing in action. *Application Requirements:* Application. **Deadline:** continuous.

Contact Roland Lapointe, Director, Maine Bureau of Veterans Services, State House Station 117, Augusta, ME 04333-0117. *E-mail:* mvs@me.ngb.army.mil. *Phone:* 207-626-4464. *Fax:* 207-626-4471. *Web site:* www.state.me.us.

Maryland

Child Care Provider Program-Maryland. Forgivable loan provides assistance for Maryland undergraduates attending a Maryland institution and pursuing studies in a child development program or an early childhood education program. Must serve as a professional day care provider in Maryland for one year for each year award received. Must maintain minimum 2.0 GPA. Contact for further information. *Academic/Career Areas:* Education. *Award:* Forgivable loan for use in freshman, sophomore, junior, or senior year; renewable. *Award amount:* $500–$2000. *Number of awards:* 100–150. *Eligibility Requirements:* Applicant must be enrolled or expecting to enroll full or part-time at a two-year or four-year institution or university; resident of Maryland and studying in Maryland. Available to U.S. citizens. *Application Requirements:* Application, transcript. **Deadline:** June 15.

Contact Margaret Crutchley, Office of Student Financial Assistance, Maryland Higher Education Commission, 839 Bestgate Road, Suite 400, Annapolis, MD 21401-3013. *E-mail:* ofsamail@mhec.state.md.us. *Phone:* 410-260-4545. *Fax:* 410-260-3203. *Web site:* www.mhec.state.md.us.

Delegate Scholarship Program-Maryland. Delegate scholarships help Maryland residents attending Maryland degree-granting institutions, certain career schools, or nursing diploma schools. May attend out-of-state institution if Maryland Higher Education Commission deems major to be unique and not offered at a Maryland institution. Free Application for Federal Student Aid may be required. Students interested in this program should apply by contacting their legislative district delegate. *Award:* Scholarship for use in freshman, sophomore, junior, senior, or graduate year; not renewable. *Award amount:* $200–$12,981. *Number of awards:* up to 3500. *Eligibility Requirements:* Applicant must be enrolled or expecting to enroll full or part-time at a two-year, four-year, or technical institution or university; resident of Maryland and studying in Maryland. Available to U.S. citizens. *Application Requirements:* Application, financial need analysis. **Deadline:** continuous.

Contact Barbara Fantom, Office of Student Financial Assistance, Maryland Higher Education Commission, 839 Bestgate Road, Suite 400,

Annapolis, MD 21401-3013. *E-mail:* osfamail@mhec.state.md.us. *Phone:* 410-260-4547. *Fax:* 410-260-3200. *Web site:* www.mhec.state.md.us.

Developmental Disabilities and Mental Health Workforce Tuition Assistance Program. Provides tuition assistance to students who are service employees that provide direct support or care to individuals with developmental disabilities or mental disorders. Must be a Maryland resident attending a Maryland college. Minimum 2.0 GPA. *Academic/Career Areas:* Health and Medical Sciences; Nursing; Social Services; Special Education; Therapy/Rehabilitation. *Award:* Forgivable loan for use in freshman, sophomore, junior, senior, or graduate year; renewable. *Award amount:* $500–$3000. *Number of awards:* 300–400. *Eligibility Requirements:* Applicant must be enrolled or expecting to enroll full or part-time at a two-year or four-year institution or university; resident of Maryland and studying in Maryland. Applicant or parent of applicant must have employment or volunteer experience in designated career field. Available to U.S. citizens. *Application Requirements:* Application, transcript. **Deadline:** July 1.

Contact Gerrie Rogers, Office of Student Financial Assistance, Maryland Higher Education Commission, 839 Bestgate Road, Suite 400, Annapolis, MD 21401. *E-mail:* osfamail@mhec.state.md.us. *Phone:* 410-260-4574. *Fax:* 410-260-3203. *Web site:* www.mhec.state.md.us.

Distinguished Scholar Award—Maryland. Renewable award for Maryland students enrolled full-time at Maryland institutions. National Merit Scholar Finalists automatically offered award. Others may qualify for the award in satisfying criteria of a minimum 3.7 GPA or in combination with high test scores, or for Talent in Arts competition in categories of music, drama, dance, or visual arts. Must maintain annual 3.0 GPA in college for award to be renewed. Contact for further details. *Award:* Scholarship for use in freshman, sophomore, junior, or senior year; renewable. *Award amount:* up to $3000. *Number of awards:* up to 2000. *Eligibility Requirements:* Applicant must be high school student; planning to enroll or expecting to enroll full-time at a two-year or four-year institution or university; resident of Maryland and studying in Maryland. Available to U.S. citizens. *Application Requirements:* Application, test scores, transcript. **Deadline:** March 1.

Contact Monica Tipton, Office of Student Financial Assistance, Maryland Higher Education Commission, 839 Bestgate Road, Suite 400, Annapolis, MD 21401-3013. *E-mail:* ofsamail@mhec.state.md.us. *Phone:* 410-260-4568. *Fax:* 410-260-3200. *Web site:* www.mhec.state.md.us.

Distinguished Scholar-Teacher Education Awards. Up to $3,000 award for Maryland high school seniors who have received the Distinguished Scholar Award. Recipient must enroll as a full-time undergraduate in a Maryland institution and pursue a program of study leading to a Maryland teaching certificate. Must maintain annual 3.0 GPA for renewal. Must teach in a Maryland public school one year for each year award is received. *Academic/Career Areas:* Education. *Award:* Forgivable loan for use in freshman, sophomore, junior, or senior year; renewable. *Award amount:* up to $3000. *Number of awards:* 20–80. *Eligibility Requirements:* Applicant must be high school student; planning to enroll or expecting to enroll full-time at a two-year or four-year institution or university; resident of Maryland and studying in Maryland. Applicant must have 3.0 GPA or higher. Available to U.S. citizens. *Application Requirements:* Application, test scores, transcript, must be recipient of the Distinguished Scholar Award. **Deadline:** continuous.

Contact Monica Tipton, Office of Student Financial Assistance, Maryland Higher Education Commission, 839 Bestgate Road, Suite 400, Annapolis, MD 21401-3013. *E-mail:* ofsamail@mhec.state.md.us. *Phone:* 410-260-4568. *Fax:* 410-260-3200. *Web site:* www.mhec.state.md.us.

Educational Assistance Grants—Maryland. Award for Maryland residents accepted or enrolled in a full-time undergraduate degree or certificate program at a Maryland institution or hospital nursing school. Must submit financial aid form by March 1. Must earn 2.0 GPA in college to maintain award. *Award:* Grant for use in freshman, sophomore, junior, or senior year; renewable. *Award amount:* $400–$2700. *Number of awards:* 11,000–20,000. *Eligibility Requirements:* Applicant must be enrolled or expecting to enroll full-time at a two-year or four-year institution or university; resident of Maryland and studying in Maryland. Available to U.S. citizens. *Application Requirements:* Application, financial need analysis. **Deadline:** March 1.

Contact Barbara Fantom, Office of Student Financial Assistance, Maryland Higher Education Commission, 839 Bestgate Road, Suite 400, Annapolis, MD 21401-3013. *E-mail:* osfamail@mhec.state.md.us. *Phone:* 410-260-4547. *Fax:* 410-260-3200. *Web site:* www.mhec.state.md.us.

Edward T. Conroy Memorial Scholarship Program. Scholarship for dependents of deceased or 100% disabled U.S. Armed Forces personnel, the son, daughter, or surviving spouse of a victim of the September 11, 2001, terrorist attacks who died as a result of the attacks on the World Trade Center in New York City, the attack on the Pentagon in Virginia, or the crash of United Airlines Flight 93 in Pennsylvania; a POW/MIA of the Vietnam Conflict or his/her son or daughter; the son, daughter or surviving spouse (who has not remarried), of a state or local public safety employee or volunteer who died in the line of duty; or a state or local public safety employee or volunteer who was 100% disabled in the line of duty. Must be Maryland resident at time of disability. Submit applicable VA certification. Must be at least 16 years of age and attend Maryland institution. *Award:* Scholarship for use in freshman, sophomore, junior, senior, or graduate year; renewable. *Award amount:* up to $12,981. *Number of awards:* up to 70. *Eligibility Requirements:* Applicant must be age 16-24; enrolled or expecting to enroll full or part-time at a two-year or four-year institution or university; resident of Maryland and studying in Maryland. Available to U.S. citizens. *Application Requirements:* Application, birth and death certificate, and disability papers. **Deadline:** July 30.

Contact Margaret Crutchley, Office of Student Financial Assistance, Maryland Higher Education Commission, 839 Bestgate Road, Suite 400, Annapolis, MD 21401-3013. *E-mail:* osfamail@mhec.state.md.us. *Phone:* 410-260-4545. *Fax:* 410-260-3203. *Web site:* www.mhec.state.md.us.

Firefighter, Ambulance, and Rescue Squad Member Tuition Reimbursement Program—Maryland. Award intended to reimburse members of rescue organizations serving Maryland communities for tuition costs of course work towards a degree or certificate in fire service or medical technology. Must attend a two- or four-year school in Maryland. Minimum 2.0 GPA. *Academic/Career Areas:* Fire Sciences; Health and Medical Sciences; Trade/Technical Specialties. *Award:* Scholarship for use in freshman, sophomore, junior, or senior year; not renewable. *Award amount:* $200–$4000. *Number of awards:* 100–300. *Eligibility Requirements:* Applicant must be enrolled or expecting to enroll full or part-time at a two-year or four-year institution or university; resident of Maryland and studying in Maryland. Applicant or parent of applicant must have employment or volunteer experience in police/firefighting. Available to U.S. citizens. *Application Requirements:* Application, transcript. **Deadline:** July 1.

Contact Gerrie Rogers, Office of Student Financial Assistance, Maryland Higher Education Commission, 839 Bestgate Road, Suite 400, Annapolis, MD 21401-3013. *E-mail:* ofsamail@mhec.state.md.us. *Phone:* 410-260-4574. *Fax:* 410-260-3203. *Web site:* www.mhec.state.md.us.

Graduate and Professional Scholarship Program—Maryland. Graduate and professional scholarships provide need-based financial assistance to students attending a Maryland school of medicine, dentistry, law, pharmacy, social work, or nursing. Funds are provided to specific Maryland colleges and universities. Students must demonstrate financial need and be Maryland residents. Contact institution financial aid office for more information. *Academic/Career Areas:* Dental Health/Services; Health and Medical Sciences; Law/Legal Services; Nursing; Social Services. *Award:* Scholarship for use in freshman, sophomore, junior, senior, graduate, or postgraduate years; renewable. *Award amount:* $1000–$5000. *Number of awards:* 40–200. *Eligibility Requirements:* Applicant must be enrolled or expecting to enroll full or part-time at a four-year institution or university; resident of Maryland and studying in Maryland. Available to U.S. citizens. *Application Requirements:* Application, financial need analysis. **Deadline:** March 1.

Contact Maryland Higher Education Commission, 839 Bestgate Road, Suite 400, Annapolis, MD 21401-3013. *Web site:* www.mhec.state.md.us.

Guaranteed Access Grant—Maryland. Award for Maryland resident enrolling full-time in an undergraduate program at a Maryland institution. Must be under 22 at time of first award and begin college within one year of completing high school in Maryland with a minimum 2.5 GPA. Must have an annual family income less than 130% of the federal poverty level guideline. *Award:* Grant for use in freshman, sophomore, junior, or senior year; renewable. *Award amount:* $400–$10,200. *Number of awards:* up to 1000. *Eligibility Requirements:* Applicant must be enrolled or expecting to enroll full-time at a two-year or four-year institution or university; resident of Maryland and studying in Maryland. Applicant must have 2.5 GPA or higher. Available to U.S. citizens. *Application Requirements:* Application, financial need analysis, transcript. **Deadline:** continuous.

Contact Theresa Lowe, Office of Student Financial Assistance, Maryland Higher Education Commission, 839 Bestgate Road, Suite 400, Annapolis, MD 21401-3013. *E-mail:* osfamail@mhec.state.md.us. *Phone:* 410-260-4555. *Fax:* 410-260-3200. *Web site:* www.mhec.state.md.us.

Hope for Nontraditional Students-Community College Transfer Scholarship Program. Award available to students who transfer with minimum 3.0 GPA and 60 credits from a Maryland two-year college to a Maryland four-year college. Annual family income limit is $95,000. Must agree to work in Maryland for up to three years. Funds are limited. *Award:* Forgivable loan for use in junior or senior year; renewable. *Award amount:* up to $3000. *Eligibility Requirements:* Applicant must be enrolled or expecting to enroll full-time at a four-year institution or university; resident of Maryland and studying in Maryland. Applicant must have 3.0 GPA or higher. Available to U.S. citizens. *Application Requirements:* Application, financial need analysis, transcript. **Deadline:** March 1.

Contact Office of Student Financial Assistance, Maryland Higher Education Commission, 839 Bestgate Road, Suite 400, Annapolis, MD 21401. *E-mail:* osfamail@mhec.state.md.us. *Phone:* 410-260-4565. *Fax:* 410-260-3202. *Web site:* www.mhec.state.md.us.

Hope Scholarship. Student must be a high school senior at the time of application and must enroll in an eligible major. Family income may not exceed $95,000

Additional State Aid Programs

annually. Recipients must agree to work in the state of Maryland for one year for each year they accept the award. Funds are limited. *Academic/Career Areas*: Agriculture; Arts; Business/Consumer Services; Communications; Foreign Language; Health and Medical Sciences; Home Economics; Humanities; Literature/English/Writing; Natural Resources; Political Science; Social Sciences. *Award*: Forgivable loan for use in freshman, sophomore, junior, or senior year; renewable. *Award amount*: $1000–$3000. *Eligibility Requirements*: Applicant must be high school student; planning to enroll or expecting to enroll full-time at a two-year or four-year institution or university; resident of Maryland and studying in Maryland. Applicant must have 3.0 GPA or higher. Available to U.S. citizens. *Application Requirements*: Application, financial need analysis, transcript. **Deadline:** March 1.

> **Contact** Office of Financial Assistance, Maryland Higher Education Commission, 839 Bestgate Road, Suite 400, Annapolis, MD 21401. *E-mail:* osfamail@mhec.state.md.us. *Phone:* 410-260-4565. *Fax:* 410-260-3202. *Web site:* www.mhec.state.md.us.

J.F. Tolbert Memorial Student Grant Program. Available to Maryland residents attending a private career school in Maryland with at least 18 clock hours per week. *Award*: Grant for use in freshman or sophomore year; not renewable. *Award amount*: up to $300. *Number of awards*: 1000. *Eligibility Requirements*: Applicant must be enrolled or expecting to enroll at a technical institution; resident of Maryland and studying in Maryland. Available to U.S. citizens. *Application Requirements*: Application, financial need analysis. **Deadline:** continuous.

> **Contact** Carla Rich, Office of Student Financial Assistance, Maryland Higher Education Commission, 839 Bestgate Road, Suite 400, Annapolis, MD 21401-3013. *E-mail:* osfamail@mhec.state.md.us. *Phone:* 410-260-4513. *Fax:* 410-260-3200. *Web site:* www.mhec.state.md.us.

Janet L. Hoffmann Loan Assistance Repayment Program. Provides assistance for repayment of loan debt to Maryland residents working full-time in nonprofit organizations and state or local governments. Must submit Employment Verification Form and Lender verification form. *Academic/Career Areas*: Education; Law/Legal Services; Nursing; Social Services; Therapy/Rehabilitation. *Award*: Grant for use in freshman, sophomore, junior, senior, or graduate year; not renewable. *Award amount*: up to $7500. *Number of awards*: up to 400. *Eligibility Requirements*: Applicant must be enrolled or expecting to enroll at an institution or university; resident of Maryland and studying in Maryland. Available to U.S. citizens. *Application Requirements*: Application, transcript, IRS 1040 form. **Deadline:** September 30.

> **Contact** Marie Janiszewski, Office of Student Financial Assistance, Maryland Higher Education Commission, 839 Bestgate Road, Suite 400, Annapolis, MD 21401. *E-mail:* osfamail@mhec.state.md.us. *Phone:* 410-260-4569. *Fax:* 410-260-3203. *Web site:* www.mhec.state.md.us.

Maryland State Nursing Scholarship and Living Expenses Grant. Renewable grant for Maryland residents enrolled in a two- or four-year Maryland institution nursing degree program. Recipients must agree to serve as a full-time nurse in a Maryland shortage area and must maintain a 3.0 GPA in college. Application deadline is June 30. Submit Free Application for Federal Student Aid. *Academic/Career Areas*: Nursing. *Award*: Forgivable loan for use in freshman, sophomore, junior, senior, or graduate year; renewable. *Award amount*: $200–$3000. *Number of awards*: up to 600. *Eligibility Requirements*: Applicant must be enrolled or expecting to enroll full or part-time at a two-year or four-year institution or university; resident of Maryland and studying in Maryland. Applicant must have 3.0 GPA or higher. Available to U.S. citizens. *Application Requirements*: Application, financial need analysis, transcript. **Deadline:** June 30.

> **Contact** Marie Janiszewski, Office of Student Financial Assistance, Maryland Higher Education Commission, 839 Bestgate Road, Suite 400, Annapolis, MD 21401-3013. *E-mail:* ofsamail@mhec.state.md.us. *Phone:* 410-260-4569. *Fax:* 410-260-3203. *Web site:* www.mhec.state.md.us.

Maryland Teacher Scholarship. Available to Maryland residents attending a college in Maryland with a major in teacher education. Must be seeking initial teaching certification. Must work as public school teacher within the state of Maryland. Funds are limited. *Academic/Career Areas*: Education; Special Education. *Award*: Forgivable loan for use in freshman, sophomore, junior, senior, graduate, or postgraduate years; renewable. *Award amount*: $1000–$5000. *Eligibility Requirements*: Applicant must be enrolled or expecting to enroll full or part-time at a two-year or four-year institution or university; resident of Maryland and studying in Maryland. Applicant must have 3.0 GPA or higher. Available to U.S. citizens. *Application Requirements*: Application, transcript. **Deadline:** March 1.

> **Contact** Scholarship Administration, Maryland Higher Education Commission, 839 Bestgate Road, Suite 400, Annapolis, MD 21401. *E-mail:* osfamail@mhec.state.md.us. *Phone:* 410-260-4565. *Fax:* 410-260-3202. *Web site:* www.mhec.state.md.us.

Part-time Grant Program-Maryland. Funds provided to Maryland colleges and universities. Eligible students must be enrolled on a part-time basis (6-11 credits) in an undergraduate degree program. Must demonstrate financial need and also be Maryland resident. Contact financial aid office at institution for more information. *Award:* Grant for use in freshman, sophomore, junior, or senior year; renewable. *Award amount:* $200–$1000. *Number of awards:* 1800–9000. *Eligibility Requirements:* Applicant must be enrolled or expecting to enroll part-time at a two-year or four-year institution or university; resident of Maryland and studying in Maryland. Available to U.S. citizens. *Application Requirements:* Application, financial need analysis. **Deadline:** March 1.

Contact Maryland Higher Education Commission, 839 Bestgate Road, Suite 400, Annapolis, MD 21401-3013. *Web site:* www.mhec.state.md.us.

Physical and Occupational Therapists and Assistants Grant Program. For Maryland residents training as physical, occupational therapists or therapy assistants at Maryland postsecondary institutions. Recipients must provide one year of service for each full, or partial, year of award. Service must be to handicapped children in a Maryland facility that has, or accommodates and provides services to, such children. Minimum 2.0 GPA. *Academic/Career Areas:* Therapy/Rehabilitation. *Award:* Forgivable loan for use in freshman, sophomore, junior, senior, or graduate year; renewable. *Award amount:* up to $2000. *Number of awards:* up to 10. *Eligibility Requirements:* Applicant must be enrolled or expecting to enroll full-time at a two-year or four-year institution or university; resident of Maryland and studying in Maryland. Available to U.S. citizens. *Application Requirements:* Application, transcript. **Deadline:** July 1.

Contact Gerrie Rogers, Office of Student Financial Assistance, Maryland Higher Education Commission, 839 Bestgate Road, Suite 400, Annapolis, MD 21401. *E-mail:* ssamail@mhec.state.md.us. *Phone:* 410-260-4574. *Fax:* 410-260-3203. *Web site:* www.mhec.state.md.us.

Science and Technology Scholarship. Provides assistance to full-time students in an academic program that will address career shortage areas in the state (computer science, engineering, biological sciences, mathematics, and physical sciences). Must be Maryland resident. Must have cumulative unweighted 3.0 GPA in grades 9-first semester of senior year if applying as a high school student. College applicants must have a cumulative average of 3.0 or greater to apply. Funds are limited. *Academic/Career Areas:* Biology; Chemical Engineering; Civil Engineering; Computer Science/Data Processing; Earth Science; Electrical Engineering/Electronics; Engineering/Technology; Engineering-Related Technologies; Fire Sciences; Physical Sciences and Math. *Award:* Forgivable loan for use in freshman, sophomore, junior, or senior year; renewable. *Award amount:* $1000–$3000. *Eligibility Requirements:* Applicant must be enrolled or expecting to enroll full-time at a two-year or four-year institution or university; resident of Maryland and studying in Maryland. Applicant must have 3.0 GPA or higher. Available to U.S. citizens. *Application Requirements:* Application, transcript. **Deadline:** March 1.

Contact Scholarship Administration, Maryland Higher Education Commission, 839 Bestgate Road, Suite 400, Annapolis, MD 21401. *E-mail:* ssamail@mhec.state.md.us. *Phone:* 410-260-4565. *Fax:* 410-260-3202. *Web site:* www.mhec.state.md.us.

Senatorial Scholarships—Maryland. Renewable award for Maryland residents attending a Maryland degree-granting institution, nursing diploma school, or certain private career schools. May be used out-of-state only if Maryland Higher Education Commission deems major to be unique and not offered at Maryland institution. *Award:* Scholarship for use in freshman, sophomore, junior, senior, or graduate year; renewable. *Award amount:* $200–$2000. *Number of awards:* up to 7000. *Eligibility Requirements:* Applicant must be enrolled or expecting to enroll full or part-time at a two-year, four-year, or technical institution or university; resident of Maryland and studying in Maryland. Available to U.S. citizens. *Application Requirements:* Financial need analysis, test scores, application to Legislative District Senator. **Deadline:** March 1.

Contact Barbara Fantom, Office of Student Financial Assistance, Maryland Higher Education Commission, 839 Bestgate Road, Suite 400, Annapolis, MD 21401-3013. *E-mail:* osfamail@mhec.state.md.us. *Phone:* 410-260-4547. *Fax:* 410-260-3202. *Web site:* www.mhec.state.md.us.

Sharon Christa McAuliffe Teacher Education—Critical Shortage Grant Program. Renewable awards for Maryland residents who are college juniors, seniors, or graduate students enrolled in a Maryland teacher education program. Must agree to enter profession in a subject designated as a critical shortage area. Must teach in Maryland for one year for each award year. Renewable for one year. *Academic/Career Areas:* Education. *Award:* Forgivable loan for use in junior, senior, or graduate year; renewable. *Award amount:* $200–$12,981. *Number of awards:* up to 137. *Eligibility Requirements:* Applicant must be enrolled or expecting to enroll full or part-time at a four-year institution or university; resident of Maryland and studying in Maryland. Applicant must have 3.0 GPA or higher. Available to U.S. citizens. *Application Requirements:* Application, essay, resume, transcript. **Deadline:** December 31.

Contact Margaret Crutchley, Office of Student Financial Assistance, Maryland Higher Education Commission, 839 Bestgate Road, Suite 400, Annapolis, MD 21401-3013. *E-mail:* ofsamail@mhec.state.md.us. *Phone:* 410-260-4545. *Fax:* 410-260-3203. *Web site:* www.mhec.state.md.us.

Additional State Aid Programs

William Kapell International Piano Competition and Festival. Quadrennial international piano competition for ages 18-33. $80 application fee. Competition takes place at the Clarice Smith Performing Arts Center at the University of Maryland July 16-25, 2003. Next competition will be in 2007. *Academic/Career Areas:* Performing Arts. *Award:* Prize for use in freshman, sophomore, junior, senior, graduate, or postgraduate years; not renewable. *Award amount:* $1000–$20,000. *Number of awards:* up to 12. *Eligibility Requirements:* Applicant must be age 18-33; enrolled or expecting to enroll at an institution or university and must have an interest in music. Available to U.S. and non-U.S. citizens. *Application Requirements:* Application, applicant must enter a contest, autobiography, photo, portfolio, references, CD or audiocassette of performance. *Fee:* $80. **Deadline:** February 1.

Contact Dr. Christopher Patton, Coordinator, Clarice Smith Performing Arts Center at Maryland, Suite 3800, University of Maryland, College Park, MD 20742-1625. *E-mail:* kapell@deans.umd.edu. *Phone:* 301-405-8174. *Fax:* 301-405-5977. *Web site:* www.claricesmithcenter.umd.edu.

Massachusetts

Christian A. Herter Memorial Scholarship. Renewable award for Massachusetts residents who are in the 10th-11th grades and whose socio-economic backgrounds and environment may inhibit their ability to attain educational goals. Must exhibit severe personal or family-related difficulties, medical problems, or have overcome a personal obstacle. Provides up to 50% of the student's calculated need, as determined by Federal methodology, at the college of their choice within the continental U.S. *Award:* Scholarship for use in freshman, sophomore, junior, or senior year; renewable. *Number of awards:* 25. *Eligibility Requirements:* Applicant must be high school student; planning to enroll or expecting to enroll full-time at a two-year, four-year, or technical institution or university and resident of Massachusetts. Applicant must have 2.5 GPA or higher. Available to U.S. citizens. *Application Requirements:* Application, autobiography, financial need analysis, interview, references. **Deadline:** March 31.

Contact Ken Smith, Massachusetts Office of Student Financial Assistance, 454 Broadway, Suite 200, Revere, MA 02151. *E-mail:* osfa@osfa.mass.edu. *Phone:* 617-727-9420. *Fax:* 617-727-0667. *Web site:* www.osfa.mass.edu.

Higher Education Coordinating Council—Tuition Waiver Program. Renewable award is tuition exemption for up to four years. Available to active members of Air Force, Army, Navy, Marines, or Coast Guard who are residents of Massachusetts. For use at a Massachusetts college or university. Deadlines vary. Contact veterans coordinator at college. *Award:* Scholarship for use in freshman, sophomore, junior, or senior year; renewable. *Eligibility Requirements:* Applicant must be enrolled or expecting to enroll full or part-time at a two-year or four-year institution or university; resident of Massachusetts and studying in Massachusetts. Available to U.S. citizens. Applicant must have served in the Air Force, Army, Coast Guard, Marine Corp, or Navy. *Application Requirements:* Application, financial need analysis.

Contact college financial aid office, Massachusetts Office of Student Financial Assistance. *Web site:* www.osfa.mass.edu.

Massachusetts Assistance for Student Success Program. Provides need-based financial assistance to Massachusetts residents to attend undergraduate postsecondary institutions in Connecticut, Maine, Massachusetts, New Hampshire, Pennsylvania, Rhode Island, Vermont, and District of Columbia. High school seniors may apply. Timely filing of FAFSA required. *Award:* Grant for use in freshman, sophomore, junior, or senior year; not renewable. *Award amount:* $300–$2900. *Number of awards:* 32,000–35,000. *Eligibility Requirements:* Applicant must be enrolled or expecting to enroll full-time at a two-year, four-year, or technical institution or university; resident of Massachusetts and studying in Connecticut, District of Columbia, Maine, Massachusetts, New Hampshire, Pennsylvania, Rhode Island, or Vermont. Available to U.S. citizens. *Application Requirements:* Financial need analysis, FAFSA. **Deadline:** May 1.

Contact Scholarship Information, Massachusetts Office of Student Financial Assistance, 454 Broadway, Suite 200, Revere, MA 02151. *Web site:* www.osfa.mass.edu.

Massachusetts Cash Grant Program. A need-based grant to assist with mandatory fees and non-state supported tuition, this supplemental award is available to Massachusetts residents who are undergraduates at two-year colleges, four-year colleges and universities in Massachusetts. Must file FAFSA before May 1. Contact college financial aid office for information. *Award:* Grant for use in freshman, sophomore, junior, or senior year; not renewable. *Award amount:* $150–$1900. *Eligibility Requirements:* Applicant must be enrolled or expecting to enroll full-time at a two-year or four-year institution or university; resident of Massachusetts and studying in Massachusetts. Available to U.S. citizens. *Application Requirements:* Financial need analysis, FAFSA. **Deadline:** continuous.

Contact college financial aid office, Massachusetts Office of Student Financial Assistance. *Web site:* www.osfa.mass.edu.

Massachusetts Gilbert Matching Student Grant Program. Must be permanent Massachusetts resident for at least one year and attending an independent, regionally accredited Massachusetts school or school of nursing full time. File the Free Application for Federal

Student Aid after January 1. Contact college financial aid office for complete details and deadlines. *Award:* Grant for use in freshman, sophomore, junior, or senior year; not renewable. *Award amount:* $200–$2500. *Eligibility Requirements:* Applicant must be enrolled or expecting to enroll full-time at a four-year institution or university; resident of Massachusetts and studying in Massachusetts. Available to U.S. citizens. *Application Requirements:* Financial need analysis, FAFSA.

Contact college financial aid office, Massachusetts Office of Student Financial Assistance. *Web site:* www.osfa.mass.edu.

Massachusetts Part-time Grant Program. Award for permanent Massachusetts resident for at least one year enrolled part-time in a state-approved postsecondary school. Recipient must not have first bachelor's degree. FAFSA must be filed before May 1. Contact college financial aid office for further information. *Award:* Grant for use in freshman, sophomore, junior, or senior year; not renewable. *Award amount:* $150–$1450. *Eligibility Requirements:* Applicant must be enrolled or expecting to enroll part-time at a two-year, four-year, or technical institution or university; resident of Massachusetts and studying in Massachusetts. Available to U.S. citizens. *Application Requirements:* Financial need analysis, FAFSA. **Deadline:** May 1.

Contact college financial aid office, Massachusetts Office of Student Financial Assistance. *Web site:* www.osfa.mass.edu.

Massachusetts Public Service Grant Program. Scholarships for children and/or spouses of deceased members of fire, police, and corrections departments who were killed in the line of duty. For Massachusetts residents attending Massachusetts institutions. *Award:* Grant for use in freshman, sophomore, junior, or senior year; not renewable. *Award amount:* $330–$2500. *Eligibility Requirements:* Applicant must be enrolled or expecting to enroll full-time at a four-year institution or university; resident of Massachusetts and studying in Massachusetts. Applicant or parent of applicant must have employment or volunteer experience in police/firefighting. Available to U.S. citizens. *Application Requirements:* FAFSA. **Deadline:** May 1.

Contact Alison Leary, Massachusetts Office of Student Financial Assistance, 454 Broadway, Suite 200, Revere, MA 02151. *E-mail:* osfa@osfa.mass.edu. *Phone:* 617-727-9420. *Fax:* 617-727-0667. *Web site:* www.osfa.mass.edu.

New England Regional Student Program (New England Board of Higher Education). For residents of Connecticut, Maine, Massachusetts, New Hampshire, Rhode Island, and Vermont. Through Regional Student Program, students pay reduced out-of-state tuition at public colleges or universities in other New England states when enrolling in certain majors not offered at public institutions in home state. *Award:* Scholarship for use in freshman, sophomore, junior, senior, or graduate year; renewable. *Eligibility Requirements:* Applicant must be enrolled or expecting to enroll full or part-time at a two-year or four-year institution or university; resident of Connecticut, Maine, Massachusetts, New Hampshire, Rhode Island, or Vermont and studying in Connecticut, Maine, Massachusetts, New Hampshire, Rhode Island, or Vermont. Available to U.S. citizens. *Application Requirements:* College application. **Deadline:** continuous.

Contact Wendy Lindsay, Director of Regional Student Program, New England Board of Higher Education, 45 Temple Place, Boston, MA 02111-1305. *E-mail:* rsp@nebhe.org. *Phone:* 617-357-9620 Ext. 111. *Fax:* 617-338-1577. *Web site:* www.nebhe.org.

Performance Bonus Grant Program. One-time award to residents of Massachusetts enrolled in a Massachusetts postsecondary institution. Minimum 3.0 GPA required. Timely filing of FAFSA required. Must be sophomore, junior or senior level undergraduate. *Award:* Grant for use in sophomore, junior, or senior year; not renewable. *Award amount:* $350–$500. *Eligibility Requirements:* Applicant must be enrolled or expecting to enroll full-time at a two-year or four-year institution or university; resident of Massachusetts and studying in Massachusetts. Applicant must have 3.0 GPA or higher. Available to U.S. citizens. *Application Requirements:* Financial need analysis, FAFSA. **Deadline:** May 1.

Contact Scholarship Information, Massachusetts Office of Student Financial Assistance, 454 Broadway, Suite 200, Revere, MA 02151. *Phone:* 617-727-9420. *Fax:* 617-727-0667. *Web site:* www.osfa.mass.edu.

Tomorrow's Teachers Scholarship Program. Tuition waver for graduating high school senior ranking in top 25% of class. Must be a resident of Massachusetts and pursue a bachelor's degree at a public college or university in the Commonwealth. Must commit to teach for four years in a Massachusetts public school. *Academic/Career Areas:* Education. *Award:* Scholarship for use in freshman, sophomore, junior, or senior year; renewable. *Eligibility Requirements:* Applicant must be high school student; planning to enroll or expecting to enroll full-time at a four-year institution or university; resident of Massachusetts and studying in Massachusetts. Applicant must have 3.5 GPA or higher. Available to U.S. citizens. *Application Requirements:* Application, essay, references, transcript. **Deadline:** February 15.

Contact Alison Leary, Massachusetts Office of Student Financial Assistance, 454 Broadway, Suite 200, Revere, MA 02151. *E-mail:* osfa@osfa.mass.edu. *Phone:* 617-727-9420. *Fax:* 617-727-0667. *Web site:* www.osfa.mass.edu.

Additional State Aid Programs

Tuition Waiver (General)—Massachusetts. Need-based tuition waiver for full-time students. Must attend a Massachusetts public institution of higher education and be a permanent Massachusetts resident. File the Free Application for Federal Student Aid after January 1. Award is for undergraduate use. Contact school financial aid office for more information. *Award:* Scholarship for use in freshman, sophomore, junior, or senior year; renewable. *Award amount:* $175–$1300. *Eligibility Requirements:* Applicant must be enrolled or expecting to enroll full-time at a two-year or four-year institution or university; resident of Massachusetts and studying in Massachusetts. Available to U.S. citizens. *Application Requirements:* Application, financial need analysis, FAFSA. **Deadline:** May 1.

Contact college financial aid office, Massachusetts Office of Student Financial Assistance. *Web site:* www.osfa.mass.edu.

Michigan

Michigan Adult Part-time Grant. Grant for part-time, needy, independent undergraduates at an approved, degree-granting Michigan college or university. Eligibility is limited to two years. Must be Michigan resident. Deadlines determined by college. *Award:* Grant for use in freshman, sophomore, junior, or senior year; not renewable. *Award amount:* up to $600. *Eligibility Requirements:* Applicant must be enrolled or expecting to enroll part-time at a two-year or four-year institution or university; resident of Michigan and studying in Michigan. Available to U.S. citizens. *Application Requirements:* Application, financial need analysis.

Contact Program Director, Michigan Bureau of Student Financial Assistance, PO Box 30466, Lansing, MI 48909-7966. *Web site:* www.michigan.gov/mistudentaid.

Michigan Competitive Scholarship. Awards limited to tuition. Must maintain a C average and meet the college's academic progress requirements. Must file Free Application for Federal Student Aid. Deadlines: February 21 and March 21. Must be Michigan resident. Renewable award of $1300 for undergraduate study at a Michigan institution. *Award:* Scholarship for use in freshman, sophomore, junior, or senior year; renewable. *Award amount:* $100–$1300. *Eligibility Requirements:* Applicant must be enrolled or expecting to enroll at a two-year or four-year institution or university; resident of Michigan and studying in Michigan. Available to U.S. citizens. *Application Requirements:* Application, financial need analysis, test scores, FAFSA.

Contact Scholarship and Grant Director, Michigan Bureau of Student Financial Assistance, PO Box 30466, Lansing, MI 48909. *Web site:* www.michigan.gov/mistudentaid.

Michigan Educational Opportunity Grant. Need-based program for Michigan residents who are at least half-time undergraduates attending public Michigan colleges. Must maintain good academic standing. Deadline determined by college. Award of up to $1000. *Award:* Grant for use in freshman, sophomore, junior, or senior year; not renewable. *Award amount:* up to $1000. *Eligibility Requirements:* Applicant must be enrolled or expecting to enroll full or part-time at a two-year or four-year institution or university; resident of Michigan and studying in Michigan. Available to U.S. citizens. *Application Requirements:* Application, financial need analysis.

Contact Program Director, Michigan Bureau of Student Financial Assistance, PO Box 30466, Lansing, MI 48909-7966. *Web site:* www.michigan.gov/mistudentaid.

Michigan Indian Tuition Waiver. Renewable award provides free tuition for Native-Americans of one-quarter or more blood degree who attend a Michigan public college or university. Must be a Michigan resident for at least one year. For more details and deadlines contact college financial aid office. *Award:* Scholarship for use in freshman, sophomore, junior, senior, graduate, or postgraduate years; renewable. *Eligibility Requirements:* Applicant must be American Indian/Alaska Native; enrolled or expecting to enroll full or part-time at a two-year or four-year institution or university; resident of Michigan and studying in Michigan. Available to U.S. and Canadian citizens. *Application Requirements:* Application, driver's license.

Contact Harriet Moran, Executive Assistant to Programs, Inter-Tribal Council of Michigan, Inc., 405 East Easterday Avenue, Sault Ste. Marie, MI 49783. *E-mail:* itchmm@yahoo.com. *Phone:* 906-632-6896. *Fax:* 906-632-1810. *Web site:* www.itcmi.org.

Michigan Tuition Grants. Need-based program. Students must attend a Michigan private, nonprofit, degree-granting college. Must file the Free Application for Federal Student Aid and meet the college's academic progress requirements. Deadlines: February 21 and March 21. Must be Michigan resident. Renewable award of $2750. *Award:* Grant for use in freshman, sophomore, junior, or senior year; renewable. *Award amount:* $100–$2750. *Eligibility Requirements:* Applicant must be enrolled or expecting to enroll at a two-year or four-year institution or university; resident of Michigan and studying in Michigan. Available to U.S. citizens. *Application Requirements:* Application, financial need analysis, FAFSA.

Contact Scholarship and Grant Director, Michigan Bureau of Student Financial Assistance, PO Box 30466, Lansing, MI 48909-7966. *Web site:* www.michigan.gov/mistudentaid.

Michigan Veterans Trust Fund Tuition Grant Program. Tuition grant of $2,800 for children of Michigan veterans who died on active duty or subse-

Appendix D

quently declared 100% disabled as the result of service-connected illness or injury. Must be 17 to 25 years old, be a Michigan resident, and attend a private or public institution in Michigan. *Award:* Grant for use in freshman, sophomore, junior, or senior year; renewable. *Award amount:* up to $2800. *Eligibility Requirements:* Applicant must be age 17-25; enrolled or expecting to enroll full-time at a two-year, four-year, or technical institution or university; resident of Michigan and studying in Michigan. Applicant or parent must meet one or more of the following requirements: general military experience; retired from active duty; disabled or killed as a result of military service; prisoner of war; or missing in action. *Application Requirements:* Application. **Deadline:** continuous.

> **Contact** Phyllis Ochis, Department of Military and Veterans Affairs, Michigan Veterans Trust Fund, 2500 South Washington Avenue, Lansing, MI 48913. *Phone:* 517-483-5469. *Web site:* www.michigan.gov/dmva.

Tuition Incentive Program (TIP)-Michigan. Award for Michigan residents who receive or have received Medicaid for required period of time through the Family Independence Agency. Scholarship provides two years tuition towards an associate's degree at a Michigan college or university. Apply before graduating from high school or earning General Education Development diploma. *Award:* Scholarship for use in freshman or sophomore year; renewable. *Eligibility Requirements:* Applicant must be high school student; planning to enroll or expecting to enroll full or part-time at a two-year or four-year institution or university; resident of Michigan and studying in Michigan. Available to U.S. citizens. *Application Requirements:* Application, financial need analysis. **Deadline:** continuous.

> **Contact** Program Director, Michigan Bureau of Student Financial Assistance, PO Box 30466, Lansing, MI 48909. *Web site:* www.michigan.gov/mistudentaid.

Minnesota

Advanced Placement/International Baccalaureate Degree Program. A non-need-based grant available for incoming Freshman who had an average score of 3 or higher on five AP courses or an average score of 4 or higher on 5 IB courses. Must be a Minnesota resident and attend a college in Minnesota. *Award:* Grant for use in freshman or sophomore year; not renewable. *Award amount:* $300–$700. *Number of awards:* 300. *Eligibility Requirements:* Applicant must be high school student; planning to enroll or expecting to enroll full or part-time at a two-year or four-year institution or university; resident of Minnesota and studying in Minnesota. Available to U.S. citizens. *Application Requirements:* Application, test scores. **Deadline:** continuous.

> Contact Brenda Larter, Minnesota Higher Education Services Office, 1450 Energy Park Drive, Suite 350, St. Paul, MN 55108-5227. *E-mail:* larter@heso.state.mn.us. *Phone:* 651-642-0567 Ext. 3417. *Fax:* 651-642-0675. *Web site:* www.mheso.state.mn.us.

Leadership, Excellence and Dedicated Service Scholarship. Awarded to high school seniors who enlist in the Minnesota National Guard. The award recognizes demonstrated leadership, community services and potential for success in the Minnesota National Guard. *Award:* Scholarship for use in freshman year; not renewable. *Award amount:* $1000. *Number of awards:* 30. *Eligibility Requirements:* Applicant must be high school student and planning to enroll or expecting to enroll full or part-time at a two-year, four-year, or technical institution or university. Applicant must have served in the Air Force National Guard or Army National Guard. *Application Requirements:* Application, essay, references, transcript. **Deadline:** March 15.

> **Contact** Barbara O'Reilly, Education Services Officer, Minnesota Department of Military Affairs, Veterans Services Building, 20 West 12th Street, St. Paul, MN 55155-2098. *E-mail:* barbara.oreilly@mn.ngb.army.mil. *Phone:* 651-282-4508. *Web site:* www.dma.state.mn.us.

Minnesota Educational Assistance for War Orphans. War orphans may qualify for $750 per year. Must have lost parent through service-related death. Children of deceased veterans may qualify for free tuition at State university, college, or vocational or technical schools, but not at University of Minnesota. Must have been resident of Minnesota for at least two years. *Award:* Grant for use in freshman, sophomore, junior, or senior year; renewable. *Award amount:* $750. *Eligibility Requirements:* Applicant must be enrolled or expecting to enroll full or part-time at a two-year, four-year, or technical institution or university; resident of Minnesota and studying in Minnesota. Available to U.S. citizens. Applicant or parent must meet one or more of the following requirements: general military experience; retired from active duty; disabled or killed as a result of military service; prisoner of war; or missing in action. *Application Requirements:* Application, financial need analysis. **Deadline:** continuous.

> **Contact** Terrence Logan, Management Analyst IV, Minnesota Department of Veterans' Affairs, 20 West 12th Street, Second Floor, St. Paul, MN 55155-2079. *Phone:* 651-296-2652. *Fax:* 651-296-3954. *Web site:* www.state.mn.us/ebranch/mdva.

Minnesota Indian Scholarship Program. One time award for Minnesota Native-Americans Indian. Contact for deadline information. *Award:* Scholarship for use in freshman, sophomore, junior, or senior year; not renewable. *Eligibility Requirements:* Applicant must be American Indian/Alaska Native; enrolled or expecting to enroll full or part-time at a two-year, four-year, or

Additional State Aid Programs

technical institution or university and resident of Minnesota. Available to U.S. citizens. *Application Requirements:* Application.

Contact Lea Perkins, Director, Minnesota Indian Scholarship Office, Minnesota Department of CFL 1500 Highway 36W, Roseville, MN 55113-4266. *Phone:* 800-657-3927.

Minnesota Nurses Loan Forgiveness Program. This program offers loan repayment to registered nurse and licensed practical nurse students who agree to practice in a Minnesota nursing home or an Intermediate Care Facility for persons with mental retardation for a minimum one-year service obligation after completion of training. Candidates must apply while still in school. Up to 10 selections per year contingent upon state funding. *Academic/Career Areas:* Health and Medical Sciences; Nursing. *Award:* Grant for use in senior or graduate year; not renewable. *Award amount:* up to $3000. *Number of awards:* up to 10. *Eligibility Requirements:* Applicant must be enrolled or expecting to enroll full or part-time at a two-year, four-year, or technical institution or university. Available to U.S. citizens. *Application Requirements:* Application, essay. **Deadline:** December 1.

Contact Karen Welter, Minnesota Department of Health, 121 East Seventh Place, Suite 460, PO Box 64975, St. Paul, MN 55164-0975. *E-mail:* karen.welter@health.state.mn.us. *Phone:* 651-282-6302. *Web site:* www.health.state.mn.us.

Minnesota Reciprocal Agreement. Renewable tuition waiver for Minnesota residents. Waives all or part of non-resident tuition surcharge at public institutions in Iowa, Kansas, Michigan, Missouri, Nebraska, North Dakota, South Dakota, and Wisconsin. Deadline is last day of academic term. *Award:* Scholarship for use in freshman, sophomore, junior, senior, or graduate year; renewable. *Eligibility Requirements:* Applicant must be enrolled or expecting to enroll full or part-time at a two-year or four-year institution or university; resident of Minnesota and studying in Iowa, Kansas, Michigan, Missouri, Nebraska, North Dakota, South Dakota, or Wisconsin. Available to U.S. citizens. *Application Requirements:* Application.

Contact Minnesota Higher Education Services Office, 1450 Energy Park Drive, Suite 350, St. Paul, MN 55108-5227. *Phone:* 651-642-0567 Ext. 1. *Web site:* www.mheso.state.mn.us.

Minnesota Safety Officers' Survivor Program. Grant for eligible survivors of Minnesota public safety officer killed in the line of duty. Safety officers who have been permanently or totally disabled in the line of duty are also eligible. Must be used at a Minnesota institution participating in State Grant Program. Write for details. Must submit proof of death or disability and Public Safety Officers Benefit Fund Certificate. Must apply each year. Can be renewed for four years. *Award:* Grant for use in freshman, sophomore, junior, or senior year; not renewable. *Award amount:* up to $7088. *Eligibility Requirements:* Applicant must be enrolled or expecting to enroll full or part-time at a two-year, four-year, or technical institution or university and studying in Minnesota. Applicant or parent of applicant must have employment or volunteer experience in police/firefighting. Available to U.S. citizens. *Application Requirements:* Application, proof of death/disability. **Deadline:** continuous.

Contact Minnesota Higher Education Services Office, 1450 Energy Park Drive, Suite 350, St. Paul, MN 55108-5227. *Phone:* 651-642-0567 Ext. 1. *Web site:* www.mheso.state.mn.us.

Minnesota State Grant Program. Need-based grant program available for Minnesota residents attending Minnesota colleges. Student covers 46% of cost with remainder covered by Pell Grant, parent contribution and state grant. Students apply with FAFSA and college administers the program on campus. *Award:* Grant for use in freshman, sophomore, junior, or senior year; not renewable. *Award amount:* $100–$7770. *Number of awards:* 71,000. *Eligibility Requirements:* Applicant must be age 17; enrolled or expecting to enroll full or part-time at a two-year, four-year, or technical institution or university; resident of Minnesota and studying in Minnesota. Available to U.S. citizens. *Application Requirements:* Application, financial need analysis. **Deadline:** June 30.

Contact Minnesota Higher Education Services Office, 1450 Energy Park Drive, Suite 350, St. Paul, MN 55108. *Phone:* 651-642-0567 Ext. 1. *Web site:* www.mheso.state.mn.us.

Minnesota State Veterans' Dependents Assistance Program. Tuition assistance to dependents of persons considered to be prisoner-of-war or missing in action after August 1, 1958. Must be Minnesota resident attending Minnesota two- or four-year school. *Award:* Scholarship for use in freshman, sophomore, junior, or senior year; renewable. *Eligibility Requirements:* Applicant must be enrolled or expecting to enroll at a two-year or four-year institution; resident of Minnesota and studying in Minnesota. Available to U.S. citizens. Applicant or parent must meet one or more of the following requirements: general military experience; retired from active duty; disabled or killed as a result of military service; prisoner of war; or missing in action. *Application Requirements:* Application. **Deadline:** continuous.

Contact Minnesota Higher Education Services Office, 1450 Energy Park Drive, Suite 350, St. Paul, MN 55108-5227. *Web site:* www.mheso.state.mn.us.

Minnesota VA Educational Assistance for Veterans. One-time $750 stipend given to veterans who have used up all other federal funds, yet have time

Financial Aid 101

remaining on their delimiting period. Applicant must be a Minnesota resident and must be attending a Minnesota college or university, but not the University of Minnesota. *Award:* Grant for use in freshman, sophomore, junior, or senior year; not renewable. *Award amount:* $750. *Eligibility Requirements:* Applicant must be enrolled or expecting to enroll full or part-time at a two-year, four-year, or technical institution or university; resident of Minnesota and studying in Minnesota. Available to U.S. citizens. Applicant must have general military experience. *Application Requirements:* Application, financial need analysis. **Deadline:** continuous.

Contact Terrence Logan, Management Analyst IV, Minnesota Department of Veterans' Affairs, 20 West 12th Street, Second Floor, St. Paul, MN 55155-2079. *Phone:* 651-296-2652. *Fax:* 651-296-3954. *Web site:* www.state.mn.us/ebranch/mdva.

Postsecondary Child Care Grant Program—Minnesota. One-time grant available for students not receiving MFIP. Based on financial need. Cannot exceed actual child care costs or maximum award chart (based on income). Must be Minnesota resident. For use at Minnesota two- or four-year school. *Award:* Grant for use in freshman, sophomore, junior, or senior year; not renewable. *Award amount:* $300–$2600. *Eligibility Requirements:* Applicant must be enrolled or expecting to enroll full or part-time at a two-year or four-year institution or university; resident of Minnesota and studying in Minnesota. Available to U.S. citizens. *Application Requirements:* Application, financial need analysis. **Deadline:** continuous.

Contact Minnesota Higher Education Services Office, 1450 Energy Park Drive, Suite 350, St. Paul, MN 55108-5227. *Phone:* 651-642-0567 Ext. 1. *Web site:* www.mheso.state.mn.us.

Mississippi

Critical Needs Teacher Loan/Scholarship. Eligible applicants will agree to employment immediately upon degree completion as a full-time classroom teacher in a public school located in a critical teacher shortage area in the state of Mississippi. Must verify the intention to pursue a first bachelor's degree in teacher education. Award covers tuition and required fees, average cost of room and meals plus a $500 allowance for books. Must be enrolled at a Mississippi college or university. *Academic/Career Areas:* Education. *Award:* Forgivable loan for use in freshman, sophomore, junior, or senior year; not renewable. *Eligibility Requirements:* Applicant must be enrolled or expecting to enroll full or part-time at a four-year institution or university and studying in Mississippi. Applicant must have 2.5 GPA or higher. Available to U.S. citizens. *Application Requirements:* Application, test scores, transcript. **Deadline:** March 31.

Contact Mississippi State Student Financial Aid, 3825 Ridgewood Road, Jackson, MS 39211-6453. *Phone:* 800-327-2980. *Web site:* www.ihl.state.ms.us.

Higher Education Legislative Plan (HELP). Eligible applicant must be resident of Mississippi and be freshmen and/or sophomore student who graduated from high school within the immediate past two years. Must demonstrate need as determined by the results of the Free Application for Federal Student Aid, documenting an average family adjusted gross income of $36,500 or less over the prior two years. Must be enrolled full-time at a Mississippi college or university, have a cumulative grade point average of 2.5 and have scored 20 on the ACT. *Award:* Scholarship for use in freshman or sophomore year; renewable. *Eligibility Requirements:* Applicant must be enrolled or expecting to enroll full-time at a four-year institution or university; resident of Mississippi and studying in Mississippi. Applicant must have 2.5 GPA or higher. Available to U.S. citizens. *Application Requirements:* Application, financial need analysis, test scores, transcript, FAFSA. **Deadline:** March 31.

Contact Mississippi State Student Financial Aid, 3825 Ridgewood Road, Jackson, MS 39211-6453. *Phone:* 800-327-2980. *Web site:* www.ihl.state.ms.us.

Mississippi Law Enforcement Officers and Firemen Scholarship Program. Award for dependents and spouses of policemen or firemen who were killed or disabled in the line of duty. Must be a Mississippi resident and attend a state-supported college or university. The award is a full tuition waiver. Contact for deadline. *Award:* Scholarship for use in freshman, sophomore, junior, or senior year; renewable. *Eligibility Requirements:* Applicant must be enrolled or expecting to enroll full-time at a two-year or four-year institution or university; resident of Mississippi and studying in Mississippi. Applicant or parent of applicant must have employment or volunteer experience in police/firefighting. Available to U.S. citizens. *Application Requirements:* Application, driver's license, references. **Deadline:** continuous.

Contact Board of Trustees, Mississippi State Student Financial Aid, 3825 Ridgewood Road, Jackson, MS 39211-6453. *Web site:* www.ihl.state.ms.us.

Mississippi Eminent Scholars Grant. Award for high-school seniors who are residents of Mississippi. Applicants must achieve a grade point average of 3.5 after a minimum of seven semesters in high school and must have scored 29 on the ACT. Must enroll full-time at an eligible Mississippi college or university. *Award:* Grant for use in freshman year; renewable. *Award amount:* up to $2500. *Eligibility Requirements:* Applicant must be high school student; planning to enroll or expecting to enroll full-time at a four-year institution or

Additional State Aid Programs

university; resident of Mississippi and studying in Mississippi. Applicant must have 3.5 GPA or higher. Available to U.S. citizens. *Application Requirements:* Application, test scores, transcript. **Deadline:** September 15.

Contact Mississippi State Student Financial Aid, 3825 Ridgewood Road, Jackson, MS 39211-6453. *Phone:* 800-327-2980. *Web site:* www.ihl.state.ms.us.

Mississippi Health Care Professions Loan/Scholarship Program. Renewable award for junior and senior undergraduates studying psychology, speech pathology or occupational therapy. Must be Mississippi residents attending four-year universities in Mississippi. Must fulfill work obligation in Mississippi or pay back as loan. Renewable award for graduate student enrolled in physical therapy. *Academic/Career Areas:* Health and Medical Sciences; Therapy/Rehabilitation. *Award:* Forgivable loan for use in junior, senior, or graduate year; renewable. *Award amount:* $1500–$3000. *Eligibility Requirements:* Applicant must be enrolled or expecting to enroll full-time at a four-year institution or university; resident of Mississippi and studying in Mississippi. Available to U.S. citizens. *Application Requirements:* Application, driver's license, references, transcript. **Deadline:** March 31.

Contact Board of Trustees, Mississippi State Student Financial Aid, 3825 Ridgewood Road, Jackson, MS 39211-6453. *Web site:* www.ihl.state.ms.us.

Mississippi Leveraging Educational Assistance Partnership (LEAP). Award for Mississippi residents enrolled for full-time study at a Mississippi college or university. Based on financial need. Deadline varies with each institution. Contact college financial aid office. *Award:* Grant for use in freshman, sophomore, junior, or senior year; not renewable. *Award amount:* $100–$1500. *Eligibility Requirements:* Applicant must be enrolled or expecting to enroll full-time at a two-year or four-year institution or university; resident of Mississippi and studying in Mississippi. Available to U.S. citizens. *Application Requirements:* Application, financial need analysis, FAFSA. **Deadline:** continuous.

Contact Student Financial Aid Office, Mississippi State Student Financial Aid. *Web site:* www.ihl.state.ms.us.

Mississippi Resident Tuition Assistance Grant. Must be a resident of Mississippi enrolled full-time at an eligible Mississippi college or university. Must maintain a minimum 2.5 GPA each semester. MTAG awards may be up to $500 per academic year for freshmen and sophomores and $1,000 per academic year for juniors and seniors. Funds will be made available to eligible participants for eight (8) semesters or the normal time required to complete the degree program, whichever comes first. *Award:* Grant for use in freshman, sophomore, junior, or senior year; renewable. *Award amount:* $500–$1000. *Eligibility Requirements:* Applicant must be enrolled or expecting to enroll full-time at a two-year or four-year institution or university; resident of Mississippi and studying in Mississippi. Applicant must have 2.5 GPA or higher. Available to U.S. citizens. *Application Requirements:* Application, test scores, transcript. **Deadline:** September 15.

Contact Mississippi State Student Financial Aid, 3825 Ridgewood Road, Jackson, MS 39211-6453. *Phone:* 800-327-2980. *Web site:* www.ihl.state.ms.us.

Nursing Education BSN Program—Mississippi. Renewable award for Mississippi undergraduates in junior or senior year pursuing nursing programs in Mississippi in order to earn BSN degree. Include transcript and references with application. Must agree to employment in professional nursing (patient care) in Mississippi. *Academic/Career Areas:* Nursing. *Award:* Forgivable loan for use in junior or senior year; renewable. *Award amount:* up to $2000. *Eligibility Requirements:* Applicant must be enrolled or expecting to enroll full or part-time at a four-year institution or university; resident of Mississippi and studying in Mississippi. Applicant must have 2.5 GPA or higher. Available to U.S. citizens. *Application Requirements:* Application, driver's license, financial need analysis, references, transcript. **Deadline:** March 31.

Contact Board of Trustees, Mississippi State Student Financial Aid, 3825 Ridgewood road, Jackson, MS 39211-6453. *Web site:* www.ihl.state.ms.us.

William F. Winter Teacher Scholar Loan Program. Awarded to Mississippi residents pursuing a teaching career. Must be enrolled full-time in a program leading to a Class A certification and maintain a 2.5 GPA. Must agree to teach one year for each year award is received. *Academic/Career Areas:* Education. *Award:* Forgivable loan for use in freshman, sophomore, junior, or senior year; renewable. *Award amount:* $1000–$3000. *Eligibility Requirements:* Applicant must be enrolled or expecting to enroll full-time at a two-year or four-year institution or university; resident of Mississippi and studying in Mississippi. Applicant must have 2.5 GPA or higher. Available to U.S. citizens. *Application Requirements:* Application, driver's license, references, transcript. **Deadline:** March 31.

Contact Board of Trustees, Mississippi State Student Financial Aid, 3825 Ridgewood Road, Jackson, MS 39211-6453. *Web site:* www.ihl.state.ms.us.

Missouri

Advantage Missouri Program. Applicant must be seeking a program of instruction in a designated high demand field. High demand fields are determined each year. Borrower must work in Missouri in the high-demand field for one year for every year the loan is received to be forgiven. For Missouri residents. Must attend a postsecondary institution in Missouri. *Award:* Forgivable loan for use in freshman, sophomore, junior, or senior year; not renewable. *Award amount:* $2500. *Eligibility Requirements:* Applicant must be enrolled or expecting to enroll full-time at a two-year, four-year, or technical institution or university; resident of Missouri and studying in Missouri. Available to U.S. citizens. *Application Requirements:* Application, financial need analysis. **Deadline:** April 1.

Contact MOSTARS Information Center, Missouri Coordinating Board for Higher Education, 3515 Amazonas Drive, Jefferson City, MO 65109. *E-mail:* icweb@mocbhe.gov. *Phone:* 800-473-6757 Ext. 1. *Fax:* 573-751-6635. *Web site:* www.mostars.com.

Charles Gallagher Student Assistance Program. Available to Missouri residents attending Missouri colleges or universities full-time. Must be undergraduates with financial need. May reapply for up to a maximum of ten semesters. Free Application for Federal Student Aid (FAFSA) or a renewal must be received by the central processor by April 1 to be considered. *Award:* Grant for use in freshman, sophomore, junior, or senior year; not renewable. *Award amount:* $100–$1500. *Eligibility Requirements:* Applicant must be enrolled or expecting to enroll full-time at a two-year, four-year, or technical institution or university; resident of Missouri and studying in Missouri. Available to U.S. citizens. *Application Requirements:* Financial need analysis. **Deadline:** April 1.

Contact MOSTARS Information Center, Missouri Coordinating Board for Higher Education, 3515 Amazonas Drive, Jefferson City, MO 65109. *E-mail:* icweb@mocbhe.gov. *Phone:* 800-473-6757 Ext. 1. *Fax:* 573-751-6635. *Web site:* www.mostars.com.

John Charles Wilson Scholarship. One-time award to members in good standing of IAAI or the immediate family of a member or must be sponsored by an IAAI member. Must enroll or plan to enroll full-time in an accredited college or university that offers courses in police or fire sciences. Application available at Web site. Deadline is February 15. *Academic/Career Areas:* Fire Sciences; Law Enforcement/Police Administration. *Award:* Scholarship for use in freshman or graduate year; not renewable. *Award amount:* $500–$1000. *Number of awards:* 5. *Eligibility Requirements:* Applicant must be enrolled or expecting to enroll full-time at a two-year or four-year institution or university. Available to U.S. and non-U.S. citizens. *Application Requirements:* Application, essay, references, transcript. **Deadline:** February 15.

Contact Marsha Sipes, Office Manager, International Association of Arson Investigators Educational Foundation, Inc., 12770 Boenker Road, Bridgeton, MO 63044. *E-mail:* iaai@firearson.com.

Phone: 314-739-4224. *Fax:* 314-739-4219. *Web site:* www.fire-investigators.org/.

Marguerite Ross Barnett Memorial Scholarship. Applicant must be employed (at least 20 hours per week) and attending school part-time. Must be Missouri resident and enrolled at a participating Missouri postsecondary school. Awards not available during summer term. Minimum age is 18. *Award:* Scholarship for use in freshman, sophomore, junior, or senior year; not renewable. *Award amount:* $849–$1557. *Eligibility Requirements:* Applicant must be age 18; enrolled or expecting to enroll part-time at a two-year or four-year institution or university; resident of Missouri and studying in Missouri. Available to U.S. citizens. *Application Requirements:* Application, financial need analysis. **Deadline:** April 1.

Contact MOSTARS Information Center, Missouri Coordinating Board for Higher Education, 3515 Amazonas Drive, Jefferson City, MO 65109. *E-mail:* icweb@mocbhe.gov. *Phone:* 800-473-6757 Ext. 1. *Fax:* 573-751-6635. *Web site:* www.mostars.com.

Missouri College Guarantee Program. Available to Missouri residents attending Missouri colleges full-time. Minimum 2.5 GPA required. Must have participated in high school extracurricular activities. *Award:* Grant for use in freshman, sophomore, junior, or senior year; not renewable. *Award amount:* $100–$4600. *Eligibility Requirements:* Applicant must be enrolled or expecting to enroll full-time at a two-year or four-year institution or university; resident of Missouri and studying in Missouri. Applicant must have 2.5 GPA or higher. Available to U.S. citizens. *Application Requirements:* Financial need analysis, test scores. **Deadline:** April 1.

Contact MOSTARS Information Center, Missouri Coordinating Board for Higher Education, 3515 Amazonas Drive, Jefferson City, MO 65109. *E-mail:* icweb@mocbhe.gov. *Phone:* 800-473-6757 Ext. 1. *Fax:* 573-751-6635. *Web site:* www.mostars.com.

Missouri Higher Education Academic Scholarship (Bright Flight). Awards of $2000 for Missouri high school seniors. Must be in top 3% of Missouri SAT or ACT scorers. Must attend Missouri institution as full-time undergraduate. May reapply for up to ten semesters. Must be Missouri resident and U.S. citizen. *Award:* Scholarship for use in freshman, sophomore, junior, or senior year; not renewable. *Award amount:* $2000. *Eligibility Requirements:* Applicant must be high school student; planning to enroll or expecting to enroll full-time at a two-year, four-year, or technical institution or university; resident of Missouri and studying in Missouri. Available to U.S. citizens. *Application Requirements:* Test scores. **Deadline:** July 31.

Contact MOSTARS Information Center, Missouri Coordinating Board for Higher Education, 3515 Amazonas Drive, Jefferson City, MO 65109. *E-mail:*

Additional State Aid Programs

icweb@mocbhe.gov. *Phone:* 800-473-6757 Ext. 1. *Fax:* 573-751-6635. *Web site:* www.mostars.com.

Missouri Minority Teaching Scholarship. Award may be used any year up to four years at an approved, participating Missouri institution. Scholarship is for minority Missouri residents in teaching programs. Recipients must commit to teach for five years in a Missouri public elementary or secondary school. Graduate students must teach math or science. Otherwise, award must be repaid. *Academic/Career Areas:* Education. *Award:* Scholarship for use in freshman, sophomore, junior, senior, or graduate year; renewable. *Award amount:* $3000. *Number of awards:* 100. *Eligibility Requirements:* Applicant must be of African, Chinese, Hispanic, Indian, or Japanese heritage; American Indian/Alaska Native, Asian/Pacific Islander, or Black (non-Hispanic); enrolled or expecting to enroll full-time at a two-year or four-year institution or university; resident of Missouri and studying in Missouri. Applicant must have 3.5 GPA or higher. Available to U.S. citizens. *Application Requirements:* Application, essay, financial need analysis, references, test scores, transcript. **Deadline:** February 15.

Contact Laura Harrison, Administrative Assistant II, Missouri Department of Elementary and Secondary Education, PO Box 480, Jefferson City, MO 65102-0480. *E-mail:* lharriso@mail.dese.state.mo.us. *Phone:* 573-751-1668. *Fax:* 573-526-3580. *Web site:* www.dese.state.mo.us.

Missouri Teacher Education Scholarship (General). Nonrenewable award for Missouri high school seniors or Missouri resident college students. Must attend approved teacher training program at Missouri institution. Nonrenewable. Must rank in top 15% of high school class on ACT/SAT. Merit-based award. *Academic/Career Areas:* Education. *Award:* Scholarship for use in freshman, sophomore, junior, or senior year; not renewable. *Award amount:* $2000. *Number of awards:* 200–240. *Eligibility Requirements:* Applicant must be enrolled or expecting to enroll full-time at a two-year or four-year institution or university; resident of Missouri and studying in Missouri. Applicant must have 3.5 GPA or higher. Available to U.S. citizens. *Application Requirements:* Application, essay, references, test scores, transcript. **Deadline:** February 15.

Contact Laura Harrison, Administrative Assistant II, Missouri Department of Elementary and Secondary Education, PO Box 480, Jefferson City, MO 65102-0480. *E-mail:* lharriso@mail.dese.state.mo.us. *Phone:* 573-751-1668. *Fax:* 573-526-3580. *Web site:* www.dese.state.mo.us.

Montana

High School Honor Scholarship. Scholarship provides a one-year non-renewable fee waiver of tuition and registration and is awarded to graduating high school seniors from accredited high schools in Montana. 500 scholarships are awarded each year averaging $2,000 per recipient. The value of the award varies, depending on the tuition and registration fee at each participating college. Must have a minimum 3.0 GPA, meet all college preparatory requirements and be enrolled in an accredited high school for at least three years prior to graduation. Awarded to highest-ranking student in class attending a participating school. Contact high school counselor to apply. Deadline: April 15. *Award:* Scholarship for use in freshman year; not renewable. *Award amount:* $2000. *Number of awards:* 500. *Eligibility Requirements:* Applicant must be high school student; planning to enroll or expecting to enroll full or part-time at a two-year or four-year institution or university; resident of Montana and studying in Montana. Applicant must have 3.0 GPA or higher. Available to U.S. citizens. *Application Requirements:* Application, transcript. **Deadline:** April 15.

Contact high school counselor, Montana Guaranteed Student Loan Program, Office of Commissioner of Higher Education. *Web site:* www.mgslp.state.mt.us.

Indian Student Fee Waiver. Fee waiver awarded by the Montana University System to undergraduate and graduate students meeting the criteria. Amount varies depending upon the tuition and registration fee at each participating college. Students must provide documentation of one-fourth Indian blood or more; must be a resident of Montana for at least one year prior to enrolling in school and must demonstrate financial need. Full-or part-time study qualifies. Complete and submit the FAFSA by March 1 and a Montana Indian Fee Waiver application form. Contact the financial aid office at the college of attendance to determine eligibility. *Award:* Scholarship for use in freshman, sophomore, junior, senior, or graduate year; renewable. *Award amount:* $2000. *Number of awards:* 600. *Eligibility Requirements:* Applicant must be American Indian/Alaska Native; enrolled or expecting to enroll full or part-time at a two-year or four-year institution or university; resident of Montana and studying in Montana. Available to U.S. citizens. *Application Requirements:* Application, financial need analysis, FAFSA. **Deadline:** March 1.

Contact Sally Speer, Grants and Scholarship Coordinator, Montana Guaranteed Student Loan Program, Office of Commissioner of Higher Education, 2500 Broadway, PO Box 203101, Helena, MT 59620-3101. *E-mail:* sspeer@mgslp.state.mt.us. *Phone:* 406-444-0638. *Fax:* 406-444-1869. *Web site:* www.mgslp.state.mt.us.

Life Member Montana Federation of Garden Clubs Scholarship. Applicant must be at least a sophomore, majoring in conservation, horticulture, park or forestry, floriculture, greenhouse management, land management, or related subjects. Must be in need of

Financial Aid 101

Appendix D

assistance. Must have a potential for a successful future. Must be ranked in upper half of class or have a minimum 2.8 GPA. Must be a Montana resident and all study must be done in Montana. Deadline: May 1. *Academic/Career Areas:* Biology; Earth Science; Horticulture/Floriculture; Landscape Architecture. *Award:* Scholarship for use in sophomore, junior, or senior year; not renewable. *Award amount:* $1000. *Number of awards:* 1. *Eligibility Requirements:* Applicant must be enrolled or expecting to enroll full-time at a four-year institution or university; resident of Montana and studying in Montana. Available to U.S. citizens. *Application Requirements:* Autobiography, financial need analysis, photo, references, transcript. **Deadline:** May 1.

Contact Elizabeth Kehmeier, Life Members Scholarship Chairman, Montana Federation of Garden Clubs, 214 Wyant Lane, Hamilton, MT 59840. *Phone:* 406-363-5693.

Montana Higher Education Opportunity Grant. This grant is awarded based on need to undergraduate students attending either part-time or full-time who are residents of Montana and attending participating Montana schools. Awards are limited to the most needy students. A specific major or program of study is not required. This grant does not need to be repaid, and students may apply each year. Apply by filing a Free Application for Federal Student Aid by March 1 and contacting the financial aid office at the admitting college. *Award:* Grant for use in freshman, sophomore, junior, or senior year; not renewable. *Award amount:* $400–$600. *Number of awards:* 500. *Eligibility Requirements:* Applicant must be enrolled or expecting to enroll full or part-time at a two-year or four-year institution or university; resident of Montana and studying in Montana. Available to U.S. citizens. *Application Requirements:* Financial need analysis, FAFSA. **Deadline:** March 1.

Contact Sally Speer, Grants and Scholarship Coordinator, Montana Guaranteed Student Loan Program, Office of Commissioner of Higher Education, 2500 Broadway, PO Box 203101, Helena, MT 59620-3101. *E-mail:* sspeer@mgslp.state.mt.us. *Phone:* 406-444-0638. *Fax:* 406-444-1869. *Web site:* www.mgslp.state.mt.us.

Montana Tuition Assistance Program—Baker Grant. Need-based grant for Montana residents attending participating Montana schools who have earned at least $2,575 during the previous calendar year. Must be enrolled full time. Grant does not need to be repaid. Award covers the first undergraduate degree or certificate. Apply by filing a Free Application for Federal Student Aid by March 1 and contacting the financial aid office at the admitting college. *Award:* Grant for use in freshman, sophomore, junior, or senior year; not renewable. *Award amount:* $100–$1000. *Eligibility Requirements:* Applicant must be enrolled or expecting to enroll full-time at a two-year or four-year institution or university; resident of Montana and studying in Montana. Available to U.S. citizens. *Application Requirements:* Financial need analysis, FAFSA. **Deadline:** March 1.

Contact Sally Speer, Grants and Scholarship Coordinator, Montana Guaranteed Student Loan Program, Office of Commissioner of Higher Education, 2500 Broadway, PO Box 203101, Helena, MT 59620-3101. *E-mail:* sspeer@mgslp.state.mt.us. *Phone:* 406-444-0638. *Fax:* 406-444-1869. *Web site:* www.mgslp.state.mt.us.

Nebraska

Nebraska National Guard Tuition Credit. Renewable award for members of the Nebraska National Guard. Pays 75% of enlisted soldier's tuition until he or she has received a baccalaureate degree. *Award:* Scholarship for use in freshman, sophomore, junior, or senior year; renewable. *Number of awards:* up to 1200. *Eligibility Requirements:* Applicant must be enrolled or expecting to enroll full or part-time at a two-year, four-year, or technical institution or university; resident of Nebraska and studying in Nebraska. Applicant must have served in the Air Force National Guard or Army National Guard. *Application Requirements:* Application. **Deadline:** continuous.

Contact Cindy York, Administrative Assistant, Nebraska National Guard, 1300 Military Road, Lincoln, NE 68508-1090. *Phone:* 402-309-7143. *Fax:* 402-309-7128. *Web site:* www.neguard.com.

Nebraska Scholarship Assistance Program. Available to undergraduates attending a participating postsecondary institution in Nebraska. Available to Pell Grant recipients only. Nebraska residency required. Awards determined by each participating institution. Contact financial aid office at respective institution for more information. *Award:* Scholarship for use in freshman, sophomore, junior, or senior year; not renewable. *Eligibility Requirements:* Applicant must be enrolled or expecting to enroll full or part-time at a two-year, four-year, or technical institution or university; resident of Nebraska and studying in Nebraska. *Application Requirements:* Financial need analysis. **Deadline:** continuous.

Contact financial aid office at college or university, State of Nebraska Coordinating Commission for Postsecondary Education. *Web site:* www.ccpe.state.ne.us.

Nebraska State Scholarship Award Program. Available to undergraduates attending a participating postsecondary institution in Nebraska. Available to Pell Grant recipients only. Nebraska residency not required. Awards determined by each participating institution. Contact financial aid office at respective institution for more details. *Award:* Scholarship for use in freshman,

Additional State Aid Programs

sophomore, junior, or senior year; not renewable. *Eligibility Requirements*: Applicant must be enrolled or expecting to enroll full or part-time at an institution or university and studying in Nebraska. *Application Requirements*: Financial need analysis. **Deadline:** continuous.

Contact financial aid office at college or university, State of Nebraska Coordinating Commission for Postsecondary Education. *Web site:* www.ccpe.state.ne.us.

Postsecondary Education Award Program—Nebraska. Available to undergraduates attending a participating private, nonprofit postsecondary institution in Nebraska. Available to Pell Grant recipients only. Nebraska residency required. Awards determined by each participating institution. Contact financial aid office at respective institution for more information. *Award:* Scholarship for use in freshman, sophomore, junior, or senior year; not renewable. *Eligibility Requirements*: Applicant must be enrolled or expecting to enroll full or part-time at a two-year or four-year institution; resident of Nebraska and studying in Nebraska. Available to U.S. citizens. *Application Requirements*: Financial need analysis. **Deadline:** continuous.

Contact financial aid office at college or university, State of Nebraska Coordinating Commission for Postsecondary Education. *Web site:* www.ccpe.state.ne.us.

Nevada

Nevada Student Incentive Grant. Award available to Nevada residents for use at an accredited Nevada college or university. Must show financial need. Any field of study eligible. High school students may not apply. One-time award of up to $5000. Contact financial aid office at local college. *Award:* Grant for use in freshman, sophomore, junior, or senior year; not renewable. *Award amount:* $100–$5000. *Number of awards:* 400–800. *Eligibility Requirements*: Applicant must be enrolled or expecting to enroll full or part-time at a two-year, four-year, or technical institution or university; resident of Nevada and studying in Nevada. Available to U.S. citizens. *Application Requirements*: Application, financial need analysis. **Deadline:** continuous.

Contact Financial Aid Office at local college, Nevada Department of Education, 700 East 5th Street, Carson City, NV 89701.

New Hampshire

Leveraged Incentive Grant Program. Award open to New Hampshire residents attending school in New Hampshire. Must be in sophomore, junior, or senior year. Award based on financial need and merit. Contact financial aid office for more information and deadline. *Award:* Grant for use in sophomore, junior, or senior year; not renewable. *Award amount:* $200–$7500. *Eligibility Requirements*: Applicant must be enrolled or expecting to enroll full-time at a two-year or four-year institution or university; resident of New Hampshire and studying in New Hampshire. Available to U.S. citizens. *Application Requirements*: Application, financial need analysis.

Contact Financial Aid Office, New Hampshire Postsecondary Education Commission. *Web site:* www.state.nh.us/postsecondary.

New Hampshire Career Incentive Program. Forgivable loans available to New Hampshire residents attending New Hampshire institutions in programs leading to certification in special education, foreign language education or licensure as an LPN, RN or an Associate, Baccalaureate or advanced nursing degree. Must work in shortage area following graduation. Deadline: June 1 for fall or December 15 for spring. Foreign language or special education students must be juniors, seniors or graduate students with a 3.0 GPA or higher. Forgivable loan is not automatically renewable. Applicant must reapply. *Academic/Career Areas:* Foreign Language; Nursing; Special Education. *Award:* Forgivable loan for use in freshman, sophomore, junior, senior, graduate, or postgraduate years; not renewable. *Award amount:* $1000–$3000. *Eligibility Requirements*: Applicant must be enrolled or expecting to enroll full-time at a two-year, four-year, or technical institution or university; resident of New Hampshire and studying in New Hampshire. Available to U.S. citizens. *Application Requirements*: Application, financial need analysis, references, transcript.

Contact Melanie K. Deshaies, Program Assistant, New Hampshire Postsecondary Education Commission, 3 Barrell Court, Suite 300, Concord, NH 03301-8512. E-mail: mdeshaies@pec.state.nh.us. Phone: 603-271-2555 Ext. 356. Fax: 603-271-2696. Web site: www.state.nh.us/postsecondary.

New Hampshire Incentive Program (NHIP). One-time grants for New Hampshire residents attending school in New Hampshire, Connecticut, Maine, Massachusetts, Rhode Island, or Vermont. Must have financial need. Deadline is May 1. Complete Free Application for Federal Student Aid. Grant is not automatically renewable. Applicant must reapply. *Award:* Grant for use in freshman, sophomore, junior, or senior year; not renewable. *Award amount:* $125–$1000. *Number of awards:* 3000–3500. *Eligibility Requirements*: Applicant must be enrolled or expecting to enroll full or part-time at a two-year, four-year, or technical institution or university; resident of New Hampshire and studying in Connecticut, Maine, Massachusetts, New Hampshire, Rhode Island, or Vermont. Available to U.S. citizens. *Application Requirements*: Application, financial need analysis. **Deadline:** May 1.

Contact Sherrie Tucker, Program Assistant, New Hampshire Postsecondary Education Commission, 3 Barrell Court, Suite 300, Concord, NH 03301-8512.

Financial Aid 101 www.petersons.com

Appendix D

E-mail: stucker@pec.state.nh.us. *Phone:* 603-271-2555 Ext. 355. *Fax:* 603-271-2696. *Web site:* www.state.nh.us/postsecondary.

Nursing Leveraged Scholarship Loan Program. Forgivable loan available to New Hampshire residents enrolled part- or full-time as a graduate or undergraduate in an approved nursing program at a New Hampshire institute of higher education. Must demonstrate financial need. Loan forgiven through service in New Hampshire as a nurse. Contact Financial Aid Office for deadline. *Academic/Career Areas:* Nursing. *Award:* Forgivable loan for use in freshman, sophomore, junior, senior, or graduate year; not renewable. *Award amount:* $100–$2000. *Eligibility Requirements:* Applicant must be enrolled or expecting to enroll full or part-time at a two-year, four-year, or technical institution or university; resident of New Hampshire and studying in New Hampshire. Available to U.S. citizens. *Application Requirements:* Application, financial need analysis.

Contact Financial Aid Office/HS Guidance Office, New Hampshire Postsecondary Education Commission. *Web site:* www.state.nh.us/postsecondary.

Scholarships for Orphans of Veterans—New Hampshire. Awards for New Hampshire residents whose parent died as a result of service in WWI, WWII, the Korean Conflict, or the Southeast Asian Conflict. Parent must have been a New Hampshire resident at time of death. Possible full tuition and $1000 per year with automatic renewal on reapplication. Contact department for application deadlines. Must be under 26. Must include proof of eligibility and proof of parent's death. *Award:* Grant for use in freshman, sophomore, junior, or senior year; renewable. *Award amount:* up to $1000. *Number of awards:* 1–10. *Eligibility Requirements:* Applicant must be age 16-25; enrolled or expecting to enroll full-time at a two-year or four-year institution or university and resident of New Hampshire. Available to U.S. citizens. Applicant or parent must meet one or more of the following requirements: general military experience; retired from active duty; disabled or killed as a result of military service; prisoner of war; or missing in action. *Application Requirements:* Application, VA approval.

Contact Melanie K. Deshaies, Program Assistant, New Hampshire Postsecondary Education Commission, 3 Barrell Court, Suite 300, Concord, NH 03301-8543. *E-mail:* mdeshaies@pec.state.nh.us. *Phone:* 603-271-2555 Ext. 356. *Fax:* 603-271-2696. *Web site:* www.state.nh.us/postsecondary.

New Jersey

Dana Christmas Scholarship for Heroism. One-time, non-renewable college scholarship will recognize and honor young for exceptional acts of heroism. The scholarship may be used for undergraduate or graduate higher education expenses. Must be current New Jersey resident and at time of act of heroism. *Award:* Scholarship for use in freshman, sophomore, junior, senior, or graduate year; not renewable. *Award amount:* up to $10,000. *Number of awards:* up to 5. *Eligibility Requirements:* Applicant must be age 21 or under; enrolled or expecting to enroll at a four-year institution or university and resident of New Jersey. Available to U.S. citizens. *Application Requirements:* Application. **Deadline:** October 15.

Contact New Jersey Higher Education Student Assistance Authority, PO Box 540, Trenton, NJ 08625-0540. *Phone:* 800-792-8670. *Web site:* www.hesaa.org.

Edward J. Bloustein Distinguished Scholars. Renewable scholarship for students who place in the top 10% of their classes and have a minimum combined SAT score of 1260, or are ranked first, second or third in their class as of the end of the junior year. Must be New Jersey resident. Must attend a New Jersey two-year college, four-year college or university, or approved programs at proprietary institutions. Deadline for Spring term is March 1 and for Fall term is October 1. *Award:* Scholarship for use in freshman, sophomore, junior, or senior year; renewable. *Award amount:* $1000. *Eligibility Requirements:* Applicant must be high school student; planning to enroll or expecting to enroll full-time at a two-year or four-year institution or university; resident of New Jersey and studying in New Jersey. Available to U.S. citizens. *Application Requirements:* Application, test scores.

Contact New Jersey Higher Education Student Assistance Authority, PO Box 540, Trenton, NJ 08625-0540. *Phone:* 800-792-8670. *Web site:* www.hesaa.org.

New Jersey Educational Opportunity Fund Grants. Grants up to $4150 per year. Must be a New Jersey resident for at least twelve consecutive months and attend a New Jersey institution. Must be from a disadvantaged background as defined by EOF guidelines. EOF grant applicants must also apply for financial aid. EOF recipients may qualify for the Martin Luther King Physician/Dentistry Scholarships for graduate study at a professional institution. *Academic/Career Areas:* Dental Health/Services; Health and Medical Sciences. *Award:* Grant for use in freshman, sophomore, junior, senior, or graduate year; renewable. *Award amount:* up to $4150. *Eligibility Requirements:* Applicant must be enrolled or expecting to enroll full-time at a four-year institution or university; resident of New Jersey and studying in New Jersey. Available to U.S. citizens. *Application Requirements:* Application, financial need analysis.

Contact Sandra Rollins, Associate Director of Financial Aid, University of Medicine and Dentistry of NJ School of Osteopathic Medicine, 40 East Laurel Road, Primary Care Center 119, Stratford, NJ

Additional State Aid Programs

08084. *E-mail:* rollins@umdnj.edu. *Phone:* 856-566-6008. *Fax:* 856-566-6015. *Web site:* www.umdnj.edu.

New Jersey War Orphans Tuition Assistance. Renewable award for New Jersey residents who are high school seniors ages 16-21 and who are children of veterans killed or disabled in duty, missing in action, or prisoner-of-war. For use at a two- or four-year college or university. Write for more information. Deadlines: October 1 for fall semester and March 1 for spring semester. *Award:* Scholarship for use in freshman, sophomore, junior, or senior year; renewable. *Award amount:* $2000–$5000. *Eligibility Requirements:* Applicant must be high school student; age 16-21; planning to enroll or expecting to enroll full-time at a two-year or four-year institution or university and resident of New Jersey. Applicant or parent must meet one or more of the following requirements: general military experience; retired from active duty; disabled or killed as a result of military service; prisoner of war; or missing in action. *Application Requirements:* Application, transcript.

Contact Patricia Richter, Grants Manager, New Jersey Department of Military and Veterans Affairs, PO Box 340, Trenton, NJ 08625-0340. *E-mail:* patricia.richter@njdmava.state.nj.us. *Phone:* 609-530-6854. *Fax:* 609-530-6970.

NJSA Scholarship Program. One-time award for legal residents of New Jersey enrolled in an accredited architecture program. Minimum 2.5 GPA required. Must show evidence of financial need, scholarship, and promise in architecture. Submit portfolio and $5 application fee. *Academic/Career Areas:* Architecture. *Award:* Scholarship for use in sophomore, junior, senior, or graduate year; not renewable. *Award amount:* $1500–$3000. *Eligibility Requirements:* Applicant must be enrolled or expecting to enroll full-time at a four-year, or technical institution or university and resident of New Jersey. Applicant must have 2.5 GPA or higher. Available to U.S. citizens. *Application Requirements:* Application, essay, financial need analysis, portfolio, references, transcript. *Fee:* $5. **Deadline:** April 25.

Contact Robert Zaccone, President, AIA New Jersey Scholarship Foundation, Inc., 212 White Avenue, Old Tappan, NJ 07675-7411. *Fax:* 201-767-5541.

Outstanding Scholar Recruitment Program. Students who meet the eligibility criteria and enroll as first-time freshmen at participating New Jersey institutions receive annual scholarship awards of up to $7500. The award amounts vary on a sliding scale depending on class rank and combined SAT scores. Must maintain a B average for renewal. Deadline March 1 for Spring term, October 1 for Fall term. *Award:* Scholarship for use in freshman, sophomore, junior, or senior year; renewable. *Award amount:* up to $7500. *Eligibility Requirements:* Applicant must be high school student; planning to enroll or expecting to enroll at an institution or university and studying in New Jersey. *Application Requirements:* Test scores.

Contact New Jersey Higher Education Student Assistance Authority, PO Box 540, Trenton, NJ 08625-0540. *Phone:* 800-792-8670. *Web site:* www.hesaa.org.

Survivor Tuition Benefits Program. Provides tuition for spouses and dependents of law enforcement officers, fire, or emergency services personnel killed in the line of duty. Recipients must be enrolled in an undergraduate degree program at a college or university in New Jersey as either half-time or full-time students. Deadline March 1 for Spring term, October 1 for Fall term. *Award:* Scholarship for use in freshman, sophomore, junior, or senior year; renewable. *Eligibility Requirements:* Applicant must be enrolled or expecting to enroll full or part-time at a four-year institution or university; resident of New Jersey and studying in New Jersey. Applicant or parent of applicant must have employment or volunteer experience in police/firefighting. Available to U.S. citizens. *Application Requirements:* Application.

Contact New Jersey Higher Education Student Assistance Authority, PO Box 540, Trenton, NJ 08625-0540. *Phone:* 800-792-8670. *Web site:* www.hesaa.org.

Tuition Assistance for Children of POW/MIAs. Assists children of military service personnel declared missing in action or prisoner-of-war after January 1, 1960. Must be a resident of New Jersey. Renewable grants provide tuition for undergraduate study in New Jersey. Apply by October 1 for fall, March 1 for spring. Must be high school senior to apply. *Award:* Scholarship for use in freshman, sophomore, junior, or senior year; renewable. *Eligibility Requirements:* Applicant must be high school student; planning to enroll or expecting to enroll full-time at a two-year or four-year institution; resident of New Jersey and studying in New Jersey. Available to U.S. citizens. Applicant or parent must meet one or more of the following requirements: general military experience; retired from active duty; disabled or killed as a result of military service; prisoner of war; or missing in action. *Application Requirements:* Application, transcript.

Contact Patricia Richter, Grants Manager, New Jersey Department of Military and Veterans Affairs, PO Box 340, Trenton, NJ 08625-0340. *E-mail:* patricia.richter@njdmava.state.nj.us. *Phone:* 609-530-6854. *Fax:* 609-530-6970.

Urban Scholars. Renewable scholarship to high achieving students attending public secondary schools in the State's urban and economically distressed areas of New Jersey. Students must rank in the top 10% of their class and have a GPA of at least 3.0 at the end of their junior year. Must be New Jersey resident. Must attend a New Jersey two-year college, four-year college or university, or approved programs at proprietary institutions. Students do not apply directly for scholarship consideration. Deadline March 1 for Spring term, October 1 for Fall term. *Award:* Scholarship for use in freshman, sophomore, junior, or senior year; renewable. *Award amount:* $1000. *Eligibility Requirements:* Applicant must be high school student; planning to enroll or expecting to enroll full-time at a two-year or four-year institution or university; resident of New Jersey and studying in New Jersey. Applicant must have 3.0 GPA or higher. Available to U.S. citizens. *Application Requirements:* Application, test scores.

Contact New Jersey Higher Education Student Assistance Authority, PO Box 540, Trenton, NJ 08625-0540. *Phone:* 800-792-8670. *Web site:* www.hesaa.org.

Veterans' Tuition Credit Program—New Jersey. Award for veterans who served in the armed forces between December 31, 1960, and May 7, 1975. Must have been a New Jersey resident at time of induction or discharge or for one year prior to application. Apply by October 1 for fall, March 1 for spring. Renewable award of $200-$400. *Award:* Scholarship for use in freshman, sophomore, junior, or senior year; renewable. *Award amount:* $200–$400. *Eligibility Requirements:* Applicant must be enrolled or expecting to enroll full or part-time at a two-year, four-year, or technical institution or university and resident of New Jersey. Available to U.S. citizens. Applicant must have general military experience. *Application Requirements:* Application.

Contact Patricia Richter, Grants Manager, New Jersey Department of Military and Veterans Affairs, PO Box 340, Trenton, NJ 08625-0340. *E-mail:* patricia.richter@njdmava.state.nj.us. *Phone:* 609-530-6854. *Fax:* 609-530-6970.

New Mexico

3% Scholarship Program. Award equal to tuition and required fees for New Mexico residents who are undergraduate students attending public postsecondary institutions in New Mexico. Contact financial aid office of any public postsecondary institution in New Mexico for deadline. *Award:* Scholarship for use in freshman, sophomore, junior, senior, or graduate year; not renewable. *Eligibility Requirements:* Applicant must be enrolled or expecting to enroll full or part-time at a two-year or four-year institution or university; resident of New Mexico and studying in New Mexico. Available to U.S. citizens. *Application Requirements:* Application.

Contact Maria Barele, Financial Specialist, New Mexico Commission on Higher Education, PO Box 15910, Santa Fe, NM 87506-5910. *Phone:* 505-827-4026. *Fax:* 505-827-7392. *Web site:* www.nmche.org.

Allied Health Student Loan Program—New Mexico. Renewable loans for New Mexico residents enrolled in an undergraduate allied health program. Loans can be forgiven through service in a medically underserved area or can be repaid. Penalties apply for failure to provide service. May borrow up to $12,000 per year for four years. *Academic/Career Areas:* Dental Health/Services; Health and Medical Sciences; Nursing; Social Sciences; Therapy/Rehabilitation. *Award:* Forgivable loan for use in freshman, sophomore, junior, or senior year; renewable. *Award amount:* up to $12,000. *Number of awards:* 1–40. *Eligibility Requirements:* Applicant must be enrolled or expecting to enroll full or part-time at a two-year or four-year institution or university; resident of New Mexico and studying in New Mexico. Available to U.S. citizens. *Application Requirements:* Application, financial need analysis, transcript, FAFSA. **Deadline:** July 1.

Contact Maria Barele, Financial Specialist, New Mexico Commission on Higher Education, PO Box 15910, Santa Fe, NM 87506-5910. *Phone:* 505-827-4026. *Fax:* 505-827-7392. *Web site:* www.nmche.org.

Children of Deceased Veterans Scholarship—New Mexico. Award for New Mexico residents who are children of veterans killed or disabled as a result of service, prisoner of war, or veterans missing-in-action. Must be between ages 16 to 26. For use at New Mexico schools for undergraduate study. Submit parent's death certificate and DD form 214. *Award:* Scholarship for use in freshman, sophomore, junior, or senior year; renewable. *Award amount:* $250–$600. *Eligibility Requirements:* Applicant must be age 16-26; enrolled or expecting to enroll full or part-time at an institution or university; resident of New Mexico and studying in New Mexico. Applicant or parent must meet one or more of the following requirements: general military experience; retired from active duty; disabled or killed as a result of military service; prisoner of war; or missing in action. *Application Requirements:* Application, transcript. **Deadline:** continuous.

Contact Alan Martinez, Manager of State Benefits, New Mexico Veterans' Service Commission, PO Box 2324, Sante Fe, NM 87504. *Phone:* 505-827-6300. *Fax:* 505-827-6372. *Web site:* www.state.nm.us/veterans.

Legislative Endowment Scholarships. Awards for undergraduate students with substantial financial need who are attending public postsecondary institutions in New Mexico. Preference given to returning adult students at two-year and four-year institutions and students transferring from two-year to four-year institutions. Deadline set by each institution. Must be resident of New Mexico. Contact financial aid office of any New Mexico public postsecondary institution to apply. *Award:* Scholarship for use in freshman, sophomore, junior, or senior year; not renewable. *Award amount:* $1000–$2500. *Eligibility Requirements:* Applicant must be enrolled or expecting to enroll full or part-time at a two-year or four-year institution or university; resident of

Additional State Aid Programs

New Mexico and studying in New Mexico. Available to U.S. citizens. *Application Requirements*: Application, financial need analysis, FAFSA.

Contact Maria Barele, Financial Specialist, New Mexico Commission on Higher Education, PO Box 15910, Santa Fe, NM 87506-5910. *Phone*: 505-827-7383. *Fax*: 505-827-7392. *Web site*: www.nmche.org.

Lottery Success Scholarships. Awards equal to 100% of tuition at New Mexico public postsecondary institution. Must have New Mexico high school degree and be enrolled at New Mexico public college or university in first regular semester following high school graduation. Must obtain 2.5 GPA during this semester. May be eligible for up to eight consecutive semesters of support. Deadlines vary by institution. Apply through financial aid office of any New Mexico public postsecondary institution. *Award*: Scholarship for use in freshman, sophomore, junior, or senior year; renewable. *Eligibility Requirements*: Applicant must be enrolled or expecting to enroll full-time at a two-year or four-year institution; resident of New Mexico and studying in New Mexico. Applicant must have 2.5 GPA or higher. Available to U.S. citizens. *Application Requirements*: Application.

Contact Maria Barele, Financial Specialist, New Mexico Commission on Higher Education, PO Box 15910, Santa Fe, NM 87506-5910. *Phone*: 505-827-4026. *Fax*: 505-827-7392. *Web site*: www.nmche.org.

New Mexico Competitive Scholarship. Scholarship available to encourage out-of-state students who have demonstrated high academic achievement to enroll in public institutions of higher education in New Mexico. One-time award for undergraduate students. Deadlines set by each institution. Contact financial aid office of any New Mexico public postsecondary institution to apply. *Award*: Scholarship for use in freshman, sophomore, junior, or senior year; not renewable. *Award amount*: $100. *Eligibility Requirements*: Applicant must be enrolled or expecting to enroll full or part-time at a two-year or four-year institution or university and studying in New Mexico. Applicant must have 3.0 GPA or higher. Available to U.S. citizens. *Application Requirements*: Application, essay, references, test scores.

Contact Maria Barele, Financial Specialist, New Mexico Commission on Higher Education, PO Box 15910, Santa Fe, NM 87506-5910. *Phone*: 505-827-4026. *Fax*: 505-827-7392. *Web site*: www.nmche.org.

New Mexico Scholars' Program. Several scholarships to encourage New Mexico high school graduates to enroll in college at a public or selected private nonprofit postsecondary institution in New Mexico before their 22nd birthday. Selected private colleges are College of Santa Fe, St. John's College in Santa Fe, and College of the Southwest. Must have graduated in top 5% of their class or obtained an ACT score of 25 or SAT score of 1140. One-time scholarship for tuition, books, and fees. Contact financial aid office at college to apply. *Award*: Scholarship for use in freshman, sophomore, junior, or senior year; not renewable. *Eligibility Requirements*: Applicant must be age 22 or under; enrolled or expecting to enroll full or part-time at a two-year or four-year institution; resident of New Mexico and studying in New Mexico. Available to U.S. citizens. *Application Requirements*: Application, financial need analysis, test scores, FAFSA.

Contact Maria Barele, Financial Specialist, New Mexico Commission on Higher Education, PO Box 15910, Santa Fe, NM 87506-5910. *Phone*: 505-827-4026. *Fax*: 505-827-7392. *Web site*: www.nmche.org.

New Mexico Student Incentive Grant. Several grants available for resident undergraduate students attending public and selected private nonprofit institutions in New Mexico. Must demonstrate financial need. To apply contact financial aid office at any public or private nonprofit postsecondary institution in New Mexico. *Award*: Grant for use in freshman, sophomore, junior, or senior year; not renewable. *Award amount*: $200–$2500. *Eligibility Requirements*: Applicant must be enrolled or expecting to enroll at a two-year or four-year institution or university; resident of New Mexico and studying in New Mexico. Available to U.S. citizens. *Application Requirements*: Application, financial need analysis, FAFSA.

Contact Maria Barele, Financial Specialist, New Mexico Commission on Higher Education, PO Box 15910, Santa Fe, NM 87506-5910. *Phone*: 505-827-4026. *Fax*: 505-827-7392. *Web site*: www.nmche.org.

New Mexico Vietnam Veterans' Scholarship. Renewable award for Vietnam veterans who are New Mexico residents attending state-sponsored schools. Must have been awarded the Vietnam Campaign medal. Submit DD214. Must include discharge papers. *Award*: Scholarship for use in freshman, sophomore, junior, or senior year; renewable. *Award amount*: up to $1554. *Eligibility Requirements*: Applicant must be enrolled or expecting to enroll at an institution or university; resident of New Mexico and studying in New Mexico. Available to U.S. citizens. Applicant must have general military experience. *Application Requirements*: Application. **Deadline**: continuous.

Contact Alan Martinez, Manager State Benefits, New Mexico Veterans' Service Commission, PO Box 2324, Sante Fe, NM 87504. *Phone*: 505-827-6300. *Fax*: 505-827-6372. *Web site*: www.state.nm.us/veterans.

Nursing Student Loan-for-Service Program. Award for New Mexico residents accepted or enrolled in nursing program at New Mexico public postsecondary

Financial Aid 101 — www.petersons.com

Appendix D

institution. Must practice as nurse in designated health professional shortage area in New Mexico. Award dependent upon financial need but may not exceed $12,000. Deadline: July 1. *Academic/Career Areas:* Nursing. *Award:* Forgivable loan for use in freshman, sophomore, junior, or senior year; not renewable. *Award amount:* up to $12,000. *Eligibility Requirements:* Applicant must be enrolled or expecting to enroll full or part-time at a two-year or four-year institution; resident of New Mexico and studying in New Mexico. Available to U.S. citizens. *Application Requirements:* Application, financial need analysis, FAFSA. **Deadline:** July 1.

Contact Maria Barele, Financial Specialist, New Mexico Commission on Higher Education, PO Box 15910, Santa Fe, NM 87506-5910. *Phone:* 505-827-4026. *Fax:* 505-827-7392. *Web site:* www.nmche.org.

Vietnam Veterans' Scholarship Program. Award for New Mexico residents who are Vietnam veterans enrolled in undergraduate or master's-level course work at public or selected private New Mexico postsecondary institutions. Award may include tuition, required fees, and book allowance. Contact financial aid office of any public or eligible private New Mexico postsecondary institution for deadline. *Award:* Scholarship for use in freshman, sophomore, junior, senior, or graduate year; not renewable. *Eligibility Requirements:* Applicant must be enrolled or expecting to enroll full or part-time at a two-year or four-year institution; resident of New Mexico and studying in New Mexico. Available to U.S. citizens. Applicant must have general military experience. *Application Requirements:* Application, certification by the NM Veteran's commission.

Contact Maria Barele, Financial Specialist, New Mexico Commission on Higher Education, PO Box 15910, Santa Fe, NM 87506-5910. *Phone:* 505-827-4026. *Fax:* 505-827-7392. *Web site:* www.nmche.org.

New York

New York Aid for Part-time Study (APTS). Renewable scholarship provides tuition assistance to part-time students who are New York residents attending New York-accredited institutions. Deadlines and award amounts vary. Must be U.S. citizen. *Award:* Grant for use in freshman, sophomore, junior, or senior year; renewable. *Award amount:* up to $2000. *Eligibility Requirements:* Applicant must be enrolled or expecting to enroll part-time at a two-year or four-year institution; resident of New York and studying in New York. Available to U.S. citizens. *Application Requirements:* Application.

Contact Student Information, New York State Higher Education Services Corporation, 99 Washington Avenue, Room 1320, Albany, NY 12255. *Phone:* 518-473-3887. *Fax:* 518-474-2839. *Web site:* www.hesc.com.

New York Educational Opportunity Program (EOP). Renewable award for New York resident attending New York college/university for undergraduate study. For educationally and economically disadvantaged students; includes educational assistance such as tutoring. Contact prospective college for information. *Award:* Scholarship for use in freshman, sophomore, junior, or senior year; renewable. *Eligibility Requirements:* Applicant must be enrolled or expecting to enroll full-time at a two-year or four-year institution or university; resident of New York and studying in New York. Available to U.S. citizens. *Application Requirements:* Application, financial need analysis, transcript.

Contact Student Information, New York State Higher Education Services Corporation, 99 Washington Avenue, Room 1320, Albany, NY 12255. *Web site:* www.hesc.com.

New York Lottery Leaders of Tomorrow (Lot) Scholarship. The goal of this program is to reinforce the lottery's education mission by awarding four-year scholarships, $1000 per year for up to four years. One scholarship is available to every New York high school, public or private, that awards a high school diploma. *Award:* Scholarship for use in freshman, sophomore, junior, or senior year; renewable. *Award amount:* $1000. *Eligibility Requirements:* Applicant must be high school student; planning to enroll or expecting to enroll full-time at a two-year, four-year, or technical institution or university; resident of New York and studying in New York. Applicant must have 3.0 GPA or higher. Available to U.S. citizens. *Application Requirements:* Application, essay, transcript. **Deadline:** March 19.

Contact Betsey Morgan, Program Coordinator, CASDA-LOT (Capital Area School Development Association), The University at Albany East Campus, One University Place—A-409, Rensselaer, NY 12144-3456. *E-mail:* casdalot@uamail.albany.edu. *Phone:* 518-525-2788. *Fax:* 518-525-2797. *Web site:* www.nylottery.org/lot.

New York State Aid to Native Americans. Award for enrolled members of a New York State tribe and their children who are attending or planning to attend a New York State college and who are New York State residents. Award for full-time-students up to $1550 annually; part-time awards approximately $65 per credit hour. *Award:* Scholarship for use in freshman, sophomore, junior, or senior year; not renewable. *Award amount:* up to $1550. *Eligibility Requirements:* Applicant must be American Indian/Alaska Native; enrolled or expecting to enroll full or part-time at a two-year, four-year, or technical institution or university; resident of New York and studying in New York. *Application Requirements:* Application. **Deadline:** July 15.

Contact Native American Education Unit, New York State Education Department, New York State Higher

Additional State Aid Programs

Education Services Corporation, EBA Room 374, Albany, NY 12234. *Phone:* 518-474-0537. *Web site:* www.hesc.com.

New York State Tuition Assistance Program. Award for New York state residents attending New York postsecondary institution. Must be full-time student in approved program with tuition over $200 per year. Must show financial need and not be in default in any other state program. Renewable award of $500-$5000. *Award:* Grant for use in freshman, sophomore, junior, or senior year; renewable. *Award amount:* $500–$5000. *Number of awards:* 300,000–320,000. *Eligibility Requirements:* Applicant must be enrolled or expecting to enroll full-time at a two-year or four-year institution or university; resident of New York and studying in New York. *Application Requirements:* Application, financial need analysis. **Deadline:** May 1.

> **Contact** Student Information, New York State Higher Education Services Corporation, 99 Washington Avenue, Room 1320, Albany, NY 12255. *Web site:* www.hesc.com.

New York Vietnam Veterans Tuition Awards. Scholarship for veterans who served in Vietnam. Must be a New York resident attending a New York institution. Renewable award of $500-$1000. Deadline: May 1. Must establish eligibility by September 1. *Award:* Scholarship for use in freshman, sophomore, junior, or senior year; renewable. *Award amount:* $500–$1000. *Eligibility Requirements:* Applicant must be enrolled or expecting to enroll full or part-time at a two-year, four-year, or technical institution or university; resident of New York and studying in New York. Applicant must have served in the Air Force, Army, Marine Corp, or Navy. *Application Requirements:* Application, financial need analysis. **Deadline:** May 1.

> **Contact** Student Information, New York State Higher Education Services Corporation, 99 Washington Avenue, Room 1320, Albany, NY 12255. *Web site:* www.hesc.com.

Regents Award for Child of Veteran. Award for students whose parent, as a result of service in U.S. Armed Forces during war or national emergency, died; suffered a 40% or more disability; or is classified as missing in action or a prisoner of war. Veteran must be current New York State resident or have been so at time of death. Must be New York resident attending, or planning to attend, college in New York State. Must establish eligibility before applying for payment. *Award:* Scholarship for use in freshman, sophomore, junior, or senior year; not renewable. *Award amount:* $450. *Eligibility Requirements:* Applicant must be enrolled or expecting to enroll full-time at a two-year or four-year institution or university; resident of New York and studying in New York. Available to U.S. citizens. Applicant or parent must meet one or more of the following requirements: general military experience; retired from active duty; disabled or killed as a result of military service; prisoner of war; or missing in action. *Application Requirements:* Application, proof of eligibility. **Deadline:** May 1.

> **Contact** Student Information, New York State Higher Education Services Corporation, 99 Washington Avenue, Room 1320, Albany, NY 12255. *Web site:* www.hesc.com.

Regents Professional Opportunity Scholarships. Award for New York State residents pursuing career in certain licensed professions. Must attend New York State college. Priority given to economically disadvantaged members of minority group underrepresented in chosen profession and graduates of SEEK, College Discovery, EOP, and HEOP. Must work in New York State in chosen profession one year for each annual payment. *Award:* Forgivable loan for use in freshman, sophomore, junior, senior, or graduate year; not renewable. *Award amount:* $1000–$5000. *Eligibility Requirements:* Applicant must be enrolled or expecting to enroll full-time at a two-year or four-year institution or university; resident of New York and studying in New York. Available to U.S. citizens. *Application Requirements:* Application. **Deadline:** May 1.

> **Contact** Scholarship Processing Unit-New York State Education Department, New York State Higher Education Services Corporation, EBA Room 1078, Albany, NY 12234. *Phone:* 518-486-1319. *Web site:* www.hesc.com.

Scholarships for Academic Excellence. Renewable awards of up to $1500 for academically outstanding New York State high school graduates planning to attend an approved postsecondary institution in New York State. For full-time study only. Contact high school guidance counselor to apply. *Award:* Scholarship for use in freshman, sophomore, junior, or senior year; renewable. *Award amount:* $500–$1500. *Number of awards:* 8000. *Eligibility Requirements:* Applicant must be high school student; planning to enroll or expecting to enroll full-time at a four-year institution or university; resident of New York and studying in New York. Available to U.S. citizens. *Application Requirements:* Application.

> **Contact** Student Information, New York State Higher Education Services Corporation, 99 Washington Avenue, Room 1320, Albany, NY 12255. *Web site:* www.hesc.com.

World Trade Center Memorial Scholarship. Renewable awards of up to the average cost of attendance at a State University of New York four-year college. Available to the families and financial dependents of victims who died or were severely and permanently disabled as a result of the Sept. 11, 2001 terrorist attacks on the U.S.A and the rescue and recovery efforts. *Award:* Scholarship for use in freshman, sophomore, junior, or senior year; renewable. *Eligibility Requirements:* Applicant must be enrolled or expecting to enroll full-time at a two-year or four-year institution or

Financial Aid 101

www.petersons.com

university and resident of New York. Available to U.S. citizens. *Application Requirements:* Application. **Deadline:** May 1.

Contact HESC Scholarship Unit, New York State Higher Education Services Corporation, 99 Washington Avenue, Room 1320, Albany, NY 12255. *Phone:* 518-402-6494. *Web site:* www.hesc.com.

Young Scholars Contest. The Young Scholars Contest is a research essay competition on a predetermined theme in the humanities. New York State high school students who are legal residents of the state are eligible. Further information, guidelines and deadlines are available at Web site www.nyhumanities.org. *Award:* Scholarship for use in freshman year; not renewable. *Award amount:* $250–$5000. *Number of awards:* 6–18. *Eligibility Requirements:* Applicant must be high school student; planning to enroll or expecting to enroll full-time at a two-year or four-year institution or university and resident of New York. Available to U.S. and non-U.S. citizens. *Application Requirements:* Applicant must enter a contest, essay.

Contact New York Council for the Humanities, 150 Broadway, Suite 1700, New York, NY 10038. *Web site:* www.nyhumanities.org.

North Carolina

Incentive Scholarship for Native Americans. Merit-based award with a required public service component. Maximum award $3000 per academic year. Must be graduate of a North Carolina high school enrolled at North Carolina institution. Must submit tribal enrollment card. Minimum 2.5 GPA required. *Award:* Scholarship for use in freshman, sophomore, junior, or senior year; renewable. *Award amount:* up to $3000. *Number of awards:* up to 200. *Eligibility Requirements:* Applicant must be American Indian/Alaska Native; enrolled or expecting to enroll full-time at a four-year institution; resident of North Carolina and studying in North Carolina. Applicant must have 2.5 GPA or higher. Available to U.S. citizens. *Application Requirements:* Application, financial need analysis, tribal enrollment card. **Deadline:** continuous.

Contact Ms. Mickey Locklear, Director, Education Talent Search, North Carolina Commission of Indian Affairs, 217 West Jones Street, Raleigh, NC 27603. *E-mail:* mickey.locklear@ncmail.net. *Phone:* 919-733-5998. *Fax:* 919-733-1207.

North Carolina Legislative Tuition Grant Program. Renewable aid for North Carolina residents attending approved private colleges or universities within the state. Must be enrolled full-time in an undergraduate program not leading to a religious vocation. Contact college financial aid office for deadlines. *Award:* Grant for use in freshman, sophomore, junior, or senior year; renewable. *Award amount:* $1500–$1800. *Eligibility Requirements:* Applicant must be enrolled or expecting to enroll full-time at a two-year or four-year institution or university; resident of North Carolina and studying in North Carolina. Available to U.S. citizens. *Application Requirements:* Application.

Contact Bill Carswell, Manager of Scholarship and Grant Division, North Carolina State Education Assistance Authority, PO Box 13663, Research Triangle, NC 27709-3663. *Web site:* www.cfnc.org.

North Carolina National Guard Tuition Assistance Program. For members of the North Carolina Air and Army National Guard who will remain in the service for two years following the period for which assistance is provided. Applicants must reapply for each academic period. For use at approved North Carolina institutions. Deadline: last day of late registration period set by the school. Applicant must currently be serving in the Air National Guard or Army National Guard. Annual maximum (July 1 through June 30) of $2000. Career maximum of $8000. *Award:* Grant for use in freshman, sophomore, junior, or senior year; not renewable. *Award amount:* up to $2000. *Eligibility Requirements:* Applicant must be enrolled or expecting to enroll full or part-time at a two-year, four-year, or technical institution or university and studying in North Carolina. Available to U.S. citizens. Applicant must have served in the Air Force National Guard or Army National Guard. *Application Requirements:* Application.

Contact Capt. Miriam Gray, Education Services Officer, North Carolina National Guard, 4105 Reedy Creek Road, Raleigh, NC 27607-6410. *E-mail:* miriam.gray@nc.ngb.army.mil. *Phone:* 800-621-4136 Ext. 6272. *Fax:* 919-664-6520. *Web site:* www.nc.ngb.army.mil.

North Carolina Police Corps Scholarship. Selected participants must attend a four-year institution full-time. May receive up to $10,000 per year with a maximum of $30,000. Complete 24-week training course receiving $400 per week while in residence and serve four years in selected law enforcement agency. Must have physical, background investigation, drug test, and psychological evaluation. *Award:* Scholarship for use in freshman, sophomore, junior, senior, or graduate year; renewable. *Award amount:* $7500–$10,000. *Number of awards:* 15–30. *Eligibility Requirements:* Applicant must be enrolled or expecting to enroll full-time at a four-year institution or university. Available to U.S. citizens. *Application Requirements:* Application, autobiography, essay, interview, photo, references, test scores, transcript. **Deadline:** November 15.

Contact Neil Woodcock, Director, NC Police Corps, North Carolina Police Corps, NC Department of Crime Control and Public Safety, 4710 Mail Service Center, Raleigh, NC 27699-4710. *E-mail:*

Additional State Aid Programs

nwoodcock@nccrimecontrol.org. *Phone:* 919-773-2823. *Fax:* 919-773-2845. *Web site:* www.ncpolicecorps.org.

North Carolina Sheriffs' Association Undergraduate Criminal Justice Scholarships. One-time award for full-time North Carolina resident undergraduate students majoring in criminal justice at a University of North Carolina school. Priority given to child of any North Carolina law enforcement officer. Letter of recommendation from county sheriff required. *Academic/Career Areas:* Criminal Justice/Criminology; Law Enforcement/Police Administration. *Award:* Scholarship for use in freshman, sophomore, junior, or senior year; not renewable. *Award amount:* $1000–$2000. *Number of awards:* up to 10. *Eligibility Requirements:* Applicant must be enrolled or expecting to enroll full-time at a four-year institution; resident of North Carolina and studying in North Carolina. Applicant or parent of applicant must have employment or volunteer experience in police/firefighting. Available to U.S. citizens. *Application Requirements:* Essay, financial need analysis, references, transcript. **Deadline:** continuous.

Contact Sharon Scott, Assistant, Scholarship and Grant Division, North Carolina State Education Assistance Authority, PO Box 13663, Research Triangle, NC 27709-3663. *Web site:* www.cfnc.org.

North Carolina Student Incentive Grant. Renewable award for North Carolina residents who are enrolled full-time in an undergraduate program not leading to a religious vocation at a North Carolina postsecondary institution. Must demonstrate substantial financial need. Must complete Free Application for Student Aid. Must be U.S. citizen and must maintain satisfactory academic progress. Offered by NCSEAA through College Foundation, Inc. Visit Web site at www.cfnc.org. *Award:* Grant for use in freshman, sophomore, junior, or senior year; renewable. *Award amount:* $200–$1500. *Eligibility Requirements:* Applicant must be enrolled or expecting to enroll full-time at a two-year or four-year institution or university; resident of North Carolina and studying in North Carolina. Available to U.S. citizens. *Application Requirements:* Financial need analysis. **Deadline:** March 15.

Contact Bill Carswell, Manager of Scholarship and Grant Division, North Carolina State Education Assistance Authority, PO Box 13663, Research Triangle, NC 27709-3663. *Web site:* www.cfnc.org.

North Carolina Student Loan Program for Health, Science, and Mathematics. Renewable award for North Carolina residents studying health-related fields, or science or math education. Based on merit, need, and promise of service as a health professional or educator in an underserved area of North Carolina. Need two co-signers. Submit surety statement. *Academic/Career Areas:* Dental Health/Services; Health Administration; Health and Medical Sciences; Nursing; Physical Sciences and Math; Therapy/Rehabilitation. *Award:* Forgivable loan for use in freshman, sophomore, junior, senior, or graduate year; renewable. *Award amount:* $3000–$8500. *Eligibility Requirements:* Applicant must be enrolled or expecting to enroll full-time at a two-year or four-year institution or university; resident of North Carolina and studying in North Carolina. Available to U.S. citizens. *Application Requirements:* Application, financial need analysis, transcript. **Deadline:** June 1.

Contact Edna Williams, Manager, Selection and Origination, HSM Loan Program, North Carolina State Education Assistance Authority, PO Box 14223, Research Triangle, NC 27709-4223. *Phone:* 919-549-8614. *Web site:* www.cfnc.org.

North Carolina Teaching Fellows Scholarship Program. Renewable award for North Carolina high school seniors pursuing teaching careers. Must agree to teach in a North Carolina public or government school for four years or repay award. Must attend one of the 14 approved schools in North Carolina. Merit-based. Must interview at the local level and at the regional level as a finalist. *Academic/Career Areas:* Education. *Award:* Forgivable loan for use in freshman, sophomore, junior, or senior year; renewable. *Award amount:* $6500. *Number of awards:* up to 400. *Eligibility Requirements:* Applicant must be high school student; planning to enroll or expecting to enroll full-time at a four-year institution; resident of North Carolina and studying in North Carolina. Applicant must have 3.5 GPA or higher. Available to U.S. citizens. *Application Requirements:* Application, essay, interview, references, test scores, transcript. **Deadline:** October 31.

Contact Ms. Sherry Woodruff, Program Officer, North Carolina Teaching Fellows Commission, 3739 National Drive, Suite 210, Raleigh, NC 27612. *E-mail:* tfellows@ncforum.org. *Phone:* 919-781-6833 Ext. 103. *Fax:* 919-781-6527. *Web site:* www.teachingfellows.org.

North Carolina Veterans' Scholarships Class I. Renewable awards for children of veterans who were killed or died in wartime service or died as a result of service-connected condition incurred in wartime service as defined in the law. Parent must have been a North Carolina resident at time of entry into service. Duration of the scholarship is four academic years (8 semesters) if used within 8 years. Free tuition, a room allowance, a board allowance, and exemption from certain mandatory fees as set forth in the law in Public, Community & Technical Colleges/Institutions. Award is $4500 per nine-month academic year in Private Colleges & Junior Colleges. No limit on number awarded each year. See Web site for details and where to procure an application. Deadline is May 30. *Award:* Scholarship for use in freshman, sophomore, junior, or senior year; renewable. *Award amount:* up to $4500. *Eligibility Requirements:* Applicant must be enrolled or expecting to enroll full or part-time at a two-year, four-year, or technical institution or university and studying in North Carolina. Available to U.S. citizens. Applicant or parent must meet one or more of the following requirements: general military experience; retired from active duty; disabled or killed as a result of military service; prisoner of war; or missing in action. *Application Requirements:* Application, financial need analysis, interview, transcript. **Deadline:** May 30.

Contact Charles F. Smith, Director, North Carolina Division of Veterans' Affairs, 325 North Salisbury Street, Raleigh, NC 27603. *Phone:* 919-733-3851. *Fax:* 919-733-2834.

North Carolina Veterans' Scholarships Class I-B. Renewable awards for children of veterans rated by U.S.DVA as 100% disabled due to wartime service as defined in the law, and currently or at time of death drawing compensation for such disability. Parent must have been a North Carolina resident at time of entry into service. Duration of the scholarship is four academic years (8 semesters) if used within 8 years. Free tuition and exemption from certain mandatory fees as set forth in the law in Public, Community & Technical Colleges/Institutions. See Web site for details and where to procure an application. $1500 per nine month academic year in Private Colleges & Junior Colleges. No limit on number awarded each year. Deadline is May 30. *Award:* Scholarship for use in freshman, sophomore, junior, or senior year; renewable. *Award amount:* up to $1500. *Eligibility Requirements:* Applicant must be enrolled or expecting to enroll full or part-time at a two-year, four-year, or technical institution or university and studying in North Carolina. Available to U.S. citizens. Applicant or parent must meet one or more of the following requirements: general military experience; retired from active duty; disabled or killed as a result of military service; prisoner of war; or missing in action. *Application Requirements:* Application, financial need analysis, interview, transcript. **Deadline:** May 30.

Contact Charles F. Smith, Director, North Carolina Division of Veterans' Affairs, 325 North Salisbury Street, Raleigh, NC 27603. *Phone:* 919-733-3851. *Fax:* 919-733-2834.

North Carolina Veterans' Scholarships Class II. Renewable awards for children of veterans rated by U.S.DVA as much as 20% but less than 100% disabled due to wartime service as defined in the law, or was awarded Purple Heart Medal for wounds received. Parent must have been a North Carolina resident at time of entry into service. Duration of the scholarship is four academic years (8 semesters) if used within 8 years. Free tuition and exemption from certain mandatory fees as set forth in the law in Public, Community & Technical Colleges/Institutions. See Web site for details and where to procure an application. $4500 per nine month academic year in Private Colleges & Junior Colleges. 100 awarded each year. Deadline is March 31. *Award:* Scholarship for use in freshman, sophomore, junior, or senior year; renewable. *Award amount:* up to $4500. *Number of awards:* 100. *Eligibility Requirements:* Applicant must be enrolled or expecting to enroll full or part-time at a two-year, four-year, or technical institution or university and studying in North Carolina. Available to U.S. citizens. Applicant or parent must meet one or more of the following requirements: general military experience; retired from active duty; disabled or killed as a result of military service; prisoner of war; or missing in action. *Application Requirements:* Application, financial need analysis, interview, transcript. **Deadline:** March 31.

Contact Charles F. Smith, Director, North Carolina Division of Veterans' Affairs, 325 North Salisbury Street, Raleigh, NC 27603. *Phone:* 919-733-3851. *Fax:* 919-733-2834.

North Carolina Veterans' Scholarships Class III. Renewable awards for children of a veteran who died or was, at time of death, drawing a pension for total and permanent disability as rated by U.S.DVA, was honorably discharged and does not a qualify for Class I, II, or IV, scholarships, or served in a combat zone or waters adjacent to a combat zone and received a campaign badge or medal and does not qualify under Class I, II, IV, or V. Parent must have been a North Carolina resident at time of entry into service. Duration of the scholarship is four academic years (8 semesters) if used within eight years. Free tuition and exemption from certain mandatory fees as set forth in the law in Public, Community & Technical Colleges/Institutions. $4500 per nine month academic year in Private Colleges & Junior Colleges. See Web site for details and where to procure an application. 100 awarded each year. Deadline is March 31. *Award:* Scholarship for use in freshman, sophomore, junior, or senior year; renewable. *Award amount:* up to $4500. *Number of awards:* 100. *Eligibility Requirements:* Applicant must be enrolled or expecting to enroll full or part-time at a two-year, four-year, or technical institution or university and studying in North Carolina. Available to U.S. citizens. Applicant or parent must meet one or more of the following requirements: general military experience; retired from active duty; disabled or killed as a result of military service; prisoner of war; or missing in action. *Application Requirements:* Application, financial need analysis, interview, transcript. **Deadline:** March 31.

Contact Charles F. Smith, Director, North Carolina Division of Veterans' Affairs, 325 North Salisbury Street, Raleigh, NC 27603. *Phone:* 919-733-3851. *Fax:* 919-733-2834.

North Carolina Veterans' Scholarships Class IV. Renewable awards for children of a veteran who was a POW or MIA. Parent must have been a North Carolina resident at time of entry into service. Duration of the scholarship is four academic years (8 semesters) if used within eight years. No limit on number awarded per year. The student receives free tuition, a room allowance, a board allowance, and exemption from certain mandatory fees as set forth in the law in public, community, and technical colleges or institutions. The scholarship is $4500 per nine-month academic year in private colleges and junior colleges. Deadline is May 30. *Award:* Scholarship for use in freshman, sophomore, junior, or senior year; renewable. *Award amount:* up to $4500. *Eligibility Requirements:* Applicant must be enrolled or expecting to enroll full or part-time at a two-year, four-year, or technical institution or university and studying in North Carolina. Available to U.S. citizens. Applicant or parent must meet one or more of the following requirements: general military experience; retired from active duty; disabled or killed as a result of military service; prisoner of war; or missing in action. *Application Requirements:* Application, financial need analysis, interview, transcript. **Deadline:** May 31.

Contact Charles F. Smith, Director, North Carolina Division of Veterans' Affairs, 325 North Salisbury Street, Raleigh, NC 27603. *Phone:* 919-733-3851. *Fax:* 919-733-2834.

State Contractual Scholarship Fund Program—North Carolina. Renewable award for North Carolina residents already attending an approved private college or university in the state in pursuit of an undergraduate degree. Must have financial need. Contact college financial aid office for deadline and information. May not be enrolled in a program leading to a religious vocation. *Award:* Scholarship for use in freshman, sophomore, junior, or senior year; renewable. *Award amount:* up to $1100. *Eligibility Requirements:* Applicant must be enrolled or expecting to enroll full or part-time at a two-year or four-year institution or university; resident of North Carolina and studying in North Carolina. Available to U.S. citizens. *Application Requirements:* Financial need analysis.

Contact Bill Carswell, Manager of Scholarship and Grant Division, North Carolina State Education Assistance Authority, PO Box 13663, Research Triangle, NC 27709-3663. *Web site:* www.cfnc.org.

North Dakota

North Dakota Department of Transportation Engineering Grant. Educational grants for civil or construction engineering, or civil engineering technology, are awarded to students who have completed one year of course study at an institution of higher learning in North Dakota. Recipients must agree to work for the Department for a period of time at least equal to the grant period or repay the grant at 6% interest. Minimum 2.0 GPA required. *Academic/Career Areas:* Civil Engineering; Engineering/Technology. *Award:* Grant for use in sophomore, junior, or senior year; renewable. *Award amount:* $2000. *Number of awards:* 1–10. *Eligibility Requirements:* Applicant must be enrolled or expecting to enroll full-time at a four-year, or technical institution and studying in North Dakota. Available to U.S. citizens. *Application Requirements:* Application, financial need analysis, interview, transcript. **Deadline:** continuous.

Contact Lorrie Pavlicek, Human Resources Manager, North Dakota Department of Transportation, 503, 38th Street South, Fargo, ND 58103. *E-mail:* lpavlice@state.nd.us. *Phone:* 701-239-8934. *Fax:* 701-239-8939. *Web site:* www.state.nd.us/dot/.

North Dakota Indian College Scholarship Program. Renewable award to Native-Americans residents of North Dakota. Priority given to full-time undergraduate students. Minimum 2.0 GPA required. *Award:* Scholarship for use in freshman, sophomore, junior, senior, or graduate year; renewable. *Award amount:* $700–$2000. *Number of awards:* up to 150. *Eligibility Requirements:* Applicant must be American Indian/Alaska Native; enrolled or expecting to enroll full-time at a two-year, four-year, or technical institution or university and resident of North Dakota. Available to U.S. citizens. *Application Requirements:* Application, financial need analysis, transcript, proof of tribal enrollment. **Deadline:** July 15.

Contact Rhonda Schauer, SAA Director, North Dakota University System, 600 East Boulevard Avenue, Department 215, Bismarck, ND 58505-0230. *Phone:* 701-328-9661. *Web site:* www.ndus.nodak.edu.

North Dakota Indian Scholarship Program. Assists Native-Americans North Dakota residents in obtaining a college education. Priority given to full-time undergraduate students and those having a 3.5 GPA or higher. Certification of tribal enrollment required. For use at North Dakota institution. *Award:* Scholarship for use in freshman, sophomore, junior, senior, or graduate year; renewable. *Award amount:* $700–$2000. *Number of awards:* 120–150. *Eligibility Requirements:* Applicant must be American Indian/Alaska Native; enrolled or expecting to enroll at a two-year or four-year institution or university; resident of North Dakota and studying in North Dakota. Applicant must have 3.5 GPA or higher. *Application Requirements:* Application, financial need analysis, transcript. **Deadline:** July 15.

Contact Rhonda Schauer, Coordinator of American Indian Higher Education, State of North Dakota, 600 East Boulevard, Department 215, Bismarck, ND 58505-0230. *Phone:* 701-328-2166. *Web site:* www.ndus.nodak.edu.

North Dakota Scholars Program. Provides scholarships equal to cost of tuition at the public colleges in North Dakota for North Dakota residents. Must score at or above the 95th percentile on ACT and rank in top twenty percent of high school graduation class. Must take ACT in fall. For high school seniors with a minimum 3.5 GPA. Application deadline is October ACT test date. *Award:* Scholarship for use in freshman, sophomore, junior, or senior year; renewable. *Number of awards:* 45–50. *Eligibility Requirements:* Applicant must be high school student; planning to enroll or expecting to enroll full-time at a two-year or four-year institution or university; resident of North Dakota and studying in

North Dakota. Applicant must have 3.5 GPA or higher. Available to U.S. citizens. *Application Requirements:* Application, test scores.

Contact Peggy Wipf, Director of Financial Aid, State of North Dakota, 600 East Boulevard, Department 215, Bismarck, ND 58505-0230. *Phone:* 701-328-4114. *Web site:* www.ndus.nodak.edu.

North Dakota Student Financial Assistance Grants. Aids North Dakota residents attending an approved college or university in North Dakota. Must be enrolled in a program of at least nine months in length. *Award:* Grant for use in freshman, sophomore, junior, or senior year; not renewable. *Award amount:* up to $600. *Number of awards:* 2500–2600. *Eligibility Requirements:* Applicant must be enrolled or expecting to enroll full-time at a two-year or four-year institution or university; resident of North Dakota and studying in North Dakota. Available to U.S. citizens. *Application Requirements:* Application, financial need analysis. **Deadline:** April 15.

Contact Peggy Wipf, Director of Financial Aid, State of North Dakota, 600 East Boulevard, Department 215, Bismarck, ND 58505-0230. *Phone:* 701-328-4114. *Web site:* www.ndus.nodak.edu.

Ohio

Ohio Academic Scholarship Program. Award for academically outstanding Ohio residents planning to attend an approved Ohio college. Must be a high school senior intending to enroll full-time. Award is renewable for up to four years. Must rank in upper quarter of class or have a minimum GPA of 3.5. *Award:* Scholarship for use in freshman, sophomore, junior, or senior year; renewable. *Award amount:* $2000. *Number of awards:* 1000. *Eligibility Requirements:* Applicant must be high school student; planning to enroll or expecting to enroll full-time at a two-year or four-year institution; resident of Ohio and studying in Ohio. Applicant must have 3.5 GPA or higher. Available to U.S. citizens. *Application Requirements:* Application, test scores, transcript. **Deadline:** February 23.

Contact Sarina Wilks, Program Administrator, Ohio Board of Regents, PO Box 182452, Columbus, OH 43218-2452. *E-mail:* swilks@regents.state.oh.us. *Phone:* 614-752-9528. *Fax:* 614-752-5903. *Web site:* www.regents.state.oh.us.

Ohio Instructional Grant. Award for low- and middle-income Ohio residents attending an approved college or school in Ohio or Pennsylvania. Must be enrolled full-time and have financial need. Average award is $630. May be used for any course of study except theology. *Award:* Grant for use in freshman, sophomore, junior, or senior year; renewable. *Award amount:* $210–$3750. *Eligibility Requirements:* Applicant must be enrolled or expecting to enroll full-time at a two-year or four-year institution or university; resident of Ohio and studying in Ohio or Pennsylvania. Available to U.S. citizens. *Application Requirements:* Application, financial need analysis. **Deadline:** October 1.

Contact Charles Shahid, Assistant Director, Ohio Board of Regents, PO Box 182452, Columbus, OH 43218-2452. *E-mail:* cshahid@regents.state.oh.us. *Phone:* 614-644-9595. *Fax:* 614-752-5903. *Web site:* www.regents.state.oh.us.

Ohio Missing in Action and Prisoners of War Orphans Scholarship. Renewable award aids children of Vietnam conflict servicemen who have been classified as missing in action or prisoner of war. Must be an Ohio resident, be 16-21, and be enrolled full-time at an Ohio college. Full tuition awards. *Award:* Scholarship for use in freshman, sophomore, junior, or senior year; renewable. *Number of awards:* 1–5. *Eligibility Requirements:* Applicant must be age 16-21; enrolled or expecting to enroll full-time at a two-year or four-year institution; resident of Ohio and studying in Ohio. Available to U.S. citizens. Applicant or parent must meet one or more of the following requirements: general military experience; retired from active duty; disabled or killed as a result of military service; prisoner of war; or missing in action. *Application Requirements:* Application. **Deadline:** July 1.

Contact Sue Minturn, Program Administrator, Ohio Board of Regents, PO Box 182452, Columbus, OH 43218-2452. *E-mail:* sminturn@regents.state.oh.us. *Phone:* 614-752-9536. *Fax:* 614-752-5903. *Web site:* www.regents.state.oh.us.

Ohio National Guard Scholarship Program. Scholarships are for undergraduate studies at an approved Ohio postsecondary institution. Applicants must enlist for six years of Selective Service Reserve Duty in the Ohio National Guard. Scholarship pays 100% instructional and general fees for public institutions and an average of cost of public schools is available for private schools. Must be 18 years of age or older. Award is renewable. Deadlines: July 1, November 1, February 1, April 1. *Award:* Scholarship for use in freshman, sophomore, junior, or senior year; renewable. *Award amount:* up to $3000. *Number of awards:* 3500–10,000. *Eligibility Requirements:* Applicant must be age 18; enrolled or expecting to enroll full or part-time at a two-year, four-year, or technical institution or university and studying in Ohio. Available to U.S. citizens. Applicant must have served in the Air Force National Guard or Army National Guard. *Application Requirements:* Application.

Contact Mrs. Toni Davis, Grants Administrator, Ohio National Guard, 2825 West Dublin Granville Road, Columbus, OH 43235-2789. *E-mail:* toni.davis@tagoh.org. *Phone:* 614-336-7032. *Fax:* 614-336-7318.

Additional State Aid Programs

Ohio Safety Officers College Memorial Fund. Renewable award covering up to full tuition is available to children and surviving spouses of peace officers and fire fighters killed in the line of duty in any state. Children must be under 26 years of age. Must be an Ohio resident and enroll full-time or part-time at an Ohio college or university. *Award:* Scholarship for use in freshman, sophomore, junior, or senior year; renewable. *Number of awards:* 50–65. *Eligibility Requirements:* Applicant must be age 25 or under; enrolled or expecting to enroll full or part-time at a two-year or four-year institution or university; resident of Ohio and studying in Ohio. Applicant or parent of applicant must have employment or volunteer experience in police/firefighting. Available to U.S. citizens. *Application Requirements:* **Deadline:** continuous.

Contact Barbara Metheney, Program Administrator, Ohio Board of Regents, PO Box 182452, Columbus, OH 43218-2452. *E-mail:* bmethene@regents.state.oh.us. *Phone:* 614-752-9535. *Fax:* 614-752-5903. *Web site:* www.regents.state.oh.us.

Ohio Student Choice Grant Program. Renewable award available to Ohio residents attending private colleges within the state. Must be enrolled full time in a bachelor's degree program. Do not apply to state. Check with financial aid office of college. *Award:* Grant for use in freshman, sophomore, junior, or senior year; renewable. *Award amount:* up to $1038. *Eligibility Requirements:* Applicant must be enrolled or expecting to enroll full-time at a four-year institution; resident of Ohio and studying in Ohio. Available to U.S. citizens. *Application Requirements:* **Deadline:** continuous.

Contact Barbara Metheney, Program Administrator, Ohio Board of Regents, PO Box 182452, Columbus, OH 43218-2452. *E-mail:* bmethene@regents.state.oh.us. *Phone:* 614-752-9535. *Fax:* 614-752-5903. *Web site:* www.regents.state.oh.us.

Ohio War Orphans Scholarship. Aids Ohio residents attending an eligible college in Ohio. Must be between the ages of 16-21, the child of a disabled or deceased veteran, and enrolled full-time. Renewable up to five years. Amount of award varies. Must include Form DD214. *Award:* Scholarship for use in freshman, sophomore, junior, or senior year; renewable. *Number of awards:* 300–450. *Eligibility Requirements:* Applicant must be age 16-21; enrolled or expecting to enroll full-time at a two-year or four-year institution; resident of Ohio and studying in Ohio. Available to U.S. citizens. Applicant or parent must meet one or more of the following requirements: general military experience; retired from active duty; disabled or killed as a result of military service; prisoner of war; or missing in action. *Application Requirements:* Application. **Deadline:** July 1.

Contact Sue Minturn, Program Administrator, Ohio Board of Regents, PO Box 182452, Columbus, OH 43218-2452. *E-mail:* sminturn@regents.state.oh.us. *Phone:* 614-752-9536. *Fax:* 614-752-5903. *Web site:* www.regents.state.oh.us.

Part-time Student Instructional Grant. Renewable grants for part-time undergraduates who are Ohio residents. Award amounts vary. Must attend an Ohio institution. *Award:* Grant for use in freshman, sophomore, or junior year; renewable. *Eligibility Requirements:* Applicant must be enrolled or expecting to enroll part-time at a two-year or four-year institution or university; resident of Ohio and studying in Ohio. Available to U.S. citizens. *Application Requirements:* Application, financial need analysis. **Deadline:** continuous.

Contact Barbara Metheney, Program Administrator, Ohio Board of Regents, PO Box 182452, Columbus, OH 43218-2452. *E-mail:* bmethene@regents.state.oh.us. *Phone:* 614-752-9535. *Fax:* 614-752-5903. *Web site:* www.regents.state.oh.us.

Robert C. Byrd Honors Scholarship. Renewable award for graduating high school seniors who demonstrate outstanding academic achievement. Each Ohio high school receives applications by January of each year. School can submit one application for each 200 students in the senior class. *Award:* Scholarship for use in freshman, sophomore, junior, or senior year; renewable. *Award amount:* $1500. *Eligibility Requirements:* Applicant must be high school student; planning to enroll or expecting to enroll at a two-year or four-year institution or university and resident of Ohio. Applicant must have 3.5 GPA or higher. Available to U.S. citizens. *Application Requirements:* Application, test scores. **Deadline:** March 10.

Contact Charles Shahid, Program Coordinator, Ohio Board of Regents, PO Box 182452, Columbus, OH 43218-2452. *E-mail:* cshahid@regents.state.oh.us. *Phone:* 614-644-5959. *Fax:* 614-752-5903. *Web site:* www.regents.state.oh.us.

Oklahoma

Academic Scholars Program. Encourages students of high academic ability to attend institutions in Oklahoma. Renewable up to four years. ACT or SAT scores must fall between 99.5 and 100th percentiles, or be designated as a National Merit Scholar or finalist. *Award:* Scholarship for use in freshman, sophomore, junior, or senior year; renewable. *Award amount:* $3500–$5500. *Eligibility Requirements:* Applicant must be high school student; planning to enroll or expecting to enroll full-time at a two-year or four-year institution or university and studying in Oklahoma. Available to U.S. and non-U.S. citizens. *Application Requirements:* Application, test scores, transcript. **Deadline:** continuous.

Appendix D

Contact Oklahoma State Regents for Higher Education, PO Box 108850, Oklahoma City, OK 73101-8850. *E-mail:* studentinfo@osrhe.edu. *Phone:* 800-858-1840. *Fax:* 405-225-9230. *Web site:* www.okhighered.org.

Future Teacher Scholarship—Oklahoma. Open to outstanding Oklahoma high school graduates who agree to teach in shortage areas. Must rank in top 15% of graduating class or score above 85th percentile on ACT or similar test, or be accepted in an educational program. Students nominated by institution. Reapply to renew. Must attend college/university in Oklahoma. Contact institution's financial aid office for application deadline. *Academic/Career Areas:* Education. *Award:* Scholarship for use in freshman, sophomore, junior, senior, or graduate year; not renewable. *Award amount:* up to $1500. *Eligibility Requirements:* Applicant must be enrolled or expecting to enroll full or part-time at a two-year or four-year institution or university; resident of Oklahoma and studying in Oklahoma. Available to U.S. and non-U.S. citizens. *Application Requirements:* Application, essay, test scores, transcript.

Contact Oklahoma State Regents for Higher Education, PO Box 108850, Oklahoma City, OK 73101-8850. *Phone:* 800-858-1840. *Fax:* 405-225-9230. *Web site:* www.okhighered.org.

Oklahoma Tuition Aid Grant. Award for Oklahoma residents enrolled at an Oklahoma institution at least part-time per semester in a degree program. May be enrolled in two- or four-year or approved vocational-technical institution. Award of up to $1000 per year. Application is made through FAFSA. *Award:* Grant for use in freshman, sophomore, junior, senior, or graduate year; renewable. *Award amount:* $200–$1000. *Number of awards:* 23,000. *Eligibility Requirements:* Applicant must be enrolled or expecting to enroll full or part-time at a two-year, four-year, or technical institution or university; resident of Oklahoma and studying in Oklahoma. Available to U.S. citizens. *Application Requirements:* Application, financial need analysis, FAFSA. **Deadline:** April 30.

Contact Oklahoma State Regents for Higher Education, PO Box 3020, Oklahoma City, OK 73101-3020. *E-mail:* otaginfo@otag.org. *Phone:* 405-225-9456. *Fax:* 405-225-9392. *Web site:* www.okhighered.org.

Regional University Baccalaureate Scholarship. Renewable award for Oklahoma residents attending one of 11 participating Oklahoma public universities. Must have an ACT composite score of at least 30 or be a National Merit Semifinalist or commended student. In addition to the award amount, each recipient also will receive a resident tuition waiver from the institution. Must maintain a 3.25 GPA. Deadlines vary depending upon the institution attended. *Award:* Scholarship for use in freshman, sophomore, junior, or senior year; renewable. *Award amount:* $3000. *Eligibility Requirements:* Applicant must be enrolled or expecting to enroll full-time at an institution or university; resident of Oklahoma and studying in Oklahoma. *Application Requirements:* Application.

Contact Oklahoma State Regents for Higher Education, PO Box 108850, Oklahoma City, OK 73101-8850. *E-mail:* studentinfo@osrhe.edu. *Phone:* 800-858-1840. *Fax:* 405-225-9230. *Web site:* www.okhighered.org.

Oregon

American Ex-Prisoner of War Scholarships: Peter Connacher Memorial Scholarship. Renewable award for American prisoners-of-war and their descendants. Written proof of prisoner-of-war status and discharge papers from the U.S. Armed Forces must accompany application. Statement of relationship between applicant and former prisoner-of-war is required. See Web site at www.osac.state.or.us for details. *Award:* Scholarship for use in freshman, sophomore, junior, or senior year; renewable. *Award amount:* $1150. *Number of awards:* 4. *Eligibility Requirements:* Applicant must be enrolled or expecting to enroll at a two-year or four-year institution and resident of Oregon. Available to U.S. citizens. Applicant or parent must meet one or more of the following requirements: general military experience; retired from active duty; disabled or killed as a result of military service; prisoner of war; or missing in action. *Application Requirements:* Application, essay, financial need analysis, transcript. **Deadline:** March 1.

Contact Director of Grant Programs, Oregon Student Assistance Commission, 1500 Valley River Drive, Suite 100, Eugene, OR 97401-7020. *E-mail:* awardinfo@mercury.osac.state.or.us. *Phone:* 800-452-8807 Ext. 7395. *Web site:* www.osac.state.or.us.

Children, Adult, and Family Services Scholarship. One-time award for graduating high school seniors, GED recipients, and college students currently or formerly in foster care or an Independent Living Program (ILP) financially supported through the Oregon State Office for Services to Children and Families. Must attend an Oregon public college. Visit Web site for more details (www.osac.state.or.us). *Award:* Scholarship for use in freshman, sophomore, junior, senior, or graduate year; not renewable. *Eligibility Requirements:* Applicant must be enrolled or expecting to enroll at a two-year or four-year institution; resident of Oregon and studying in Oregon. Available to U.S. citizens. *Application Requirements:* Application, essay, financial need analysis, references, transcript, activity chart. **Deadline:** March 1.

Contact Director of Grant Programs, Oregon Student Assistance Commission, 1500 Valley River Drive, Suite 100, Eugene, OR 97401-7020. *E-mail:*

awardinfo@mercury.osac.state.or.us. *Phone:* 800-452-8807 Ext. 7395. *Web site:* www.osac.state.or.us.

Dorothy Campbell Memorial Scholarship. Renewable award for female Oregon high school senior with a minimum 2.75 GPA. Must submit essay describing strong, continuing interest in golf and the contribution that sport has made to applicant's development. *Award:* Scholarship for use in freshman, sophomore, junior, or senior year; renewable. *Award amount:* $1500. *Number of awards:* 2. *Eligibility Requirements:* Applicant must be high school student; planning to enroll or expecting to enroll at a four-year institution; female; resident of Oregon; studying in Oregon and must have an interest in golf. Available to U.S. citizens. *Application Requirements:* Application, essay, financial need analysis, test scores, transcript, activity chart. **Deadline:** March 1.

Contact Director of Grant Programs, Oregon Student Assistance Commission, 1500 Valley River Drive, Suite 100, Eugene, OR 97401-7020. *E-mail:* awardinfo@mercury.osac.state.or.us. *Phone:* 800-452-8807 Ext. 7395. *Web site:* www.osac.state.or.us.

Former Foster Children Scholarship. Must have been a ward of the court and in legal custody of the State Office for Services to Children and Families (now Children, Adult, and Family Services) for 12 months between ages 16 and 21. Must enroll in college within 3 years of the earlier of high school graduation (or equivalent) or removal from the care of Services to Children and Families. *Award:* Scholarship for use in freshman, sophomore, junior, or senior year; renewable. *Award amount:* $3012. *Number of awards:* 13. *Eligibility Requirements:* Applicant must be enrolled or expecting to enroll at an institution or university; resident of Oregon and studying in Oregon. *Application Requirements:* Application, essay, financial need analysis, transcript, activity chart, FAFSA. **Deadline:** March 1.

Contact Director of Grant Programs, Oregon Student Assistance Commission, 1500 Valley River Drive, Suite 100, Eugene, OR 97401-7020. *E-mail:* awardinfo@mercury.osac.state.or.us. *Phone:* 800-452-8807 Ext. 7395. *Web site:* www.osac.state.or.us.

Glenn Jackson Scholars Scholarships (OCF). Award for graduating high school seniors who are dependents of employees or retirees of Oregon Department of Transportation or Parks and Recreation Department. Employees must have worked in their department at least three years. Award for maximum twelve undergraduate quarters or six quarters at a two-year institution. Must be U.S. citizen or permanent resident. Visit Web site (www.osac.state.or.us) for more details. *Award:* Scholarship for use in freshman, sophomore, junior, or senior year; renewable. *Award amount:* $2500. *Number of awards:* 2. *Eligibility Requirements:* Applicant must be high school student; planning to enroll or expecting to enroll at a four-year institution and resident of Oregon. Applicant or parent of applicant must be affiliated with Oregon Department of Transportation Parks and Recreation. Applicant or parent of applicant must have employment or volunteer experience in designated career field. Available to U.S. citizens. *Application Requirements:* Application, essay, financial need analysis, references, transcript, activity chart. **Deadline:** March 1.

Contact Director of Grant Programs, Oregon Student Assistance Commission, 1500 Valley River Drive, Suite 100, Eugene, OR 97401-7020. *E-mail:* awardinfo@mercury.osac.state.or.us. *Phone:* 800-452-8807 Ext. 7395. *Web site:* www.osac.state.or.us.

Lawrence R. Foster Memorial Scholarship. One-time award to students enrolled or planning to enroll in a public health degree program. First preference given to those working in the public health field and those pursuing a graduate degree in public health. Undergraduates entering junior or senior year health programs may apply if seeking a public health career, and not private practice. Prefer applicants from diverse cultures. Must provide 3 references. Additional essay required. Must be resident of Oregon. *Academic/Career Areas:* Health and Medical Sciences. *Award:* Scholarship for use in junior, senior, graduate, or postgraduate years; not renewable. *Award amount:* $4167. *Number of awards:* 6. *Eligibility Requirements:* Applicant must be enrolled or expecting to enroll at a four-year institution and resident of Oregon. Available to U.S. citizens. *Application Requirements:* Application, essay, financial need analysis, references, transcript, activity chart. **Deadline:** March 1.

Contact Director of Grant Programs, Oregon Student Assistance Commission, 1500 Valley River Drive, Suite 100, Eugene, OR 97401-7020. *E-mail:* awardinfo@mercury.osac.state.or.us. *Phone:* 800-452-8807 Ext. 7395. *Web site:* www.osac.state.or.us.

Oregon Occupational Safety and Health Division Workers Memorial Scholarship. Available to Oregon residents who are the dependents or spouses of an Oregon worker who was killed or permanently disabled on the job. Submit essay of 500 words or less titled "How has the injury or death of your parent or spouse affected or influenced your decision to further your education?" See Web site for more details. (www.osac.state.or.us) *Award:* Scholarship for use in freshman, sophomore, junior, senior, or graduate year; not renewable. *Award amount:* $4786. *Number of awards:* 1. *Eligibility Requirements:* Applicant must be enrolled or expecting to enroll at a two-year or four-year institution and resident of Oregon. Applicant or parent of applicant must have employment or volunteer experience in designated career field. Available to U.S. citizens. *Application Require-*

ments: Application, essay, financial need analysis, test scores, transcript, workers compensation claim number. **Deadline:** March 1.

> **Contact** Director of Grant Programs, Oregon Student Assistance Commission, 1500 Valley River Drive, Suite 100, Eugene, OR 97401-7020. *E-mail:* awardinfo@mercury.osac.state.or.us. *Phone:* 800-452-8807 Ext. 7395. *Web site:* www.osac.state.or.us.

Oregon Scholarship Fund Community College Student Award. Scholarship open to Oregon residents enrolled or planning to enroll in Oregon community college programs. May apply for one additional year. *Award:* Scholarship for use in freshman or sophomore year; not renewable. *Eligibility Requirements:* Applicant must be enrolled or expecting to enroll at a two-year institution; resident of Oregon and studying in Oregon. Available to U.S. citizens. *Application Requirements:* Application, essay, financial need analysis, transcript, activity chart. **Deadline:** March 1.

> **Contact** Director of Grant Programs, Oregon Student Assistance Commission, 1500 Valley River Drive, Suite 100, Eugene, OR 97401-7020. *E-mail:* awardinfo@mercury.osac.state.or.us. *Phone:* 800-452-8807 Ext. 7395. *Web site:* www.osac.state.or.us.

Oregon Scholarship Fund Transfer Student Award. Award open to Oregon residents who are currently enrolled in their second year at a community college and are planning to transfer to a four-year college in Oregon. Prior recipients may apply for one additional year. *Award:* Scholarship for use in junior or senior year; not renewable. *Eligibility Requirements:* Applicant must be enrolled or expecting to enroll at a four-year institution; resident of Oregon and studying in Oregon. Available to U.S. citizens. *Application Requirements:* Application, essay, financial need analysis, transcript, activity chart. **Deadline:** March 1.

> **Contact** Director of Grant Programs, Oregon Student Assistance Commission, 1500 Valley River Drive, Suite 100, Eugene, OR 97401-7020. *E-mail:* awardinfo@mercury.osac.state.or.us. *Phone:* 800-452-8807 Ext. 7395. *Web site:* www.osac.state.or.us.

Oregon Student Assistance Commission Employee and Dependent Scholarship. One-time award for current permanent employee of the Oregon Student Assistance Commission or legally dependent children of employee. Also available to dependent children of an employee who retires, is permanently disabled, or deceased directly from employment at OSAC. Dependent must enroll full time. Employee may enroll part time. *Award:* Scholarship for use in freshman, sophomore, junior, or senior year; not renewable. *Award amount:* $500. *Number of awards:* 7. *Eligibility Requirements:* Applicant must be enrolled or expecting to enroll full or part-time at an institution or university and resident of Oregon. *Application Requirements:* Application, essay, financial need analysis, transcript. **Deadline:** March 1.

> **Contact** Director of Grant Programs, Oregon Student Assistance Commission, 1500 Valley River Drive, Suite 100, Eugene, OR 97401-7020. *E-mail:* awardinfo@mercury.osac.state.or.us. *Phone:* 800-452-8807 Ext. 7395. *Web site:* www.osac.state.or.us.

Oregon Trucking Association Scholarship. One scholarship available to a child of an Oregon Trucking Association member, or child of employee of member. Applicants must be Oregon residents who are graduating high school seniors from an Oregon high school. One-time award. *Award:* Scholarship for use in freshman year; not renewable. *Award amount:* $750. *Number of awards:* 4. *Eligibility Requirements:* Applicant must be high school student; planning to enroll or expecting to enroll at a four-year institution and resident of Oregon. Applicant or parent of applicant must have employment or volunteer experience in designated career field. Available to U.S. citizens. *Application Requirements:* Application, essay, financial need analysis, references, transcript, activity chart. **Deadline:** March 1.

> **Contact** Director of Grant Programs, Oregon Student Assistance Commission, 1500 Valley River Drive, Suite 100, Eugene, OR 97401-7020. *E-mail:* awardinfo@mercury.osac.state.or.us. *Phone:* 800-452-8807 Ext. 7395. *Web site:* www.osac.state.or.us.

Pennsylvania

Educational Gratuity Program. This program is for eligible dependents of 100% disabled or deceased veteran whose disability was incurred during a period or war or armed conflict. Must be a Pennsylvania resident attending a Pennsylvania school. *Award:* Grant for use in freshman, sophomore, junior, or senior year; renewable. *Award amount:* up to $500. *Eligibility Requirements:* Applicant must be age 16-23; enrolled or expecting to enroll full-time at a two-year, four-year, or technical institution or university; resident of Pennsylvania and studying in Pennsylvania. Available to U.S. citizens. Applicant must have general military experience. *Application Requirements:* Application, driver's license, financial need analysis, transcript. **Deadline:** continuous.

> **Contact** Michelle Zimmerman, Clerk Typist, Pennsylvania Bureau for Veterans Affairs, Fort Indiantown Gap, Annville, PA 17003-5002. *E-mail:* michzimmer@state.pa.us. *Phone:* 717-861-8910. *Fax:* 717-861-8589. *Web site:* sites.state.pa.us/PA_Exec/Military_Affairs/va/.

New Economy Technology Scholarships. Renewable award for Pennsylvania residents pursuing a degree

Additional State Aid Programs

in science or technology at a PHEAA-approved Pennsylvania school. Must maintain minimum 3.0 GPA. Must commence employment in Pennsylvania in field related to student's program within one year after completion of studies. Must work one year for each year scholarship was awarded. *Academic/Career Areas:* Science, Technology and Society. *Award:* Scholarship for use in freshman, sophomore, junior, or senior year; renewable. *Award amount:* up to $3000. *Eligibility Requirements:* Applicant must be enrolled or expecting to enroll full or part-time at a two-year, four-year, or technical institution; resident of Pennsylvania and studying in Pennsylvania. Applicant must have 3.0 GPA or higher. *Application Requirements:* Application, FAFSA. **Deadline:** December 31.

Contact PHEAA State Grant and Special Programs Division, Pennsylvania Higher Education Assistance Agency, 1200 North Seventh Street, Harrisburg, PA 17102-1444. *Phone:* 800-692-7392. *Web site:* www.pheaa.org.

Pennsylvania State Grant. Award for Pennsylvania residents attending an approved postsecondary institution as undergraduates in a program of at least two years duration. Renewable for up to eight semesters if applicants show continued need and academic progress. Submit Free Application for Federal Student Aid. *Award:* Grant for use in freshman, sophomore, junior, or senior year; renewable. *Award amount:* $300–$3300. *Number of awards:* up to 151,000. *Eligibility Requirements:* Applicant must be enrolled or expecting to enroll full or part-time at a two-year, four-year, or technical institution or university and resident of Pennsylvania. Available to U.S. and Canadian citizens. *Application Requirements:* Application, financial need analysis. **Deadline:** May 1.

Contact Keith New, Director of Communications and Press Office, Pennsylvania Higher Education Assistance Agency, 1200 North Seventh Street, Harrisburg, PA 17102-1444. *E-mail:* knew@pheaa.org. *Phone:* 717-720-2509. *Fax:* 717-720-3903. *Web site:* www.pheaa.org.

Postsecondary Education Gratuity Program. Waiver of tuition and fees for children of Pennsylvania police officers, firefighters, rescue or ambulance squad members, corrections facility employees or National Guard members who died in the line of duty after January 1, 1976. Must be a resident of Pennsylvania 25 years old or younger and enrolled full time as an undergraduate student at a Pennsylvania community college, state-owned institution or state-related institution. Award is for a maximum of 5 years. Application deadline March 31. *Award:* Grant for use in freshman, sophomore, junior, or senior year; renewable. *Eligibility Requirements:* Applicant must be age 25 or under; enrolled or expecting to enroll full-time at a two-year or four-year institution or university; resident of Pennsylvania and studying in Pennsylvania. *Application Requirements:* Application. **Deadline:** March 31.

Contact PHEAA State Grant and Special Programs Division, Pennsylvania Higher Education Assistance Agency, 1200 North Seventh Street, Harrisburg, PA 17102-1444. *Phone:* 800-692-7392. *Web site:* www.pheaa.org.

Veterans Grant—Pennsylvania. Renewable awards for Pennsylvania residents who are qualified veterans attending an approved undergraduate program full-time. Up to $3300 for in-state study or $800 for out-of-state study. Deadlines: May 1 for all renewal applicants, new applicants who plan to enroll in an undergraduate baccalaureate degree program, and those in college transfer programs at two-year public or junior colleges; August 1 for all first-time applicants who plan to enroll in a business, trade, or technical school; a hospital school of nursing; or a two-year terminal program at a community, junior, or four-year college. *Award:* Grant for use in freshman, sophomore, junior, or senior year; renewable. *Award amount:* $800–$3300. *Eligibility Requirements:* Applicant must be enrolled or expecting to enroll full-time at a two-year, four-year, or technical institution or university and resident of Pennsylvania. Available to U.S. citizens. Applicant must have general military experience. *Application Requirements:* Application.

Contact Keith New, Director of Communications and Press Office, Pennsylvania Higher Education Assistance Agency, 1200 North Seventh Street, Harrisburg, PA 17102-1444. *E-mail:* knew@pheaa.org. *Phone:* 717-720-2509. *Fax:* 717-720-3903. *Web site:* www.pheaa.org.

Puerto Rico

Robert C. Byrd Honor Scholarships. This grant is sponsored by the Puerto Rico Department of Education and is granted to gifted students. These are students chosen from public and private schools who graduate from high school and are admitted to an accredited university in Puerto Rico or in the United States and who show promise to complete a college career. It is granted for a period of four years if the student maintains a satisfactory academic progress. Must be a U.S. citizen and rank in the upper quarter of class or have a minimum 3.5 GPA. *Award:* Scholarship for use in freshman, sophomore, junior, or senior year; renewable. *Award amount:* $1500. *Number of awards:* 74–85. *Eligibility Requirements:* Applicant must be high school student and planning to enroll or expecting to enroll full-time at a four-year institution or university. Applicant must have 3.5 GPA or higher. Available to U.S. citizens. *Application Requirements:* Application, financial need analysis, interview, portfolio, references, test scores, transcript. **Deadline:** May 30.

Contact Eligio Hernandez, Director, Puerto Rico Department of Education, PO Box 190759, San Juan, PR 00919-0759. *E-mail:* hernandez_eli@de.gobierno.pr. *Phone:* 787-754-

1015. *Fax:* 787-758-2281. *Web site:* www.de.gobierno.pr/eduportal/default.htm.

Rhode Island

Rhode Island Higher Education Grant Program. Grants for residents of Rhode Island attending an approved school in the U.S., Canada, or Mexico. Based on need. Renewable for up to four years if in good academic standing. Applications accepted January 1 through March 1. Several awards of variable amounts. Must be U.S. citizen or registered alien. *Award:* Grant for use in freshman, sophomore, junior, or senior year; not renewable. *Award amount:* $250–$750. *Number of awards:* 10,000–12,000. *Eligibility Requirements:* Applicant must be enrolled or expecting to enroll full or part-time at a two-year, four-year, or technical institution or university and resident of Rhode Island. Available to U.S. citizens. *Application Requirements:* Application, financial need analysis. **Deadline:** March 1.

Contact Mary Ann Welch, Director of Program Administration, Rhode Island Higher Education Assistance Authority, 560 Jefferson Boulevard, Warwick, RI 02886. *E-mail:* mawelch@riheaa.org. *Phone:* 401-736-1170. *Fax:* 401-732-3541. *Web site:* www.riheaa.org.

South Carolina

Educational Assistance for Certain War Veteran's Dependents—South Carolina. Renewable aid to South Carolina Disabled Veterans' dependents under age 26. Veterans must have had wartime service in World War II, the Vietnam War, Persian Gulf or the Korean War. Must have received the Purple Heart or Medal of Honor. Applicant must show DD214 (birth certificate and VA rating). For undergraduate study at any South Carolina state-supported college. Must be South Carolina resident. *Award:* Scholarship for use in freshman, sophomore, junior, or senior year; renewable. *Eligibility Requirements:* Applicant must be age 18-26; enrolled or expecting to enroll full or part-time at a two-year, four-year, or technical institution or university; resident of South Carolina and studying in South Carolina. Available to U.S. citizens. Applicant or parent must meet one or more of the following requirements: general military experience; retired from active duty; disabled or killed as a result of military service; prisoner of war; or missing in action. *Application Requirements:* Application. **Deadline:** continuous.

Contact Ms. Lauren Hugg, Free Tuition Assistant, South Carolina Division of Veterans Affairs, 1801 Assembly Street, Room 141, Columbia, SC 29201. *Phone:* 803-255-4317. *Fax:* 803-255-4257.

Legislative Incentives for Future Excellence Program. Scholarship for students from South Carolina to attend an institution of higher education in South Carolina. For students attending a four-year institution, two of these three criteria must be met: 1) minimum 3.0 GPA, 2) 1100 SAT or 24 ACT, or 3) graduate in the top 30% of class. Students attending a two-year or technical college must have a 3.0 GPA, SAT and class rank requirements are waived. *Award:* Scholarship for use in freshman, sophomore, junior, senior, or graduate year; renewable. *Award amount:* $3700–$5090. *Eligibility Requirements:* Applicant must be enrolled or expecting to enroll full-time at a two-year, four-year, or technical institution or university; resident of South Carolina and studying in South Carolina. Applicant must have 3.0 GPA or higher. Available to U.S. citizens. *Application Requirements:* Test scores, transcript. **Deadline:** continuous.

Contact Bichevia Green, LIFE Scholarship Coordinator, South Carolina Commission on Higher Education, 1333 Main Street, Suite 200, Columbia, SC 29201. *E-mail:* bgreen@che400.state.sc.us. *Phone:* 803-737-2280. *Fax:* 803-737-2297. *Web site:* www.che400.state.sc.us.

Palmetto Fellows Scholarship Program. Renewable award for qualified high school seniors in South Carolina to attend a four-year South Carolina institution. Must rank in top 5% of class at the end of sophomore or junior year, earn a 3.5 GPA on a 4.0 scale, and score at least 1200 on the SAT or 27 on the ACT. Submit official transcript, test scores, and application by established deadline (usually January 15th of senior year). *Award:* Scholarship for use in freshman, sophomore, junior, senior, or graduate year; renewable. *Award amount:* up to $6700. *Eligibility Requirements:* Applicant must be high school student; planning to enroll or expecting to enroll full-time at a four-year institution or university; resident of South Carolina and studying in South Carolina. Applicant must have 3.5 GPA or higher. Available to U.S. citizens. *Application Requirements:* Application, test scores, transcript. **Deadline:** January 15.

Contact Ms. Sherry Hubbard, Coordinator, South Carolina Commission on Higher Education, 1333 Main Street, Suite 200, Columbia, SC 29201. *E-mail:* shubbard@che400.state.sc.us. *Phone:* 803-737-2260. *Fax:* 803-737-2297. *Web site:* www.che400.state.sc.us.

South Carolina Hope Scholarship. One-year merit-based scholarship for eligible first-time entering freshmen attending a four-year institution. Minimum 3.0 GPA. *Award:* Scholarship for use in freshman year; not renewable. *Award amount:* $2650. *Eligibility Requirements:* Applicant must be enrolled or expecting to enroll full-time at a four-year institution or university; resident of South Carolina and studying in South Carolina. Applicant must have 3.0 GPA or higher. Available to U.S. citizens. *Application Requirements:* Transcript. **Deadline:** continuous.

Additional State Aid Programs

Contact Bichevia Green, Life/Hope Scholarship Coordinator, South Carolina Commission on Higher Education, 1333 Main Street, Suite 200, Columbia, SC 29201. *E-mail:* bgreen@che400.state.sc.us. *Phone:* 803-737-2280. *Fax:* 803-737-2297. *Web site:* www.che400.state.sc.us.

South Carolina Need-Based Grants Program. Need-based grant awarded based on results of Free Application for Federal Student Aid. A student may receive up to $2500 annually for full-time and up to $1250 annually for part-time. The grant must be applied toward the cost of attendance at a South Carolina college for up to eight full-time equivalent terms. Student must be degree-seeking. *Award:* Grant for use in freshman, sophomore, junior, senior, or graduate year; renewable. *Award amount:* up to $2500. *Eligibility Requirements:* Applicant must be enrolled or expecting to enroll full or part-time at a two-year, four-year, or technical institution or university; resident of South Carolina and studying in South Carolina. Available to U.S. citizens. *Application Requirements:* Financial need analysis. **Deadline:** continuous.

Contact Ms. Sherry Hubbard, Coordinator, South Carolina Commission on Higher Education, 1333 Main Street, Suite 200, Columbia, SC 29201. *E-mail:* shubbard@che400.state.sc.us. *Phone:* 803-737-2260. *Fax:* 803-737-2297. *Web site:* www.che400.state.sc.us.

South Carolina Teacher Loan Program. One-time awards for South Carolina residents attending four-year postsecondary institutions in South Carolina. Recipients must teach in the South Carolina public school system in a critical-need area after graduation. 20% of loan forgiven for each year of service. Write for additional requirements. *Academic/Career Areas:* Education; Special Education. *Award:* Forgivable loan for use in freshman, sophomore, junior, senior, or graduate year; not renewable. *Award amount:* $2500–$5000. *Number of awards:* up to 1121. *Eligibility Requirements:* Applicant must be enrolled or expecting to enroll full or part-time at a four-year institution or university; resident of South Carolina and studying in South Carolina. Applicant must have 3.0 GPA or higher. *Application Requirements:* Application, test scores. **Deadline:** June 1.

Contact Jennifer Jones-Gaddy, Vice President, South Carolina Student Loan Corporation, PO Box 21487, Columbia, SC 29221. *E-mail:* jgaddy@slc.sc.edu. *Phone:* 803-798-0916. *Fax:* 803-772-9410. *Web site:* www.slc.sc.edu.

South Carolina Tuition Grants Program. Assists South Carolina residents attending one of twenty approved South Carolina Independent colleges. Freshmen must be in upper 3/4 of high school class or have SAT score of at least 900. Upper-class students must complete 24 semester hours per year to be eligible. *Award:* Grant for use in freshman, sophomore, junior, or senior year; renewable. *Award amount:* $100–$3240. *Number of awards:* up to 11,000. *Eligibility Requirements:* Applicant must be enrolled or expecting to enroll full-time at a two-year or four-year institution; resident of South Carolina and studying in South Carolina. Available to U.S. citizens. *Application Requirements:* Application, financial need analysis, test scores, transcript, FAFSA. **Deadline:** June 30.

Contact Toni Cave, Financial Aid Counselor, South Carolina Tuition Grants Commission, 101 Business Park Boulevard, Suite 2100, Columbia, SC 29203-9498. *E-mail:* toni@sctuitiongrants.org. *Phone:* 803-896-1120. *Fax:* 803-896-1126. *Web site:* www.sctuitiongrants.com.

South Dakota

Education Benefits for Dependents of POWs and MIAs. Children and spouses of prisoners of war, or of persons listed as missing in action, are entitled to attend a state-supported school without the payment of tuition or mandatory fees provided they are not eligible for equal or greater federal benefits. File SDDVA for E-12 available at financial aid offices. Must be a South Dakota resident intending to study in South Dakota. *Award:* Scholarship for use in freshman, sophomore, junior, or senior year; not renewable. *Eligibility Requirements:* Applicant must be enrolled or expecting to enroll at an institution or university; resident of South Dakota and studying in South Dakota. Available to U.S. citizens. Applicant or parent must meet one or more of the following requirements: general military experience; retired from active duty; disabled or killed as a result of military service; prisoner of war; or missing in action. *Application Requirements:* Application.

Contact Dr. Lesta V. Turchen, Senior Administrator, South Dakota Board of Regents, 306 East Capitol Avenue, Suite 200, Pierre, SD 57501-3159. *Phone:* 605-773-3455. *Fax:* 605-773-2422. *Web site:* www.ris.sdbor.edu.

Haines Memorial Scholarship. One-time scholarship for South Dakota public university students who are sophomores, juniors, or seniors having at least a 2.5 GPA and majoring in a teacher education program. Include resume with application. Must be South Dakota resident. *Academic/Career Areas:* Education. *Award:* Scholarship for use in sophomore, junior, or senior year; not renewable. *Award amount:* $2150. *Number of awards:* 1. *Eligibility Requirements:* Applicant must be enrolled or expecting to enroll at an institution or university; resident of South Dakota and studying in South Dakota. Applicant must have 2.5 GPA or higher. *Application Requirements:* Application, autobiography, essay, resume. **Deadline:** February 25.

Contact South Dakota Board of Regents, 306 East Capitol Avenue, Suite 200, Pierre, SD 57501-3159. *Web site:* www.ris.sdbor.edu.

Appendix D

South Dakota Aid to Dependents of Deceased Veterans. Program provides free tuition for children of deceased veterans who are under the age of 25, are residents of South Dakota, and whose mother or father was killed in action or died of other causes while on active duty. ("Veteran" for this purpose is as defined by South Dakota Codified Laws.) Parent must have been a bona fide resident of SD for at least six months immediately preceding entry into active service. Eligibility is for state-supported schools only. Must use SDDVA form E-12 available at financial aid offices. *Award:* Scholarship for use in freshman, sophomore, junior, or senior year; not renewable. *Eligibility Requirements:* Applicant must be age 25 or under; enrolled or expecting to enroll at a two-year or four-year institution; resident of South Dakota and studying in South Dakota. Available to U.S. citizens. Applicant or parent must meet one or more of the following requirements: general military experience; retired from active duty; disabled or killed as a result of military service; prisoner of war; or missing in action. *Application Requirements:* Application.

Contact Dr. Lesta V. Turchen, Senior Administrator, South Dakota Board of Regents, 306 East Capitol Avenue, Suite 200, Pierre, SD 57501-3159. *Phone:* 605-773-3455. *Fax:* 605-773-2422. *Web site:* www.ris.sdbor.edu.

South Dakota Board of Regents Senior Citizens Tuition Assistance. Award for tuition assistance for any postsecondary academic year of study to senior citizens age 65 and older. Write for further details. Must be a South Dakota resident and attend a school in South Dakota. *Award:* Scholarship for use in freshman, sophomore, junior, or senior year; not renewable. *Eligibility Requirements:* Applicant must be age 65; enrolled or expecting to enroll at an institution or university; resident of South Dakota and studying in South Dakota. *Application Requirements:* Application. **Deadline:** continuous.

Contact South Dakota Board of Regents, 306 East Capitol Avenue, Suite 200, Pierre, SD 57501-3159. *Web site:* www.ris.sdbor.edu.

South Dakota Board of Regents State Employee Tuition Assistance. Award for South Dakota state employees for any postsecondary academic year of study in South Dakota institution. Must be U.S. citizen. Write for requirements and other details. *Award:* Scholarship for use in freshman, sophomore, junior, or senior year; not renewable. *Eligibility Requirements:* Applicant must be enrolled or expecting to enroll at an institution or university; resident of South Dakota and studying in South Dakota. Applicant or parent of applicant must have employment or volunteer experience in designated career field. Available to U.S. citizens. *Application Requirements:* **Deadline:** continuous.

Contact South Dakota Board of Regents, 306 East Capitol Avenue, Suite 200, Pierre, SD 57501-3159. *Web site:* www.ris.sdbor.edu.

South Dakota Education Benefits for National Guard Members. Guard members who meet the requirements for admission are eligible for a 50% reduction in undergraduate tuition charges at any state-supported school for up to a maximum of four academic years. Provision also covers one program of study, approved by the State Board of Education, at any state vocational school. Must be state resident and member of the SD Army or Air Guard throughout period for which benefits are sought. Must contact financial aid office for full details and forms at time of registration. *Award:* Scholarship for use in freshman, sophomore, junior, or senior year; not renewable. *Eligibility Requirements:* Applicant must be enrolled or expecting to enroll at a two-year, four-year, or technical institution or university; resident of South Dakota and studying in South Dakota. Available to U.S. citizens. Applicant must have served in the Air Force National Guard or Army National Guard. *Application Requirements:* Application.

Contact Dr. Lesta V. Turchen, Senior Administrator, South Dakota Board of Regents, 306 East Capitol Avenue, Suite 200, Pierre, SD 57501-3159. *Phone:* 605-773-3455. *Fax:* 605-773-2422. *Web site:* www.ris.sdbor.edu.

South Dakota Education Benefits for Veterans. Certain veterans are eligible for free undergraduate tuition assistance at state-supported schools provided they are not eligible for educational payments under the GI Bill or any other federal educational program. Contact financial aid office for full details and forms. May receive one month of free tuition for each month of qualifying service (minimum one year, maximum four years). Must be resident of South Dakota. *Award:* Scholarship for use in freshman, sophomore, junior, or senior year; not renewable. *Eligibility Requirements:* Applicant must be enrolled or expecting to enroll at an institution or university; resident of South Dakota and studying in South Dakota. Available to U.S. citizens. Applicant must have general military experience. *Application Requirements:* Application, DD Form 214.

Contact Dr. Lesta V. Turchen, Senior Administrator, South Dakota Board of Regents, 306 East Capitol Avenue, Suite 200, Pierre, SD 57501-3159. *Phone:* 605-773-3455. *Fax:* 605-773-2422. *Web site:* www.ris.sdbor.edu.

Tennessee

Minority Teaching Fellows Program/Tennessee. Forgivable loan for minority Tennessee residents pursuing teaching careers. High school applicant minimum 2.75 GPA. Must be in the top quarter of the class or score an 18 on ACT. College applicant minimum 2.50 GPA. Submit statement of intent, test scores, and

Additional State Aid Programs

transcripts with application and two letters of recommendation. Must teach one year per year of award or repay as a loan. *Academic/Career Areas:* Education; Special Education. *Award:* Forgivable loan for use in freshman, sophomore, junior, or senior year; renewable. *Award amount:* $5000. *Number of awards:* 19–29. *Eligibility Requirements:* Applicant must be American Indian/Alaska Native, Asian/Pacific Islander, Black (non-Hispanic), or Hispanic; enrolled or expecting to enroll full-time at a two-year or four-year institution or university; resident of Tennessee and studying in Tennessee. Available to U.S. citizens. *Application Requirements:* Application, essay, references, test scores, transcript. **Deadline:** April 15.

> **Contact** Kathy Stripling, Scholarship Coordinator, Tennessee Student Assistance Corporation, 404 James Robertson Parkway, Suite 1950, Parkway Towers, Nashville, TN 37243-0820. *E-mail:* kathy.stripling@state.tn.us. *Phone:* 615-741-1346. *Fax:* 615-741-6101. *Web site:* www.state.tn.us/tsac.

Ned McWherter Scholars Program. Assists Tennessee residents with high academic ability. Must have high school GPA of at least 3.5 and have scored in top 5% of SAT or ACT. Must attend college in Tennessee. Only high school seniors may apply. *Award:* Scholarship for use in freshman, sophomore, junior, or senior year; renewable. *Award amount:* $6000. *Number of awards:* 55. *Eligibility Requirements:* Applicant must be high school student; planning to enroll or expecting to enroll full-time at a two-year or four-year institution or university; resident of Tennessee and studying in Tennessee. Applicant must have 3.5 GPA or higher. Available to U.S. citizens. *Application Requirements:* Application, test scores, transcript. **Deadline:** February 15.

> **Contact** Kathy Stripling, Scholarship Coordinator, Tennessee Student Assistance Corporation, Suite 1950, Parkway Towers, Nashville, TN 37243-0820. *E-mail:* kathy.stripling@state.tn.us. *Phone:* 615-741-1346. *Fax:* 615-741-6101. *Web site:* www.state.tn.us/tsac.

Tennessee Student Assistance Award Program. Assists Tennessee residents attending an approved college or university within the state. Complete a Free Application for Federal Student Aid form. Apply January 1. FAFSA must be processed by May 1 for priority consideration. *Award:* Grant for use in freshman, sophomore, junior, or senior year; renewable. *Award amount:* $100–$2130. *Number of awards:* 26,000. *Eligibility Requirements:* Applicant must be enrolled or expecting to enroll full or part-time at a two-year, four-year, or technical institution or university; resident of Tennessee and studying in Tennessee. Available to U.S. citizens. *Application Requirements:* Application, financial need analysis. **Deadline:** May 1.

> Contact Naomi Derryberry, Grant and Scholarship Administrator, Tennessee Student Assistance Corporation, Suite 1950, Parkway Towers, Nashville, TN 37243-0820. *E-mail:* naomi.derryberry@state.tn.us. *Phone:* 615-741-1346. *Fax:* 615-741-6101. *Web site:* www.state.tn.us/tsac.

Tennessee Teaching Scholars Program. Forgivable loan for college juniors, seniors, and college graduates admitted to an education program in Tennessee with a minimum GPA of 2.5. Students must commit to teach in a Tennessee public school one year for each year of the award. *Academic/Career Areas:* Education. *Award:* Forgivable loan for use in junior, senior, or graduate year; not renewable. *Award amount:* $1000–$4200. *Number of awards:* 30–250. *Eligibility Requirements:* Applicant must be enrolled or expecting to enroll full or part-time at a four-year institution or university; resident of Tennessee and studying in Tennessee. Applicant must have 2.5 GPA or higher. Available to U.S. citizens. *Application Requirements:* Application, references, test scores, transcript, letter of intent. **Deadline:** April 15.

> **Contact** Mike McCormack, Scholarship Administrator, Tennessee Student Assistance Corporation, Suite 1950, Parkway Towers, Nashville, TN 37243-0820. *E-mail:* mike.mccormack@state.tn.us. *Phone:* 615-741-1346. *Fax:* 615-741-6101. *Web site:* www.state.tn.us/tsac.

Texas

Academic Common Market Waiver. For Texas residents who are students pursuing a degree in a field of study not offered in Texas. May qualify for special tuition rates. Deadlines vary by institution. Must be studying in the South. *Award:* Scholarship for use in freshman, sophomore, junior, senior, or graduate year; renewable. *Eligibility Requirements:* Applicant must be enrolled or expecting to enroll full or part-time at an institution or university; resident of Texas and studying in Alabama, Arkansas, Florida, Georgia, Kentucky, Louisiana, Mississippi, Missouri, Oklahoma, South Carolina, Tennessee, or Virginia. Available to U.S. citizens. *Application Requirements:* Application.

> **Contact** Linda McDonough, Associate Program Director, Texas Higher Education Coordinating Board, PO Box 12788, Austin, TX 78711-2788. *E-mail:* grantinfo@thecb.state.tx.us. *Phone:* 512-427-6525. *Web site:* www.collegefortexans.com.

Border County Waiver. Award provides waiver of nonresident tuition for students of neighboring states (Louisiana, Oklahoma, Arkansas and New Mexico). Must attend a Texas public institution. Deadline varies by institution. Contact the registrar's office for details. *Award:* Scholarship for use in freshman, sophomore, junior, or senior year; not renewable. *Eligibility Require-*

Financial Aid 101   www.petersons.com

ments: Applicant must be enrolled or expecting to enroll at a four-year institution or university; resident of Arkansas, Louisiana, New Mexico, or Oklahoma and studying in Texas. *Application Requirements:* Application.

Contact Financial Aid Office at college, Texas Higher Education Coordinating Board, PO Box 12788, Austin, TX 78711-2788. *E-mail:* grantinfo@thecb.state.tx.us. *Phone:* 512-427-6101. *Fax:* 512-427-6127. *Web site:* www.collegefortexans.com.

Conditional Grant Program. A grant that provides female minorities financial education assistance up to $6,000 per year for approved degree plans. At present, it is for civil engineering or computer science degrees. Must be a Texas resident and study in Texas. *Academic/Career Areas:* Civil Engineering; Computer Science/Data Processing. *Award:* Grant for use in freshman, sophomore, junior, or senior year; renewable. *Award amount:* up to $6000. *Number of awards:* 25. *Eligibility Requirements:* Applicant must be American Indian/Alaska Native, Asian/Pacific Islander, Black (non-Hispanic), or Hispanic; enrolled or expecting to enroll full-time at a four-year institution; female; resident of Texas and studying in Texas. Applicant must have 2.5 GPA or higher. Available to U.S. citizens. *Application Requirements:* Application, essay, interview, references, test scores, transcript. **Deadline:** March 1.

Contact Minnie Brown, Program Coordinator, Texas Department of Transportation, 125 East 11th Street, Austin, TX 78701-2483. *E-mail:* mbrown2@dot.state.tx.us. *Phone:* 512-416-4979. *Fax:* 512-416-4980. *Web site:* www.dot.state.tx.us.

Early Childhood Care Provider Student Loan Repayment. Award will repay student loans for child-care workers with a degree in Early Child Development. Must be employed at a licensed facility and work a minimum of 31 hours per week. Must agree to provide service for two years. *Award:* Scholarship for use in freshman, sophomore, junior, or senior year; not renewable. *Award amount:* up to $3830. *Eligibility Requirements:* Applicant must be enrolled or expecting to enroll at an institution or university. Applicant or parent of applicant must have employment or volunteer experience in designated career field. Available to U.S. citizens. *Application Requirements:* Application. **Deadline:** continuous.

Contact Special Accounts, Texas Higher Education Coordinating Board, PO Box 12788, Austin, TX 78711. *E-mail:* grantinfo@thecb.state.tx.us. *Web site:* www.collegefortexans.com.

Early High School Graduation Scholarships. Award of $1000 for Texas residents who have completed the requirements for graduation from a Texas high school in no more than 36 consecutive months. Eligibility continues until full $1000 tuition award is received. Must submit high school certificate of eligibility to Coordinating Board. For more information, contact your high school counselor. *Award:* Scholarship for use in freshman year; not renewable. *Award amount:* $1000. *Eligibility Requirements:* Applicant must be high school student; planning to enroll or expecting to enroll full or part-time at a two-year, four-year, or technical institution or university; resident of Texas and studying in Texas. Available to U.S. citizens. *Application Requirements:* Application. **Deadline:** continuous.

Contact Texas Higher Education Coordinating Board, PO Box 12788, Austin, TX 78711-2788. *E-mail:* grantinfo@thecb.state.tx.us. *Phone:* 800-242-3062 Ext. 6387. *Web site:* www.collegefortexans.com.

Educational Aides Exemption. Assist certain educational aides by exempting them from payment of tuition and fees at public colleges or universities in Texas. Applicants must have worked as an educational aide in a Texas public school for at least one year and must be enrolled in courses required for teacher certification. Contact your college or university financial aid office for information on applying for this scholarship. Application cycles are as follows: Fall, June 1 through February 1; Spring, November 1 through July 1; and Summer, April 1 through October 1. *Academic/Career Areas:* Education. *Award:* Scholarship for use in freshman, sophomore, junior, or senior year; not renewable. *Award amount:* up to $605. *Eligibility Requirements:* Applicant must be enrolled or expecting to enroll at a four-year institution or university; resident of Texas and studying in Texas. *Application Requirements:* Application, financial need analysis.

Contact Financial Aid Office at college, Texas Higher Education Coordinating Board, PO Box 12788, Austin, TX 78711-2788. *E-mail:* grantinfo@thecb.state.tx.us. *Phone:* 512-427-6101. *Fax:* 512-427-6127. *Web site:* www.collegefortexans.com.

Exemption for Disabled in the Line of Duty Peace Officers. Renewable award for persons who were injured in the line of duty while serving as Peace Officers. Must be Texas resident and attend a public college or university in Texas. Submit documentation of disability from employer. For more information see registrar. *Award:* Scholarship for use in freshman, sophomore, junior, or senior year; renewable. *Eligibility Requirements:* Applicant must be enrolled or expecting to enroll at a four-year institution or university; resident of Texas and studying in Texas. Applicant or parent of applicant must have employment or volunteer experience in police/firefighting. *Application Requirements:* Application, form letter.

Contact Texas Higher Education Coordinating Board, PO Box 12788, Austin, TX 78711. *E-mail:* grantinfo@thecb.state.tx.us. *Web site:* www.collegefortexans.com.

Additional State Aid Programs

Fifth-year Accounting Student Scholarship Program. One-time award for students enrolled as fifth-year accounting students at a Texas institution. Must sign statement confirming intent to take the written exam for the purpose of being granted a certificate of CPA to practice in Texas. Contact college/university financial aid office for application information. *Academic/Career Areas:* Accounting. *Award:* Scholarship for use in senior or graduate year; not renewable. *Award amount:* up to $3000. *Eligibility Requirements:* Applicant must be enrolled or expecting to enroll full or part-time at a four-year institution or university and studying in Texas. Available to U.S. and non-U.S. citizens. *Application Requirements:* Application, financial need analysis, transcript, letter of intent. **Deadline:** continuous.

Contact Financial Aid Office at college, Texas Higher Education Coordinating Board, PO Box 12788, Austin, TX 78711-2788. *E-mail:* grantinfo@thecb.state.tx.us. *Phone:* 512-427-6101. *Fax:* 512-427-6127. *Web site:* www.collegefortexans.com.

Firefighter Exemption Program—Texas. One-time award assists firemen enrolled in fire science courses as part of a fire science curriculum. Award is exemption from tuition and laboratory fees at publicly supported Texas colleges. Contact the admissions/registrar's office for information on how to apply. *Academic/Career Areas:* Applied Sciences; Physical Sciences and Math; Trade/Technical Specialties. *Award:* Scholarship for use in freshman, sophomore, junior, or senior year; not renewable. *Eligibility Requirements:* Applicant must be enrolled or expecting to enroll full or part-time at a two-year, four-year, or technical institution; resident of Texas and studying in Texas. Applicant or parent of applicant must have employment or volunteer experience in fire service or police/firefighting. Available to U.S. citizens. *Application Requirements:* Application. **Deadline:** continuous.

Contact Financial Aid Office at college, Texas Higher Education Coordinating Board, PO Box 12788, Austin, TX 78711-2788. *E-mail:* grantinfo@thecb.state.tx.us. *Phone:* 512-427-6101. *Fax:* 512-427-6127. *Web site:* www.collegefortexans.com.

Good Neighbor Scholarship Waiver. Renewable aid for students residing in Texas who are citizens of another country of the Americas and intend to return to their country upon completion of the course of study. Must attend public college in Texas. Student will be exempt from tuition. *Award:* Scholarship for use in freshman, sophomore, junior, or senior year; renewable. *Eligibility Requirements:* Applicant must be Canadian or Latin American/Caribbean citizenship; enrolled or expecting to enroll full or part-time at a two-year, four-year, or technical institution or university and studying in Texas. Available to Canadian and non-U.S. citizens. *Application Requirements:* Application, test scores, transcript. **Deadline:** March 15.

Contact Texas Higher Education Coordinating Board, PO Box 12788, Austin, TX 78711-2788. *E-mail:* grantinfo@thecb.state.tx.us. *Phone:* 800-242-3062. *Web site:* www.collegefortexans.com.

Leveraging Educational Assistance Partnership Program (LEAP) (formerly SSIG). Renewable award available to residents of Texas attending public colleges or universities in Texas. Must be enrolled at least half-time and show financial need. Deadlines vary by institution. Contact the college/university financial aid office for application information. *Award:* Grant for use in freshman, sophomore, junior, or senior year; renewable. *Award amount:* up to $1250. *Eligibility Requirements:* Applicant must be enrolled or expecting to enroll full or part-time at a two-year, four-year, or technical institution or university; resident of Texas and studying in Texas. Available to U.S. citizens. *Application Requirements:* Financial need analysis, FAFSA.

Contact Financial Aid Office at college, Texas Higher Education Coordinating Board, PO Box 12788, Austin, TX 78711-2788. *E-mail:* grantinfo@thecb.state.tx.us. *Phone:* 512-427-6101. *Fax:* 512-427-6127. *Web site:* www.collegefortexans.com.

License Plate Insignia Scholarship. One-time award to Texas residents enrolled at least half-time at public or private nonprofit senior colleges and universities in Texas. Must demonstrate financial need. Contact financial aid office at college for deadlines and application. *Award:* Scholarship for use in freshman, sophomore, junior, or senior year; not renewable. *Eligibility Requirements:* Applicant must be enrolled or expecting to enroll full or part-time at a four-year institution or university; resident of Texas and studying in Texas. *Application Requirements:* Application, financial need analysis.

Contact Financial Aid Office at college, Texas Higher Education Coordinating Board, PO Box 12788, Austin, TX 78711-2788. *E-mail:* grantinfo@thecb.state.tx.us. *Phone:* 512-427-6101. *Fax:* 512-427-6127. *Web site:* www.collegefortexans.com.

Military Stationed in Texas Waiver. Award provides tuition waiver for nonresident military personnel stationed in Texas. Limited to public institutions only. Contact financial aid office at college for deadline and application. *Award:* Scholarship for use in freshman, sophomore, junior, or senior year; not renewable. *Eligibility Requirements:* Applicant must be enrolled or expecting to enroll at an institution or university and studying in Texas. Applicant must have general military experience. *Application Requirements:* Application.

Contact Financial Aid Office at college, Texas Higher Education Coordinating Board, PO Box 12788, Austin, TX 78711-2788. *E-mail:* grantinfo@thecb.state.tx.us. *Phone:* 512-427-6101. *Fax:* 512-427-6127. *Web site:* www.collegefortexans.com.

Appendix D

Outstanding Rural Scholar Program. Award enables rural communities to sponsor a student going into health professions. The students must agree to work in that community once they receive their degree. Must be Texas resident entering a Texas institution on a full-time basis. Must demonstrate financial need. *Academic/Career Areas:* Health and Medical Sciences. *Award:* Scholarship for use in freshman, sophomore, junior, or senior year; renewable. *Eligibility Requirements:* Applicant must be enrolled or expecting to enroll full-time at a four-year institution or university; resident of Texas and studying in Texas. Applicant must have 3.0 GPA or higher. *Application Requirements:* Application, financial need analysis, transcript, nomination.

Contact Center for Rural Health Initiatives, Texas Higher Education Coordinating Board, PO Drawer 1708, Austin, TX 78767. *E-mail:* grantinfo@thecb.state.tx.us. *Phone:* 512-479-8891. *Web site:* www.collegefortexans.com.

Physician Assistant Loan Reimbursement Program. Award will repay loans for physician assistants working in rural Texas counties. Must have worked at least 12 consecutive months in a rural Texas county designated medically underserved. Can be renewed for up to four years. *Award:* Grant for use in freshman, sophomore, junior, or senior year; renewable. *Award amount:* up to $5000. *Eligibility Requirements:* Applicant must be enrolled or expecting to enroll at an institution or university. Applicant or parent of applicant must have employment or volunteer experience in designated career field. Available to U.S. citizens. *Application Requirements:* Application.

Contact Financial Aid Office at college, Texas Higher Education Coordinating Board, PO Box 12788, Austin, TX 78711-2788. *E-mail:* grantinfo@thecb.state.tx.us. *Phone:* 512-427-6101. *Fax:* 512-427-6127. *Web site:* www.collegefortexans.com.

Professional Nurses' Student Loan Repayment. Award for licensed nurses practicing in Texas to pay off student loans. Must demonstrate financial need. *Award:* Scholarship for use in freshman, sophomore, junior, or senior year; not renewable. *Award amount:* up to $2000. *Eligibility Requirements:* Applicant must be enrolled or expecting to enroll at an institution or university. Applicant or parent of applicant must have employment or volunteer experience in designated career field. *Application Requirements:* Application, financial need analysis. **Deadline:** January 15.

Contact Grants and Special Programs Office, Texas Higher Education Coordinating Board, PO Box 12788, Austin, TX 78711. *E-mail:* grantinfo@thecb.state.tx.us. *Phone:* 800-242-3062. *Web site:* www.collegefortexans.com.

Professional Nursing Scholarships. Several awards for Texas residents enrolled at least half-time in a nursing program leading to a professional degree at a Texas institution. Contact school financial aid office for further information. *Academic/Career Areas:* Nursing. *Award:* Scholarship for use in freshman, sophomore, junior, or senior year; not renewable. *Award amount:* up to $3000. *Eligibility Requirements:* Applicant must be enrolled or expecting to enroll full or part-time at a four-year institution or university; resident of Texas and studying in Texas. Available to U.S. citizens. *Application Requirements:* Application, financial need analysis, test scores, transcript.

Contact Student Services Division, Texas Higher Education Coordinating Board, PO Box 12788, Austin, TX 78711-2788. *E-mail:* grantinfo@thecb.state.tx.us. *Phone:* 800-242-3062. *Web site:* www.collegefortexans.com.

Teach for Texas Conditional Grant Program. This is a student loan with cancellation provisions for teaching. Prospective teachers must be enrolled in degree programs leading to certification in a teaching field designated as having a critical shortage of teachers, or agree to teach in a Texas community certified as experiencing a critical shortage of teachers. For upper division college students only. *Academic/Career Areas:* Education. *Award:* Forgivable loan for use in junior or senior year; not renewable. *Award amount:* up to $11,800. *Eligibility Requirements:* Applicant must be enrolled or expecting to enroll full or part-time at a four-year institution or university; resident of Texas and studying in Texas. Applicant must have 2.5 GPA or higher. Available to U.S. citizens. *Application Requirements:* Application, financial need analysis, references. **Deadline:** continuous.

Contact Special Accounts Servicing, Texas Higher Education Coordinating Board, PO Box 12788, Austin, TX 78711-2788. *E-mail:* grantinfo@thecb.state.tx.us. *Phone:* 800-242-3062. *Web site:* www.collegefortexans.com.

Texas National Guard Tuition Assistance Program. Provides exemption from the payment of tuition to certain members of the Texas National Guard, Texas Air Guard or the State Guard. Must be Texas resident and attend school in Texas. Visit the TNG Web site at: www.agd.state.tx.us/education_office/state_tuition.htm. *Award:* Scholarship for use in freshman, sophomore, junior, or senior year; renewable. *Eligibility Requirements:* Applicant must be enrolled or expecting to enroll at an institution or university; resident of Texas and studying in Texas. Applicant must have served in the Air Force National Guard, Army National Guard, or Navy National Guard. *Application Requirements:* Application.

Contact State Adjutant General's Office, Texas Higher Education Coordinating Board, PO Box 5218/AGTX-PAE, Austin, TX 78763-5218. *Phone:* 512-465-5001. *Web site:* www.collegefortexans.com.

Additional State Aid Programs

Texas Tuition Exemption for Blind/Deaf Students. Renewable award aids certain blind or deaf students by exempting them from payment of tuition and fees at public colleges or universities in Texas. Must be a resident of Texas. Deadlines vary. Must submit certificate of deafness or blindness. Contact the admissions/registrar's office for application information. *Award:* Scholarship for use in freshman, sophomore, junior, or senior year; renewable. *Eligibility Requirements:* Applicant must be enrolled or expecting to enroll full or part-time at a two-year, four-year, or technical institution or university; resident of Texas and studying in Texas. Applicant must be hearing impaired or visually impaired. Available to U.S. citizens. *Application Requirements:* Application, certificate of impairment.

Contact Financial Aid Office at college, Texas Higher Education Coordinating Board, PO Box 12788, Austin, TX 78711-2788. *E-mail:* grantinfo@thecb.state.tx.us. *Phone:* 512-427-6101. *Fax:* 512-427-6127. *Web site:* www.collegefortexans.com.

Texas Tuition Exemption for Senior Citizens-65+. Tuition exemption for Texas residents over the age of 65 at eligible Texas institutions. Pays tuition for up to six semester credit hours per semester or summer term. Nonrenewable. Awards made on a space-available basis. Contact the admissions/registrar's office for application information. *Award:* Scholarship for use in freshman, sophomore, junior, or senior year; not renewable. *Eligibility Requirements:* Applicant must be age 65; enrolled or expecting to enroll part-time at a two-year, four-year, or technical institution or university; resident of Texas and studying in Texas. Available to U.S. citizens. *Application Requirements:* Application. **Deadline:** continuous.

Contact Financial Aid Office at college, Texas Higher Education Coordinating Board, PO Box 12788, Austin, TX 78711-2788. *E-mail:* grantinfo@thecb.state.tx.us. *Phone:* 512-427-6101. *Fax:* 512-427-6127. *Web site:* www.collegefortexans.com.

Texas Tuition Exemption for Students in Foster Care or other Residential Care. Exemption from tuition and fees at Texas institution. Must have been in foster care under the conservatorship of the Department of Protection and Regulatory Services on or after 18th birthday; or on the day of the student's 14th birthday, if the student was also eligible for adoption on or after that day; or the day the student graduated from high school or completed the equivalent of a high school diploma. Must enroll as undergraduate student within three years of discharge. Must be Texas resident. Contact the admissions/registrar's office for application information. *Award:* Scholarship for use in freshman, sophomore, junior, or senior year; renewable. *Eligibility Requirements:* Applicant must be enrolled or expecting to enroll full or part-time at a two-year, four-year, or technical institution or university; resident of Texas and studying in Texas. Available to U.S. citizens. *Application Requirements:* Application. **Deadline:** continuous.

Contact Financial Aid Office at college, Texas Higher Education Coordinating Board, PO Box 12788, Austin, TX 78711-2788. *E-mail:* grantinfo@thecb.state.tx.us. *Phone:* 512-427-6101. *Fax:* 512-427-6127. *Web site:* www.collegefortexans.com.

Texas Tuition Exemption for TANF Students. Tuition and fee exemption for Texas residents who during last year of high school received financial assistance for not less than 6 months. Must enroll at Texas institution within 24 TANF months of high school graduation. Award is good for one year. Contact the admissions/registrar's office for application information. *Award:* Scholarship for use in freshman year; not renewable. *Eligibility Requirements:* Applicant must be age 21 or under; enrolled or expecting to enroll full or part-time at a two-year, four-year, or technical institution or university; single; resident of Texas and studying in Texas. *Application Requirements:* Application, financial need analysis. **Deadline:** continuous.

Contact Financial Aid Office at college, Texas Higher Education Coordinating Board, PO Box 12788, Austin, TX 78711-2788. *E-mail:* grantinfo@thecb.state.tx.us. *Phone:* 512-427-6101. *Fax:* 512-427-6127. *Web site:* www.collegefortexans.com.

Texas Tuition Exemption Program: Highest Ranking High School Graduate. Award available to Texas residents who are the top ranked seniors of their high school. Must attend a public college or university within Texas. Recipient is exempt from certain charges for first two semesters. Deadlines vary. Contact admissions/registrar's office for application information. Must provide proof of valedictorian ranking to the registrar. *Award:* Scholarship for use in freshman year; not renewable. *Eligibility Requirements:* Applicant must be enrolled or expecting to enroll full or part-time at a two-year, four-year, or technical institution or university; resident of Texas and studying in Texas. Applicant must have 3.5 GPA or higher. Available to U.S. citizens. *Application Requirements:* Transcript.

Contact Financial Aid Office at college, Texas Higher Education Coordinating Board, PO Box 12788, Austin, TX 78711-2788. *E-mail:* grantinfo@thecb.state.tx.us. *Phone:* 512-427-6101. *Fax:* 512-427-6127. *Web site:* www.collegefortexans.com.

Texas Yes! Scholarships. Texas YES! Scholarships are awarded to women and minorities, or to applicants who have participated in the educational programs sponsored by the Texas Society of Professional Engineers: MATHCOUNTS, NEDC, TEC, TEAMS, TESC. Applicants must have a 3.0 GPA. Must major in a field of engineering, be a resident of Texas and attend a postsecondary institution in Texas. Must be a high school senior. *Academic/Career Areas:* Chemical Engineering; Civil Engineering; Electrical Engineering/

Appendix D

Electronics; Engineering/Technology; Mechanical Engineering. *Award:* Scholarship for use in freshman year; not renewable. *Award amount:* $500–$1000. *Number of awards:* 3–5. *Eligibility Requirements:* Applicant must be high school student; planning to enroll or expecting to enroll full-time at an institution or university; resident of Texas and studying in Texas. Applicant must have 3.0 GPA or higher. Available to U.S. citizens. *Application Requirements:* Application, essay, references, transcript. **Deadline:** January 15.

Contact Kelly Melnyk, Assistant Director of Education Programs, Texas Engineering Foundation, Attn: Programs Director, 3501 Manor Road, PO Box 2145, Austin, TX 78768. *E-mail:* kellym@tspe.org. *Phone:* 512-472-9286. *Fax:* 512-472-2934. *Web site:* www.tspe.org.

Texas-Tuition Fee Exemption for Children of Disabled/Deceased Firemen, Peace Officers, Game Wardens, Employees of Correctional Institutions. Renewable award for children of paid or volunteer firemen, game wardens, peace officers, or custodial employees of the Department of Corrections disabled or deceased while serving in Texas. Must attend a Texas institution. Must apply before 21st birthday. Must provide certification of parent's disability or death. Contact institution's admissions or registrar's office for application information. *Award:* Scholarship for use in freshman, sophomore, or junior year; renewable. *Eligibility Requirements:* Applicant must be age 20 or under; enrolled or expecting to enroll full or part-time at a two-year, four-year, or technical institution or university; resident of Texas and studying in Texas. Applicant or parent of applicant must have employment or volunteer experience in designated career field, fire service, or police/firefighting. Available to U.S. citizens. *Application Requirements:* Application. **Deadline:** continuous.

Contact Financial Aid Office at college, Texas Higher Education Coordinating Board, PO Box 12788, Austin, TX 78711-2788. *E-mail:* grantinfo@thecb.state.tx.us. *Phone:* 512-427-6101. *Fax:* 512-427-6127. *Web site:* www.collegefortexans.com.

Toward Excellence, Access and Success (TEXAS Grant). Renewable aid for students enrolled in a public or private nonprofit, college or university in Texas. Based on need. Amount of award is determined by the financial aid office of each school. Deadlines vary. Contact the college/university financial aid office for application information. *Award:* Grant for use in freshman, sophomore, junior, or senior year; renewable. *Award amount:* up to $2800. *Eligibility Requirements:* Applicant must be enrolled or expecting to enroll full or part-time at a two-year, four-year, or technical institution or university; resident of Texas and studying in Texas. Applicant must have 2.5 GPA or higher. Available to U.S. citizens. *Application Requirements:* Application, financial need analysis, transcript. **Deadline:** continuous.

Contact Financial Aid Office at college, Texas Higher Education Coordinating Board, PO Box 12788, Austin, TX 78711-2788. *E-mail:* grantinfo@thecb.state.tx.us. *Phone:* 512-427-6101. *Fax:* 512-427-6127. *Web site:* www.collegefortexans.com.

Toward Excellence, Access, and Success (TEXAS) Grant II Program. Provides grant aid to financially needy students enrolled in Texas public two-year colleges. Complete FAFSA. Contact college financial aid office for additional assistance. *Award:* Grant for use in freshman or sophomore year; renewable. *Award amount:* up to $2600. *Eligibility Requirements:* Applicant must be enrolled or expecting to enroll full or part-time at a two-year or technical institution; resident of Texas and studying in Texas. Applicant must have 2.5 GPA or higher. Available to U.S. citizens. *Application Requirements:* Financial need analysis, transcript, FAFSA. **Deadline:** continuous.

Contact Financial Aid Office at college, Texas Higher Education Coordinating Board, PO Box 12788, Austin, TX 78711-2788. *E-mail:* grantinfo@thecb.state.tx.us. *Phone:* 512-427-6101. *Fax:* 512-427-6127. *Web site:* www.collegefortexans.com.

Train our Teachers Award. Awarded to employed child care workers seeking credentials or an associate degree in child development. Must agree to work 18 consecutive months in a licensed child care facility. Must attend a Texas institution. For more details and deadlines see Web site: www.collegefortexans.com. *Award:* Scholarship for use in freshman or sophomore year; not renewable. *Award amount:* up to $1000. *Number of awards:* up to 2000. *Eligibility Requirements:* Applicant must be enrolled or expecting to enroll at an institution or university and studying in Texas. Applicant or parent of applicant must have employment or volunteer experience in designated career field. *Application Requirements:* Application.

Contact Financial Aid Office at college, Texas Higher Education Coordinating Board, PO Box 12788, Austin, TX 78711-2788. *E-mail:* grantinfo@thecb.state.tx.us. *Phone:* 512-427-6101. *Fax:* 512-427-6127. *Web site:* www.collegefortexans.com.

Tuition and Fee Exemption for Children of Prisoners of War or Persons Missing in Action-Texas. Renewable award assists children of prisoners of war or veterans classified as missing in action. Must be a Texas resident and attend a public college or university within Texas. Submit proof of service and proof of MIA/POW status. Award is exemption from tuition and fees. Must be under 21 years of age. Contact the admissions/registrar's office for application information. *Award:* Scholarship for use in freshman, sophomore, junior, or senior year; renewable. *Eligibility Requirements:* Applicant must be age 20 or under; enrolled or expecting to enroll at a two-year, four-year, or technical institution or university; resident of Texas and studying in Texas. Applicant or parent must meet

Additional State Aid Programs

one or more of the following requirements: general military experience; retired from active duty; disabled or killed as a result of military service; prisoner of war; or missing in action. *Application Requirements:* Application, proof of service and MIA/POW status. **Deadline:** continuous.

> Contact Financial Aid Office at college, Texas Higher Education Coordinating Board, PO Box 12788, Austin, TX 78711-2788. *E-mail:* grantinfo@thecb.state.tx.us. *Phone:* 512-427-6101. *Fax:* 512-427-6127. *Web site:* www.collegefortexans.com.

Tuition Equalization Grant (TEG) Program. Renewable award for Texas residents enrolled at least half-time at an independent college or university within the state. Based on financial need. Deadlines vary by institution. Must not be receiving athletic scholarship. Contact college/university financial aid office for application information. *Award:* Grant for use in freshman, sophomore, junior, or senior year; renewable. *Award amount:* up to $3572. *Eligibility Requirements:* Applicant must be enrolled or expecting to enroll full or part-time at a two-year or four-year institution or university; resident of Texas and studying in Texas. Available to U.S. citizens. *Application Requirements:* Financial need analysis, FAFSA.

> Contact Financial Aid Office at college, Texas Higher Education Coordinating Board, PO Box 12788, Austin, TX 78711-2788. *E-mail:* grantinfo@thecb.state.tx.us. *Phone:* 512-427-6101. *Fax:* 512-427-6127. *Web site:* www.collegefortexans.com.

Tuition Exemptions for Texas Veterans (Hazelwood Act). Renewable tuition and partial fee exemptions for Texas veterans who have been honorably discharged after at least 180 days of active duty. Must be a Texas resident at time of entry into service. Must have exhausted federal education benefits. Contact the admissions/registrar's office for information on how to apply. Must be used at a Texas public institution. *Award:* Scholarship for use in freshman, sophomore, junior, or senior year; renewable. *Award amount:* $980. *Eligibility Requirements:* Applicant must be enrolled or expecting to enroll full or part-time at a two-year, four-year, or technical institution or university; resident of Texas and studying in Texas. Available to U.S. citizens. Applicant or parent must meet one or more of the following requirements: general military experience; retired from active duty; disabled or killed as a result of military service; prisoner of war; or missing in action. *Application Requirements:* Application. **Deadline:** continuous.

> Contact Financial Aid Office at college, Texas Higher Education Coordinating Board, PO Box 12788, Austin, TX 78711-2788. *E-mail:* grantinfo@thecb.state.tx.us. *Phone:* 512-427-6101. *Fax:* 512-427-6127. *Web site:* www.collegefortexans.com.

Vocational Nursing Scholarships. Scholarships for Texas residents must be enrolled in a vocational nursing program at an institution in Texas. Deadline varies. *Academic/Career Areas:* Nursing. *Award:* Scholarship for use in freshman or sophomore year; not renewable. *Award amount:* up to $1500. *Eligibility Requirements:* Applicant must be enrolled or expecting to enroll full or part-time at a four-year institution or university; resident of Texas and studying in Texas. Available to U.S. citizens. *Application Requirements:* Application, financial need analysis, test scores, transcript.

> Contact Texas Higher Education Coordinating Board, PO Box 12788, Austin, TX 78711-2788. *E-mail:* grantinfo@thecb.state.tx.us. *Web site:* www.collegefortexans.com.

Utah

Leveraging Educational Assistance Partnership (LEAP). Available to students with substantial financial need for use at participating Utah schools. Contact Financial Aid Office of specific school for application requirements and deadlines. Must be Utah resident. *Award:* Grant for use in freshman, sophomore, junior, or senior year; renewable. *Award amount:* up to $2500. *Number of awards:* up to 3000. *Eligibility Requirements:* Applicant must be enrolled or expecting to enroll full or part-time at a two-year, four-year, or technical institution or university; resident of Utah and studying in Utah. Available to U.S. citizens. *Application Requirements:* Application, financial need analysis. **Deadline:** continuous.

> **Contact** Financial Aid Office, Utah State Board of Regents. *Web site:* www.uheaa.org.

New Century Scholarship. Scholarship for qualified high school graduates of Utah. Must attend Utah state-operated college. Award depends on number of hours student enrolled. Please contact for further eligibility requirements. Eligible recipients receive an award equal to 75% of tuition for 60 credit hours toward the completion of a bachelor's degree. For more details see Web site: www.utahsbr.edu. *Award:* Scholarship for use in junior or senior year; renewable. *Award amount:* $500–$1000. *Eligibility Requirements:* Applicant must be high school student; planning to enroll or expecting to enroll full or part-time at a four-year institution or university; resident of Utah and studying in Utah. Available to U.S. citizens. *Application Requirements:* Application, test scores, transcript, GPA/copy of enrollment verification from an eligible Utah 4-year institute. **Deadline:** continuous.

> **Contact** Angie Loving, Manager for Programs/Administration, State of Utah, 3 Triad Center, Suite 500, Salt Lake City, UT 84180-1205. *E-mail:* aloving@utahsbr.edu. *Phone:* 801-321-7124. *Fax:* 801-321-7199. *Web site:* www.utahsbr.edu.

Financial Aid 101

Appendix D

T.H. Bell Teaching Incentive Loan-Utah. Renewable awards for Utah residents who are high school seniors and wish to pursue teaching careers. Award pays for tuition and fees at a Utah institution. Must agree to teach in a Utah public school or pay back loan through monthly installments. Must be a U.S. citizen. *Academic/Career Areas:* Education; Special Education. *Award:* Forgivable loan for use in freshman, sophomore, junior, or senior year; renewable. *Number of awards:* 50. *Eligibility Requirements:* Applicant must be high school student; planning to enroll or expecting to enroll full-time at a two-year or four-year institution or university; resident of Utah and studying in Utah. Available to U.S. citizens. *Application Requirements:* Application, essay, test scores, transcript. **Deadline:** March 29.

Contact Diane DeMan, Executive Secretary, Utah State Office of Education, 250 East 500 South, Salt Lake City, UT 84111. *Phone:* 801-538-7741. *Fax:* 801-538-7973. *Web site:* www.usoe.k12.ut.us/cert/scholarships/scholars.htm.

Terrel H. Bell Teaching Incentive Loan. Designed to provide financial assistance to outstanding Utah students pursuing a degree in education. The incentive loan funds full-time tuition and general fees for eight semesters. After graduation/certification the loan may be forgiven if the recipient teaches in a Utah public school or accredited private school (K-12). Loan forgiveness is done on a year-for-year basis. For more details see Web site: www.utahsbr.edu. *Academic/Career Areas:* Education. *Award:* Forgivable loan for use in freshman, sophomore, junior, or senior year; renewable. *Award amount:* $600–$1500. *Number of awards:* 365. *Eligibility Requirements:* Applicant must be enrolled or expecting to enroll full-time at a two-year or four-year institution or university; resident of Utah and studying in Utah. Available to U.S. citizens. *Application Requirements:* Application, essay, test scores, transcript. **Deadline:** March 31.

Contact Angie Loving, Manager for Programs and Administration, State of Utah, 3 Triad Center, Suite 550, Salt Lake City, UT 84180. *E-mail:* aloving@utahsbr.edu. *Phone:* 801-321-7124. *Fax:* 801-321-7199. *Web site:* www.utahsbr.edu.

Utah Educationally Disadvantaged Program. Renewable award for residents of Utah who are disadvantaged and attending an eligible institution in Utah. Must demonstrate need and satisfactory progress. Contact financial aid office of participating institution. *Award:* Scholarship for use in freshman, sophomore, junior, or senior year; renewable. *Eligibility Requirements:* Applicant must be enrolled or expecting to enroll at a two-year or four-year institution; resident of Utah and studying in Utah. Applicant must be hearing impaired, learning disabled, physically disabled, or visually impaired. *Application Requirements:* Application. **Deadline:** continuous.

Contact Lynda Reid, Administrative Assistant, Utah State Board of Regents, 60 South 400 West, The Board of Regents Building, The Gateway, Salt Lake City, UT 84101-1284. *Phone:* 801-321-7207. *Fax:* 801-321-7299. *Web site:* www.uheaa.org.

Utah Engineering and Computer Science Program (UECLP). A loan forgiveness program to recruit and train engineering, computer science and related technology students to assist in providing for and advancing the intellectual and economic welfare of the state. *Academic/Career Areas:* Computer Science/Data Processing; Engineering/Technology; Engineering-Related Technologies. *Award:* Forgivable loan for use in junior or senior year; renewable. *Award amount:* $1500–$5000. *Number of awards:* 90–110. *Eligibility Requirements:* Applicant must be enrolled or expecting to enroll full-time at a four-year institution or university; resident of Utah and studying in Utah. Applicant must have 3.0 GPA or higher. Available to U.S. citizens. *Application Requirements:* Application, test scores, transcript. **Deadline:** continuous.

Contact Chalmers Gail Norris, Executive Director of UHEAA of the Utah State Board of Regents, Utah State Board of Regents, 60 South 400 West, Salt Lake City, UT 84101. *Fax:* 801-321-7299. *Web site:* www.uheaa.org.

Utah Society of Professional Engineers Scholarship. One-time award for entering freshman pursuing studies in the field of engineering (civil, chemical, electrical, or engineering related technologies.) Minimum 3.0 GPA required. Must be a U.S. citizen and Utah resident attending school in Utah. Application deadline is March 27. *Academic/Career Areas:* Chemical Engineering; Civil Engineering; Economics; Electrical Engineering/Electronics; Engineering/Technology; Engineering-Related Technologies; Mechanical Engineering. *Award:* Scholarship for use in freshman year; not renewable. *Award amount:* $1000. *Number of awards:* 1. *Eligibility Requirements:* Applicant must be high school student; planning to enroll or expecting to enroll full-time at a four-year institution or university; resident of Utah and studying in Utah. Applicant must have 3.0 GPA or higher. Available to U.S. citizens. *Application Requirements:* Application, essay, resume, references, test scores, transcript, certification. **Deadline:** March 27.

Contact Tom McNamee, Scholarship Coordinator, Utah Society of Professional Engineers, 488 East Winchester Street, Suite 400, Murray, UT 84107. *E-mail:* tmcnamee@sisna.com. *Web site:* www.uspeonline.com.

Utah Tuition Waiver. Renewable awards ranging from partial to full tuition waivers at eligible Utah institutions. A limited number of waivers are available for nonresidents. Deadlines vary by institutions. Contact Financial Aid Office. *Award:* Scholarship for use in freshman, sophomore, junior, senior, or graduate year; renewable. *Eligibility Requirements:* Applicant must be enrolled or expecting to enroll full or part-time at a two-year or four-year institution and studying in Utah. Available to U.S. and non-U.S. citizens. *Application Requirements:* Application, financial need analysis, interview.

> Contact Lynda Reid, Administrative Assistant, Utah State Board of Regents, 60 South 400 West, The Board of Regents Building, The Gateway, Salt Lake City, UT 84101-1284. *Phone:* 801-321-7207. *Fax:* 801-321-7299. *Web site:* www.uheaa.org.

Vermont

Vermont Incentive Grants. Renewable grants for Vermont residents based on financial need. Must meet needs test. Must be college undergraduate or graduate student enrolled full-time at an approved postsecondary institution. Only available to U.S. citizens or permanent residents. *Award:* Grant for use in freshman, sophomore, junior, senior, or graduate year; renewable. *Award amount:* $500–$9100. *Eligibility Requirements:* Applicant must be enrolled or expecting to enroll full-time at an institution or university and resident of Vermont. Available to U.S. citizens. *Application Requirements:* Application, financial need analysis. **Deadline:** continuous.

> **Contact** Grant Program, Vermont Student Assistance Corporation, PO Box 2000, Winooski, VT 05404-2000. *Phone:* 802-655-9602. *Fax:* 802-654-3765. *Web site:* www.vsac.org.

Vermont Non-degree Student Grant Program. Renewable grants for Vermont residents enrolled in non-degree programs at colleges, vocational centers, and high school adult courses. May receive funds for two enrollment periods per year, up to $690 per course, per semester. Award based upon financial need. *Award:* Grant for use in freshman or sophomore year; renewable. *Award amount:* up to $690. *Eligibility Requirements:* Applicant must be enrolled or expecting to enroll at an institution or university and resident of Vermont. *Application Requirements:* Application, financial need analysis. **Deadline:** continuous.

> **Contact** Grant Program, Vermont Student Assistance Corporation, PO Box 2000, Winooski, VT 05404-2000. *Phone:* 802-655-9602. *Fax:* 802-654-3765. *Web site:* www.vsac.org.

Vermont Part-time Student Grants. For undergraduates carrying less than twelve credits per semester who have not received a bachelor's degree. Must be Vermont resident. Based on financial need. Complete Vermont Financial Aid Packet to apply. May be used at any approved postsecondary institution. *Award:* Grant for use in freshman, sophomore, junior, or senior year; renewable. *Award amount:* $250–$6830. *Eligibility Requirements:* Applicant must be enrolled or expecting to enroll part-time at an institution or university and resident of Vermont. *Application Requirements:* Application, financial need analysis. **Deadline:** continuous.

> **Contact** Grant Program, Vermont Student Assistance Corporation, PO Box 2000, Winooski, VT 05404-2000. *Phone:* 802-655-9602. *Fax:* 802-654-3765. *Web site:* www.vsac.org.

Virginia

General Mills Scholars Program/Internship. Scholarships and paid summer internships awarded to college sophomores and juniors majoring in accounting, business (sales interest), computer science, engineering, finance, human resources, information systems, information technology or marketing at a UNCF member college or university. Minimum 3.5 GPA required. Prospective applicants should complete the Student Profile found at Web site: www.uncf.org. *Academic/Career Areas:* Accounting; Business/Consumer Services; Computer Science/Data Processing; Engineering/Technology. *Award:* Scholarship for use in sophomore or junior year; not renewable. *Award amount:* $5000. *Eligibility Requirements:* Applicant must be Black (non-Hispanic) and enrolled or expecting to enroll full-time at a four-year institution or university. Applicant must have 3.5 GPA or higher. Available to U.S. citizens. *Application Requirements:* Application, financial need analysis, test scores. **Deadline:** February 14.

> **Contact** Program Services Department, United Negro College Fund, 8260 Willow Oaks Corporate Drive, Fairfax, VA 22031. *Web site:* www.uncf.org.

Mary Marshall Practical Nursing Scholarships. Award for practical nursing students who are Virginia residents. Must attend a nursing program in Virginia. Recipient must agree to work in Virginia after graduation. Minimum 3.0 GPA required. Recipients may reapply up to three years for an award. *Academic/Career Areas:* Nursing. *Award:* Scholarship for use in freshman, sophomore, junior, or senior year; not renewable. *Award amount:* $150–$500. *Eligibility Requirements:* Applicant must be enrolled or expecting to enroll full or part-time at a two-year or technical institution; resident of Virginia and studying in Virginia. Applicant must have 3.0 GPA or higher. Available to U.S. citizens. *Application Requirements:* Application, financial need analysis, references, transcript. **Deadline:** June 30.

> Contact Norma Marrin, Business Manager/Policy Analyst, Virginia Department of Health, Office of Health Policy and Planning, PO Box 2448, Richmond, VA 23218-2448. *E-mail:* nmarrin@vdh.state.va.us. *Phone:* 804-371-4090. *Fax:* 804-371-0116. *Web site:* www.vdh.state.va.us/primcare/index.html.

Mary Marshall Registered Nursing Program Scholarships. Award for registered nursing students who are Virginia residents. Must attend a nursing program in Virginia. Recipient must agree to work in Virginia after graduation. Minimum 3.0 GPA required. Recipient may reapply up to three years for an award. *Academic/Career*

Areas: Nursing. *Award:* Scholarship for use in freshman, sophomore, junior, or senior year; not renewable. *Award amount:* $1200–$2000. *Number of awards:* 60–100. *Eligibility Requirements:* Applicant must be enrolled or expecting to enroll full- or part-time at a two-year or four-year institution or university; resident of Virginia and studying in Virginia. Applicant must have 3.0 GPA or higher. Available to U.S. citizens. *Application Requirements:* Application, financial need analysis, references, transcript. **Deadline:** June 30.

> **Contact** Norma Marrin, Business Manager/Policy Analyst, Virginia Department of Health, Office of Health Policy and Planning, PO Box 2448, Richmond, VA 23218-2448. *E-mail:* nmarrin@udh.state.va.us. *Phone:* 804-371-4090. *Fax:* 804-371-0116. *Web site:* www.vdh.state.va.us/primcare/index.html.

Virginia Tuition Assistance Grant Program (Private Institutions). Renewable awards of approximately $3,000 each for undergraduate, graduate, and first professional degree students attending an approved private, nonprofit college within Virginia. Must be a Virginia resident and be enrolled full-time. Not to be used for religious study. Preferred deadline July 31. Others are wait-listed. Contact college financial aid office. The application process is handled by the participating colleges' financial aid office. *Award:* Grant for use in freshman, sophomore, junior, senior, or graduate year; renewable. *Award amount:* $3000. *Number of awards:* 15,000. *Eligibility Requirements:* Applicant must be enrolled or expecting to enroll full-time at a four-year institution; resident of Virginia and studying in Virginia. *Application Requirements:* Application. **Deadline:** July 31.

> **Contact** Financial Aid Office at participating institution, State Council of Higher Education for Virginia, James Monroe Building, 10th Floor, 101 North 14th Street, Richmond, VA 23219. *Web site:* www.schev.edu.

Virginia War Orphans Education Program. Scholarships for postsecondary students between ages 16 and 25 to attend Virginia state supported institutions. Must be child or surviving child of veteran who has either 1. been permanently or totally disabled due to war or other armed conflict; 2. died as a result of war or other armed conflict or 3. been listed as a POW or MIA. Parent must also meet Virginia residency requirements. Contact for application procedures and deadline. *Award:* Scholarship for use in freshman, sophomore, junior, senior, or graduate year; renewable. *Eligibility Requirements:* Applicant must be age 16-25; enrolled or expecting to enroll at a two-year, four-year, or technical institution or university and studying in Virginia. Applicant or parent must meet one or more of the following requirements: general military experience; retired from active duty; disabled or killed as a result of military service; prisoner of war; or missing in action. *Application Requirements:* Application.

Contact Beth Tonn, Administrative Assistant, Virginia Department of Veterans' Affairs, Poff Federal Building, 270 Franklin Road, S.W., Room 503, Roanoke, VA 24011-2215. *Phone:* 540-857-7104. *Fax:* 540-858-7573. *Web site:* www.vdva.vipnet.org/education_state.htm.

Virginia War Orphans Education Program. Grant is equal to tuition-free education for up to 48 months. One of the applicant's parents must have served in the armed forces of the United States and be permanently and totally disabled due to war or other armed conflict, died as a result of war or other armed conflict or be listed as a prisoner of war (POW) or missing in action (MIA). Must be a resident of Virginia studying in Virginia. *Award:* Grant for use in freshman, sophomore, junior, or senior year; renewable. *Eligibility Requirements:* Applicant must be age 16-25; enrolled or expecting to enroll at an institution or university; resident of Virginia and studying in Virginia. Available to U.S. citizens. Applicant or parent must meet one or more of the following requirements: general military experience; retired from active duty; disabled or killed as a result of military service; prisoner of war; or missing in action. *Application Requirements:* Application.

> **Contact** Commonwealth of Virginia Department of Veterans' Affairs, 270 Franklin Road SW, Room 503, Poff Federal Building, Roanoke, VA 24011-2215.

Walter Reed Smith Scholarship. Award for full-time female undergraduate student who is a descendant of a Confederate soldier, studying nutrition, home economics, nursing, business administration, or computer science. Must carry a minimum of 12 credit hours each semester and have a minimum 3.0 GPA. Submit letter of endorsement from sponsoring chapter of the United Daughters of the Confederacy. *Academic/Career Areas:* Business/Consumer Services; Computer Science/Data Processing; Food Science/Nutrition; Home Economics; Nursing. *Award:* Scholarship for use in freshman, sophomore, junior, or senior year; renewable. *Award amount:* $800–$1000. *Number of awards:* 1–2. *Eligibility Requirements:* Applicant must be enrolled or expecting to enroll full-time at a four-year institution or university and female. Applicant or parent of applicant must be member of United Daughters of the Confederacy. Applicant must have 3.0 GPA or higher. Available to U.S. citizens. *Application Requirements:* Application, essay, financial need analysis, photo, references, self-addressed stamped envelope, transcript. **Deadline:** February 15.

> **Contact** Second Vice President General, United Daughters of the Confederacy, 328 North Boulevard, Richmond, VA 23220-4057. *Phone:* 804-355-1636. *Web site:* www.hqudc.org.

Washington

American Indian Endowed Scholarship. Awarded to financially needy undergraduate and graduate students with close social and cultural ties to a Native-Americans community. Must be Washington resident, enrolled full-time at Washington School. Deadline is May 15. *Award:* Scholarship for use in freshman, sophomore, junior, senior, or graduate year; renewable. *Award amount:* $1000–$2000. *Number of awards:* 10–15. *Eligibility Requirements:* Applicant must be American Indian/Alaska Native; enrolled or expecting to enroll full-time at a two-year, four-year, or technical institution or university; resident of Washington and studying in Washington. Available to U.S. citizens. *Application Requirements:* Application, financial need analysis. **Deadline:** May 15.

Contact John Klacik, Washington Higher Education Coordinating Board, 917 Lakeridge Way SW, PO Box 43430, Olympia, WA 98504-3430. *E-mail:* johnk@hecb.wa.gov. *Phone:* 360-755-7851. *Fax:* 360-753-7808. *Web site:* www.hecb.wa.gov.

Educational Opportunity Grant. Annual grants of $2500 to encourage financially needy, placebound students to complete bachelor's degree. Must be unable to continue education due to family or work commitments, health concerns, financial needs, or similar. Must be Washington residents, live in one of 13 designated counties, and have completed two years of college. Grant only used at eligible four-year colleges in Washington. Applications accepted beginning in April and following months until funds are depleted. *Award:* Grant for use in junior or senior year; not renewable. *Award amount:* $2500. *Eligibility Requirements:* Applicant must be enrolled or expecting to enroll at a four-year institution or university; resident of Washington and studying in Washington. Available to U.S. citizens. *Application Requirements:* Application, financial need analysis.

Contact Betty Gebhardt, Washington Higher Education Coordinating Board, 917 Lakeridge Way SW, PO Box 43430, Olympia, WA 98504-3430. *E-mail:* bettyg@hecb.wa.gov. *Phone:* 360-753-7852. *Fax:* 360-753-7808. *Web site:* www.hecb.wa.gov.

State Need Grant. Grants for undergraduate students with significant financial need. Must be Washington resident and attend school in Washington. Must have family income equal or less than 55% of state median. *Award:* Grant for use in freshman, sophomore, junior, or senior year; not renewable. *Award amount:* $1900–$4000. *Eligibility Requirements:* Applicant must be enrolled or expecting to enroll full or part-time at a two-year, four-year, or technical institution or university; resident of Washington and studying in Washington. Available to U.S. citizens. *Application Requirements:* Application, financial need analysis. **Deadline:** continuous.

Contact John Klacik, Washington Higher Education Coordinating Board, 917 Lakeridge Way SW, PO Box 43430, Olympia, WA 98504-3430. *E-mail:* johnk@hecb.wa.gov. *Phone:* 360-753-7851. *Fax:* 360-753-7808. *Web site:* www.hecb.wa.gov.

Washington Award for Vocational Excellence. Tuition-only award for those completing a vocational education program as graduating seniors or community/technical college students who have completed first year of a two-year program. The scholarship is for 6 quarters or 4 semesters. Three are awarded in each of 49 legislative districts in the state. Must be a Washington State resident attending a postsecondary institution in Washington State. *Award:* Grant for use in freshman or sophomore year; renewable. *Award amount:* $3486–$7796. *Number of awards:* 147. *Eligibility Requirements:* Applicant must be enrolled or expecting to enroll full or part-time at a two-year, four-year, or technical institution or university; resident of Washington and studying in Washington. Available to U.S. and non-U.S. citizens. *Application Requirements:* Application, essay, references. **Deadline:** March 1.

Contact Lee Williams, Program Administrator, Washington State Workforce Training and Education Coordinating Board, 128 Tenth Avenue SW, PO Box 43105, Olympia, WA 98504-3105. *E-mail:* lwilliams@wtb.wa.gov. *Phone:* 360-586-3321. *Fax:* 360-586-5862. *Web site:* www.wtb.wa.gov/wave-abt.html.

Washington Award for Vocational Excellence (WAVE). Award to honor three vocational students from each of the state's 49 legislative districts. Grants for up to two years of undergraduate resident tuition. Must be enrolled in Washington high school, skills center, or technical college at time of application. Complete 360 hours in single vocational program in high school or one year at technical college. Contact principal or guidance counselor for more information. *Award:* Grant for use in freshman, sophomore, junior, or senior year; renewable. *Eligibility Requirements:* Applicant must be enrolled or expecting to enroll full-time at a two-year, four-year, or technical institution or university; resident of Washington and studying in Washington. Available to U.S. citizens. *Application Requirements:* **Deadline:** continuous.

Contact John Klacik, Washington Higher Education Coordinating Board, 917 Lakeridge Way, SW, PO Box 43430, Olympia, WA 98504-3430. *E-mail:* johnk@hecb.wa.gov. *Phone:* 360-753-7851. *Fax:* 360-753-7808. *Web site:* www.hecb.wa.gov.

Washington National Guard Scholarship Program. A state funded retention incentive/loan program for both Washington Army and Air Guard members meeting all eligibility requirements. The loans are forgiven if the soldier/airman completes their service requirements. Failure to meet/complete service obligations incurs the requirement to repay the loan plus 8%

Appendix D

interest. Minimum 2.5 GPA required. Deadline is April 30. *Award:* Forgivable loan for use in freshman, sophomore, junior, or senior year; not renewable. *Award amount:* $200–$4000. *Number of awards:* up to 60. *Eligibility Requirements:* Applicant must be enrolled or expecting to enroll full or part-time at a two-year, four-year, or technical institution or university and resident of Washington. Applicant must have 2.5 GPA or higher. Available to U.S. and non-U.S. citizens. Applicant must have served in the Air Force National Guard or Army National Guard. *Application Requirements:* Application, transcript, enlistment/extension documents. **Deadline:** April 30.

Contact Mark M. Rhoden, Educational Services Officer, Washington National Guard, Building 15, Camp Murray, Tacoma, WA 98430-5073. *E-mail:* mark.rhoden@wa.ngb.army.mil. *Phone:* 253-512-8899. *Fax:* 253-512-8936. *Web site:* www.washingtonguard.com/education/education.htm.

Washington Promise Scholarship. College scholarships to low- and middle-income students in high school. Must either rank in top 15 percent of senior class or score a combined 1200 on SAT or 27 on ACT on first attempt. Family income cannot exceed 135% of state median family income. Must be Washington resident, attend a Washington school. School must identify applicants. Contact principal or guidance counselor for more information. *Award:* Scholarship for use in freshman or sophomore year; renewable. *Award amount:* up to $1000. *Eligibility Requirements:* Applicant must be high school student; planning to enroll or expecting to enroll full or part-time at a two-year, four-year, or technical institution or university; resident of Washington and studying in Washington. Available to U.S. citizens. *Application Requirements:* Financial need analysis. **Deadline:** continuous.

Contact John Klacik, Washington Higher Education Coordinating Board, 917 Lakeridge Way SW, PO Box 43430, Olympia, WA 98504-3430. *E-mail:* johnk@hecb.wa.gov. *Phone:* 360-753-7851. *Fax:* 360-753-7808. *Web site:* www.hecb.wa.gov.

Washington Scholars Program. Awarded to three high school students from each of the 49 state legislative districts. Must be Washington resident and enroll in college or university in Washington. Scholarships equal up to four years of full-time resident undergraduate tuition and fees. Contact principal or guidance counselor for more information. *Award:* Grant for use in freshman, sophomore, junior, or senior year; renewable. *Eligibility Requirements:* Applicant must be high school student; planning to enroll or expecting to enroll full-time at a four-year institution or university; resident of Washington and studying in Washington. Available to U.S. citizens. *Application Requirements:* **Deadline:** continuous.

Contact John Klacik, Washington Higher Education Coordinating Board, 917 Lakeridge Way SW, PO Box 43430, Olympia, WA 98504-3430. *E-mail:* johnk@hecb.wa.gov. *Phone:* 360-753-7851. *Fax:* 360-753-7808. *Web site:* www.hecb.wa.gov.

West Virginia

Higher Education Adult Part-time Student Grant Program. Program to assist needy adult students to continue their education on a part-time basis. Also has a component in which 25% of the funding may be utilized for students enrolled in workforce and skill development programs. Contact institution financial aid office for more information and deadlines. *Award:* Grant for use in freshman, sophomore, junior, or senior year; not renewable. *Eligibility Requirements:* Applicant must be enrolled or expecting to enroll full or part-time at a two-year, four-year, or technical institution or university; resident of West Virginia and studying in West Virginia. Available to U.S. citizens. *Application Requirements:* Application, financial need analysis.

Contact Judy Kee, Financial Aid Manager, West Virginia Higher Education Policy Commission-Office of Financial Aid and Outreach Services, 1018 Kanawha Boulevard, East, Suite 700, Charleston, WV 25301. *E-mail:* kee@hepc.wvnet.edu. *Phone:* 304-558-4618. *Fax:* 304-558-4622. *Web site:* www.hepc.wvnet.edu.

Promise Scholarship. Renewable award for West Virginia residents. Minimum 3.0 GPA and combined ACT score of 21 or 1000 on the SAT. Provides full-tuition scholarship to a state college or university in West Virginia or an equivalent scholarship to an in-state private college. Financial resources are not a factor. *Award:* Scholarship for use in freshman, sophomore, junior, or senior year; renewable. *Award amount:* $3000. *Number of awards:* 3500. *Eligibility Requirements:* Applicant must be high school student; planning to enroll or expecting to enroll full-time at a two-year or four-year institution or university; resident of West Virginia and studying in West Virginia. Applicant must have 3.0 GPA or higher. Available to U.S. citizens. *Application Requirements:* Application, financial need analysis, test scores, transcript. **Deadline:** January 31.

Contact Robert Morgenstern, Executive Director, West Virginia Higher Education Policy Commission-Office of Financial Aid and Outreach Services, Promise Scholarship, 1018 Kanawha Boulevard, Suite 700, Charleston, WV 25301. *E-mail:* morgenstern@hepc.wvnet.edu. *Phone:* 304-558-4417. *Fax:* 304-558-3264. *Web site:* www.hepc.wvnet.edu.

Underwood-Smith Teacher Scholarship Program. For West Virginia residents at West Virginia institutions pursuing teaching careers. Must have a 3.25 GPA after completion of two years of course work. Must teach two years in West Virginia public schools for each year the award is received. Recipients will be required to sign an agreement acknowledging an understanding of the program's requirements and their willingness to repay the award if appropriate teaching service is not rendered. *Academic/Career Areas*: Education. *Award*: Scholarship for use in junior, senior, or graduate year; renewable. *Award amount*: up to $5000. *Number of awards*: 53. *Eligibility Requirements*: Applicant must be enrolled or expecting to enroll full-time at a four-year institution or university; resident of West Virginia and studying in West Virginia. Available to U.S. citizens. *Application Requirements*: Application, essay, references. **Deadline:** March 1.

Contact Michelle Wicks, Scholarship Coordinator, West Virginia Higher Education Policy Commission-Office of Financial Aid and Outreach Services, 1018 Kanawha Boulevard East, Suite 700, Charleston, WV 25301. *E-mail:* wicks@hepc.wvnet.edu. *Phone:* 304-558-4618. *Fax:* 304-558-4622. *Web site:* www.hepc.wvnet.edu.

West Virginia Division of Veterans' Affairs War Orphans Education Program. Renewable waiver of tuition award for West Virginia residents who are children of deceased veterans. Parent must have died of war-related service-connected disability. Must be ages 16-23. Minimum 2.5 GPA required. Must attend a state-supported West Virginia postsecondary institution. Deadline: July 1 and December 1. *Award*: Scholarship for use in freshman, sophomore, junior, senior, or graduate year; renewable. *Eligibility Requirements*: Applicant must be age 16-23; enrolled or expecting to enroll full or part-time at a two-year, four-year, or technical institution or university; resident of West Virginia and studying in West Virginia. Applicant must have 2.5 GPA or higher. Available to U.S. citizens. Applicant or parent must meet one or more of the following requirements: general military experience; retired from active duty; disabled or killed as a result of military service; prisoner of war; or missing in action. *Application Requirements*: Application, references.

Contact Ms. Linda Walker, Secretary, West Virginia Division of Veterans' Affairs, 1321 Plaza East, Suite 101, Charleston, WV 25301-1400. *E-mail:* wvdva@state.wv.us. *Phone:* 304-668-3661. *Fax:* 304-668-3662.

West Virginia Engineering, Science & Technology Scholarship Program. For students attending West Virginia institutions full time pursuing a career in engineering, science or technology. Must have a 3.0 GPA on a 4.0 scale. Must work in the fields of engineering, science or technology in West Virginia one year for each year the award is received. *Academic/Career Areas*: Electrical Engineering/Electronics; Engineering/Technology; Engineering-Related Technologies; Science, Technology and Society. *Award*: Scholarship for use in freshman, sophomore, junior, or senior year; renewable. *Award amount*: up to $3000. *Number of awards*: 300. *Eligibility Requirements*: Applicant must be enrolled or expecting to enroll full-time at a two-year, four-year, or technical institution or university and studying in West Virginia. Applicant must have 3.0 GPA or higher. Available to U.S. citizens. *Application Requirements*: Application, essay, test scores, transcript. **Deadline:** March 1.

Contact Michelle Wicks, Scholarship Coordinator, West Virginia Higher Education Policy Commission-Office of Financial Aid and Outreach Services, 1018 Kanawha Boulevard East, Suite 700, Charleston, WV 25301. *E-mail:* wicks@hepc.wvnet.edu. *Phone:* 304-558-4618. *Fax:* 304-558-4622. *Web site:* www.hepc.wvnet.edu.

West Virginia Higher Education Grant Program. For West Virginia residents attending an approved nonprofit degree-granting college or university in West Virginia or Pennsylvania. Must be enrolled full-time. Based on financial need and academic merit. Award covers tuition and fees. *Award*: Grant for use in freshman, sophomore, junior, or senior year; renewable. *Award amount*: $350–$2718. *Number of awards*: 10,500–10,800. *Eligibility Requirements*: Applicant must be enrolled or expecting to enroll full-time at a two-year or four-year institution or university; resident of West Virginia and studying in Pennsylvania or West Virginia. Available to U.S. citizens. *Application Requirements*: Application, financial need analysis, test scores, transcript. **Deadline:** March 1.

Contact Robert Long, Grant Program Coordinator, West Virginia Higher Education Policy Commission-Office of Financial Aid and Outreach Services, 1018 Kanawha Boulevard East, Suite 700, Charleston, WV 25301-2827. *E-mail:* long@hepc.wvnet.edu. *Phone:* 888-825-5707. *Fax:* 304-558-4622. *Web site:* www.hepc.wvnet.edu.

Wisconsin

Handicapped Student Grant—Wisconsin. One-time awards available to residents of Wisconsin who have severe or profound hearing or visual impairment. Must be enrolled at least half-time at a nonprofit institution. If the handicap prevents the student from attending a Wisconsin school, the award may be used out-of-state in a specialized college. *Award*: Grant for use in freshman, sophomore, junior, or senior year; not renewable. *Award amount*: $250–$1800. *Eligibility Requirements*: Applicant must be enrolled or expecting to enroll full or part-time at a two-year, four-year, or technical institution or university and resident of Wisconsin. Applicant must be hearing impaired or visually impaired. Available to U.S. and non-U.S. citizens. *Application Requirements*: Application, financial need analysis. **Deadline:** continuous.

Contact Sandra Thomas, Wisconsin Higher Educational Aid Board, PO Box 7885, Madison, WI 53707-7885. *E-mail:*

sandy.thomas@heab.state.wi.us. *Phone:* 608-266-0888. *Fax:* 608-267-2808. *Web site:* www.heab.state.wi.us.

Minnesota-Wisconsin Reciprocity Program. Wisconsin residents may attend a Minnesota public institution and pay the reciprocity tuition charged by Minnesota institution. All programs are eligible except doctoral programs in medicine, dentistry, and veterinary medicine. *Award:* Scholarship for use in freshman, sophomore, junior, or senior year; renewable. *Eligibility Requirements:* Applicant must be enrolled or expecting to enroll full or part-time at a two-year, four-year, or technical institution or university; resident of Wisconsin and studying in Minnesota. Available to U.S. citizens. *Application Requirements:* Application. **Deadline:** continuous.

Contact Cindy Lehrman, Wisconsin Higher Educational Aid Board, PO Box 7885, Madison, WI 53707-7885. *E-mail:* cindy.lehrman@heab.state.wi.us. *Phone:* 608-267-2209. *Fax:* 608-267-2808. *Web site:* www.heab.state.wi.us.

Minority Retention Grant-Wisconsin. Provides financial assistance to African-American, Native-Americans, Hispanic, and former citizens of Laos, Vietnam, and Cambodia, for study in Wisconsin. Must be Wisconsin resident, enrolled at least half-time in a two-year or four-year nonprofit college, and must show financial need. *Award:* Grant for use in sophomore, junior, senior, or graduate year; not renewable. *Award amount:* $250–$2500. *Eligibility Requirements:* Applicant must be American Indian/Alaska Native, Asian/Pacific Islander, Black (non-Hispanic), or Hispanic; enrolled or expecting to enroll full or part-time at a two-year, four-year, or technical institution; resident of Wisconsin and studying in Wisconsin. Available to U.S. and non-U.S. citizens. *Application Requirements:* Application, financial need analysis. **Deadline:** continuous.

Contact Mary Lou Kuzdas, Program Coordinator, Wisconsin Higher Educational Aid Board, PO Box 7885, Madison, WI 53707-7885. *E-mail:* mary.kuzdas@heab.state.wi.us. *Phone:* 608-267-2212. *Fax:* 608-267-2808. *Web site:* www.heab.state.wi.us.

Nursing Student Loan Program. Provides forgivable loans to students enrolled in a nursing program. Must be a Wisconsin resident studying in Wisconsin. Application deadline is May 3. *Academic/Career Areas:* Nursing. *Award:* Forgivable loan for use in freshman, sophomore, junior, or senior year; not renewable. *Award amount:* $250–$3000. *Eligibility Requirements:* Applicant must be enrolled or expecting to enroll full or part-time at a two-year, four-year, or technical institution or university; resident of Wisconsin and studying in Wisconsin. Available to U.S. and non-U.S. citizens. *Application Requirements:* Application, financial need analysis. **Deadline:** May 3.

Contact Alice Winters, Program Coordinator, Wisconsin Higher Educational Aid Board, PO Box 7885, Madison, WI 53707-7885. *E-mail:* alice.winters@heab.state.wi.us. *Phone:* 608-267-2213. *Fax:* 608-267-2808. *Web site:* www.heab.state.wi.us.

Talent Incentive Program—Wisconsin. Assists residents of Wisconsin who are attending a nonprofit institution in Wisconsin and have substantial financial need. Must meet income criteria, be considered economically and educationally disadvantaged and be enrolled at least half-time. *Award:* Grant for use in freshman, sophomore, junior, or senior year; renewable. *Award amount:* $600–$1800. *Eligibility Requirements:* Applicant must be enrolled or expecting to enroll full or part-time at a two-year, four-year, or technical institution or university; resident of Wisconsin and studying in Wisconsin. Available to U.S. and non-U.S. citizens. *Application Requirements:* Application, financial need analysis. **Deadline:** continuous.

Contact John Whitt, Program Coordinator, Wisconsin Higher Educational Aid Board, PO Box 7885, Madison, WI 53707-7885. *E-mail:* john.whitt@heab.state.wi.us. *Phone:* 608-266-1665. *Fax:* 608-267-2808. *Web site:* www.heab.state.wi.us.

Teacher of the Visually Impaired Loan Program. Provides forgivable loans to students who enroll in programs that lead to be certified as a teacher of the visually impaired or an orientation and mobility instructor. Must be a Wisconsin resident. For study in Wisconsin, Illinois, Iowa and Michigan. *Award:* Forgivable loan for use in freshman, sophomore, junior, senior, or postgraduate years; not renewable. *Award amount:* $250–$10,000. *Eligibility Requirements:* Applicant must be enrolled or expecting to enroll full or part-time at a two-year, four-year, or technical institution or university; resident of Wisconsin and studying in Illinois, Iowa, Michigan, or Wisconsin. Available to U.S. and non-U.S. citizens. *Application Requirements:* Application, financial need analysis. **Deadline:** continuous.

Contact John Whitt, Program Coordinator, Wisconsin Higher Educational Aid Board, PO Box 7885, Madison, WI 53707-7885. *E-mail:* john.whitt@heab.state.wi.us. *Phone:* 608-266-0888. *Fax:* 608-267-2808. *Web site:* www.heab.state.wi.us.

Tuition and Fee Reimbursement Grants. Up to 85% tuition and fee reimbursement for Wisconsin veterans who were discharged from active duty within the last 10 years. Undergraduate courses must be completed at accredited Wisconsin schools. Those attending Minnesota public colleges, universities, and technical schools that have a tuition reciprocity agreement with Wisconsin also may qualify. Must meet military service requirements. Application must be received no later than 60 days after the completion of the course. *Award:* Grant for use in freshman, sopho-

Additional State Aid Programs

more, junior, or senior year; renewable. *Eligibility Requirements*: Applicant must be enrolled or expecting to enroll full-time at a two-year, four-year, or technical institution or university; resident of Wisconsin and studying in Minnesota or Wisconsin. Available to U.S. citizens. Applicant must have general military experience. *Application Requirements*: Application.

Contact Mr. Steve Olson, Public Relations Officer, Wisconsin Department of Veterans Affairs, PO Box 7843, Madison, WI 53707-7843. *Phone*: 608-266-1311. *Web site*: dva.state.wi.us.

Wisconsin Academic Excellence Scholarship. Renewable award for high school seniors with the highest GPA in graduating class. Must be a Wisconsin resident. Award covers tuition for up to four years. Must maintain 3.5 GPA for renewal. Scholarships of up to $2250 each. Must attend a nonprofit Wisconsin institution full-time. *Award*: Scholarship for use in freshman, sophomore, junior, or senior year; renewable. *Award amount*: $250–$2250. *Eligibility Requirements*: Applicant must be high school student; planning to enroll or expecting to enroll full-time at a two-year, four-year, or technical institution or university; resident of Wisconsin and studying in Wisconsin. Applicant must have 3.5 GPA or higher. Available to U.S. and non-U.S. citizens. *Application Requirements*: Transcript. **Deadline**: continuous.

Contact Alice Winters, Program Coordinator, Wisconsin Higher Educational Aid Board, PO Box 7885, Madison, WI 53707-7885. *E-mail*: alice.winters@heab.state.wi.us. *Phone*: 608-267-2213. *Fax*: 608-267-2808. *Web site*: www.heab.state.wi.us.

Wisconsin Department of Veterans Affairs Retraining Grants. Renewable award for veterans, unmarried spouses of deceased veterans, or dependents of deceased veterans. Must be resident of Wisconsin and attend an institution in Wisconsin. Veteran must be recently unemployed and show financial need. Must enroll in a vocational or technical program that can reasonably be expected to lead to employment. Course work at four-year colleges or universities does not qualify as retraining. *Award*: Grant for use in freshman or sophomore year; renewable. *Award amount*: up to $3000. *Eligibility Requirements*: Applicant must be enrolled or expecting to enroll full or part-time at a technical institution; resident of Wisconsin and studying in Wisconsin. Applicant or parent must meet one or more of the following requirements: general military experience; retired from active duty; disabled or killed as a result of military service; prisoner of war; or missing in action. *Application Requirements*: Application, financial need analysis.

Contact Mr. Steve Olson, Public Relations Officer, Wisconsin Department of Veterans Affairs, PO Box 7843, Madison, WI 53707-7843. *Phone*: 608-266-1311. *Web site*: dva.state.wi.us.

Wisconsin Higher Education Grants (WHEG). Grants for residents of Wisconsin attending a campus of the University of Wisconsin or Wisconsin Technical College. Must be enrolled at least half-time and show financial need. Renewable for up to five years. *Award*: Grant for use in freshman, sophomore, junior, or senior year; not renewable. *Award amount*: $250–$1800. *Eligibility Requirements*: Applicant must be enrolled or expecting to enroll full or part-time at a two-year, four-year, or technical institution or university; resident of Wisconsin and studying in Wisconsin. Available to U.S. and non-U.S. citizens. *Application Requirements*: Application, financial need analysis. **Deadline**: continuous.

Contact Sandra Thomas, Program Coordinator, Wisconsin Higher Educational Aid Board, PO Box 7885, Madison, WI 53707-7885. *E-mail*: sandy.thomas@heab.state.wi.us. *Phone*: 608-266-0888. *Fax*: 608-267-2808. *Web site*: www.heab.state.wi.us.

Wisconsin National Guard Tuition Grant. Renewable award for active members of the Wisconsin National Guard in good standing, who successfully complete a course of study at a qualifying school. Award covers full tuition, excluding fees, not to exceed undergraduate tuition charged by University of Wisconsin-Madison. Must have a minimum 2.0 GPA. *Award*: Grant for use in freshman, sophomore, junior, or senior year; renewable. *Award amount*: up to $1927. *Number of awards*: up to 4000. *Eligibility Requirements*: Applicant must be enrolled or expecting to enroll full or part-time at a two-year, four-year, or technical institution or university and resident of Wisconsin. Applicant must have 2.5 GPA or higher. Available to U.S. citizens. Applicant must have served in the Air Force National Guard or Army National Guard. *Application Requirements*: Application. **Deadline**: continuous.

Contact Karen Behling, Tuition Grant Administrator, Department of Military Affairs, PO Box 14587, Madison, WI 53714-0587. *E-mail*: karen.behling@dma.state.wi.us. *Phone*: 608-242-3159. *Fax*: 608-242-3154. *Web site*: wisconsinguard.com.

Wisconsin Native American Student Grant. Grants for Wisconsin residents who are at least one-quarter American-Indian. Must be attending a college or university within the state. Renewable for up to five years. Several grants of up to $1100. *Award*: Grant for use in freshman, sophomore, junior, or senior year; renewable. *Award amount*: $250–$1100. *Eligibility Requirements*: Applicant must be American Indian/Alaska Native; enrolled or expecting to enroll full or part-time at a two-year, four-year, or technical institution or university; resident of Wisconsin and studying in Wisconsin. Available to U.S. and non-U.S. citizens. *Application Requirements*: Application, financial need analysis. **Deadline**: continuous.

Financial Aid 101

Appendix D

Contact Sandra Thomas, Program Coordinator, Wisconsin Higher Educational Aid Board, PO Box 7885, Madison, WI 53707-7885. *E-mail:* sandy.thomas@heab.state.wi.us. *Phone:* 608-266-0888. *Fax:* 608-267-2808. *Web site:* www.heab.state.wi.us.

Wisconsin Tuition Grant Program. Available to Wisconsin residents who are enrolled at least half-time in degree or certificate programs at independent, nonprofit colleges or universities in Wisconsin. Must show financial need. *Award:* Grant for use in freshman, sophomore, junior, or senior year; not renewable. *Award amount:* $250–$2350. *Eligibility Requirements:* Applicant must be enrolled or expecting to enroll full or part-time at a four-year institution or university; resident of Wisconsin and studying in Wisconsin. Available to U.S. and non-U.S. citizens. *Application Requirements:* Application, financial need analysis. **Deadline:** continuous.

Contact Mary Lou Kuzdas, Program Coordinator, Wisconsin Higher Educational Aid Board, PO Box 7885, Madison, WI 53707-7885. *E-mail:* mary.kuzdas@heab.state.wi.us. *Phone:* 608-267-2212. *Fax:* 608-267-2808. *Web site:* www.heab.state.wi.us.

Wisconsin Veterans Part-time Study Reimbursement Grant. Open only to Wisconsin veterans and dependents of deceased Wisconsin veterans. Renewable for continuing study. Contact office for more details. Application deadline is no later than sixty days after the course completion. Veterans may be reimbursed up to 85% of tuition and fees. *Award:* Grant for use in freshman, sophomore, junior, or senior year; renewable. *Award amount:* $300–$1100. *Eligibility Requirements:* Applicant must be enrolled or expecting to enroll part-time at an institution or university; resident of Wisconsin and studying in Wisconsin. Available to U.S. citizens. Applicant or parent must meet one or more of the following requirements: general military experience; retired from active duty; disabled or killed as a result of military service; prisoner of war; or missing in action. *Application Requirements:* Application.

Contact Mr. Steve Olson, Public Relations Officer, Wisconsin Department of Veterans Affairs, PO Box 7843, Madison, WI 53707-7843. *Phone:* 608-266-1311. *Web site:* dva.state.wi.us.

Wyoming

Douvas Memorial Scholarship. Available to Wyoming residents who are first-generation Americans. Must be between 18-22 years old. Must be used at any Wyoming public institution of higher education for study freshman year. *Award:* Scholarship for use in freshman year; not renewable. *Award amount:* $500. *Number of awards:* 1. *Eligibility Requirements:* Applicant must be age 18-22; enrolled or expecting to enroll at a two-year or four-year institution or university; resident of Wyoming and studying in Wyoming. *Application Requirements:* Application. **Deadline:** April 18.

Contact Wyoming Department of Education, 2300 Capitol Avenue, Hathaway Building, 2nd Floor, Cheyenne, WY 82002-0050.

Superior Student in Education Scholarship—Wyoming. Available to Wyoming high school graduates who have demonstrated high academic achievement and plan to teach in Wyoming public schools. Award is for tuition at Wyoming institutions. Must maintain 3.0 GPA. *Academic/Career Areas:* Education. *Award:* Scholarship for use in freshman, sophomore, junior, or senior year; renewable. *Number of awards:* 16–80. *Eligibility Requirements:* Applicant must be enrolled or expecting to enroll full-time at a two-year or four-year institution or university; resident of Wyoming and studying in Wyoming. Applicant must have 3.0 GPA or higher. Available to U.S. citizens. *Application Requirements:* Application, references, test scores, transcript. **Deadline:** October 31.

Contact Joel Anne Berrigan, Assistant Director, Scholarships, State of Wyoming, administered by University of Wyoming, PO Box 3335, Laramie, WY 82071-3335. *E-mail:* finaid@uwyo.edu. *Phone:* 307-766-2117. *Fax:* 307-766-3800.

Vietnam Veterans Award/Wyoming. Available to Wyoming residents who served in the armed forces between August 5, 1964, and May 7, 1975, and received a Vietnam service medal. Award is free tuition at the University of Wyoming or a state (WY) community college. *Award:* Scholarship for use in freshman, sophomore, junior, or senior year; renewable. *Eligibility Requirements:* Applicant must be enrolled or expecting to enroll full or part-time at a two-year or four-year institution or university; resident of Wyoming and studying in Wyoming. Available to U.S. citizens. Applicant must have general military experience. *Application Requirements:* Application. **Deadline:** continuous.

Contact Joel Anne Berrigan, Assistant Director, Scholarships, State of Wyoming, administered by University of Wyoming, PO Box 3335, Laramie, WY 82071-3335. *E-mail:* finaid@uwyo.edu. *Phone:* 307-766-2117. *Fax:* 307-766-3800.